NINETEENTH-CENTURY RELIGION, LITERATURE AND SOCIETY

NINETEENTH-CENTURY RELIGION, LITERATURE AND SOCIETY

General Editor:
Naomi Hetherington

Volume II

Mission and Reform

Edited by Angharad Eyre

LONDON AND NEW YORK

First published 2020
by Routledge
2 Park Square, Milton Park, Abingdon, Oxon OX14 4RN

and by Routledge
52 Vanderbilt Avenue, New York, NY 10017

Routledge is an imprint of the Taylor & Francis Group, an informa business

© 2020 selection and editorial matter, Naomi Hetherington and Angharad Eyre; individual owners retain copyright in their own material.

The right of Naomi Hetherington and Angharad Eyre to be identified as the author[/s] of the editorial material, and of the authors for their individual chapters, has been asserted in accordance with sections 77 and 78 of the Copyright, Designs and Patents Act 1988.

All rights reserved. No part of this book may be reprinted or reproduced or utilised in any form or by any electronic, mechanical, or other means, now known or hereafter invented, including photocopying and recording, or in any information storage or retrieval system, without permission in writing from the publishers.

Trademark notice: Product or corporate names may be trademarks or registered trademarks, and are used only for identification and explanation without intent to infringe.

British Library Cataloguing-in-Publication Data
A catalogue record for this book is available from the British Library

Library of Congress Cataloging-in-Publication Data
A catalog record for this book has been requested

ISBN: 978-1-138-56315-5 (set)
eISBN: 978-1-351-27236-0 (set)
ISBN: 978-1-138-57283-6 (volume II)
eISBN: 978-1-351-27220-9 (volume II)

Typeset in Times New Roman
by Apex CoVantage, LLC

CONTENTS

Editor's acknowledgements	x
Acknowledgements	xi
Introduction to Volume II: Mission and Reform	1

PART 1
The Foreign Mission Movement **11**

1.1 Gaining Support **13**

1 Extracts from *Dialogue between a Minister and a Parishioner concerning the Church Missionary Society*, c. 1830–1839 — 16

1.2 Children **25**

2 E. M. I., 'Lessons from Heathen Lands', 1843–1844 — 29

3 Extracts from John Campbell, *Worlds Displayed for the Benefit of Young People by a Familiar History of Some of their Inhabitants*, 1802 — 34

1.3 Women and Authority in the Mission Field **39**

4 Extracts from *Memoirs of Female Labourers in the Missionary Cause*, 1839 — 43

5 Extracts from *Female Missionary Intelligencer*, 1853 — 47

6 Pandita Ramabai, 'Report', 1892 — 52

1.4 Masculinity and Leadership **57**

7 Extracts from *Soldiership and Christianity: Being a Review of the Memoirs of the Late Hedley Vicars*, 1856 — 61

CONTENTS

8 Review of *Vikings of Today*, 1895   70

9 Extracts from A. F. Childe, *Good out of Evil; or, the History of Adjai the African Slave-Boy*, 1850   72

1.5 Ethnography and Anthropology   **79**

10 Extracts from Robert Moffat, *Missionary Labours and Scenes in Southern Africa*, 1843   83

11 Extracts from George Taplin [and James Ngunaitponi], *The Narrinyeri*, 1879   88

1.6 Biblical History, Geography and Travel Writing   **95**

12 Charlotte Elizabeth Tonna, 'Palestine', 1826   99

13 Anon., 'Lebanon and its Cedars', 1854   103

14 Constance Maynard, Contributions to *Hermes* (Westfield College Newsletter), 1898–1900 (i) 'A Few Pages from a Diary'; (ii) 'A Few Pages from a Diary (continued)'; (iii) 'Letter from the Mistress'   106

PART 2
Home Missions   **115**

2.1 Unitarian Home Missionary Board   **117**

15 [John Relly Beard], 'Unitarian Home Missionary Board', 1853   120

2.2 University Settlements   **125**

16 Frederick Rogers, *The New Movement at the Universities and What May Come of it, by a Whitechapel Man*, 1886   129

17 Lady Margaret Hall's Old Student Old Student Association Newsletter, 1894–1897 (i) 'The Women's University Settlement'; (ii) 'Opening of the Lady Margaret Hall New Buildings'; (iii) 'Proposed LMH Settlement'; (iv) 'The Settlement'   132

2.3 Revivalism   **137**

18 Extracts from Phoebe Palmer, *Four Years in the Old World: Comprising the Travels, Incidents, and Evangelical Labors of Dr and Mrs Palmer in England, Ireland, Scotland and Wales*, 1866   141

CONTENTS

19 Extracts from Maurice Davies, 'The "Twelve Days' Mission"', 1874   148

20 Extracts from Society of St John the Evangelist
    (the Holy Cross), *The Book of the Mission*, 1870   153

2.4 The Salvation Army   **157**

21 Extract from William Booth, *Orders and Regulations for
    Field Officers*, 1886   161

22 Extracts from *The War Cry*, 1895–1896
    (i) '*Quenched*: Rescue Report for 1895'; (ii) 'Married Women
    Warriors' (26 January 1895); (iii) 'Married Women Warriors'
    (13 April 1895); (iv) 'Women Warriors' (11 April 1896)   163

2.5 The Mission to the Jews   **173**

23 Extracts from London Society for Promoting Christianity
    Amongst the Jews, 'Abstract of the 27th Report', 1835   177

24 'A Visit to the Chapel of the Hebrew Christian Brethren
    in London by a Converted Israelite', 1832   181

25 Extracts from Osborn W. Trenery Heighway, *Leila Ada:
    The Jewish Convert, an Authentic Memoir*, 1852   183

**PART 3
Reforming Private Life**   **189**

3.1 Temperance   **191**

26 William Gaskell, 'Dread Memories!', 'A Mother's
    Death-Song for her Child', 'Parting Words' and 'Heaven
    to Thee!', 1839   195

27 *The Importance of Sobriety Illustrated by the Evils of
    Intemperance*, 1850   199

3.2 Sabbatarianism   **205**

28 *Sabbath Occupations, c.* 1820   208

29 Edward Capern, 'The Rural Postman', 1859   213

3.3 Fidelity in the Upper Classes   **217**

30 'Letter to a Friend in the Higher Circles of Society', 1831   221

CONTENTS

31 Extracts from Arthur Selous, *The Young Governess: A Tale for Girls*, c. 1870–1879 ... 225

3.4 Education ... 231

32 Extracts from Dinah Craik, *Bread upon the Waters*, 1852 ... 235

33 G. F. B., *Charlie Brame: or What Came of Loitering*, 1870 ... 240

34 Mary B. G. Slade, 'The Missionary Meeting', 1887 ... 243

PART 4
Social and Political Reform ... 247

4.1 Abolitionism ... 249

35 Extracts from [Susanna Watts and Elizabeth Heyrick], 'Remarks on the Descent of the Africans from Ham', 1825 ... 253

36 Extracts from Isaac Nelson, *Slavery Supported by the American Churches and Countenanced by Recent Proceedings in the Free Church of Scotland*, 1847 ... 260

4.2 Prison Reform ... 267

37 Extracts from Mary Carpenter, 'On Reformatory Schools and their Present Position', 1855 ... 271

38 Extracts from Walter Lowe Clay, *The Prison Chaplain: A Memoir of the Reverend John Clay B.D. Late Chaplain of the Preston Gaol*, 1861 ... 274

39 Extracts from [Fred W. Robinson], *Female Life in Prison: By a Prison Matron*, 1862 ... 280

4.3 Philanthropic Organisations ... 285

40 Extracts from Clara Collet, 'George Gissing's Novels', 1891 ... 289

41 Extracts from *Baroness Burdett Coutts: A Sketch of her Public Life and Work*, 1893 ... 293

4.4 Social Purity ... 299

42 'On the Repeal of the CD Act in India', 1888 ... 303

43 Extracts from J. E. H. [Ellice Hopkins], *Is it Natural?*, 1885 ... 306

4.5 Christian Socialism ... 311

CONTENTS

44 Extracts from Stewart Headlam, 'The Service of Humanity' and
'The Stage', 1882   315

45 Extracts from Eliza and John Trevor, *The Labour Church Hymn
Book*, 1895   319

46 Extracts from John Clifford, *Socialism and the Teaching of
Christ*, 1897   325

4.6 Women's Suffrage   **331**

47 Extracts from [Barbara Bodichon], 'How to Utilize the Powers
of Women', 1859   335

48 Emily Wilding Davison, 'The Price of Liberty', 1914   340

49 Extracts from Gertrude Spielmann, Woman's Place in the
Synagogue', 1813–1814   343

EDITOR'S ACKNOWLEDGEMENTS

I would like to thank the archivists and librarians who have helped to make this project possible. Thanks are especially due to the John Rylands Library, University of Manchester, for funding a three-week, early-career fellowship that enabled me to study the archive of the Unitarian College and manuscripts of the Gaskells – and for the permission to reproduce the Unitarian Home Missionary source.

I am very grateful to Oliver Mahony, archivist at Lady Margaret Hall, University of Oxford, for welcoming me to the LMH archive and for providing copies of the articles from LMH's *Old Students' Association Newsletter*.

Thanks to Denise Anderson at the University of Edinburgh Library for her assistance in providing a copy of Isaac Nelson's *Slavery Supported by the American Churches and Countenanced by Recent Proceedings in the Free Church of Scotland*.

I am also grateful to Josh King, Melvin Shuetz and Jennifer Borderud at Baylor University Library for their help in identifying appropriate sources for this volume.

I have been incredibly fortunate to work with my fellow editors on this project, all of whom have contributed to how I was able to conceptualise and contextualise this volume. I would especially like to thank Naomi Hetherington for bringing me on board, for her ever-supportive leadership and for all her suggestions of sources. I have also been lucky enough to be able to draw on the expertise of friends and colleagues, especially Rebecca Styler, Nadia Valman and Lara Atkin, whose help and suggestions for sources for this volume have been invaluable.

Finally, I would also like to express my gratitude to Kimberley Smith, Simon Alexander and Sarahjayne Smith at Routledge for their oversight of this project from its early days to its successful completion in what has been an unprecedented global crisis.

Angharad Eyre

ACKNOWLEDGEMENTS

The publishers would like to thank the following for permission to reprint their material:

Armstrong Browning Library, Baylor University, Waco, Texas for permission to reprint:

Anon., *Dialogue between A Minister and a Parishioner concerning the Church Missionary Society* ([London]: Church Missionary Society, *c.* 1830–9), pp. 1–12.

G. F. B., *Charlie Brame: or what came of Loitering* (London: Society for Promoting Christian Knowledge, 1870), pp. 5–15.

Royal London Hospital Archives for permission to reprint Anon., review of 'Vikings of Today', *London Hospital Gazette* (1895), pp. 52–3.

Queen Mary Archives for permission to reprint Constance Maynard, 'A Few Pages from a Diary', *Hermes*, 12 (1898), Queen Mary Archives, WFD/23/3, pp. 8–10; Constance Maynard, 'A Few Pages from a Diary (Continued)', *Hermes*, 13 (1899), Queen Mary Archives, WFD/23/3, pp. 13–15; and Constance Maynard, 'Letter from the Mistress', *Hermes*, 17 (1900), Queen Mary Archives, WFD/23/3, pp. 10–12.

Manchester Library, Unitarian College Collection for permission to reprint 'Unitarian Home Missionary Board', privately circulated, 1853, University of Manchester Library, Unitarian College Collection, UCC 1/6/2/3.

Lady Margaret Hall Archives for permission to reprint 'The Women's University Settlement', *Old Students' Association Newsletter* (Oxford: Lady Margaret Hall, 1894), pp. 10–13; 'Opening of the Lady Margaret Hall New Buildings' and 'Proposed LMH Settlement', *Old Students' Association Newsletter* (Oxford: Lady Margaret Hall, 1896), pp. 12–18, 19–23; and 'The Settlement', *Old Students' Association Newsletter* (Oxford: Lady Margaret Hall, 1897), pp. 10–11.

ACKNOWLEDGEMENTS

The University of Edinburgh Library for permission to reprint Isaac Nelson, *Slavery Supported by the American Churches and Countenanced by Recent Proceedings in the Free Church of Scotland* (Edinburgh: Charles Ziegler, 1847), pp. 2–7. [abridged]

London School of Economics Women's Library for permission to reprint Emily Wilding Davison, 'The Price of Liberty', *Suffragette*, 5 June 1914, p. 129.

The British Library for permission to reprint:

E. M. I., 'Lessons from Heathen Lands', in *Missionary Stories* (London: John Snow, 1843–4), pp. 3–8.

John Campbell, *Worlds Displayed for the Benefit of Young People by a Familiar History of Some of their Inhabitants*, in *The Juvenile Cabinet of Travels and Narratives for the Amusement and Instruction of Young Persons* (London: Francis Westley, 1825), pp. 101–2, 105–7, 124, 126–29, 137. [abridged]

Anon., *Memoirs of Female Labourers in the Missionary Cause* (Bath: [n.p.], 1839), Introduction by Richard Knill, pp. v–vii, 1–9.

Editorial, *Female Missionary Intelligencer*, 1 [1853] (Dublin: SPFEE, 1854), pp. 1–4, 15–17.

Pandita Ramabai, 'Report', *Report of the Annual Meeting of the Ramabai Association* (Boston: Geo. H. Ellis, 1892), pp. 21–7.

Anon., *Soldiership and Christianity: Being a Review of the Memoirs of the Late Hedley Vicars* (London: Ward and Co., 1856), pp. 3–16. [abridged]

A. F. Childe, *Good out of Evil; or, the History of Adjai the African Slave-Boy* (London: Wertheim and Macintosh, 1850), pp. 80–97, 100–1, 108–10, 114–21. [abridged]

Robert Moffat, *Missionary Labours and Scenes in Southern Africa* (London: John Snow, 1843), pp. 1–15. [abridged]

George Taplin [and James Ngunaitponi], *The Narrinyeri*, in Woods (ed.), *The Native Tribes of South Australia* (Adelaide: Wigg and Son, 1879), pp. 1–2, 34–36, 48–51, 128–9. [abridged]

Charlotte Elizabeth Tonna, 'Palestine', in *Osric: A Missionary Tale, with The Garden and Other Poems* [1826] (Dublin: Curry, [n.d.]), pp. 43–8.

ACKNOWLEDGEMENTS

Anon., 'Lebanon and its Cedars', *Sunday at Home*, 1 (May 1854), pp. 6–7.

Frederick Rogers, *The New Movement at the Universities and What May Come of it, by a Whitechapel Man* ([n.p.]: [n.p.], [1886]).

Phoebe Palmer, *Four Years in the Old World: Comprising the Travels, Incidents, and Evangelical Labors of Dr and Mrs Palmer in England, Ireland, Scotland and Wales* (New York: [n.p.], 1866), pp. v, 84–85, 90–98, 106–7, 110–12. [abridged]

Maurice Davies, 'The "Twelve Days' Mission"', in *Orthodox London: Or Phases of Religious Life in the Church of England*, 2nd edn (London: Tinsley Brothers, 1874), pp. 267, 269–71, 274–78, 279–82. [abridged]

Society of St John the Evangelist (the Holy Cross), *The Book of the Mission* (London: [n.p.], [1870]), pp. iv–v, 17–19.

William Booth, extracts from *Orders and Regulations for Field Officers* (London: Salvation Army, 1886), pp. 322–3.

'"Quenched": Rescue Report for 1895', *The War Cry*, 23 November 1895, p. 4.

'Married Women Warriors', *The War Cry*, 26 January 1895, p. 7.

'Married Women Warriors,' *The War Cry*, 13 April 1895, p. 13.

'Women Warriors', *The War Cry*, 11 April 1896, p. 5.

London Society for Promoting Christianity Amongst the Jews, 'Abstract of the 27th Report', supplement to *Jewish Intelligence*, 1835, pp. 6–8, 15–16. [abridged]

'A Visit to the Chapel of the Hebrew Christian Brethren in London by a Converted Israelite', *The Christian Lady's Friend and Family Repository*, May 1832, pp. 421–3.

Osborn W. Trenery Heighway, *Leila Ada: The Jewish Convert, an Authentic Memoir* [1852] (London: Partridge, Oakey and Co., 1854), pp. vii–xiii, 88–96. [abridged]

William Gaskell, 'Dread Memories', 'A Mother's Death-Song for her Child', 'Parting Words' and 'Heaven to Thee!', in *Temperance Rhymes* (London: Simpkin, Marshall and Co., 1839), pp. 15–17, 23, 67–9, 70–1. [abridged]

The Importance of Sobriety Illustrated by the Evils of Intemperance (London: RTS, *c.* 1850), pp. 1–7.

ACKNOWLEDGEMENTS

Sabbath Occupations (London: Religious Tract Society, *c.* 1820), pp. 1–8.

Edward Capern, 'The Rural Postman', in *Poems* (London: W. Kent and Co., 1859), pp. 9–13.

'Letter to a Friend in the Higher Circles of Society', *Christian Lady's Friend and Family Repository*, November 1831, pp. 101–5.

Arthur Selous, *The Young Governess: A Tale for Girls* (London: Griffith, Farran, Okeden and Welsh, *c.* 1870–9), pp. 17–18, 26, 28–29, 39, 106–14. [abridged]

Dinah Craik, *Bread upon the Waters*, in *Bread upon the Waters; A Family in Love; A Low Marriage; The Double House* [Governesses' Benevolent Institution, 1852] (Leipzig: Bernhard Tauchnitz, 1865), pp. 50–59, 70–72. [abridged]

Mary B. G. Slade, 'The Missionary Meeting', in *For Week Evening Entertainment* (London: Sunday School Union, 1887), pp. 1–4.

Susanna Watts and Elizabeth Heyrick, 'Remarks on the Descent of the Africans from Ham', *The Humming Bird, or Morsels of Information on the Subject of Slavery*, 1, 2, January 1825, pp. 35–38, 39–45. [abridged]

Mary Carpenter, 'On Reformatory Schools and their Present Position', in Jelinger Symons (ed.), *On the Reformation of Young Offenders: A Collection of Pamphlets, Papers and Speeches on Reformatories and the Various Views Held on the Subject of Juvenile Crime and its Treatment* (London: G. Routledge and Co., 1855), pp. 131–35, 138. [abridged]

Walter Lowe Clay, *The Prison Chaplain: A Memoir of the Reverend John Clay B.D. Late Chaplain of the Preston Gaol* (Cambridge: Macmillan, 1861), pp. vii–viii, 351–352, 356–361, 364–366, 368–370. [abridged]

[Fred W. Robinson], *Female Life in Prison: By a Prison Matron*, 2 vols (London: Hurst and Blackett, 1862), vol. 1, pp. 1–9, 44–50. [abridged]

Clara Collet, 'George Gissing's Novels', *Charity Organisation Review*, May 1891, pp. 375–380. [abridged]

Baroness Burdett Coutts: A Sketch of her Public Life and Work, 1893, pp. 15–19, 21–3, 25–7, 105–10, 176–80. [abridged]

'On the Repeal of the CD Act in India', *The Sentinel*, September 1888, pp. 109–110.

xiv

ACKNOWLEDGEMENTS

J. E. H. [Ellice Hopkins], *Is it Natural?* (London: Hatchards, [1885]), pp. 3–13. [abridged]

Stewart Headlam, *The Service of Humanity and other Sermons* (London: J. Hodges, 1882), pp. 1, 3–7, 11, 13–18. [abridged]

Eliza and John Trevor, *The Labour Church Hymn Book* (Manchester: Labour Church Institute, [1895]), pp. 1–7. [abridged]

John Clifford, *Socialism and the Teaching of Christ*, Fabian Tract no. 78 (London: Fabian Society, 1897), pp. 2–7, 10–11. [abridged]

Barbara Bodichon, *English Woman's Journal*, 3 (March 1859), pp. 34–35, 39–44, 46–47. [abridged]

Gertrude Spielmann, 'Woman's Place in the Synagogue', *Jewish Review*, 4 (1913–14), pp. 24–28, 31–34, 36. [abridged]

Disclaimer

The publishers have made every effort to contact authors/copyright holders of works reprinted in *Nineteenth-Century Religion, Literature and Society*. This has not been possible in every case, however, and we would welcome correspondence from those individuals/companies whom we have been unable to trace.

INTRODUCTION TO VOLUME II: MISSION AND REFORM

One of the great embodiments of the nineteenth century's deeply religious character was the mission movement. Inspired by the late-eighteenth-century evangelical revival in the Protestant Church, British missionaries established a foreign mission field that outran the limits even of the British empire, as they sought to fulfil their Biblical instruction to take the word of God 'into all the world' (Mark 16:15).[1] Meanwhile, the home mission movement aimed to bring true Christianity to those living in Britain yet outside the faith, such as the Jewish population and the working classes. More generally, a mission of reform took hold in the domestic realm, starting with the evangelical reformation of morals but progressing to social and political reforms that paved the way for the twentieth century's democratic welfare state.

The impact of the evangelical revival on nineteenth-century culture has been well debated, but it is usually agreed that this was greatest from the beginning of the century to the 1860s. Though some scholars have suggested that religious influence waned after this point, this volume provides evidence that religion was very much alive in late-Victorian and Edwardian society, with religious discourse flourishing in the prose of reformers, socialists and feminists alike at the turn of the century.[2] Indeed, it can be seen that religion was at the heart of all the major reforming movements of the day. Moreover, the extensive and specific impact of mission on nineteenth-century culture cannot be ignored. This volume draws attention to how the pervasive presence of religious mission in society informed literature's representation of reform movements, and how the writings of missionary and reform movements contributed to the development of literary genres.

Contexts

Probably the most important context for mission and reform in the nineteenth century was the late-eighteenth-century evangelical revival. However, other revivals were also significant. The Church of England's 'High Church' Oxford Movement – started by individuals including John Keble, John Henry Newman and Edward Pusey – sought to re-establish doctrine and ritual from the Church's Catholic origins.[3] In the late nineteenth century, the Holiness Movement spread

1

amongst evangelicals, as low-church Methodists renewed vital religion in mass meetings and Anglicans combated the Church of England's growing ritualism.[4] As Elisabeth Jay has shown, the effects of these revivals are visible in the work of Victorian novelists such as Anthony Trollope, Charles Kingsley, George Eliot and Thomas Hardy.[5]

The foreign mission movement itself has been well studied, especially in the field of history and postcolonial studies.[6] Through the nineteenth century, Protestant missionaries from America and mainland Europe as well as England massively expanded the scope of international missionary activity.[7] Initially, cross-denominational evangelicalism inspired often working-class-led missionary efforts, but the Wesleyan Methodists and Anglicans soon established their own highly-organised missions around the world, with the Church of England extending the episcopal system across the empire.[8] Missionary activity was often prompted by evangelical millenarian beliefs, which prophesied that when Christianity had been taken into all the world, the end of days, as predicted by Revelations, would take place. This theory especially motivated the domestic mission to the Jews, as it was believed that the second coming of Christ was dependent on the conversion of the Jews and their return to Israel.[9] Mission work was also inspired by more moderate and Incarnation-based Christian beliefs about England's responsibility to the lives of the 'heathen' in both its overseas territories and its city slums at home.[10]

The involvement of missions in the work of empire has been a great field of debate; missionaries' contributions to anthropology, cartography and other geographical and scientific disciplines are undeniable, and this, combined with their physical presence, certainly functioned as a form of imperial power.[11] However, on the ground, missionaries often maintained a distance between themselves and what they often saw as the corrupting influences of colonial authorities.[12] Recent work on the involvement of women, families and emotions in mission has led to fascinatingly nuanced studies of the interactions between missionaries and indigenous populations, with greater attention paid to the voices of these populations where they can be heard.[13] In this volume, works about and by two indigenous Christian converts, the Indian social reformer Pandita Ramabai and the African Bishop Samuel Crowther, demonstrate the complex relationship of missionary converts to the empire and white missionary supporters (see this volume, Women and authority in the mission field, and Masculinity and leadership). Meanwhile, the voice of a mission guide, James Ngunaitponi, can be distinguished within the work of the missionary George Taplin, representing the south Australian indigenous community (see this volume, Ethnography and anthropology).

In addition to inspiring missions, the evangelical revival in particular led to public campaigns to reform the morals of the general population, aiming to establish a pious society at all levels and implant vital religion at the heart of the domestic sphere. Reforms like the temperance movement encouraged Christians to moderation, which would lead to more harmonious domestic relations. Meanwhile Sabbatarians campaigned in Parliament for an end to Sunday working and exhorted the faithful to refrain from any secular activity on this day, including the reading of fiction (the movement also produced suitable Sunday reading materials). The Sunday School movement worked to reform the morals of working-class youth, with the establishment of working-class respectability as its legacy.[14] And Christian periodicals and education societies aimed to infiltrate the drawing rooms of the upper classes and encourage the higher echelons of society to more vital religion and more faithful attendance at church (referred to as fidelity in faith).[15] As well as forming the background to many Victorian domestic novels – either as a motive in novels such as Dinah Craik's *John Halifax Gentleman*, or as a satirical target, as in Thackeray's *Vanity Fair* or Wilkie Collins's *The Moonstone*[16] – these reforms also led to the development of new literary genres – for example, temperance literature by evangelicals such as Sarah Stickney-Ellis and William Gaskell.[17]

Beyond reforming behaviour, evangelicals were inspired by the doctrine of practical piety to take part in wider social reforms, taking up causes such as abolitionism and prison reform.[18] In the later nineteenth century, Incarnation theology prompted the same impetus to social activism in High Church adherents.[19] Some Christians, believing that society could only be saved if their faith was at the heart of social organisation, went as far as joining radical political movements such as socialism and suffragism.[20] And Christians weren't the only ones who believed religion should be part of politics – as Anne Summers has argued, by the turn of the century Jewish women such as Gertrude Spielmann were also raising their voices to suggest that religion could provide an answer to the Woman Question.[21]

Religious mission, reform and writing: overarching themes

In addition to providing a variety of perspectives on the themes identified by scholarship on religious activity in the nineteenth century, some overarching themes in mission and reform writing emerge from the sources included in this volume; these relate to the ways religious individuals thought about the world, the role of religion in society and how to represent and change the world through their literary productions.

Perhaps the most obvious theme that emerges from the sources in this volume is how religious individuals, including the clergy, felt called upon to be involved in every aspect of the world, from the problems of the slums, to prison reform and women's right to vote. Because nineteenth-century religion was so involved in the world, religious discourse often existed on many sides of a social question. Debates were not simply between religious reformers and secular conservatives: sometimes religious reformers joined secular reformers in opposition to the more conservative religious population; at other times secular reformers joined religious movements against secular conservatism. Churches were not always on the humane, progressive side of a question.[22] For example, Walter Lowe Clay's *The Prison Chaplain: A Memoir of the Reverend John Clay B.D. Late Chaplain of the Preston Gaol* sets out how contemporary religious and secular discourse, which removed the idea of punishment from penal theory, was not in alignment with how all Christians believed religious society should treat criminals and sinners, and that progressive ideas such as removing children from the general prison population and into reformatory schools were not always supported by prison chaplains. Similarly, Isaac Nelson's *Slavery Supported by the American Churches and Countenanced by Recent Proceedings in the Free Church of Scotland* and Susanna Watts and Elizabeth Heyrick's 'Remarks on the Descent of the Africans from Ham' argue against certain publications by fellow Christians which they saw as countenancing the system of slavery in the United States.[23]

Significantly, Christianity could offer an alternative perspective on the world – a lens that also took in the supernatural, which saw time differently and located the nineteenth century within a Biblical timeline connecting it directly with the times of Jesus and the imminent time to come, as set out in Revelations.[24] In this volume, this tendency can particularly be seen in foreign missionary texts, such as John Campbell's *Worlds Displayed*, which imagines travelling through heaven and hell, meeting converts from all periods of history; or the scientific works of Moffat and Taplin, which endeavour to trace the descendancy of indigenous populations from Biblical tribes. Millenarian belief in the literally imminent second coming of Christ was widespread across denominations at various points in the nineteenth century, lending an urgency to religious activism that can be sensed in the texts of home missions and revivals – especially the Mission to the Jews. This urgent sense of prophecies coming to pass made the social mores of the nineteenth century seem unimportant to Christian socialists and feminists, leading them, like Emily Wilding Davison in 'The Price of Liberty', to reject worldly political systems such as capitalism and patriarchy.[25] In their world view, God's authority trumped that of the world.

Women's use of religious authority to justify their engagement in public movements is particularly evident in the sources of this volume. The number of women authors suggests that religious women had little difficulty becoming involved in mission and reform activities. Aspects of philanthropy and social work, such as financially supporting missions and working in Sunday schools, were encouraged among women as demonstrating appropriate femininity; Alison Twells has argued that women's domestic mission was interpreted expansively by some congregations.[26] Some of the women authors in this volume had authorisation from clergymen to write for the cause – for example, the anonymous author of *Memoirs of Female Labourers* is introduced by the Reverend Richard Knill, and A. F. Childe's publication of her biography of the convert Samuel Crowther was encouraged by her local minister. Other women who appear in this volume, such as Phoebe Palmer and Salvation Army officers, refer to their religious calling, which left them no choice but to follow a missionary life. However, such prioritising of God's law over society's was not unproblematic. Emily Wilding Davison's justification of militant feminism's opposition to national law and order expresses the psychological pain this path involved for women. And while one of the young

INTRODUCTION TO VOLUME II

protagonists of Arthur Selous's novel, *The Young Governess*, confidently declares, '*No* one has a right to forbid what the Church commands,' her friend, the clergyman's daughter, demurs that the Church also commands obedience to 'the powers that be'.[27] The radical potential of evangelicalism for the extension of women's activities could always be hedged by conservative Churchmen.

Finally, the sources in this volume show that religious mission, including that experienced by religious individuals in a range of reform work, inspired literary production, and how this writing interacted with more canonical Victorian literature. Scholars have identified the missionary movement as an important context for novels of this period: most famously, Dickens caricatured zealous foreign and home mission supporters in Mrs Jellyby and Mrs Pardiggle in *Bleak House*, and Charlotte Brontë's missionary anti-hero, St John Rivers, in *Jane Eyre* has been likened to the real-life Henry Martyn.[28] Moreover, the mission movement itself produced a vast amount of written material, from letters and memoirs to popular science and travel writing.[29] And social reformers used poetry, hymns and novels to advance their causes, in addition to the periodicals and reports one might expect. This volume reflects the variety of genres used by mission and reform writers, and reveals the different effects created by this diversification. For example, the silver-fork novel of Arthur Selous and the temperance poetry of William Gaskell brought artistry to the temperance and fidelity movements, which were usually sustained by Religious Tract Society productions. Similarly, the multi-faceted, developing genre of nineteenth-century biography was used by numerous societies and movements to create sympathy for converts, inspire others to support missions, or to provide a focal point for a particular issue. As Elisabeth Jay has argued, developments in the biography form had implications not only for nonfiction, but also for novels.[30] On the other side of the coin, novels were important to those involved in social reform. As the reform movement inspired novelists like Dickens and Gissing, the reformers in turn praised their novels for contributing to the cause by representing social problems, and suggested them as examples and styles to be emulated.[31]

Structure and sources

The first half of this volume explores mission in the nineteenth century, first looking at material concerned with the foreign mission movement, and then material on home missions. The second half of the volume explores reform, starting with reform on a more domestic level – the evangelical reform of morals and manners – and moving on to more overtly political reform movements. The texts chosen to represent missions and reform movements offer a view of religiously-inspired activity across the period, from abolitionist writings of the 1820s to suffragette manifestos in the first decade of the twentieth century. The texts also present a glimpse into the rich mine that is nineteenth-century popular and periodical writing: in sourcing texts about mission and social reform that are less well known, I approached the organisational publications of the RTS, the Church Missionary Society, the Salvation Army and women's colleges – to name just a few. Many of the texts reproduced in this volume are anonymous – the product of an organisational position and spirit rather than a magisterial Author. Often when these sorts of texts are attributable, the writer is little-known today; where more well-known figures are included, the text selected has usually not received the attention it perhaps deserves. Whether written by a professional author or an enthusiastic supporter of a movement, the texts reveal remarkable similarities in this sort of writing throughout the century, as similar themes and textual strategies emerge consistently across missions and movements.

To include a wide range of texts, and to represent a range of themes, it was evidently necessary to abridge longer texts. One method of abridgement has been to omit the longer, discursive footnotes so beloved of many Victorian writers. This has only been done where the footnotes were considered tangential and not essential for understanding the text. Shorter and more necessary footnotes appear exactly as in the original text.

There are necessarily some overlaps and connections between sections. For example, the activities carried out by home missions such as the Salvation Army are related to reform movements such as temperance, prison reform and the social purity campaigns, and some publications, like the *Christian Ladies' Friend*, reflected their readers' interest in multiple missions and causes. The line between private and public reform is difficult to draw; the topic of education, for example, was both an instrument of moral improvement and a social institution requiring reform. In practice, I have usually allowed the nature of the material to determine a topic's placement – while the education system was a target of political reform by the turn of the century, most Victorian religious writing on education was aimed at influencing individuals.

All sections, apart from that covering the foreign mission movement, organise material by the different mission organisations or reform movements that produced them, as these provide a variety of perspectives on the topic at hand. However, texts produced by the foreign mission movement's organisations were often quite similar; many missionary societies were interdenominational, and much of their published output was written in a way that might appeal to the broadest audience. More appropriate here was the organisation of material into themes, covering the sorts of individuals involved in the foreign mission movement, such as women, men and children, and the activities associated with or influenced by mission work. In all sections, sources were selected to represent as many different mission and reform organisations, Christian denominations, and nationalities as possible. Moreover, to demonstrate the relationship between literature and the mission and reform movements, sources chosen also represent a variety of different written genres.

The first section, the Foreign Mission Movement, presents material reflecting the experiences of, and the discourses around, children, women and men in the mission field. Sources illustrate the roles these groups were expected to play, including male and female converts such as Pandita Ramabai and Samuel

INTRODUCTION TO VOLUME II

Crowther, who went on to work in the mission movement. This section also provides examples of how those associated with the foreign missionary movement communicated knowledge and theories about the world back to England in the forms of travel writing, poetry and contributions to the new scientific disciplines of ethnography and anthropology.

The second section, Home Missions, presents material from a number of different denominational and organisational missions in England. Anglicans involved in higher education, Unitarians in Manchester, Anglo-Catholics in London and Primitive Methodists around the country all had their own versions of home mission, and all believed in their faith's specific power to re-awaken faith in the heart of the empire. Of course, this section would not be complete without the inclusion of perhaps the best-known home mission, the Salvation Army. Finally, the Mission to the Jews is introduced as in many ways a foreign mission at home, using many of the same methods as the foreign missionary movement, including utilising the literary form of biography.

The third section, Reforming Private Life, includes a variety of texts concerned with the reform of private life in England. The methods used by reformers to change people's behaviour included political campaigns, such as that to outlaw working on Sundays, but also employed poetry and novels to convince readers to change their ways. Accordingly, the sources in this section are a mix of tracts, poems, novels, magazine articles and even plays. Education was a major tool for moral improvement and religious education organisations such as the Sunday School movement and Religious Tract Society are represented here.

The final section, Social and Political Reform, reveals the extent of religiously-inspired activity within major social reform campaigns (such as abolitionism and prison reform); the organisation of religious individuals in charity and the social purity campaign; and the religious discourse at the heart of political groups such as the Christian Socialists and the Suffragettes. Newsletters were a key genre for mobilising religious support for these campaigns, along with more mainstream journalism, but this section also provides examples of sermons and essays that dealt directly with social subjects. Indeed, the variety of textual forms used by reformers, from the sober political report of Mary Carpenter, to the fictional biography of Robinson's 'Prison Matron', to the pain-filled manifesto of Emily Wilding Davison, present the world of social and political reform as a remarkably fluid one, with boundaries and conventions yet to be drawn, in which religious individuals felt bound to engage, struggle, and write.

Notes

1 Ian Bradley, *The Call to Seriousness: The Evangelical Impact on the Victorians* (London: Cape, 1976), pp. 74–93.
2 Herbert Schlossberg, *Conflict and Crisis in the Religious Life of Victorian England* (London: Transaction Publishers, 2009), pp. 1–6.
3 Elisabeth Jay, *Faith and Doubt in Victorian Britain* (London: Macmillan, 1986), pp. 24–9; and Schlossberg, pp. 139–173.

4 Schlossberg, pp. 78–9.

5 *The Religion of the Heart: Anglican Evangelicalism and the Nineteenth-Century Novel* (Oxford: Clarendon, 1979), pp. 53, 207–43.

6 For a survey of mission historiography, see Patricia Grimshaw and Andrew May, 'Reappraisals of Mission History: An Introduction', in *Missionaries, Indigenous Peoples and Cultural Exchange*, ed. by Patricia Grimshaw and Andrew May (Eastbourne: Sussex Academic Press), pp. 2–3.

7 Bebbington, *Evangelicalism in Modern Britain: A History from the 1730s to the 1980s* (London: Unwin Hyman, 1989), p. 12.

8 Andrew Porter, 'An Overview, 1700–1914', in *Missions and Empire*, ed. by Norman Etherington (Oxford: Oxford University Press, 2005), pp. 40–63 (pp. 54–5); Schlossberg, pp. 144–8.

9 Anne Summers, *Christian and Jewish Women in Britain, 1880–1940: Living with Difference* (Palgrave Macmillan, 2017), p. 11.

10 Boyd Hilton, *The Age of Atonement: The Influence of Evangelicalism on Social and Economic Thought, 1795–1865* (Oxford: Clarendon, 1988), pp. 5–6.

11 For examples, see Helen Bethea Gardner, 'Practising Christianity, Writing Anthropology: Missionary Anthropologists and their Informants', in *Missionaries, Indigenous Peoples and Cultural Exchange*, ed. by Grimshaw and May, pp. 110–22.

12 Bebbington, *The Dominance of Evangelicalism*, pp. 106–8.

13 For examples of this scholarship see Claire McClisky, Daniel Midena and Karen Valgårda's edited collection, *Emotions and Christian Missions: Historical Perspectives* (Basingstoke: Palgrave Macmillan, 2015).

14 June Purvis, *A History of Women's Education in England* (Milton Keynes: Open University Press, 1991), pp. 15–17.

15 Jay, *Faith and Doubt*, pp. 16–18; Bebbington, *The Dominance of Evangelicalism*, pp. 201–34; and Bradley, pp. 94–118.

16 Jay, *Religion of the Heart*, pp. 4–5, 172.

17 Henrietta Twycross Martin, 'The Drunkard, the Brute and the Paterfamilias: The Temperance Fiction of the Early Victorian Writer Sarah Stickney Ellis', in *Women of Faith in Victorian Culture: Reassessing the Angel in the House*, ed. by Anne Hogan and Andrew Bradstock (London: Macmillan, 1998), pp. 6–30.

18 Hilton, pp. 5–6; pp. 16–19; pp. 203–18; Bebbington, *Evangelicalism in Modern Britain*, pp. 10–12; Bradley, pp. 119–34.

19 Schlossberg, pp. 144–8.

20 On the radical tendency of Christian Socialists, especially members of the clergy, see Edward Norman, *The Victorian Christian Socialists* (Cambridge: Cambridge University Press), pp. 1–9.

21 Summers, p. 66.

22 Hilton draws attention to how those whom he terms the 'extreme evangelicals' supported harsh criminal laws, while other evangelicals did not believe in corporal punishment, pp. 215–17.

23 On Isaac Nelson, see Daniel Ritchie, 'Anti-Slavery Orthodoxy: Isaac Nelson and the Free Church of Scotland c. 1843–65', *The Scottish Historical Review* 94 (2015).

24 Martin Spence has also identified this aspect of Victorian evangelicalism in his *Heaven on Earth: Reimagining Time and Eternity in Nineteenth-Century British Evangelicalism* (Eugene OR: Pickwick, 2015), pp. 3–6.

25 Norman, pp. 2–8.

26 Alison Twells, 'Missionary Domesticity, Global Reform and "Woman's Sphere" in Early Nineteenth-Century England', *Gender and History* 18 (2006), 266–84 (pp. 267–8).

INTRODUCTION TO VOLUME II

27 Arthur Selous, *The Young Governess, A Tale for Girls* (London: Griffith, Farran, Okeden and Welsh, [*c.* 1870–9], pp. 117–18.

28 Jay, *Religion of the Heart*, pp. 169, 171; Valentine Cunningham, ' "God and Nature Intended You for a Missionary's Wife" ' in *Women and Missions: Past and Present*, ed. by Fiona Bowie et al. (Oxford: Berg, 1993), pp. 96–8.

29 Johnston, p. 3.

30 Jay, *Religion of the Heart*, pp. 152–3; see also Linda Peterson, 'Women Writers and Self-Writing', in *Women and Literature in Britain 1800–1900*, ed. by Joanne Shattock (Cambridge: Cambridge University Press, 2001), pp. 209–30 (p. 224).

31 See Ruth Livesey, 'Reading for Character: Women Social Reformers and Narratives of the Urban Poor in Late Victorian and Edwardian London', *Journal of Victorian Culture* 9 (2004), 43–67 (pp. 43–5).

Part 1

THE FOREIGN MISSION MOVEMENT

1.1

Gaining Support

1.1 Gaining Support

The nineteenth-century's foreign missionary movement stemmed from the evangelical revival in Protestantism: evangelicals were inspired to spread Christianity across the world, and especially within the British empire (also see Volume I, Evangelical Religion). No one denomination had a monopoly in the foreign mission movement; the Church of England and nonconformist sects alike sent missionaries into the field. This activity required a great deal of support in terms of both money and people: individuals from all classes and of all ages were expected by their churches to donate money to the cause and to purchase tracts and newsletters. In dissenting religions, the missionaries themselves were mainly drawn from the working classes. Women often became collectors of missionary subscriptions – as is referred to in the source in this section – and this work was considered to be part of the appropriately feminine activity of philanthropy. Women also went into the mission field as wives of missionaries in the early century, before taking on more professional roles as teachers and nurses from the 1850s onwards (see this volume, Women and Authority in the Mission Field).

The source below is one of many tracts which would have been sold to support the mission movement financially, while at the same time aiming to garner support for the movement by educating its readers about their religious duty. Tracts took a range of forms, ranging from printed sermons to accounts of the missions and biographies of the missionaries. The Church Missionary Society in particular printed a number of sermons in the first half of the century which set out how the Bible commanded Christians to engage in and support evangelisation efforts around the world. This particular tract takes the form of a somewhat humorous dialogue, imagining the working-class characters the movement is trying to influence. It paints a picture of the religious working class as lacking the necessary education to fully understand religious texts, yet taking part in the factionalism of religion at this time by identifying themselves strongly as either 'Churchmen' or 'dissenters'. This characterisation is the basis of the tract's wry humour, as the parishioner is brought to realise that though he has set himself against missionaries, every time he takes part in a religious service he is reciting words and prayers that in fact support the mission movement.

More seriously, the tract makes clear how close attention to the words of the Bible – a tenet of Protestantism – and the words of the Church of England's prayers and services, led British Christians to believe that it was their duty to evangelise other nations. The author also draws on millenarian beliefs to argue that it is missionary activity that will bring about the Kingdom of Heaven on earth – as the Bible suggested that this would only come about when Christianity was spread across the world. Finally, the tract casts female collectors of subscriptions as Jesus's servants, further dignifying the missionary cause and its agents, and encouraging the religious public to treat the cause with respect, while giving generously.

1

DIALOGUE BETWEEN A MINISTER AND A PARISHIONER CONCERNING THE CHURCH MISSIONARY SOCIETY

([London]: Church Missionary Society, *c.* 1830–1839), pp. 1–12 [abridged]

M. GOOD morning to you, Mr. A———.

P. The same to you, Sir. Pray be seated.

M. I have called upon you, my good friend, in consequence of a conversation which, I am informed, took place between you and one of the Collectors of the Church Missionary Society. I understand that you refused to subscribe; and treated the subject with great indifference, and even rudeness.

P. Sir, I certainly refused to give any thing, and I as certainly view the cause with indifference; but I did not intend to be uncivil. My neighbour, Mr. B—, has set me against the Missionaries: not that I really know any thing about them, for or against.

M. I dare say you do not: indifference to this Cause, too commonly, arises either from the want of information, or from a wrong state of heart. But I am not come to call you to account to ME for your behaviour: I am only sorry that a concern of such moment should not be seriously considered: and I am the more surprised, because I know you take a pleasure in boasting that you are a CHURCHMAN.

P. Sir, you surprise me! What has my being a CHURCHMAN to do with the question? I was told by Mr. B—, that none but Dissenters, or those of the Church who are little better than Dissenters in their hearts, have any thing to do with Missionary Societies.

M. It is a pity, my friend, that, in a matter of such importance as Religion, you do not think for yourself. If, when you go to Church, you would but *take heed* to the WORDS you utter there, (even as the Scripture warns you to do, Eccles. V. 1.) you would not be so soon misled by such representations as those of Mr. B—. So far from CHURCHMEN having nothing to do with the Cause; in the last Report of the Church Missionary Society there are the names of more than 1200 CLERGYMEN— besides the MULTITUDE of Churchmen who are not of the Clergy. And as to the

THE CHURCH MISSIONARY SOCIETY

PROPRIETY of Churchmen being zealous in this Cause, they, of all people, one would suppose, ought to see and feel the necessity of making great exertions.

P. Well, Sir, this really is all Greek to me! I am sure I wish to be a consistent Churchman. But tell me, what has the subscribing, in order to send out Missionaries, to do with it? and how does it affect me more as a Churchman, than if I were a Dissenter?

M. Tell me first—Do you think it consistent for a man to ask things of God, when at Church, which he does not desire to have? and to PRAY for the Missionary Cause, when he feels no concern about it?

P. No, Sir, certainly not. But you do not mean to say that our Church Prayers have any thing in them about Missionaries?

M. Yes, my friend, I certainly do mean to say it; and therefore it is that I expect a Churchman, of all others, to be alive to the Cause. It is JUST POSSIBLE that a Dissenter may never, in his life, have heard a prayer put up for Missions; but YOU must undoubtedly have heard MANY, and have joined in many. But I fear there are numbers who say those Prayers, and yet never take the trouble to consider what they mean: thus mocking God. Does not the Apostle James speak of the ungodliness of those who give good words and prayers to the needy, and yet make no effort themselves to fulfil the good wishes they utter? (James ii. 14–16.) Are not you, friend A—, under this condemnation? Is not your faith *dead*, being *unfruitful*?

P. Sir, these are hard words. I do not for a moment dispute the truth and propriety of what St. James says; but God forbid that I should have been guilty of such folly and wickedness! I am sure, if you can make it appear, I will not only become a Subscriber, but commence with a good Donation, by way of making up for my past shameful neglect: for SHAMEFUL, in that case, I certainly call it! But I really have so little considered the matter, that I do not, at this moment, recollect a single word about MISSIONARIES, in the whole Church Prayers; nor do I exactly understand what 'a Missionary' means.

M. A Missionary is a person who is *sent forth, to preach the Gospel*, among those who know it not. The word MISSIONARY strictly means a person *sent*. Our Saviour was a Missionary, being *sent* into the world by our Heavenly Father, in order that we might be saved through his Gospel: (John xviii. 18. xx. 21.) Jesus *sent forth* his Disciples as Missionaries, saying, *Go ye, and teach all nations:* (Matt. xxviii. 19, 20. Mark xvi. 15, 16, 20.) And the injunction which he gave them, at the same time, to teach the nations ALL THINGS which he had commanded THEM, shows, that he intended WE should all, in our turn, either go forth ourselves, or endeavour to send forth others, to preach to those not yet converted. This is still more evident from that command of our Saviour to His Disciples, in the 9th chapter of St. Matthew; in which it is related, that *when he saw the multitudes*, who were as *sheep* without a *shepherd*, having no Preacher of the Gospel, he drew the attention of his Disciples to the abundant *harvest* of souls, and the small number of *Labourers;* and bade them make it a matter of prayer to God, that He would *send forth Labourers into His harvest:* (Matt. ix. 36–38.) I repeat, then, this was

THE FOREIGN MISSION MOVEMENT

evidently one of the things which our Saviour taught his Disciples; and therefore one of the things which His Ministers are to teach their people, to the end of time. The Church of England, you will see, has ACTED upon this principle; and teaches her members so to pray. Let us therefore return to this subject.

P. With all my heart, Sir. I still cannot call to memory any thing about Missionaries.

M. The very word 'MISSIONARIES,' or 'MISSIONS,' does not occur; but that which these words SIGNIFY most certainly does, in other terms: and it is the more remarkable that YOU should recollect nothing about it; for I observed you following in the train of mourners, at the funeral of your late friend Mr. —, only last week, and, if I mistake not, was much affected at the grave.

P. I was, indeed, Sir. Those prayers always affect me, more than any other of our Services: they are so solemn; and the occasion is so solemn. We stand literally at the brink of the grave; and I always fancy myself more immediately in the presence of God, than at any other time.

M. And did it not occur to you, that one of those Prayers, offered up at the grave, has an express reference to the grand objects of Missions?

P. No, indeed, Sir! Which of them?

M. What do you understand by these words, "That it "may please Thee, of thy gracious goodness, shortly to accomplish "the number of thine elect, and to hasten thy "kingdom"?

P. Sir, I do not clearly understand the whole of what you have repeated, though I now recollect the prayer very well. Pray, what is the meaning of it?

M. Well, my good friend, I do still hope that you are a candid and reasonable man, or I should not have taken the trouble to call upon you; and therefore I will endeavour to explain that part of the prayer which relates to Missions. You will not deny, that men, in general, are not *obedient to the laws of God;* and that they *serve* rather the law of the Devil, which is *the law of sin.*

P. Ah! there are too many of HIS servants in the world, sure enough!

M. Too many indeed! We are ALL his servants by nature. You stare my friend; but it is true, both of you and me:—*His servants ye are* (saith the Scripture) *whose works ye perform*: (John viii. 34. Rom. vi. 16.) And again: *Whosoever committeth sin, is of the Devil:* (1 John iii. 8.) We may not have committed the gross sins which some around us have; but if we have obeyed the ungodly principles of the world—if we have followed *the desires of the flesh or of the mind* rather than the holy precept of the Gospel, we have been led on by *the spirit which worketh in the children of disobedience:* (Ephes. ii. 1–3.) But I must return to the explanation of what is said, in the prayer, about "hastening the kingdom of God." The *Kingdom of God*, the *Kingdom of Christ*, and the *Kingdom of Heaven*, mentioned in various parts of the Scriptures, all mean one and the same thing: they refer to the rule and commandments of God and of Christ, as opposed to the rule and law of the Devil.—When men, through the *Spirit of God*, become *new creatures*, then they begin to give their chief affections to *heavenly things*, instead of *earthly things:*—then the commandments of God become written in their hearts,

18

THE CHURCH MISSIONARY SOCIETY

so that they constantly give heed to, and endeavour to regulate all their actions by them;—then they begin to be truly sensible and sorry for their sins; to love Jesus; to feel how much they are indebted to Him; and to love their neighbour also:—in short, Jesus then has HIS THRONE, as it were, *set up* in their hearts; He rules them; and they are already, in spirit, *members* of His kingdom. I may add, it is not UNTIL then, that we know what true happiness is; for there is no REAL enjoyment, but in godliness. *Whence come wars and fighting among you?* asks the Apostle. *Come they not hence, even of your lusts which war in your members?* (James iv. 1.) Yes, my friend, all the misery and disquietude which we see in the world may be traced to sin: and men do not know *that peace of mind which passeth understanding,* till they know and obey the Gospel.

P. Sir, I believe you—I believe you!

M. But the time will arrive, friend A—, when this Gospel shall be known and obeyed by all men (Isaiah xi. 9. Hab. ii. 14.), when *the nations shall not learn war any more* (Isaiah ii. 4.); but all shall bow down to Jesus Christ (Psalm lxxii. 11.); and, finally, when all who have served God shall have a *glorious body,* which shall be *incorruptible,* and never perish; and they shall be happy with God, and with Christ, with the holy Angels, and each other, for ever and ever: (1 Cor. xv. 51–58. 1 Thess. iv. 17.)

P. A glorious time indeed! I wish it was come!

M. Yes;—but this is the time of PREPARATION for it; now, in the kingdom of *Grace*: for ALL men shall not be saved; only those who *believe in* and *obey* the Lord Jesus: (Mark xvi. 16.) When their number is completed, then the Lord will come in His glory: (2 Thess. i. 8. Rev. vi. 11.) But we have reason to believe, from Scripture, that this will not take place till *the Gospel of Christ* shall have been preached in all nations—till *the knowledge of Him shall have covered the earth—* and the Jews; His ancient people, are also brought to believe in Him: (Matt. xxiv. 14. Rom. xi. 26.) Therefore it is that pious persons—when, through the loss of friends or relatives, or by means of any other affliction or vexation, they perceive more clearly than usual the vanities and the troubles of this life—look forward to that time, when these things shall cease from the EARTH; even when there shall be no more *sin* nor *death*; *the tears shall be wiped from all eyes, and sorrow and sighing shall flee away:* (Rev. xxi. 4.) They enter into a happy rest when they die: but their glory, and the final perfection of their happiness, (Heb. xi. 40. Rev. vi. 9–11. xiv. 13)—the destruction also of Satan, who causes so much misery in the earth—is left till that day, when they shall *shine forth as the sun in the Kingdom of their Father* (Matt. xiii. 43. Rev. xx.); *and when all the redeemed shall come to Zion, with songs and everlasting joy upon their heads:* Isaiah xxxv. 10.) Thus the prayer to which I have called your attention has a peculiar beauty and reference to this subject: "We give Thee hearty thanks, for that it hath pleased Thee to deliver this our brother out of the miseries of this sinful world; beseeching Thee, that it may please Thee, of Thy gracious goodness, shortly to accomplish the number of Thine elect, and to hasten Thy Kingdom; that we, with all those that are departed in the true faith of Thy holy Name, may have our perfect consummation and bliss, both in body and soul, in thy eternal and everlasting glory, through Jesus Christ our Lord."

P. Well, indeed it would appear so! and I thank you for this explanation. I suppose the reason I never noticed it, is, because the Burial Service has come before me so seldom.

M. It may be so. But, my friend, this is not the only part of our Church Prayers in which we profess to be interested in the conversion of those who now oppose the Lord. [...]

[...] But now let me ask you a question. You think a FUNERAL a very solemn and affecting circumstance: but which DAY OF THE YEAR ought to bring the most solemn and affecting recollections home to the soul of the Christian? When ought he more especially to remember his dying Lord, and that sin has produced all our misery, and needed the sacrifice of Jesus Christ? When ought he to consider that he is *bought with a price?* and, out of gratitude to his Saviour for purchasing for him an inheritance with blood, when ought he to devote himself most heartily to the service of Christ, and determine to do his utmost to bring OTHERS to the knowledge of the same mercy?

P. Well, Sir, I think there can be but little question upon that head: there is one day in the year, Good Friday, on which, as I suppose, we specially commemorate the death of our Saviour. I certainly think, if we have any spark of gratitude or consideration at all, it will lead us to worship Him on THAT day.

M. I am glad to hear you answer so much to the purpose. And do you not recollect, that the Christian prays on that day for the poor Jews; for the followers of the false prophet, Mahomet; for all nations who may now be in darkness or unbelief—yea, for all nations or individuals who, though they may profess Christianity, *err from the truth* of the Gospel in some essential points, and are therefore considered Heretics? Yes, the Christian longs for the time when there shall only be *one flock* and *one Shepherd*. He knows that his Redeemer, when he *set up* His *Kingdom*, did it in order that sinners of all descriptions might be converted;—he knows that it is by *the foolishness of preaching*, as by an instrument, that God generally effects this object: he is sensible, that it must be most pleasing to Him when men take an interest in the spiritual concerns of others: for Jesus then *sees the travail* (that is, the agony) *of his soul,* every time a sinner is brought to confess, and turn from the error of his ways: (Isaiah liii. 10.) In short, the Christian feels it to be his OWN interest to spread the Gospel; for—

P. But, my dear Sir, gently if you please! I remember nothing of all this on Good Friday. Where—in what part—do we pray for all these people?

M. Reach me your Prayer Book.——There; read that Collect, for Good Friday.

P. [reads] "O merciful God, who hast made all men, and hatest nothing that thou hast made; nor wouldest the death of a sinner, but rather that he should be converted and live; have mercy upon all Jews, Turks, Infidels, and Heretics; and take from them all ignorance, hardness of heart, and contempt of thy word: and so fetch them home, Blessed Lord, to thy flock, that they may be saved among the remnant of the TRUE Israelites, and be made one fold under one Shepherd,

THE CHURCH MISSIONARY SOCIETY

Jesus Christ our Lord, who liveth and reigneth with Thee and the Holy Spirit, one God world without end!"

M. Well—what say you now? God, as you must be well aware, usually works by means; more especially in taking IGNORANCE from men. How can you reasonably expect that these are to have "all ignorance and hardness of heart taken from them," if the means are not used which, with God's blessing, are calculated to produce this effect? Why do you PRAY for the thing, if you are not disposed to ASSIST in promoting it.

P. Indeed, what you say is all very true. I suppose it must be owing to this prayer coming only once in the year, that I have never taken proper notice of it.

M. Come, come, my good friend, I do not intend to let you escape thus! You conceive yourself excused for not having paid attention to the spirit of the prayers you offer, because funerals occur but seldom, and Good Friday only once a-year: in general, prayers are apt to attract attention the MORE from their only being used occasionally. But, though I have been led, by circumstances, to mention these two prayers first, they are by no means the whole, nor the half, of what I can bring forward. In the prayers you offer up on every Sabbath, both in the morning and afternoon, you mention this subject. Look at the Litany, for instance, used in the morning; what is the meaning of these words—"That it may please Thee to give to ALL NATIONS, unity, peace, and concord"? How can this ever take place, if you will not send them the *Gospel of Peace?*—Again, "That it may please Thee to bring into the way of Truth all such as have erred and are deceived." There can be no doubt that the Heathens are deceived, and that many nations calling themselves Christians have fearfully erred; but how are they to be brought into the WAY OF TRUTH, if you will not preach to them the *Word of Truth*, nor point them to JESUS, as *the Way, the Truth, and the Life?* Once more:—In the Litany you pray, "That it may please Thee to have MERCY upon all men:"—yet YOU will have NO mercy! Though you profess to hope for it in Christ yourself, and to believe *that there is no other name given among men whereby we can be saved*, you are nevertheless careless about bringing ALL MEN to the knowledge of His mercy.—Now for the Sabbath Afternoon: have the goodness to notice this prayer, which you regularly offer up: "O God, the Creator and Preserver of all mankind! we humbly beseech Thee for ALL SORTS and conditions of men; that Thou wouldest be pleased to make Thy ways known unto them, Thy saving health unto ALL NATIONS." What can be more plain and express? What is "SAVING health," but the Gospel? it is that alone which can make known to us the ways of God: and yet, when you have the opportunity, you will not subscribe, to SEND it to the nations! Is not this mockery, friend A—? Have I not proved you to be under the condemnation of which St. James speaks? that is—you give the poor perishing Heathen good WORDS, but make no effort to give them the THINGS they require.

P. Well, Sir; I have not a word to reply. I must own myself convicted. I really wonder what I can have been dreaming about for the forty years during which I have regularly attended at Church! There may be an excuse for some; but there is none for me; for if I had not known better, it has been my own fault, for not

21

paying attention to what I have been about. I see, indeed, that every Sunday of my life I have been guilty of an act of solemn mockery, at the very time when I have thought I was making myself more acceptable to God. I am almost afraid to talk any further with you, Sir. You will be proving next, that I have been praying for Missionaries EVERY DAY, and thus taking *the name of the Lord in vain.*

M. Well, I feel gratified at your honest confession: it makes me the more anxious to point out your errors,—not, I assure you, my friend, for the sake of exposing, but of correcting them. Tell me, then; Do you PRAY daily?

P. Yes, Sir, I trust I do not neglect that duty. I always have my family together, night and morning.

M. Very right.—And what Prayers do you make use of?

P. I give them one out of a book which I have here, Sir: and I generally finish with the Lord's Prayer.

M. The LORD's Prayer!—and a very good prayer it is. It occurs many times also in the CHURCH SERVICE.

P. Yes, Sir; but I always think it must be a good one; for our Lord made it Himself.

M. So think I: and as to its being repeated several times, we have an instance, in the EXAMPLE of our Lord also, that *repetitions,* if they are not *vain* ones (as I fear yours may have been), are not objectionable in the sight of God: for when the soul of Jesus was *in agony,* He made use of the same words three times (Matt. xxvi. 44.) within an hour or two. If men were more in EARNEST about their own souls and the souls of others, we should not hear of such objections. But I like this prayer the better just now, because the three first things which we ask of God in it concern Missionaries; and we may rest assured thereby, that the converting of souls to God by the preaching of the Gospel must have been very near the heart of Jesus, and very pleasing to His Heavenly Father, or He would not have made these things so considerable a part of that prayer which He gave us for daily use.

P. Indeed, Sir, you take me by surprise again!

M. What! have you forgotten your Catechism? How are you taught to reply, when you are asked the question, "What DESIREST thou of God in this prayer?" Do you not answer: "I desire my Lord God, our Heavenly Father, who is the giver of all goodness, to send His grace unto me, and to ALL PEOPLE, that we may WORSHIP Him, SERVE Him, and OBEY Him, AS WE OUGHT TO DO." The part of the prayer to which this undoubtedly refers is, *"Hallowed be thy name:"* there is the FIRST petition: and it is as much as to say, 'May Thy name be worshipped and glorified throughout the world.' But with respect to these poor creatures, who are now living in ignorance of Him, St. Paul justly asks, *How, then, shall they call on Him in whom they have not believed? and how shall they believe in Him of whom they have not heard? and how shall they hear without a preacher? and how shall they preach, except they be sent?* (Rom. x. 14, 15.) MISSIONARIES, you see, are what is wanted; and surely none can really desire the Father's name to be *hallowed,* who do not make some effort to *send forth Labourers.*

THE CHURCH MISSIONARY SOCIETY

P. Well, Sir, I really begin to fear every fresh remark you are about to make, lest it should condemn me. I never noticed the meaning of these words before, though I have often gabbled them over.

M. I will pass over the SECOND petition—*"Thy Kingdom come,"*—because I have already explained the meaning of it: it is the same as "Hasten Thy Kingdom," in the Burial Service. But mark the THIRD petition—*"Thy will be done on earth, as it is in Heaven."* What does that mean?

P. Oh, Sir, I feel all shame! I declare, if I do know, I can hardly answer you now; I am so confused.

M. Did you ever consider, HOW the will of God is done in Heaven?

P. No, Sir, I never gave it a thought.

M. In Heaven, the will of God is universally obeyed. There is not a spirit there which does not cheerfully perform it: (Ps. ciii. 20, 21.)

P. I suppose not, Sir.—It is the Angels who are in Heaven, is it not; and the souls of the righteous who have departed this life?

M. Yes—souls whose delight it has been to *do the will of God* HERE; and are now enabled to *do* it THERE, without any drawback or check. But how, let me ask, can the *will* of God be *done on earth* AS IT IS IN HEAVEN, whilst there is one person in the world opposed to that will? You will allow, that there is NOT one opposed to it in Heaven: and I repeat, whilst there is one single soul opposed to it in the world, the *will* of God is not *done on earth* AS IT IS *in Heaven.*

P. Certainly, that is very true: I cannot contradict it.

M. Ah, my friend! how many are there who daily say that prayer, and yet have never once asked themselves the question—"Am I endeavouring to do the will of God MYSELF? and am I doing what lies in my power to bring OTHERS to the knowledge and obedience of His will?"

P. That has been my case, Sir. Pray say no more. I will give you a donation for the past, according as I promised; and I will cheerfully subscribe in future.

M. I am glad to see you so determined: but I will not take it of you myself. I shall send the Collector, who called before: it will be some little encouragement to that Lady, in the work she has undertaken.

P. Be it so, Sir. I hope she will now meet with a different reception.

M. I trust she will: I am SURE she will, if you feel as you ought to do on the ocasion: for she is doing an HONOUR in soliciting you.—I perceive you stare at that saying.

P. No—no, Sir: I have heard so much to-day that has been strange to me, and yet very true, that you hardly can surprise me any more.

M. Well, certainly, if the Cause of Missions is the Cause of Jesus (which I think you will now admit), the Collectors solicit you in the STEAD of Jesus: they are His servants: and he that receiveth them, whom He sendeth, receiveth Him: (Matt. x. 40, 41. Luke x. 16. John xiii. 20.) Indeed, too many of those who DO give, seem to think it a FAVOUR done to the Collector! And they also lose sight of their own INTEREST;—for, if we are real BELIEVERS, what we give for Missionaries is, as it were, laid out upon our own estate. If we have an interest in the *Kingdom* of Christ, it must be our interest to promote the welfare of that *Kingdom,* and to hasten it forward: to say nothing of the reward we shall receive ACCORDING to our works, if they are performed in a right spirit.

P. Well, Sir, I see the thing plainer now: and as I do not labour as a Collector myself, I hope I shall, in future, be more ready to *esteem* those highly, *for their work's sake*, who do. I can only repeat, if the Lady calls again, I will endeavour to give her a proper reception.

M. Do so: and when you cry next, "O be joyful in the Lord, ALL ye lands!" may your *heart* be enabled to joy and rejoice in Him also! Farewell.

1.2

Children

1.2 Children

While lower-class British children at home were the objects of domestic missions and the Sunday School movement (see this volume, Education), children of all nationalities growing up in the empire could come under the care and instruction of missionaries. The foreign mission movement also provided a context for the religious teaching of British children: stories of converted native children were designed to draw British children's attention to how lucky they were to have been born in a Christian country, at the same time as emphasising their unworthiness in comparison with many pious native converts. Furthermore, British children were recruited as supporters and fundraisers for the foreign mission movement, and as such could be seen as little missionaries.

'Lessons from Heathen Lands' is a short children's tract, by an author known only as E. M. I., that was first published in the 1843 collection, *Missionary Stories*, and later in an American Methodist Sunday School collection, *25 Missionary Stories for Children*. It presents stories from the mission field as parables and draws out the lessons for young readers. Two of the stories are about children of the South Sea Islands and New Zealand who made sacrifices and overcame barriers just so they could attend the mission school and learn to be Christians. The stories imply that these children from 'heathen' lands are more pious than the privileged child readers in Britain, and suggest that readers should feel 'reproved' by their example and attend Sunday school more often and more promptly. The lesson is taught in three different ways: implicitly in a story, more explicitly in verse and then explained in a direct address to the reader.

Over and above the individual lessons of this book is an encompassing narrative of the child readers themselves, who are envisaged as 'little missionary collectors and subscribers' by virtue of being members of Sunday schools. This activity is compared to the exciting and culturally significant endeavour of imperial trade, and the child subscribers are designated as the 'merchants' of the missionary message being sent to the mission field thanks to their pennies. This imagery is mixed with the most ubiquitous metaphors of the missionary movement – sowing the good seed in the mission field, harvesting the souls of the heathen, labouring in the vineyard – and the children are called 'seed merchants' who are called upon to pray for the seeds to bear fruit. This overarching narrative frame suggests that, though native children can be exemplars of pious Christianity for British children to emulate, only the British children can be depicted as imperial agents and missionaries.

Worlds Displayed is an allegorical work in the style of *Pilgrim's Progress*, written by John Campbell (1766–1840) – who later became a missionary for the London Missionary Society (LMS) – and first published in 1802 (the version extracted here was taken from his later collection of stories for children). In what is eventually revealed to be a dream, the narrator visits heaven and hell. He refers to these respectively as 'the mansions of the blessed' or 'the New Jerusalem', and 'the eternal prison of the wicked'. In his advertisement for the work, he states that his purpose is to impress upon young people the connection between time and eternity. Indeed, in both heaven and hell there are characters from Campbell's contemporary era, along with those from the near past, and those from Biblical times. In this way missionary work of the nineteenth century is represented as simply a continuance of the missionary work of the Bible, and part of the same monumental Biblical history (see this volume, Biblical History, Geography and Travel Writing). Moreover, the work also stresses the connectedness of geographical places as converts and sinners from different countries are brought together in the all-encompassing space of God's 'empire' – which itself is imagined as having a complex geography including the metropolis of the 'holy city', the prison of hell, and other 'innumerable suns and worlds'.

In many ways *Worlds Displayed* invokes child readers' awareness of the nineteenth-century foreign mission movement. One effect of this is to make Biblical stories more familiar. For example, the story of the Apostle Paul is told as the 'History of a Jewish Convert', linking it with the nineteenth-century Mission to the Jews (see this volume, Mission to the Jews). And when the narrator comes to describe hell, the lesson is similar to that in 'Lessons from Heathen Lands': souls who have ended in hell despite having the advantages of growing up in a Christian country are treated far more severely than those from the non-Christian world.

2

E. M. I., 'LESSONS FROM HEATHEN LANDS'

In *Missionary Stories*
(London: John Snow, 1843–1844), pp. 3–8

Lessons from Heathen Lands

It is a pleasant and cheerful thing to stand by the water-side in some busy sea-port, and see the vessels with their cargoes all packed, their sails set, and their brave and active seamen on board, sailing away with a fair wind and a strong brisk tide, to carry their treasures to distant lands, far across the deep blue sea. Children who live in sea-port towns can understand all this; and those who do not, must try to fancy it all: the bright sunshine, the sharp sea-breeze, and the dancing waves, and then the shouts of the sailors and the splash of the restless waters mingling together, as the stately ship sails away on her long, long voyage.

Many stand on the shore to watch, but there is one who seems to look more anxiously than the rest; ah! that is the merchant, the owner of the ship, or of her cargo. Many precious things he has sent in that vessel: how he will think of her when she shall be far away! how he will hope she is safe, and that the good things she is taking will sell for a great deal of money, and that with that money other things may be bought which she shall bring home to England, that so he may "buy and sell, and get gain."

But you will say this is not a "Missionary story." Yes, it is; it is a story for all the little missionary collectors and subscribers; for all who have learned the "best use of a penny,"

> "Not on apples, or cakes, or on playthings to spend it,
> But over the seas for the heathen to send it."

Listen, dear children; you are merchants—*little seed merchants*. "The seed is the word of God;" your pennies are helping to send it abroad. Missionaries go to sow this precious seed, and the hearts of little heathen children, and of heathen men and women too, are the gardens in which they love to work. God smiles upon their labours, and his smile is like the sunshine in summer; it causes the seed to spring, and the blossom to open, and the precious fruits to ripen. And then the missionaries write home to tell us "good news from far," and we listen, and rejoice, and thank God—the God of the harvest.

Now do you see how you are merchants, and how the stories I am going to tell you are *fruits* which have come home instead of the seed you have sent out? Try to remember this, and I will tell you afterwards what you must do with the fruits, and how you must try to learn "Lessons from Heathen Lands."

One Sabbath evening, a missionary was walking up and down in the verandah before his house, in the island of Aitutaki. The sun was just setting behind the waves of the Southern Ocean, the labours of the day were over and in that cool, quiet evening hour, the missionary was lifting his heart to God, and asking a blessing on his people, his schools, and himself.

All was hushed and still, except a little rustling in the leaves of a mimosa-tree close by; he fancied a breeze was springing up, and continued his lonely walk, but again he heard the rustling, and again and again, till he felt quite sure it could not be the wind alone, so he parted the long leafy branches of the tree, and peeped beneath. What did he find there? Three little boys! Two were fast asleep in each other's arms, but the third was awake, and it was he who had stirred the mimosa leaves.

"What are you doing here, my children?" asked the missionary. "We are come to sleep here, teacher," said the boy. "And why would you sleep here? have you no home?" "Oh yes, but if we sleep here, we are sure to be quite ready when the first school-bell rings in the morning." "Do your parents know about it?" "Mine do; but these little boys have no parents, they are orphans."

Now, the nights in the South-Sea Islands are not cold and damp like ours; but the kind missionary looked round, and he felt sure a heavy rain was coming, so, rousing the sleeping ones, he led the three little fellows into the large porch of his house, where they might rest in safety; and oh! his heart rejoiced to know that thus they loved to come to school, to "hear of heaven, and learn the way."

Very like this was the story of some little black children, in New Zealand, who lived a long way from one side of a river, and their school was at the other side. There are no bridges there. Did they, therefore, stay at home? No. We will try to tell you, in verse, how *they* showed their love to their school. Cannot you fancy them, as they set off, singing some such song as this,—

> "Oh! come, with the morning's earliest ray
> Joyfully onward we take our way
> Across the wide valley or sunny plain,
> Till our teacher's distant home we gain.
> See where the walls of the school-house white
> Cheerfully gleam in the morning light;
> Many a wonderful thing is there;—
> Books which can speak, tho' no voice we hear;
> Slates which can carry our thoughts away,
> Tho' never a word with our lips we say;

E. M. I., 'LESSONS FROM HEATHEN LANDS'

And pictures and beautiful maps, to tell
Of the far-off countries where strangers dwell."

But the little ones came to a river's side,
Gently onward the wavelets glide,
But ah! neither bridge nor boat is there
To help them over the waters fair.—
Do the little travellers turn again
And retrace their steps over valley and plain?
No; with their treasured books held high,
Lightly they spring from the herbage dry,
And manfully breasting the yielding wave,
No help from bridge or from boat they crave,
Quickly they land on the opposite shore,
And soon they are safe at the school-house door.

Oh! could some of our English children feel
But a spark of the little islanders' zeal,
How soon would each vacant class be full
In our happy English Sunday-school!

Now, dear little readers, stop a minute and think; *you* could not sleep all night under a tree in England, nor could you swim across a stream, like the young New Zealanders, who have not clothes like yours to hinder them, and who can swim almost like fishes; but is there *the same feeling in your hearts?* Does not a shower, or a cold day, or a very hot day, sometimes keep *you* from school? And do you not sometimes walk idly into your place when half the business of the class is over? If it be so, and you feel reproved by these stories, then try to show your teachers that you have learned *some* good Lessons from Heathen Lands.

And now I will tell you another story about the Sabbath, not *about* children, as the others were, but still what children may profit by.

A little boat was sailing on its lonely course across the deep waters of the Southern Ocean; no island was near, no shore to be seen; wherever the poor voyagers looked, still the same wide wide sea spread around, and their hearts felt sad and heavy; for they had been six weeks upon those deep waters; their small stock of food had had grown less and less, and now a very little rice, and a few drops of oil, were all their store. They divided the rice, and ate a grain at a time, and then they dipped a little of the husk of the cocoa-nut in oil, to moisten their parched and thirsty lips. It was the Sabbath-day, and, weak and weary as they were, they raised a Sabbath hymn, and then they read together in God's holy word, and prayed that they might not die from famine on the mighty deep.

Just then a large fish appeared on the top of the waves, and played some time around the boat; the poor sailors were hungry, and the fish would have made them one good meal at least; but *it was the Sabbath-day;* they looked at it, and at each

31

other, and, after talking together, they agreed that "they would not catch fish on the Lord's-day." So they let it swim away, and again they prayed, "resting in the Lord and waiting patiently for Him;" and their prayer was heard. God led them safely across the waters to the island of Atui, and at length brought them back to their own far-off home.

These were South-Sea Islanders. A very little time before, they knew nothing of God's holy day, or of Him who is Lord of the Sabbath, and now they knew but little, or they might have thought how Jesus himself allowed his hungry disciples to seek and gather food on the Sabbath-day, for "He loved mercy better than sacrifice." But with our better *knowledge,* is our *spirit* as obedient? The Bible says, "Happy is the man that feareth always, but he that hardeneth his heart shall fall into mischief."

One more Lesson only we can put into this little book; it, too, comes from the South Seas—from the beautiful island of Rarotonga, where a missionary was one day taking his way from one station to another. On one side of him rose lofty hills, fringed with rows of spreading chesnut-trees, and the deep blue waves of the Ocean rolled on the other; his path lay beneath the shade of banana and plaintain-trees, while scattered about at some little distance from the road, were the pretty houses of the natives, each with its path of black and white pebbles leading to the door. Six or eight stone seats were ranged by the way-side, and here, in the cool of the evening, the people loved to sit, and they would often say, "Here my father or grandfather, or some great chief, used to sit, long long since." I wonder whether they ever thought how different the scene was then—their fathers had no peaceful dwellings or smiling gardens like theirs. No, for *they* had not the gospel, or English teachers to tell them how to build, or dig, or plant. But oh, was it for *this,* then, that the missionary had left his happy English home? No, he rejoiced in the increased comforts of the islanders, but he felt that his message was to their *hearts,* his chief work to sow seed *there.* And had he done this?

We will listen, for just at that moment a voice said to him, "Welcome, servant of God, who brought light to this dark island, who brought to us the word of salvation!" Ah! that was a pleasant sound, and the missionary (it was Mr. Williams) looked up, and before him stood a poor native whose hands and feet had been eaten away by a sad disease, so that he had to walk upon his knees. "And what do you know of the word of salvation?" said Mr. W. "Oh," Buteve replied, "I know about Jesus, who came into the world to save sinners, and died painfully on the cross to pay for all their sins, that so they might go to heaven." "And do all people, then, go to heaven?" "No, none but they who believe in the Lord Jesus, put away their sins and pray to God." "Then, do *you* pray?" "Oh yes, while I weed my ground, I pray, and three times a day, and in the morning and evening with my family." "And what do you say?" "I say, 'O Lord, I am a great sinner; may Jesus take away my sins, and give me his righteousness to adorn me, and his spirit to teach me, and make my heart good, and to take me to heaven when I die!'" "Well, Buteve, that is very good; but who taught you this?" "Oh, *you* taught me," said Buteve; "you brought the good word." "Ah, but I never saw you listening when I preached: how did you hear?" "Oh," said the poor man, "I take my seat by the way-side as the people pass by, and I beg a bit of the word from them: one gives me one piece, and another another piece; I put all these in my heart, and think about them; and then I pray to God, and so he teaches me to understand them."

Dear young friends, as you read of this poor cripple working in his garden, and praying to God the while, do you think of the Bible lesson, to be "diligent in business, fervent in spirit, serving God?"

And as you picture him like one of old,"sitting by the way-side begging," not for the bread which perisheth, but for heavenly food, do you remember *your* English homes, with their schools and Sabbath services? And does not another text come to your mind, "Where much is given, much shall be required?" Oh! like Buteve, the poor cripple of Rarotonga, put these things into your hearts, and then pray to God that your souls may not be like the fleece of Gideon, dry while the dew of instruction is falling all around you!

And now I have no more stories; but I have a short message *for yourselves*. One autumn a lady gave me some beautiful fruit. I put one of the stones into the garden, and soon a tiny stalk peeped out, then two bright green leaves opened, and after them, more and more. It is but a slender twig now, but it has lived through the long winter months, and, perhaps, with care and culture, it may be a tree in time. This is just what I want you to do with my stories—my fruit.

Do any of you sometimes come late to school, or even like to stay quite away? Are there any who do not "remember the Sabbath-day to keep it holy?" or who do not prize their Sabbath lessons and sermons? Ah! dear children! pick out from these stories some little good seeds for your own hearts, and then ask God to cause those seeds to spring and blossom there; then, while you care for others, you shall keep your own vineyards too; and these "Lessons from Heathen Lands" will be better to you "than the merchandize of silver, and the gain thereof than fine gold."

3

JOHN CAMPBELL, *WORLDS DISPLAYED FOR THE BENEFIT OF YOUNG PEOPLE BY A FAMILIAR HISTORY OF SOME OF THEIR INHABITANTS* [1802]

In *The Juvenile Cabinet of Travels and Narratives for the Amusement and Instruction of Young Persons* (London: Francis Westley, 1825), pp. 101–102, 105–107, 124, 126–129, 137

Advertisement

The design of this little book is to impress the minds of young people with the importance of time and eternity, and to exhibit the close connection that there is between them.

Narrative appears a pleasing and engaging way of communicating divine truth to young persons. Some may judge it, when fictitious, to be an improper instrument for cutting down the corruptions of men; but as God has so frequently used the same method, his example may be safely followed. The Old Testament contains many parables, and much of our Lord's instruction during his ministry on earth was communicated in this form. The Pilgrim's Progress, Hervey's Dialogues, and many of the Tracts published for the Cheap Repository, are of a similar kind, and are generally and justly approved, and have done much good.

Some of the passages may appear rather too terrific; but as the attack designed against obdurate and strongly fortified hearts, which is the true and scriptural description of every unrenewed soul, the shot does not appear too sharp, nor the artillery too heavy. The parable of the rich man and Lazarus is perhaps more so than any of the following lives.

That the Lord's blessing may accompany this small effort to be useful to my fellow-sinners, is my sincere prayer.

John Campbell

Worlds Displayed

One evening in May last, Apollos and I took a long walk through the fields. The sun had nearly finished his course—the whole creation around us seemed silent as death; not a breath of wind was heard; every thing combined solemnly to please the imagination, and to produce thought. We talked a while upon the wisdom and power of that God who gave being to all the beauties which surrounded us; then upon the superior excellency of that heavenly glory we soon hoped to see. By this conversation, I found my desire to depart to the happy regions of immortality greatly increased.

After our return home, I was not long asleep till the scene we had talked over came fresh into my mind, and to my delight and astonishment, a heavenly messenger addressed me thus: "I am acquainted with your desire to visit the mansions of the blessed, and am commissioned to carry you there, to exhibit to you some of the glories of that state, and afterwards to conduct you back to your present condition, till my Lord's time be fully come to fix you for ever in his everlasting kingdom." Happy tidings! I exclaimed, being overpowered with transport at the thought of beholding Jesus on his throne, at the head of his redeemed.

We mounted in the air with a quickness I can only compare to lightning. After passing innumerable suns and worlds, I enquired if we were near heaven? The angel replied with a smile, We are only in the frontiers of the Mediator's kingdom. I asked what kind of beings inhabited these vast bodies, scattered through the immensity of space? My commission, said he, is to convey and guard you to the metropolis of my Lord's empire; I cannot go beyond it: but, for your comfort let me tell you, that when you finish your course below, and enter on your glorified life, nothing shall be hid from you; then you shall know even as you are known.

We had scarcely ended this conversation, when I was desired to look directly above my head; I did so, and, to my inexpressible surprise, I saw a brightness, to which the sun bears no resemblance. Pointing to it with his finger, the angel said, That is heaven! In a moment I was surrounded with hundreds of those whom I had known upon earth, all welcoming me to their blissful, peaceful realms. Perceiving me astonished at the grandeur of their appearance, they desired me to suspend my wonder, till they brought me into the presence of Jesus. Upon this they unanimously exclaimed, "To him, to him, be all the glory!" We flew past millions of the spirits of justified men made perfect, till we came to Jesus the judge of all, of whom indeed I dare not now speak, for no tongue can utter his praise, or declare his glory.

Turning my eyes in every direction, I exclaimed, No wonder that this should be called an exceeding great and eternal weight of glory!

While I stood wondering at the Saviour, and extolling his mercy and grace to me, in redeeming me from misery, and promising soon to put me in full possession of all the glory of his kingdom, I was surprised with the noise of shouts of joy from every quarter. I asked my guide the reason of this new appearance. He replied, See a legion of angels advancing to the throne with the soul of one of your countrymen! This is his entrance to our society: every accession to our number gives rise to a new song of praise to the Lamb of God. [...]

[...] While I stood silently admiring the harmony, love, happiness, and perfect peace which universally pervaded the heavenly country, I was struck with shouts of triumph which commenced in the vicinity of our Lord's presence, and which spread like lightning over his immense empire. Enquiring into the cause, I was informed that ten careless sinners in Bohemia had been a few minutes before converted to the faith of Christ. Are you surprised at their rejoicing so heartily at this? said the angel: do not you read in the scriptures, that there is joy in heaven over one sinner that repenteth? We are deeply interested in the displays of divine mercy to men upon earth; we rejoice in the glory that redounds to our dear Lord; and in the boundless, endless felicity to which the poor sinner is thereby exalted, the prodigious misery he has thereby escaped, and a thousand other things combined with that event. Truly, you terrestrial saints see these things but darkly as through a glass, or you would feel more deeply interested in the salvation of poor perishing mortals. [...]

History of a Jewish convert

I was born in Judea, a few furlongs from Jerusalem, about a year before our Lord's appearance upon earth. I was brought up by my parents a Pharisee. The wickedness of my heart prompted me greatly to prefer, and to be much more zealous in defending the traditions, or rather the inventions of the elders, than the revelation of God in Moses and the prophets. I found these were more consonant to my corruption than the holy and righteous laws of the Lord.

Being once prevailed upon to hear a sermon by John the Baptist, I was a little affected by what he advanced, but quite offended with the coarseness of his attire, and the strictness of his tenets. I had no idea that he was sent of God, or that he was the harbinger of the Messiah.

Some time after this, I heard much about the preaching and miracles of our Saviour; but all that we Pharisees did, was to dispute about them, and generally to slight them. The resurrection of Lazarus caused a great outcry against Christ, instigated by the members of the Sanhedrim; and though I joined in the general outcry, I had my fears, lest it should be some great prophet whose character we were traducing. Though Jesus passed our house when on his last journey to Jerusalem, I did not so much as go to see him.

We were greatly alarmed on the day Jesus was crucified, by the uncommon darkness which happened, and more so by a person calling at our house, and declaring that he saw several rocks of Mount Zion rent in a most astonishing manner; also that the vail of the temple, which separated between the holy place, and the most holy, was torn from top to bottom without human hands.—Three days after, we were told that Jesus, in spite of every precaution taken by the chief priests, had burst the tomb, and got out of their hands; likewise that some who had

JOHN CAMPBELL, *WORLDS DISPLAYED*

lain long in the grave had come forth, and called upon several citizens of Jerusalem. All these things struck me exceedingly. The claim of Christ, to the character of the Jewish Messiah, appeared a matter of immense magnitude, and deserving the most attentive consideration. But the prejudice and enmity at that time prevalent against Jesus, prevented me from mentioning my inward reasoning to my dearest and nearest relations. However, I learned that some of the followers of the Messiah were preaching on Pentecost day. I instantly ran to the place where they were addressing an immense concourse. Peter was speaking with a fervour which demonstrated his own conviction of the truth of what he said.

I trembled when he boldly asserted the divinity of his Master; and when he charged our nation with murdering the Prince of Life, I cried out, with thousands more, Men and brethren, what shall we do to be saved! But O how we rejoiced, when he commanded us to believe in the Lord Jesus Christ, assuring us, if we did so, that all our sins should be forgiven; that God would even accept us, murderers of his dear Son, as righteous in his sight: that, by the death of Christ, he opened a way whereby he would eternally appear just, even when he justified the ungodly. I believed that Jesus was the Son of God,—that his death was the appointed atonement for sin, and that the Old Testament sacrifices all prefigured his one offering.

I ran home to my relations, and preached unto them the glory of Jesus. I besought them to compare the character of Jesus with Old Testament predictions, and they would look no longer for their expected deliverer,—that Jesus was the very person,—that we had most shamefully joined in the hue and cry that was raised against him, which hindered us from maturely examining the matter.

Our whole family, with many of our neighbours, sat up till midnight talking about these strange things which had happened, and I assure you they made a solemn impression upon all our minds. Some regretted that they had ever uttered a word against the Messiah, others that they had basely neglected to hear him. In short, all who were present were under deep impression of the magnitude of these matters. We did not work, and scarcely ate any thing next day. Some were alarmed lest God should inflict some dreadful judgment upon Jerusalem for the atrocious crime of crucifying the Lord of Glory. I told them, that by believing in Jesus they became the friends of God, and when inflicting his judgments, he knew well how to distinguish between friends and foes. They believed in Christ and had peace with God. We all committed ourselves to the care, guidance, and protection of God, and then sung the 18th verse of Psalm lxviii. *Thou hast ascended on high, thou hast led captivity captive; thou hast received gifts for men; yea, for the rebellious also, that the Lord God might dwell among men.* [...]

[...] We now left the Holy City amidst the hosannahs of millions. Heaven was engraven on my mind, its glory was present to my view. Said I to my conductor, I see death to me will be unspeakable gain. Truly it will be better than life. I long to depart and be with Christ. I can never now set my heart upon long life, or riches, or honour in the world, all is eclipsed by the glory of Christ. While I was thus speaking, we entered the gloomy gate which led to the mansions of the miserable. We took a general view of this extensive empire, and noticed misery in all its degrees, proportioned by infinite wisdom and power to the guilt contracted in the world. Those who had had few opportunities of obtaining the knowledge of God and his Son Jesus Christ, were beaten comparatively with few stripes; but those who had lived in countries blessed with the scriptures of truth were beaten with many. The vials of the unmixed wrath of God were perpetually pouring out upon them. Many were constantly exclaiming, O that I had never seen the word of God! O that I had never heard of Jesus Christ! O that I had never been advised and entreated to believe in him! O that I had never been born! O that I had died that day! Tell my brethren who are still alive not to come into this place of torment, for they will add to my misery by upbraiding me for shewing them such bad example, and giving them so wicked counsel.

1.3

Women and Authority in the Mission Field

1.3 Women and Authority in the Mission Field

Female missionary biography influenced the definition and evolution of women's roles in the nineteenth century. Though there was initially resistance to the idea of wives accompanying male missionaries into the field, from the 1850s and 1860s, women's missionary activity began to be professionalised as single women took on roles as missionary teachers, nurses and, eventually, doctors. By the end of the century women outnumbered men in the mission field. Through the century, different rhetoric was employed in writing about women missionaries, including by women missionaries themselves, in order to justify their activity.

Memoirs of Female Labourers in the Missionary Cause is an example of a collective biography of female missionaries written by a woman who remains anonymous. As was common practice among women writers of female missionary memoir, this 'authoress' also produced collective biographies of domestic Christian women and children, including a work titled *Early Religion seen in the Peaceful Happy Deaths of Thirteen Young Children, who Lived and Died in the Lord*. In some ways the author presents women missionaries in the tradition of child obituary literature, as in her preface she suggests that the female missionary's self-sacrificial, 'peaceful happy death' will particularly inspire emulation (for more discussion of this theme in Christianity, see Volume III, Resignation). However, the writer also uses military rhetoric when she calls on her readers to do more for the mission movement, instructing them to put on their armour and engage in the conflict between God and his enemies.

As was often the case with women's religious publishing, the introduction to *Memoirs of Female Labourers* was written by a minister – in this case, the LMS missionary, Richard Knill (1787–1857) – in a move to authorise women's missionary engagement. Knill presents women's religious activities along a spectrum: from mothers instructing their children and the local poor, through women supporting missions, to, finally, women venturing into the mission field. In this way, women's missionary work overseas is seen as a logical extension of their domestic duties. Knill also advances British women missionaries' heroism as evidence to prove that England was destined by God to extend Christianity around the world through its imperial activity. In the short verse that begins her preface, the woman editor of this work also stresses the 'grace' that has been obtained by the British race, which she believes is possible to convey to other races.

The *Female Missionary Intelligencer* was first published in 1853 by the Society for the Promotion of Female Education in the East (SPFEE). The newsletter publicised the work of the society, encouraged financial and other support for female schools of a variety of Protestant missionary societies, and recruited women to become missionary superintendents of female schools. This role of school superintendent embodies the professionalisation of women's missionary work, and the publication refers to the 'selection', 'preparation' and 'training' of both British and native women for their work in schools. However, the idea of professional, single women missionaries is in tension with the rhetoric of much of the newsletter, which focuses on the need to disseminate Christian domesticity to native communities, so that a convert would not be endangered by 'the evils of heathen intercourse in his domestic circle'. It should also be noted that, while native teachers are referred to briefly, non-western women are otherwise subsumed within a heathen mass, whose 'cry' for help enables western women's agency.

As in *Memoirs of Female Labourers*, the *Female Missionary Intelligencer* justifies women's religious work as an extension of her domestic Christian duty. Women missionaries are additionally said to be acting in imitation of the disciples in extending their influence from their immediate circle to 'all nations'. To some extent the work is presented as an opportunity – 'a field of exertion', or an outlet for women's frustrated energies. There are also some suggestions of military rhetoric, for example women's mission stations are referred to as their 'posts' and they are called on to take part in confronting the Catholic mission at Mussoorie. However, mainly the 'field' referred to is an arable one, and the metaphors of labouring in the field and bringing in a harvest of souls abound. Similarly, Christianity is depicted as 'a spring of living water', with the power to fertilise the desert of heathenism.

Pandita Ramabai (1858–1922) was given her title of 'Pandita' by a conclave of Pandits in Calcutta, in recognition of her high standard of education. Her activism on behalf of Hindu child widows in India gained her recognition in England, where she moved to pursue her education. While in England she converted to Christianity and worked as Professor of Sanskrit at Cheltenham Ladies College. While travelling in America she formed the Ramabai Association, which raised funds for a school for Hindu widows, which she established on her return to India. In her 1892 report to the Association she presents herself with the humility of a Christian missionary, though in effect this is a double, or triple humility, as she not only stresses her dependence on God, but also on the western men and women and the Hindu 'gentlemen' who support her. At the same time, she also takes on the role of a western missionary 'among a strange and hostile people in a strange land'. In this role she faces attacks from enemies and endures, like Christ, condemnation from her own people. Interestingly, she describes the Christian education of the school as producing a political subjectivity in her students that coexists with perfect feminine domesticity: the students' petitioning of the government is seen as evidence that their character is becoming that of 'the true woman'.

4

MEMOIRS OF FEMALE LABOURERS IN THE MISSIONARY CAUSE

(Bath: [n.p.], 1839), Introduction by Richard Knill, pp. v–vii; Preface, pp. 1–9

Introduction

Woman was first in the transgression, but the last at the cross, and the earliest at the tomb. "Now upon the first day of the week, very early in the morning, they came unto the sepulchre bringing the spices which they had prepared to embalm the body of their Lord."

Ten thousand instances of the sincere ardent attachment to the Saviour, are to be found in pious women of the present day. Not indeed to the mangled body which had just been taken down from the cross—but to the advancement of the glory of Christ, in extending his kingdom in the world. This is manifest in the holy, prayerful instructions of the nursery—in the devoted self-denying labours of the Sunday-school—in the frequent visits to the habitations of the poor—in the frequent prayers offered up with the sick and dying—and last, but not least, in the vast amount of funds supplied to our religious institutions through Ladies' Auxiliary Societies.

O Woman! never didst thou occupy a position of such moral grandeur as in the history of the present age. And we hail with delight every circumstance which is calculated through the Divine blessing, to elevate thy affections; to expand thy views; and to render thee more and more efficient in the service of God.

And is there anything on earth better calculated to do this, than the perusal of the Memoirs of Holy Women, who have ventured their lives for the name of the Lord Jesus—and who actually died among the Heathen, while endeavouring to lead them to Christ? This is the object which the excellent person had in view in preparing the following Memoirs, and that this object may be realized is the sincere desire of the Reader's,

Very obedient servant,

Richard Knill

A Word for the Heathen

"Christians, ye taste the heavenly grace,
Which cheers believers in the race.
Uncheered by grace, through heathen gloom,
See millions hastening to the tomb;
To heathen lands that grace convey,
Which trains the soul for endless day."

"Go ye, therefore, into all the world, and preach the gospel to every creature.—Work while it is called to-day."

This last command of the ascending adorable Saviour has not yet called forth that measure of attention and obedience from his followers that it ought to have done. And at this moment, notwithstanding all we have heard and read of Missionary efforts and operations, darkness still covers multitudes of people; and the joyful sounds of the gospel of peace are yet unheard by thousands, and tens of thousands, sitting in darkness, and in the region of the "shadow of death."

Remembering the cheering promises contained in "the Scriptures of truth" to encourage our efforts by the prospect of success,—self-reproach is surely fitting the bosoms of professing christians, while such awful accounts of prevailing darkness, idolatry and superstition, still reach our ears. Yes, kind reader, eighteen hundred years have passed away, and the above command has been but partially attended to, and but inadequately carried into operation. We have been too contented with the little that has been attempted. We have suffered ourselves to be settled in self-gratulation with the partial success of our Missionaries, forgetting the command was still binding upon us to do our utmost for the cultivation of the vast moral desert, by which our exertions are bounded on every side. While thinking with complacency on the little that has been sown, we have forgotten, with lamentable apathy, the large field that remained uncultivated; and we have sat down with rejoicing, instead of regirding on our armour, and renewing the conflict with the enemies of God and man.

If you feel, dear reader, a conviction of these truths, suffer the incidents and appeals of this little work, together with the anniversaries of the present season, to aid your resolutions, and ensure your attempting something further for the conversion of the heathen than you have hitherto aimed at. Yield yourself to the condemnation— do not shrink from the charge of selfishness, guilty as it will make you, but be humbled. And while you lament before God that it has so painfully paralized your exertions and straitened the bowels of your compassion, resolve that your present and future days shall be devoted to the glory of the Redeemer, and that henceforth your chief joy shall arise from Zion's prosperity—your delights be in works of mercy and benevolence, such as shall be fitting one redeemed from

MEMOIRS OF FEMALE LABOURERS

similar wretchedness, and brought through the rich mercy of an atoning Saviour, into union and fellowship with him here below, as an earnest of your glorification with Him above.

Be not discouraged, Christian reader, at the vast amount of work yet remaining to be done—the means are quite adequate to the proposed end; let but the Church of Christ arise and put on its strength, and the arm of Omnipotence shall nerve it to the conflict; the darkness of heathenism and idolatry shall be chased by the light of the glorious gospel; the Redeemer shall reign, whose right it is to reign from the rivers to the ends of the earth.

> "All hail! triumphant Lord,
> Eternal be thy reign;
> Behold the nations sue
> To wear thy gentle chain.
> When earth and time are known no more,
> Thy throne shall stand for ever more."

But in addition to the encouragement which the promises of the word of God afford—the blessed fruits that have already been reaped are of such a nature as to animate us to increased exertion—it is proposed in this little work to record some pleasing memorials of Women professing godliness, who hazarded their lives for the sake of the Lord Jesus, to bear his name among the degraded idolaters of heathen lands. Such women shall be held in everlasting remembrance as "fellow-helpers to the truth;" and Oh! that their example, their useful lives, and peaceful happy deaths may enkindle a like missionary spirit in the hearts of some readers, who, feeling for the state of the Heathen, shall say, "Here am I, send me." Then will the desire of the writer be accomplished, and God the Redeemer will be glorified and made known around the earth.

But, reader, dear reader, *be prompt* in your decisions and increased efforts, for time is fast flying away; the numbers of unconverted heathen who are daily dropping into eternity is painfully *large*—yes, *so it was yesterday—so it will be to-day—so it will be to-morrow*;—therefore be up and doing, and feel a holy ambition and solicitude to be a sharer in the glorious toil and undertaking. "The longest summer's day soon elapses; and he who labours from its dawn to its close, soon has to say, 'My labour is done.' The longest harvest month soon concludes, and he who toils through it all, who scorches under its heat, or droops amidst its showers, soon has to exclaim, 'The season is past, the harvest is finished.' So soon must the Christian retire from the field of labour, and retire from it for ever. Time will soon end with *those* you wish to benefit, and soon end *with you*. The missionary collector must shortly take her *last* round—the subscriber pay his *last* guinea—the missionary advocate deliver his *last* plea for the heathen—the missionary utter his *last* warning, his *last* entreaty, and exhibit for the *last* time the Lord Jesus Christ on the pole of the gospel for the healing of the people. Soon the Christian will have to offer up his *last* prayer for the success of the gospel and the influences of the Holy Spirit; and soon, soon alas, those who now claim our sympathy, prayers, tears, money, influence and labours, will be removed from our sight, our reach, and our prayers. And if unblessed with that gospel, we have it in our power to make known, they will sink in the darkness of ignorance, idolatry and depravity—into the world of hopeless despair and misery. And shall *we* look with indifference on such a scene? Shall we think of the probable, or even the possible, result of our inactivity and selfishness without shuddering at our supine, ungrateful, unfeeling hearts? O let us crowd, then, into the remainder of our little day of life all the exertion, all the benevolence and activity possible; and animated by the sure word of prophecy, and, by the triumphs of the gospel already achieved, go forward—yes, forward—onward must be the course of the active christian. Pitying the condition of helpless millions, and constrained by Immanuel's dying love, *we must go forward.* Beholding a world dead in trespasses and sins, we must mourn, and labour, and pray that the light of the glorious gospel may shine on them, and think no sacrifice of money or time too great when the claims of the Redeemer, and the misery that surrounds us are compared therewith. It is for our support that we are not engaged in a sinking cause; the promise of the Lord Jehovah is engaged for its final triumph. "He must reign;" he hath given to his son the heathen for his inheritance, and the uttermost parts of the earth for his possession. Thus with faith we may offer the prayer, *"Thy kingdom come,"* and rejoice in the prospect that the period will arrive when it shall be said by all kindreds, nations, and tongues, "Hallelujah, the Lord God omnipotent reigneth."

5

FEMALE MISSIONARY INTELLIGENCER [1853]

(Dublin: SPFEE, 1854), vol. I, pp. 1–4, 15–17

Address

The Society whose name heads this page has strong claims on the attention of all who take an interest in Christian missions. It had long been felt, that though adult converts may be gathered here and there by the faithful preaching of the Gospel in heathen lands, yet that its success must mainly be hoped for through the medium of efforts on the *rising* generation, whose fresh and comparatively unfettered minds might more readily open to receive the light than those who had grown to maturity in the midst of heathen influence. With this view, schools were begun in a very early stage of most Christian missions;—but at first (partly owing to the strong local prejudices in favour of female ignorance) they were limited to boys; and the young Christian convert, returning to his home, was necessarily exposed to all the evils of heathen intercourse in his domestic circle.

A sense of this evil, however, contributed to bring about the remedy; intelligent natives have, within a few years, begun to feel a wish that their wives and daughters should not be utterly ignorant; but about thirty years ago, the first effort was made to educate females in India, in the beginning by gathering together the poorest outcasts. Miss Cooke, afterwards Mrs. Wilson, who was sent out by the British and Foreign School Society, and Miss Bird, who voluntarily devoted herself to the same work till death removed her, were among the first labourers in this field.

In 1834, the present Society was formed; and unsustained as it has been for the most part by the public meetings and other aids usually resorted to by Missionary Societies, its workings are so little generally known, that some few words of explanation of its objects may be needed.

Its sphere is a wide one; extending from the Mediterranean eastward to China, it embraces the Malayan peninsula and archipelago, India and Ceylon, with South and West Africa.

Its object is the establishment and superintendence of schools in these regions, wherever favourable opportunities are presented—the selection and preparation at home of pious and well-educated persons to go out as superintendents, and the training and encouragement of native teachers—as also giving assistance in various ways to schools already existing.

While seeking, in all these different lines, to impart all the useful knowledge and acquirements which circumstances may render desirable and practicable, the end and chief aim kept in view by the Society is to lead the pupils to an acquaintance with Scriptural truth and a knowledge of Christ as their Saviour; on this broad Christian basis it has been established; it, therefore, includes all Protestant denominations who acknowledge as their watchword and standard the Gospel message—full and free salvation through the all-sufficient atonement of the Son of God. [...]

[...] The Society is now in the nineteenth year of its existence; it has, in the course of this time, raised £37,000, upwards of £11,000 of which was the produce of work sold at home or in the East. It has bestowed help on schools belonging to all the great Protestant missions in grants of money or work, and itself sent forth seventy-three agents, besides aiding several others sent out by other Societies or on their own resources. Of these agents, a few have returned—a few been gathered to their rest while labouring at their post; while the greater number, in connexion with this or other Societies, are still devoting themselves to the same work.

But when it is remembered that two hundred and fifty millions of women in Eastern lands are living without the Gospel, and passing into eternity "without God and without hope," can we feel too strongly the responsibility of *all* who can do anything towards the work of their evangelization? The number of female schools that would be required in India alone, reckoning one in fifteen of the population to receive Christian education, and each school to contain about one hundred children, would be 86,000; while all this Society has been able to accomplish includes, perhaps, 86! And taking a general view of all the missionary operations in India, it has been shown that while 99,855 boys are under Christian instruction, only 13,905 girls are partakers of the same blessing—that is to say, *one* to *seven.*

And India is only part of the Society's sphere: from other parts of the East—from Africa and China—the cry is alike sent forth—"Come over and help us."

Let us hope that the women of our favoured islands will not be deaf to that cry.

Extract from the Parent Society's Report

"Never was there a time so favorable for the work of female education as the present. Applications for help in grants, money, and school materials arrive from all quarters, and there are many important openings for locating teachers, were the Committee in a position to bestow salaries for their support. Two of these deserve especial mention; where, on the one hand, schools are in action, and greatly needing teachers; and, on the other, two ladies, apparently well qualified to meet their requirements, are earnestly desirous of consecrating themselves to the work. In a recent interview, the Rev. G. Pearce, with the authority which the experience of twenty-six years in India gives to his opinion, pressed upon the Committee the importance of enlarged efforts. He represented that three or four ladies might immediately occupy wide spheres of usefulness in Calcutta alone, where the native ladies of high caste are, to a considerable extent, desiring education, and, as it is believed, would not now refuse it, even if offered on a Christian basis; while the children of native converts, who multiply much faster than the means of instruction are supplied, present a field from which many precious fruits are lost to the Church of Christ for want of labourers to gather them. Were agents appointed to these posts, salaries from home would be required."

From the "North London Auxiliary's" Report

"The Rev. W. Keane, in a note regretting his absence from the meeting of the North London Auxiliary, says:—'During the six years that I was in India, I saw no aspect of the mission-field so urgent in its claims, so promising in its results, as that of native female education. I long from my heart to tell to your Society what I repeat on almost every platform of the Church Missionary Society, the heavy sufferings of the heathen women; and how I have seen your Society afford the only remedy.' The Committee therefore earnestly desire that a spirit of effectual prayer may be poured out, that the command may be obeyed, 'Pray ye, therefore, the Lord of the harvest, that He would send forth labourers unto His harvest.'"

To those Christian women who are alive to the duty of not limiting our efforts for the spiritual good of others to our own immediate neighbourhood and circle, and who desire to act in the spirit of our Divine Master's command to His disciples, who, while told to "begin at Jerusalem," were also to "go and teach *all nations*"—to such this Society offers a field for exertion ample enough for all and more than all who may be willing to work in it. But the quiet and unobtrusive character of these labours has hitherto rendered them comparatively unknown. It is to meet this difficulty that this Magazine has been established, to serve as the organ of the Society, with a view both to make it generally known, and to supply the various Working Parties and other Associations in aid of it, with the missionary information so useful and so desirable.

It is proposed that the price should be One Penny; it will be published monthly, and it is intended that it should take a brief view of the progress of the Society, and include a variety of information from foreign stations, with the latest intelligence of interest; also notices of the work sold, of the places where it is most in demand, of boxes sent, &c.

This first number, being designed to serve as a kind of handbook of reference, to introduce the Society to those previously unacquainted with it, must necessarily be in great part occupied by explanations respecting its constitution, regulations, and arrangements of all kinds. The subsequent ones will be more particularly devoted to such information as may throw light on the subject of female education and evangelization in Africa and the East. [...]

Appeal for the Formation of a School at Mussoorie

Description of Mussoorie

"If you look at the map of India, you see along the north-east the great valley of the Ganges, the Ganges running along some 1,500 or 1,600 miles into the Bay of Bengal. Then, if you take your stand at the head of the Bay of Bengal, and look to the north-west along that immense valley, you have one of the largest plains in the whole world, and beyond all debate the most densely-populated plain upon the face of the earth. If your eye could grasp it, it could run along in a straight line for 1,000 miles along a lovely plain, in breadth about 300 miles. This is the plain of the valley of the Ganges. In that single valley you have more human beings endowed with immortal souls than you have in the whole United States, and the Canadas, and Mexico, and Brazil, and the other empires of South America; in fact, more human beings than in the whole of North and South America put together: and all these British subjects are now lying prostrate at our feet, asking us what we shall make of them. The lowest range of the Himalayas run along for 1500 or 2000 miles along the side of this immense valley. This lowest range are in height something like your own highest mountains in Great Britain. Beyond this first range there is an immense valley running along, of which Nepaul is only a portion. Then you have the secondary range of the Himalayas before you, rising up to the height of 7,000 or 8,000 feet. From that valley they rise up very precipitously, and it is on the top of one of these crests or peaks that you have the establishment known under the name of Mussoorie.

"It may be asked, why do people assemble there? For the sake of the bracing breeze, and the healthfulness of the situation. I am sorry to say that the Romanists have pre-occupied the field (of education) [...] Now, then, Christian friends, what is wanted is, that this Society put forth its whole energy in counteracting the deadliness of this effect of Romanism upon the summit of Mussoorie. There are numbers who go there every year in quest of health—they are resident there, with their children. If they do not send them there, there is nothing for them to do but idle at home. But if you were to get up an Institution there, properly conducted, we should be too glad to send our children to it. Remember, moreover, that there is but a fluctuating, migratory population there. I have little doubt of the substantial reality of what is said in the Report. I have little doubt that, migratory though it be, yet there will be, as it were, an everlasting flux—so that, if there were really a good Institution founded, though it might be costly at the outset, there would be every reason to believe, nay, one might venture to say, that it would be

FEMALE MISSIONARY INTELLIGENCER

self-supporting. And what a glorious thing would that be, to have a noble Protestant Institution up there confronting that Romanizing Institution! Scarcely any Romanists go there; they are almost all Protestant children that are taught in that Institution. And what is done on the heights of Mussoorie is done in many places along the valley of the Ganges, down in Calcutta, and in other regions throughout India; and if a Protestant Institution were to succeed at Mussoorie, it would be a model for other places. Therefore, surely there is a loud call upon one and all to come forward to the help of the Lord in India."

To this appeal of Dr. Duff's in behalf of Mussoorie, we subjoin a few further particulars and statements from persons on the spot, corroborative of his testimony.

The station referred to attracts, by its refreshing and salubrious climate, numbers not only of Europeans, but of Indo-Britons, as they are called—a class rapidly increasing in number, wealth, and influence. It is the female children of this class which the efforts now contemplated is especially designed to benefit. They are rarely seut to Europe for education, and the country affording only the most scanty means of instruction for them, they grow up to the prey of the evil influence around them, being Protestant Christians in little more than the name, even if they do not adopt the baneful tenets of Popery.

No adequate means of education are provided at Mussoorie by Protestants for girls of either class, except that there are a few private seminaries of an exclusive and expensive character. The Romanists, on the other hand, quick to perceive and to profit by the supineness of Protestants, have established convents, as has been already stated, where a liberal and ornamental education is supplied at a cheap rate, and where many young females have been perverted to Popery.

To meet this evil, and to afford the required facilities for a liberal education, on pure Christian principles, to those so greatly needing it, it is proposed to establish a Female School at Mussoorie, on such terms as shall render it generally available.

The undertaking is necessarily a considerable one; for on a liberal scale only can it be expected to succeed. One thousand pounds will be required for the first two years, but after that period, on the calculation of those who are well acquainted with the locality, all demands on home resources would cease; and thus, by a little present exertion, might be opened springs of living water where now is a desert, or delusive streams only; nor can we estimate how far and wide would flow its fertilizing influence in life and blessing to the daughters of India.

6

PANDITA RAMABAI, 'REPORT'

Report of the Annual Meeting
of the Ramabai Association
(Boston: Geo. H. Ellis, 1892), pp. 21–27

To the President and Officers of the Ramabai Association

Esteemed Friends,—We, the teachers and pupils of the Shâradâ Sadana, send hearty greetings, with our gratitude and sisterly love, to you, at the beginning of the fourth year of our existence. We gratefully and heartily thank our heavenly Father, and you our friends, for the generous help and encouragement we have received from you.

This year has been full of blessings to us. Not a single day has dawned upon us without bringing some new blessing, some fresh token of God's love to us. The more we think of his kindness, the more we feel how little we deserve it, and how very unworthy we have been of it, and how very forbearing and good the dear Father has been to us all this time. The past year has not been without its trials, but they have all turned into blessings; and thus we have been enabled to realize, in a measure, the eternal truth that "no chastening for the present seemeth to be joyous, but grievous: nevertheless afterward it yieldeth the peaceable fruit of righteousness unto them which are exercised thereby."

We began our last year by asking the blessing of God on our work, and by celebrating the birthday of our little school. You may remember that we had twenty-six widows, three deserted wives, four married girls, and seven unmarried girls in our school at this time last year. Now we have thirty young widows, three deserted wives, three married girls, and seven unmarried girls studying in the Shâradâ Sadana. Of the forty-three girls, thirty-eight are boarders; and five who live in their own houses attend the school daily. The number of non-widow girls is steadily diminishing, and that of widows increasing. I have not sent a tabulated report this year; for most of the girls are those whose names, castes, ages, etc., were reported last year. Four widows and five non-widows who attended this school last year have left it for different reasons. One young widow, Krishnabai, left us just after the celebration of our last anniversary. She is, since then, happily married, and has settled into a home of her own, where she rules, the sole mistress of her household and of her loving husband's heart. We are very happy in her happiness, and wish that many of our young child-widows may have their sufferings ended in this or some other better way. The rest of the number who went away from our school left because they were taken away from us by their parents or guardians, who were afraid of the Hindu public, who talk against our school, and are very much opposed to the education and consequent independence of widows and women in general. You know very well that our school has been unpopular with the orthodox Hindus from the beginning, and is so now; and then we are met with fresh outbreaks of popular "indignation," and the Shârâdâ Sadana is stormed and attacked on all sides. It is very natural for some of the girls to fear public criticism and leave our school.

The cause of the last great storm was a sad and strange one. It so happened that a woman whom we had appointed to do the matron's work, and whom we thought to be our friend, and one who took an interest in this movement, proved to be our deadly foe. Her mischievous work was begun by tyrannizing and exercising a bad influence over the girls. For this she was promptly removed from the institution. When going away, she took a young widow with her, who also was a relative of hers. She then went into the town and identified herself with the great army of our opponents. She manufactured many false stories, and spread them through the town, and caused many people to doubt and turn against us. A terrible storm surged around us for a time, and we had to try hard to keep our ground. Although we are living in our own country and among our own people, we are continually made to feel that we are among a strange and hostile people in a strange land. We are utterly defenceless and almost friendless in this beloved land of ours. But our very weakness is a strong appeal to God, and we feel that he is on our side. We hear him say, "My grace is sufficient for thee," and realize that "he giveth power to the faint." We have trusted in him, and we know that he is able to protect and save his own. You will see by the steady increase of our numbers that our school has not suffered any loss, though our enemies have tried their best to pull it down. There are times when we see nothing but darkness thick enough to be felt on all sides; but we are soon made to see the silvery lining of the clouds that surround us. Our enemies are watching us quietly now, but God only knows whether their present silence is a calm before a great storm or not.

This year has seen us happy possessors of a home of our own. This great event in our short history is second to none except the establishment of the Shârâdâ Sadana. Your great kindness and unparalleled generosity has made it possible for us to get a place where we can lay our heads; and we thank you from the bottom of our hearts for giving a house to our school. The Shârâdâ Sadana, which only three years ago was looked upon as nothing but a castle built in the air by crackbrains, may now be counted among many living realities resting upon a very good foundation. All of us are very happy over it, and look forward with great pleasure to the day when our school will be taken into the new house after the necessary additions and repairs, etc., are finished.

We hope (D. V.) to celebrate the fourth birthday of our school in the new house. I have given all particulars concerning the newly bought house in my report to the Executive Committee, so need not report them here. The house, as it stands now, is good, and has about two and three-fourths acres of ground. It consists of two separate bungalows, one to be used as the sleeping apartment for the girls, and the other as the school, besides the spacious out-houses, cook-rooms, dining-rooms, etc. But it has no accommodation for the resident teachers and for new girls who come to us, desiring admission to the school. It is not safe to admit such girls into the school at once. They must be lodged separately for a time, and their character, etc., tested thoroughly before they be allowed to mix with the older pupils. It is, therefore, very necessary to build another small bungalow on the grounds in front of the already existing house. We need to have a fencing wall around our compound or open ground, and another dormitory for the pupils, besides a dining-room and cook-room for the resident teachers who may not take their meals with the high caste Hindu girls. These new additions and repairs will take some time, but we are doing our best to get them done quickly and cheaply.

The internal work of the school is going on in very much the same way as it was in the last year. The pupils' progress in their studies is very satisfactory. I am glad to say they are advancing in moral training also. Their several natures are becoming more and more unselfish and sweeter than ever, and their manners quite refined. The girls are very anxious to do their part of the work, and take pains to build up their character. They are now beginning to feel that they owe a duty, not to themselves only, but that they owe it also to their God, and mankind in general. They are kept well informed of what is going on in the outer world; and they feel they are no more the isolated individuals they used to be, that even the Hindu widow bears some relation and owes a duty to the world, that there are many good people who take interest in them, and that they also ought to take an interest in others. Last year when a great agitation concerning the "Age of Consent" Bill was exciting the country, and another movement in the interest of stopping the terrible opium traffic was urged among our people, the pupils of the Shâradâ Sadana were not backward in sending their petitions to the government in favor of the necessary reforms and in aiding the work of progress as far as lay in their power. The true woman, loving, sympathetic, and unselfish, is gradually making her appearance in each one of the girls. They feel for each other, help each other, and are ready to show kindness to any one without regard to caste, color, or creed. We care more for their moral training than for their literary attainments; and we look forward to the day when, by God's help, our girls will go out in the world to scatter seeds of kindness and goodness, and will be the sunbeams of the household wherein they may dwell.

We have added a new department to our school since last October. A kindergarten training class has been started, which is making good progress. Fourteen pupils and two teachers have joined the class. We may now hope to see a real Fröbel kindergarten in connection with the Shâradâ Sadana, in which the pupils who are being trained now will have ample opportunity to practise what they have learned. We did not have many visitors last year. His Highness the Maharaja of Mysore and suite visited our school early in March of 1891. His Highness donated 500 rupees to the school. Mr. Dayaram Gidumal, a judge in the Province of Sind, and a reformed Hindu gentleman, continues to show his kind interest in our work by giving a subscription of 120 rupees annually. Mrs. Somerset, of Cambridge, England, collected and sent 556 rupees as a donation. I owe a debt of gratitude to these generous donors to our school. I gratefully mention the name of Mrs. Emma H. Palmer, M.D. (an old friend of our late lamented friend, Dr. Bodley) among our donors. Mrs. Palmer has worked hard, and is still working, to get some funds to build up a "Bodley Memorial Library" in our school. The money collected by Mrs. Palmer has already amounted to over 450 rupees. And you have kindly allowed me to add the money sent by Mrs. Somerset to this Bodley Memorial Library Fund. So we may by and by hope to erect a good and lasting monument on our school grounds, sacred to the memory of our valued friend, Dr. Bodley. I am very glad of it, and am very grateful to those who are helping us in this direction. I must also mention the name of Mr. Harishchandra Vithal, a gentleman of very limited means, who has given a donation of 10 rupees to the Shâradâ Sadana. It was very kind of him to do so, and he has my thanks for his kindness.

Chundrabai, a pupil-teacher who used to teach a little in this school last year, has given up her teaching, and is now applying her whole time in studying diligently. Her place has been taken by Mrs. Mathurabai, an educated Hindu Christian lady, who has been teaching in our school from November last. She teaches very nicely, and takes great pains to do her part of the work. Our school has suffered much from outside, but we have been very fortunate in getting such good helpers. The hearty co-operation and womanly sympathy of Malanbai, Miss Kemp, Simhabai, and Mathurabai, have been a great help and comfort to me. These good ladies spare neither time nor trouble, and do their best to make the school a success. Their good example and kind and judicious treatment of the girls have done much to keep peace and order in the school. I cannot thank them enough for the unbounded interest with which they are helping our work on.

I must not forget to mention my grateful appreciation of the sympathetic co-operation and kindly help rendered to us by our good, faithful clerk, Mr. G. B. Gudrè. No one except those who know the internal condition of present Hindu society can realize how difficult it is to find a really good and faithful man to work with and in the interests of women. We could have easily found a better clerk, but could not have found a better man than Mr. Gudrè. He has tried his best to do his duty, and has always shown a true brotherly sympathy and kindness toward us.

Many thanks are also due to the members of our Advisory Board of Bombay and Poona. They have always been ready to give me their advice and help whenever I wanted them. Our good friend, Mr. Chandavarkar has shown great kindness toward us in doing the necessary legal work free of charge, when the building and ground for the school were purchased. The Hon. Mr. M. G. Ranade helped us in drawing the title-deed in correct form. Dr. R. G. Bhandakar, R. B. G. G. Gokhali, R. B. Kanitkar, and other gentlemen have been very prompt in giving their help and advice on many occasions. Rao Saheb C. N. Bhat has kindly audited our accounts, and helped us in many other ways. I take this opportunity to show my appreciation of their kindness to me, and tender my best thanks to all these gentlemen.

The kind-hearted President and other officers of our Association have been very, very kind to me. They have shown their interest in this school, and been more patient with me than ever. Their words of love and encouragement and their deep sympathy have sustained me while I was being criticised, condemned, and discouraged by my people. I cannot find words expressive enough to thank them for what they have done and are doing for India's poor widowed daughters, and for me. May He who is the Rewarder of all good and kind people bless them abundantly, and be glorified by their good deeds! With kindest regards and all best wishes for the New Year, I remain,

Very faithfully yours,

Ramabai.

1.4

Masculinity and Leadership

1.4 Masculinity and Leadership

For Victorians writing about missionary men, the extent to which Christianity affected the masculinity of their subjects could be a problem. In the same way that Victorian femininity was being discursively created during the first half of the nineteenth century, masculinity was becoming ever more defined. There was a risk that, in contrast to the active modern agents of the East India Company or the military men of the British Empire, male missionaries could be seen as emasculated by their Christianity. A response to this challenge to masculinity can be seen in the ideology of muscular Christianity, famously embodied in the writings of Charles Kingsley and Thomas and Matthew Arnold. Even before these writers, however, there was a tendency for biographers of male missionaries to use militaristic metaphors when describing religious heroism. Equally, memoirs of military men like Hedley Vicars could elide the soldier with the missionary, emphasising their shared mission to bring British, Christian civilisation to the rest of the world.

The first text in this section criticises the memoir of Hedley Vicars for encouraging the elision of war and mission. Initially the memoir is criticised for being written in such a way that others can make 'mistaken and mischievous use' of it. The reviewer argues forcibly against using the Christianity of an individual to authorise any unchristian profession, especially that of a soldier. In a way that undermines the masculinity of the military profession, they explain that it is particularly problematic for Christians to be soldiers because the military system denies the right of the individual conscience (soldiers are 'machines', not men). Interestingly, the writer supports their refusal to give Christian sanction to the military profession by referring to the slave trade, out of which also came Christian autobiographies and towards which, in the early nineteenth century, Christian culture was equivocal (see this volume, Abolitionism). Towards the end of the review the writer criticises the tendency of the female author of the memoir to use militaristic metaphors, accusing her of a profane and literal interpretation of the Bible's figurative references to warfare.

Another review, this time of an autobiography by the medical missionary William Grenfell, is included here to illustrate how, by the end of the century, muscular Christianity was very much being deployed by missionary writers. Grenfell had been a student and surgeon at the Royal London Hospital, studying under the famous surgeon Frederick Treves (writer of *The Elephant Man and Other Reminiscences*), and the review appeared in the *London Hospital Gazette*. The review establishes Grenfell's masculinity through reference to the activities he took part in while at the Royal London – it suggests he is well known as a surgeon and for his prowess in sports – and by including Treves' powerful description of the tough heroism of the Labrador missionaries, 'trying to hold their own against hostile surroundings'. Treves' description of the men's masculine determination and heroism uses the rhetoric of sports and military defence, and the review suggests that a similar rhetoric can be found in the autobiography itself. Indeed, the reviewer praises Grenfell for his ability to vigorously narrate his missionary work as a highly readable tale of adventure. However, the review also notes that the juxtaposition of excessively masculine incidents such as the slaughter of Arctic animals with Biblical quotations is too jarring for a reader, suggesting that the elision of masculinity and Christianity could be taken too far.

Another group of men holding leadership roles in the mission field, apart from white British missionaries and soldiers, were the 'native' Christian Bishops, such as Bishop Samuel Crowther, a biography of whom is extracted here. While some British Christians believed in Henry Venn's vision of a self-governing Church in the Empire, contemporary racism led others to dispute the empire's indigenous people's ability to lead the faith and undermine their claims to Victorian masculinity. The biography extracted here was written by a young woman, in the style of a Christian tract for children (see this volume, Children), and it is telling that the title emphasises his identity as a 'slave boy' while reducing his life to a simplistic object lesson – 'Good out of Evil'. Indeed, the major aspect of Crowther's work that is stressed is his conversion of his own mother and family, which is presented as a sentimental, domestic story. The main attribute for which he is praised is his humility. Otherwise, his story is only part of a larger narrative of how God was enabling missionary work in Africa through freed slaves like Crowther. The fact that this treatment of Crowther was deemed suitable enough for the young woman author to be encouraged to publish speaks volumes about the views of the English Christian community towards native clergymen. While white Christian agents in the mission field could star in their own heroic narratives, native converts would always be the surprising recipients of God's grace.

7

SOLDIERSHIP AND CHRISTIANITY: BEING A REVIEW OF THE MEMOIRS OF THE LATE HEDLEY VICARS

(London: Ward and Co., 1856), pp. 3–16 [abridged]

Soldiership and Christianity

A little book has been recently published, which has reached extraordinary circulation and celebrity, among a certain section of the religious world. Though, in itself, in some respects, a work of singular interest and beauty, we cannot but fear that it is being turned to a very mistaken and mischievous use by many, who seem to imagine that the example of a good man is of value enough to justify or consecrate a bad system. We allude to *Memorials of Captain Hedley Vicars, Ninety-seventh Regiment*. It commemorates the brief life and violent death of a young officer, who was one of the numberless victims sacrificed before Sebastopol during the late wretched war. For our own part, we must say at the outset, that utterly as we abhor the system, of which, by an accident of his life, Captain Vicars became a part, and inexpressibly painful as we feel to be some of the anomalies revealed in this volume between his character and calling, we have not a moment's hesitation or reluctance in admitting that he was an eminently christian man. Who can doubt this, who reads his letters, so full of devout fervour and sincerity? And especially who can doubt this, who observes the earnest and self-sacrificing love with which he sought to promote the highest interests and happiness of others? Whether he is engaged in instructing the poor ignorant navvies at home, or in tending with a brave and unwearied devotion his own soldiers amid the raging horrors of cholera and fever, in the Piræus, he proved himself a true disciple of Him who went about doing good. Indeed, in proportion as we come to know and admire the excellence of such men as Captain Vicars, and to feel how admirably adapted they were not only to adorn by their virtues the private circles in which they moved, but to become a blessing to society at large, the more do we feel inclined to execrate and loathe the war, by which their valuable lives were cut short, and the homes and hearts of which they were deservedly the idols, smitten with irremediable desolation. And we feel this all the more bitterly, from the profound and daily deepening conviction we have, that the war was produced by the blunders of diplomacy, and the senseless violence of popular passion; and has gained for us absolutely nothing that might not have been better secured by wise and friendly negotiation.

Gladly, however, as we acknowledge the rare excellence and beauty of Captain Vicars's character, we cannot for one instant admit the inference which some good people are disposed to draw from it, that the war-system is consistent with Christianity, or that the military profession is one which a Christian ought to pursue. The principle upon which such inference rests, is fundamentally false, and of extremely dangerous tendency; for it assumes to determine what Christianity is,—what it forbids, and what it enjoins,—not by its own authoritative canon and the obvious and prevailing spirit which pervades it, but by the practices, always imperfect and often grievously inconsistent, of its erring disciples. This is an exact reversal of the rule we ought to apply. Human conduct is to be tested by Christian principle, not Christian principle by human conduct. The form, probably, in which the argument from the example of Captain Vicars and others will be put, is this: 'If war be, as you affirm, so opposed to the spirit of Christianity, how is it possible that one whom you admit to be a truly Christian man, could have taken part in it?' Unhappily, the history of the Church in every age proves that it *is* possible for good men, whose Christian sincerity no one can question, under the blinding influence of educational prejudice to lend their sanction to practices, which are at the time felt by some, and afterwards acknowledged by all, to be utterly at variance with the religion they profess. It would be easy to cite many instances in illustration of this remark. Few, we presume, will doubt that persecution for conscience sake—subjecting men and women to imprisonment, cruel torture and death in the name of Christ—is as gross an outrage upon the spirit of the gospel as can well be imagined. And yet, no one can deny that many whose names stand conspicuous in the roll of ancient piety were persecutors in heart, and some of them in positive act. Sir Thomas More, John Knox, John Calvin, Cotton Mather, and many others, stand as examples of this inconsistency. But no one, surely, would now dream of saying, that persecution cannot be unchristian, or such good men as these would never have persecuted.

But there is another example at hand, if possible still more striking, of this extraordinary blindness to the clearest requirements of Christian obligation with which good men are sometimes smitten. And we the rather dwell upon it, as the individual to whom it refers is held in great veneration by the very class of persons who are most likely to find in the character and memory of Captain Vicars a justification for war.

There are not many who will now hesitate to acknowledge, that if ever there was a calling wholly inconsistent with Christianity, if ever there was a calling in itself inherently and irredeemably wicked, it was that of the man engaged in the African slave-trade a hundred years ago. On the other hand, if ever there lived a man whose conversion was genuine, whose whole life was an attestation of the

SOLDIERSHIP AND CHRISTIANITY

reality of the spiritual change wrought in his life and character, that man was John Newton. And yet it is notorious that for some years after he became a Christian, John Newton was engaged in the slave trade, not merely as an accessory but as a principal, without having the slightest feeling of remorse or suspicion as to the unlawfulness of his calling. Nay more, (and here we have some remarkable coincidences between his experience and that of Captain Vicars,) he declares that never did he pass hours of such spiritual elevation and devout enjoyment as when he was in command of a vessel freighted with a mass of manacled and suffocating negroes on the coast of Guinea. "I know not any calling," he says, "that seems more favourable, or affords greater advantages to an awakened mind, for promoting the life of God in the soul, especially to a person who has the command of a ship, than a seafaring life in African voyages. ... I never knew sweeter or more frequent hours of divine communion than in my two last voyages to Guinea, when I was either almost secluded from society on ship-board, or when on shore among the natives." [...]

[...] But will anybody say that because the sainted John Newton could follow the occupation of a slave-trader without any consciousness of wrong, that this diabolical trade must therefore be lawful for a Christian?

We should like to elucidate this point a little more, as we have no doubt it is found to be a sore perplexity to many who are anxious to judge righteous judgments in regard both to principles and characters. They feel that to unchristianize men who in their life and conduct exhibit marks of genuine piety, because on some one momentous point they deviate from Christian requirement, is a harsh and uncharitable proceeding. But they feel also that there is the greatest danger in granting immunity from the plain obligations of Christian morality, on the plea of piety, or out of complaisance and tenderness for individuals. Is there any way, then, of escaping out of this dilemma? Is there any way of reconciling the dictates of conscience with the judgment of charity? We think there is.

The problem to be solved is usually put in this form. Is it possible for any one to be a true Christian who lives in the habitual and conscious disregard of any important part of Christ's will? We do not see how we can avoid giving a negative answer to this question *when it is thus expressed*. But the solution, as it appears to us, depends upon the presence or absence of one word in the above proposition, and that word is "conscious." Eliminate that, and we do not hesitate to reply in the affirmative. For our own part we believe, to a certain extent, and in a certain sense, in the doctrine of development. That is, we believe that it is only gradually that the full glory and perfection of the Christian system dawns upon the Christian world. We are convinced that there never has been an era in the history of Christianity, when the Saviour, if he had appeared among his people, might not, in regard to some important points of truth and duty, have said to them as he did to Philip, "Have I been so long time with you, and yet have you not known me?" In proportion as the church advances in knowledge and wisdom, will it discover new excellencies in the teachings of Christ which had been previously veiled from its eyes. Illustrations of this are not wanting even within a very late period. The doctrine which inculcates charity to the errors of others, and teaches us that the only means of promulgation and defence which Christianity owns are the weapons of truth and love—"in meekness *instructing* those that oppose themselves"—is as old as the gospel. And yet it is only quite recently that this has been discerned by Christians. It was the received and all but universal conviction among good men, for we know not how many centuries, that in subjecting heretics to legal coercion and bodily suffering they were doing God an acceptable service. So for generations, in regard to slavery and the slave-trade. Individuals, or a small minority might have discovered and denounced the unchristian character of that infamous traffic. But it is notorious that the Christian world generally had no sense whatever of its wickedness. And so is it at this moment in regard to war and other practices.

How do we apply these remarks in our judgment of individual characters? Why thus. That in estimating the sincerity of a man's obedience to the will of Christ, we must, in charity, test him, not by the abstract and perfect criterion of that will revealed in the gospel, and at a later time perhaps discovered by the Church, but by the received and acknowledged *understanding* of that will which prevails among those by whom he has been instructed. It is the *conscious* violation of duty that incurs guilt and depraves character. There may be, no doubt, a measure of guilt attached to our ignorance or misconception of what is revealed, even though we share that in common with the generality of Christians. But such guilt is very different in character and in turpitude from that of the man "who *knew* his Lord's will and did it not." [...]

[...] Let us apply these remarks to the case of Captain Vicars. We have stated that to our minds there is something inexpressibly painful in the contrast between his Christian character, full as he was of the meekness and gentleness of Christ, and distinguished by the depth and fervour of his love towards God and man, and the bloody work—the work of vindictiveness, cruelty and death, in which he was employed. He describes his own feelings in the camp almost in the same words as John Newton in the slave-ship. "It is six months since I have been within reach of a house of prayer, or have had the opportunity of receiving the Sacrament; yet, never have I enjoyed more frequent or precious communion with my Saviour than I have found in the trenches or in my tent." To our feeling, we must admit, Captain Vicars going forth from "precious communion with his Saviour," to bayonet poor Russian peasants, or pour infernal fire upon the devoted town of Sebastopol, is as violent and revolting a contradiction, as that of John Newton, combining a similar exercise with the man-stealing and manacles of the African slave-trade. But we must remember that this excellent officer had been brought up in the atmosphere of that military Christianity, which is unhappily the prevailing religion of England, at this day, and especially in the circle in which he moved. As John Newton came in course of time as his knowledge matured, to condemn with grave severity the traffic in men, so we have little doubt that Captain Vicars, had his life been

SOLDIERSHIP AND CHRISTIANITY

spared, could not have failed, with the tenderness of conscience that he possessed, to reach the conclusion that the disciple of Him who came not to destroy men's lives but to save them, could not consistently be, (we do not use the phrase offensively, but to describe the thing really as it is) a professional homicide.

We now proceed to point out, briefly, certain features in the military calling and life, which seem to us absolutely incompatible with a perfect obedience to the will of Christ.

And first of all we must refer to the condition,—the essential, invariable, inevitable condition—on which all military service is and must ever be assumed, namely, the total surrender of individual conscience to the control and authority of another. We presume that no one competent to have a judgment on such a subject,—certainly not the admirers of Captain Hedley Vicars's character and memoirs,—will deny that the characteristic mark of a genuine Christian profession is cheerful and universal submission to the will of the Saviour, "bringing into captivity every thought to the obedience of Christ." For the Christian, at any rate, the supreme master of conscience is Christ. To this rule there is absolutely no exception, not even a regard for "father, or mother, or wife, or children, or brethren, or sisters, or life itself." That the command of the civil magistrate forms no exception, is proved by the example of prophets, apostles, and martyrs, in all ages, who have *not* deemed it right in the sight of God to obey men rather than God. But what is the law of the soldier's life?

We give the answer in the language of Sir Charles J. Napier, the hero of Scinde, from a work which he published on Military Law some years ago. After stating that the duties of a citizen may be divided into three parts, namely his duty to God, to the laws of his country, and to mankind at large, Sir Charles adds:—

"But the soldier has nothing to do with these three duties; that is to say, he has nothing to do with them in his character of a soldier. It is true that, as a man, he is a being responsible to his Creator, both for his religion and morals. But as a soldier, OBEDIENCE is the *'Law and the Prophets.' His* religion, law, and morals, are in the 'orderly book.' If that says, 'spare,' he spares. If that says, 'destroy,' he destroys. I do not speak of a Russian slave in military habit: I speak of a British soldier. The conscience of a good soldier is in the keeping of his general; who has the whole responsibility, before God and man, for what the soldiers do in obedience to his orders."[1] [...]

[...] So, again, in a remarkable debate which recently took place in Parliament, in reference to the bands playing in the Parks on Sundays, the same doctrine was most nakedly and emphatically advanced. Among the objections raised to the practice in question, one was, that in the bands ordered to play there might be some religious men, whose consciences would be wounded by being required to do what they might consider a desecration of the sabbath, and a violation of the divine law. But when this plea was put forth it was treated with the utmost contempt, as too transparent an absurdity to be entertained for a moment. What! it was said, a soldier pretend to have a conscience! Why a soldier is a machine, and ought so to regard himself! Now let it be observed that this is no exaggeration or caricature of the unbending rule of military life. It is the plain, obvious, and undeniable interpretation of its whole spirit and letter. A soldier, in regard to every point of professional duty, *is* a machine, without reason, without feelings, without conscience. Now, we strenuously and confidently deny that a Christian can put himself in a position where he must act as a mere machine. We maintain, that under no circumstances, and for no consideration whatever, is he at liberty to become the blind instrument for the performance of acts having a moral character, without consulting the voice of conscience, or paying the slightest heed to the will of his master. If there be some special act of indulgence or absolution promulgated by the great Lawgiver of Sion, for the behoof of military men, releasing *them,* in their professional capacity, from observing his laws, let it be produced. For ourselves, we must plead entire ignorance of its existence.

Now, let it be remarked, that our reasoning as to the incompatibility of a soldier's life with a Christian profession does not proceed on the assumption of the absolute unlawfulness of war. We have no right to assume that in our present argument, and we do *not* assume it. We only assume what none will be bold enough to deny, that a Government, or a general, or whoever has the command of an army, *may* undertake enterprises or order acts to be performed that are unjust and unchristian. And surely, of all other men, those who control armies have the least right to affect the possession of moral infallibility. Well, then, if an army may be commanded to do what is wrong—if, as all history testifies, all armies, (most assuredly not excepting the British army,) have, under such command, committed horrible wrongs and cruelties,—we ask, how can a Christian man put himself in a position where, *by the very conditions upon which he enters there,* he binds himself, without hesitation, without inquiry, without remorse, to perform acts which he may feel to be plainly condemned by the dictates even of his natural conscience, much more by the authoritative will of Christ. We observe that Captain Vicars tries to comfort himself on one occasion by saying, "There cannot be a doubt that it is a just war we are engaged in." We mean no disrespect to him when we say, that he was probably little qualified by position or intimate knowledge of the facts to form an impartial judgment of its justice or injustice. We have no doubt that if he had been going to fight *with* the Russians instead of against them (for which a very plausible case certainly might have been made out, especially to ardent Protestants who knew in what restless efforts for Oriental aggrandizement on the part of the Catholic Church the war had originated,) he would have pronounced for its justice with no less hesitation. Be that as it may, the question is, What right had Captain Vicars to import into the account any considerations whatever of the justice or injustice of the war? He was sworn to obey his Queen and his superior officers in whatever they prescribed him to do, be it just or unjust. And we say it again, with the utmost emphasis we can give to words, that this is a position which no Christian can consistently occupy.

SOLDIERSHIP AND CHRISTIANITY

But we remark further, that the work which a soldier has to do is utterly, deeply, revoltingly at variance with the sentiments and dispositions which a Christian ought habitually to cultivate. We are willing to believe, nay, indeed we have no doubt of it, that much of the talk in this volume, about longing to be "let loose" upon and "have a brush" with the Russians, and to die fighting for his colours, &c., is what we must be permitted to call, without meaning any offence, mere professional cant. All military men, in order to avoid the suspicion of "showing the white feather," are obliged to speak in this foolish way, as though they actually panted to be engaged in scenes of brutal conflict and wholesale slaughter, and as though the life which God had given them, so rich to many of them in the most precious feelings and relations, they could fling away with inconsiderate contempt. We must say, for ourselves, that we utterly disbelieve these professions, on the part, at least, of the best and noblest specimens of the military profession, for they are, also, the most intelligent and reflecting, who, we will do them the justice to believe, do not, cannot look forward with the ferocious animal joy they sometimes affect, to the horrible work, from which, however, when the time comes, they may feel it their duty not to shrink. This was the case, we are convinced, with Captain Vicars. Still, with all this allowance and mitigation, there is something to us altogether inexplicable in the fact, that a man holding such views as he did, and holding them with so devout and passionate an ardour, *could* bring himself to take share in such scenes as are described (not in this volume, but elsewhere) to have been enacted before Sebastopol. We will take only one out of many aspects of the case that occur to us.

Captain Vicars professed, and his whole conduct proved, beyond all suspicion, with what intense sincerity he professed, to feel the deepest concern for the salvation of others. Profoundly impressed with the infinite worth of the soul, and the incalculable peril involved in men's dying and going into the presence of God unprepared, he laboured, in season and out of season, to bring those within his reach into a state of salvation. "Oh! it is enough," he exclaims, "to make one's heart bleed to see, in one hospital after another, men dying without any kind friend or faithful minister to direct their hearts to the words of heavenly mercy, to point them to Jesus, and to refresh their souls with the water of life." Again, "Although I have often cause to grieve for my backwardness and slothfulness in the cause of Christ, yet my heart yearns over the souls of those who have not fled to the cleansing fountain of His blood for pardon and peace; and often, on rising from my knees, I have felt so powerfully drawn by the love of Christ, that I have been almost on the point of going out through the camp, to endeavour to impart to others the ground of my own peace and happiness." Now, will anybody explain to us how a man entertaining such views and feelings as these, as to the inexpressible value and importance of salvation, could nevertheless behold, and be himself an instrument in hurling scores and hundreds of immortal spirits into eternity, in what he, at any rate, must have considered an unsaved condition? "He was acting in obedience to his sovereign," we shall be told. But in the name of all that is solemn, has obedience to an earthly sovereign no limit? Is that warrant enough to lull to rest the conscience of a Christian man in the prospect and performance of deeds involving the perdition of immortal souls?

We verily believe that some good men, especially in the army, not a little bewilder their own consciences by the confused way in which they interpret and apply the figurative language of Scripture. The New Testament abounds with military imagery, the apostles naturally and wisely employing as illustrations of spiritual things those objects and events with which those whom they addressed were most familiar. But this no more implied any Christian sanction of war than the similar use they make of the boxing, and wrestling, and fighting with wild beasts, which prevailed among the ancients, implied their approval of those brutal and brutalizing spectacles; or our Saviour's comparing his second coming to that of "a thief in the night," implied a justification of house-breaking and robbery. The warfare to which Christianity summons its disciples, is against pride, avarice, ambition, malice, revenge, and other spiritual evils, many of which find their highest excitement and encouragement in the wars waged by men and nations against each other. Its testimony in regard to *these* is, that they come of men's lusts that war in their members. And yet we constantly find in this *Life of Captain Vicars,* and similar works, such expressions as "the soldier of the cross," "a good soldier of Jesus Christ," "the great Captain of our salvation," and others of kindred import, employed in, at least, a most equivocal sense, so as to leave us in doubt whether the writers do not confound the spiritual conflict, which the Christian is called upon to wage by means of "the weapons that are not carnal," with that coarse literal warfare which is carried on by material *steel* swords and bayonets,—by cannons, and howitzers and bomb-shells, and the object of which is the wholesale slaughter of human beings, by stabbing, cutting, shooting, drowning, and blowing them limb from limb with gunpowder. If we were not quite sure of the entire absence of any irreverent *intention*, such perversion of Scriptural terms would appear to us almost profane. If a racer or pugilist were to take the metaphors of the New Testament, and apply them to his own calling, we certainly should feel shocked, even though it were done seriously, and we cannot, we confess, hold it any more justifiable in the case of a soldier. [...]

[...] For our own part, we have the fullest conviction that, had Captain Vicars' life been spared, he could not have failed, as his knowledge of the Christian system became more intimate and profound, to have forced upon him the conviction, that the profession of a Christian and a soldier could not possibly be reconciled. He was but a young convert, and his intercourse had evidently been with those whose minds were unhappily warped on this point by educational prejudice and military associations. But with the New Testament in the hand of a man of so much simplicity and godly sincerity, we believe the final result would not have been doubtful. Indeed, it seems to us pretty clear, that, as it was, he *had* a lurking misgiving as to the lawfulness of his calling. For in one place he says, with great emphasis, that if he had known Christ, when he was seventeen years of

SOLDIERSHIP AND CHRISTIANITY

age, *"most certainly"* he would never have entered the army. But why not? If the military profession is perfectly in harmony with the mind of the Saviour, and if, as is repeatedly affirmed in this volume, it affords special opportunities for serving him, and making known his truth and grace, why should Captain Vicars say he would certainly never have entered upon it, had he been converted at an earlier age? This incidental revelation of what was working in his mind, seems to us pregnant with significance.

Note

1 Remarks on Military Law, &c. By Major-General Charles J. Napier, C.B., p. 5.

8

REVIEW OF
VIKINGS OF TODAY

London Hospital Gazette (1895), pp. 52–53

Vikings of To-day, **by Wilfred T. Grenfell, M.R.C.S.**
(Marshall Brothers, Paternoster Row)

This book, which has lately appeared with a preface of high commendation by Mr. F. Treves, cannot fail to interest all London Hospital men. There will be many who remember Mr. Grenfell as House-Surgeon, and as one of our best football players, as a man of daring and resource, and during the last few years a still larger number have learnt to associate his name with that splendid mission work to the North Sea Fishermen which has accomplished so much good at such insignificant cost in actual money. Mr. Grenfell, for the first time, carried the benefits of medical treatment to every rocky haven of the Labrador coast, and his work formed an invaluable adjunct to the labours of the Missionaries who have devoted themselves to the poverty-stricken English and Eskimo fishermen in that inhospitable land, where, as Mr. Treves writes, "Among fogs and icebergs a handful of determined men are trying to hold their own against hostile surroundings, and to earn a living in defiance of dreary odds."

Nothing conveys a stronger impression of the fierce struggle against nature that must be waged in Labrador, than the fact that in two of the chief settlements the mean temperature is from five to ten degrees below freezing point throughout the year. There are no cows, and tinned milk (poor substitute as it is) is rarely obtained owing to its cost; vegetables are extremely scarce, and in many parts unknown. Exposed to constant danger from extreme cold, storms, absence of proper medical treatment, and privation, the inhabitants of Labrador form a stirling example of the marvellous powers of resistance of the human race. The Eskimos have of late considerably diminished in numbers, and would, in Mr. Grenfell's opinion, run some risk of extermination but for the protecting influence of the Missionaries. In fact, one wonders why the struggle for existence in Labrador has not come to an end, so far as mankind is concerned. The answer may partly be found in the attractions of a comparatively free and wholly uncivilized life (there are no policemen in Labrador), and of the unrivalled facilities for procuring fish in these regions. Without the hugh shoals of cod, and without the seal "fishery," Labrador would no doubt have become ere this a complete desert. As it is, some thousands of whites

REVIEW OF *VIKINGS OF TODAY*

(mainly English in origin, and known as Lioynes) of Eskimos and of Indians, eke out a precarious livelihood, in addition to the numerous fishermen who also visit the coast of Labrador during the summer months.

The last return showed a total population of between twelve and thirteen thousand, and for this large number there was, until Mr. Grenfell's visit, no hospital and no good medical aid to be procured except at long and almost indefinite intervals. Taking, in the steam-launch "Albert," two other medical men (one of them being Mr. Curwen, who was formerly House-Physician to the London Hospital, the other, Mr. Bobardt of Melbourne) and two skilled Nurses, Mr. Grenfell had the satisfaction of founding, on his second voyage, a small wooden Hospital at Battle Harbour, in which the sick and injured were well cared for, and in some cases saved from a certain death. This work will no doubt be continued now that it has once been fairly started, for it cannot be believed that England and Canada, which are so directly interested in the matter, will allow the moderate sum of money annually necessary to be wanting.

In Mr. Grenfell's successive voyages many adventures were met with, his account is well illustrated from photographs, and is on the whole very good reading. Some slight criticism must however be made. The "sportsman's" instinct has led Mr. Grenfell to introduce several incidents which are somewhat repulsive to the ordinary reader, such, for instance, as the massacre of the seals and the butchering to death of a white bear (page 30). These form a striking contrast to such expressions as "so wonderfully does God remember all His creatures" (page 36), and the frequent biblical quotations and hymns. One or other, perhaps both, would have been better omitted. The same may be said of the statistical tables of the diseases met with amongst the patients (page 217), of the mythical and uninteresting tales about the discovery of Labrador, and of certain medical details as to "internal abscesses" and the like. The book moreover would have been improved by more careful arrangement of its subject matter and by the addition of an index. These are, however, but slight faults. *Vikings of To-day* deserves to be widely read, and Mr. Grenfell is to be congratulated alike for the success which attended his heroic undertaking, and for the vigour and interest with which he has narrated its history.

We have to acknowledge, with thanks, several numbers of the *St. Bartholomew's Hospital Journal;* the *St. Thomas's Hospital Gazette;* the *St. George's Hospital Gazette;* the *St. Mary's Hospital Gazette.*

9

A. F. CHILDE, *GOOD OUT OF EVIL; OR, THE HISTORY OF ADJAI THE AFRICAN SLAVE-BOY*

(London: Wertheim and Macintosh, 1850),
pp. 80–97, 100–101, 108–110, 114–121

Chapter X

You must remember, dear children, that though Adjai had been made free from the yoke of his cruel owner, and though his mind was now being cultivated, and his conscience enlightened, yet his heart was still dark, and he remained under the yoke of Satan. At length, the instructions of the faithful missionaries were blessed to their little scholar, and "God who commanded the light to shine out of darkness, shined into the heart" of the young captive, and made him doubly free.

When the missionaries were fully convinced that a work of grace had been begun in his heart, they baptized him, on the 11th of December, 1825. He then gave up his heathen name of Adjai, and received that of "Samuel Crowther," after a pious clergyman in England.

In 1826, Samuel visited this country for a short time. He longed to remain, and to learn what might qualify him to be a teacher to his countrymen; but the Lord's time had not yet fully come.

Very soon after his return to Africa, the Fourah Bay Institution, to which I have already referred, was opened, and he was admitted as the first student. He there received a measure of the wished-for instruction; and the warmest desire of his heart was in some degree granted, for he was enabled to engage in the service of Christ, which, as he now testifies from experience, is "perfect freedom." It was at this period that, taking a review of his past life, he was taught to call "the day of his captivity a blessed day, because it was the day which God had marked out for him to set out on his journey from the land of heathenism, superstition, and vice, to a place where His Gospel was preached."

In the year 1829, Samuel was married to a Christian woman, and God has given them several dear children, whose names are Abigail, Josiah, Samuel, Susanna, Juliana, and Dandeson. For many years he laboured actively and devotedly in the colony of Sierra Leone, as the schoolmaster of Regent's Town. Yet useful as he was there, the Lord had still higher work for him to do.

A. F. CHILDE, *GOOD OUT OF EVIL*

In the year 1841 three ships were fitted out by England to sail up the river Niger, which flows into the Gulf of Guinea. The object of our Queen, in sending them, was to persuade the chiefs of the nations on its banks to give up the cruel practice of selling their countrymen for slaves, and instead of this, to cultivate their land, and trade with its produce.

This was the Niger expedition, of which you have, doubtless, often heard. The ships were called the Albert, the Wilberforce, and the Soudan, which last is the name of an African river, a branch of the Niger.

As the ships were to pass not very far from the native country of Samuel Crowther, he was desired by the Committee of the Church Missionary Society to accompany them, in the capacity of native interpreter. He went accordingly, and God preserved him amidst all the danger, the sickness, and the fearful mortality which befel the expedition. He returned in safety to his family, with his desire to benefit his country deepened, and with the earnest wish that, since it had pleased God, by sickness and death, thus to disappoint the efforts of Europeans for preparing the way of the Gospel into the interior of Africa, the sons of Africa themselves might receive such instruction as should qualify them to act, not only as teachers, but as *missionaries* to their countrymen.

His desire was granted, and he was the first selected for the glorious work. He came over a second time to England, and was now admitted as a student into the college at Islington, where most of the missionaries of the Church Missionary Society are educated. While there, his consistent Christian conduct made him beloved by all who knew him. At length, after having given full proof of fitness for his great work, he was admitted, by the Lord Bishop of London, to the sacred office of the Christian ministry.

Oh think, dear children, what a solemn season the day of his ordination would be to Samuel! What emotions would crowd into his mind as he felt the Bishop's hand laid upon his head, and as he received into his own hands the Bible, with "authority to preach the Word of God!" Then would he see, more clearly than ever, the riches of that mercy which had separated him, in childhood, from his heathen home, not only that he himself might know and love the Saviour, but that he might be that Saviour's ambassador to his dark, yet still beloved land.

Yes, little Adjai, the poor black slave-boy, is now an ordained minister of the Gospel, a missionary of the Lord Jesus Christ! And where do you think he is labouring? Is he, do you suppose, feeding one of the little flocks which have been gathered into the fold of Christ at Sierra Leone? Or, is he spending his strength in travelling among the scattered villages of the interior, preaching to here a few, and there a few, besides running the risk of being again captured and enslaved? Neither of these is his sphere of duty.

The slave-trade, which had been so wonderfully made to *provide the missionary,* was made to *provide his station also.* Perhaps you do not quite understand me, so I will try to explain what I mean.

The natives of the Yoruba country, which, you will remember, was Samuel Crowther's native land, used formerly to live in scattered villages. Finding, however, that they were, in this way, unable to resist the attacks of the neighbouring tribes, who were constantly burning their villages, and carrying off the inhabitants to sell them as slaves,—it was resolved, by the Egba tribe of Yorubas, to collect together, and form a large city for mutual protection. To this they gave the name of Abbeokuta, or Under-stone. It contains from 50,000 to 70,000 inhabitants. And how do you suppose the Gospel came to be first introduced amongst this vast population? I told you that amongst the liberated Africans at Sierra Leone, many still remained *heathen*. A considerable number of these, finding that they were hindered in their idolatrous practices, by the spread of the Gospel in the colony, desired to return to their own country, that they might celebrate their heathen rites without a check. They accordingly made their way to Abbeokuta, to see whether they could comfortably settle there. On their arrival, they soon found many of their former connexions or acquaintance; and, in answer to the natural expressions of astonishment, "How is it that you are still alive and free?—From whence have you now come?"—replied, that the English had liberated them, brought them to Sierra Leone, provided for them as long as was necessary, and protected them ever since. This account filled the people of Abbeokuta with astonishment, and they exclaimed, "The English are a people dwelling nearer to God than any other." Thus, you observe, it was the *heathen* themselves, who first gave such a report as produced a decided impression in favour of the "good white men" at Sierra Leone; and so at last prepared the way for missionaries.

After a little time, several of the party who had gone to Abbeokuta, returned to the colony, and gave an account of their visit which, at length, awakened in the native *Christians* the desire to follow their example. These, however, found a difficulty such as the heathen had not experienced. As long as they remained at Sierra Leone, they enjoyed religious privileges, which they had been taught of God to prize above every other blessing. Although, therefore, they felt a strong desire to return to their native land, and to be restored to the dear relations and friends from whom they had been torn by the slave-trade, they dared not turn their backs upon the means of grace to which they owed everything, as servants of Christ. At length, they petitioned that a missionary might accompany them, and accordingly Mr. Townsend, who was then an English catechist, was sent to the Yoruba country, to learn whether there really was an opening for the Gospel, and whether the chiefs and people of Abbeokuta, in particular, were willing to receive Christian instructors among them. You can scarcely conceive the delight which this occasioned to the Yorubas who were in Sierra Leone. They had been praying that it might be brought about, and had shown that they were sincere by liberally subscribing towards the expenses of the undertaking; and now that their prayer seemed about to be answered, their joy knew no bounds. As Mr. Townsend passed down the streets they would point him out, one to another, as "the white man who was going to their own country;" and many a hearty "God bless you, massa, and go wid you!" sounded in his ears.

And how do you think, dear children, that he travelled to Badagry,—the port which is chosen as the safest line of communication between the colony and

Abbeokuta? It was in a ship which had once been a slaver, but was now the property of a Christian African merchant of the Yoruba tribe, and who himself had formerly been a slave! He had purchased this little vessel, to which he had given the honoured name of "Wilberforce," with his own money earned in business, and counted it a privilege that he was thus able to offer a free passage to the missionary to his native country. Thus the first herald of Christian *liberty* to this dark land was carried thither in a captured *slave-ship,* by a liberated *slave!*

Mr. Townsend was kindly received at Badagry. He did not, however, long remain there, but hastened on to Abbeokuta, which is about sixty miles inland. On his arrival, he found the account of the Sierra Leone emigrants to be quite true. He was led in triumph into the town, conducted by the king's son, and a body of armed men. The streets were thronged with the eager and delighted people, who shouted as he passed, "How do you do, white man? How do you do, you that are coming?" The king, whose name was Sodeke, and the chiefs also, entreated in the name of their people, that a missionary might come and dwell among them, and promised "that he should have more children to teach than he could manage."

With this good news, Mr. Townsend returned to Sierra Leone, and it was at once determined that the request of the Yoruba people should be granted. But who was to go? It was just when this question arose, that the Rev. Samuel Crowther, a native of that very tribe, and understanding that very language, was admitted to the sacred office of the ministry, and was thus ready to become an evangelist to whatever part of his native land the Lord might send him.

How clearly, then, was the finger of God seen pointing out the right sphere for his future missionary labours! He left England in October, 1843, followed by many prayers, and arrived safely in Sierra Leone on the 2nd of December, to the great joy of his countrymen, who had been anxiously expecting him, and who could scarcely believe that a black man had been actually "crowned a minister."

On the day after his arrival, which was Sunday, he, for the first time in Africa, ascended the pulpit, and presented himself before his countrymen as the messenger of Jesus Christ to their souls. Much interest was excited at seeing the service performed by a native; but instead of being puffed up by the notice he attracted, Mr. Crowther very beautifully remarks in his journal for that day, that "the question, 'who maketh thee to differ?' filled him with shame and confusion of face." It was Sacrament Sunday, and, after the morning service, he had the joy of administering the emblems of a Saviour's dying love to his dear native brethren. The season was a solemn one, and the Lord was graciously present with them. [...]

[...] They had been but a few days at Badagry, when news reached them which threw a gloom over the prospects of the Mission. Sodeke, the chief who had so earnestly entreated for the missionaries, had just died, and war had broken out, which threatened to prevent their proceeding to Abbeokuta. They were not discouraged, however, but entered, at once, upon missionary work at Badagry. A large and beautiful tree was selected for their out-of-doors church, and beneath its wide-spreading branches Mr. Crowther regularly preached, to an attentive congregation, "the truth as it is in Jesus," in the Yoruba language. His Sunday-school, too, was kept beneath the same tree. Just try, dear children, to fancy the scene,—the rays of the sun piercing the leafy roof of this new-fashioned school-room, and shining on the black faces of the forty little scholars, all eager to be able to "speak out of book," as they see their kind teacher do every Sunday! [...]

[...] Scarcely had he been three weeks at Abbeokuta, when an event occurred which, I am sure, cannot but fill your minds, as it did his, with wonder and joy. I will relate it in his own words. In his Journal for the 21st August, he thus writes:—"The text for this day in the 'Christian Almanack,' is, 'Thou art the help of the fatherless.' I have never felt the force of this text more than I have this day, as I have to relate that my *mother,* from whom I was torn away about five-and-twenty years ago, came with my brother in search of me! When she saw me she trembled. She could not believe her own eyes. We grasped one another, looking at each other with silence and great astonishment; big tears rolled down her emaciated cheeks. She trembled as she held me by the hand, and called me by the familiar names by which I well remember I used to be called by my grandmother, who has since died in slavery. We could not say much, but sat still, and cast now and then an affectionate look at each other,—a look which violence and oppression have long checked;—an affection which has nearly been extinguished by the long space of twenty-five years. Thus unsought for, after all search for me had failed, God has brought us together again, and turned our sorrow into joy!"

Have you ever heard, dear children, of such a meeting? One can scarcely fancy it. Little Adjai was torn from her arms, you will remember, a naked, ignorant slave-boy; and now he is restored to her, a faithful, intelligent Christian minister and missionary! Truly the Lord's ways are wonderful, yet all of them are wisdom and love to his own dear children! [...]

[...] Only three weeks afterwards, war was declared between the two towns, and the road between them was stopped. All that Mr. Crowther, therefore, could do, was to commend the absent members of his family to the care of that Heavenly Father who, though they knew him not, had hitherto so wonderfully preserved them. At length Abaka was entirely destroyed, and the inhabitants were brought as prisoners and slaves to Abbeokuta. Among the rest were Mr. Crowther's relations,—his two sisters, the husband of one of them, and four little nieces. The husband of his other sister, they had reason to fear, died on the march. [...]

[...] The kind brother, with the help of a few Christian friends, ransomed his sisters, his brother-in-law, and his little nieces, from slavery. Thus the little family, so long separated, after so many years of sorrow, toils, and danger, were once more united! And oh, how earnest were the prayers of that son and brother, that their union might become that of Christian fellowship, and that as he had been the means of restoring them to outward liberty, so he might also be the instrument, in the hands of God, of freeing them from spiritual bondage.

I must now return, for a short time, to Mr. Crowther's missionary labours. These were graciously owned, and abundantly blessed. Young and old, rich and poor, Chiefs and people, eagerly listened to his message. A church was erected, in which attentive congregations met to worship the true God. Neat houses, too, were built for the missionaries, which were the wonder of all the natives, who, contrasting them with their own rude huts, confessed that "white man had sense;" and both Chiefs and people would spend hours in gazing at and admiring them. Before long, a little band, who had renounced idolatry, offered themselves for Christian baptism; and amongst these was Afala, Mr. Crowther's beloved mother! Yes; God had heard the prayers of her son, and blessed his instructions. She had cast off all her former heathen practices, and in an illness which she had about this time, gave full proof that she had been "born again." With what increased affection would his heart yearn over that dear mother, since they were now related by a twofold tie; not only was he her child after the flesh, but he had become her father in Christ! After the candidates had been carefully instructed for many months, those who gave satisfactory evidence of change of heart were baptized on the 6th of February, 1848.

That was indeed an interesting and solemn day at Abbeokuta. A large congregation was gathered in the church. It was the first Christian church that had been built in the interior of Western Africa, and in it these first-fruits of missionary labour there were now to be received as members of the true Church. The two ministers were standing at the font, and before them were the candidates—three women, (one of whom was Afala) neatly dressed in white, two men, and four little children. After the baptismal service (translated into Yoruba for the occasion by Mr. Crowther,) had been read, Mr. Townsend baptized the grown-up candidates, and Mr. Crowther the little girls. These were his own nieces, whom he had redeemed from slavery, and to whom, by the custom of the country, he had now become father. He had chosen for his mother the appropriate name of *Hannah;* and surely the Jewish Hannah had no greater reason to rejoice in her Samuel, than the African Hannah had in hers.

His sisters are not yet baptized, but they have given up idolatry, and are now living with their brother, who is anxiously watching over them, and looking forward to the time when they too shall have learnt to know and love the Lord, and so the whole family be one in Christ Jesus.

The last accounts of this dear African missionary prove him to be full of zeal for the conversion of his nation, and to be as judicious as he is active. Having made great progress in translating the New Testament, from the Greek into the Yoruba language, he now wishes to begin the Old Testament also. He cannot, however, feel satisfied without being able, in this case as well as in the former, to translate immediately from the original. He therefore proposes to apply himself afresh to the study of Hebrew, and then to attempt his important task.

Thus a noble work lies before him: and, should his life be spared, it is possible that he may be still more wonderfully honoured and advanced than ever. There are many who hope to see him appointed as the first black bishop of Western Africa.

1.5

Ethnography and Anthropology

1.5 Ethnography and Anthropology

By virtue of their situations around the world, the nature of their work and their networks, missionaries were well placed to contribute to the developing fields of ethnography and anthropology. These amateur anthropologists were indebted to their native converts, guides and translators for much of their information, though these contributors were almost always unacknowledged. As the century went on missionaries began to make connections between the peoples they encountered and missionary accounts of other peoples in other regions of the world – sometimes in support of Biblical narratives such as that of the Lost Tribes of Israel (see this volume, Biblical History, Geography and Travel Writing). Data concerning languages and physical appearance of the peoples encountered was especially deployed to support such narratives. This data, along with information about kinship systems, also contributed to Victorian theories of race.

Robert Moffat (1795–1883), an LMS missionary to South Africa, was a very early contributor, sending information from his travels to the Royal Geographical Society for publication and discussion. His own book, *Missionary Labours and Scenes in Southern Africa*, is an expansive work that presents the missionary experience, its adventures and its exotic setting. In the first chapter, however, which is extracted here, Moffat focuses on the tribes that missionaries in Africa were encountering and provides his explanations for their variation. His analysis is detailed, providing data on the usual categories that ethnographers were interested in – appearance, customs and dialect – and he weighs evidence and alternative theories from a variety of sources. In this way, Moffat positions his writing as scientific discourse. However, missionaries like Moffat were largely motivated in their studies by a need to explain the current degraded state of Africa, and provide evidence that the Gospel had the ability to civilise all tribes and peoples around the world (by no means the majority view by the end of the century). As Moffat comments evaluatively on the conditions in which different tribes live, he uses Biblical references. Degraded tribes in the desert are in a kind of 'Babel', and the Hottentots were forced to migrate to the south because of the migration from the Holy Land of the sons of Ham. Moreover, when he comments on the changed nature of the missionised Basutos he uses the metaphor of planting in fertile soil, which was more common in missionary writing than in science (see this volume, Women and Authority in the Mission Field).

George Taplin (1831–1879) was a Congregationalist missionary who was posted to Southern Australia. His text, *The Narrinyeri*, was first published in 1873 and then revised for inclusion in J. D. Woods' collection, *The Native Tribes of South Australia*. The revised version is reproduced here as it is in the revisions that the hand of Taplin's aboriginal collaborator, James Ngunaitponi, can most probably be seen.[1] Taplin's work is positioned even more as scientific discourse than Moffat's, as can be seen by the precise titles and table of kinship included in the extract here. Tables and annotated figures abound in this work and, like Moffat, Taplin quotes western scientific authorities and other missionary ethnographers, with whom he was in correspondence. Also like Moffat, Taplin displays a desire to hypothesise the origins of his aboriginal tribes, and comes to a similar conclusion: the Narrinyeri, he believes, were displaced from India by the advancement of Aryan tribes. Taplin makes fewer references to the mission and the Bible than Moffat, and when he does these are clearly demarcated from more scientific passages. Interestingly, Taplin's Christian appreciation of the Narrinyeri's system of trial by jury – the Tendi – leads him to reflections on cultural relativism. He describes how the Tendi is not only very like the British system of trial by jury, but that it shows the Narrinyeri's understanding of judgement as an abstract concept, and one ultimately tied to a higher power in the heavens. He is impressed by this 'remarkable recognition' by those 'in heathen darkness', and this leads him to equivocate on whether it is an entirely good thing that the colonial rule of law has displaced the Tendi.

While missionaries took part in the imperial civilising mission, their relationship with the politics of Empire was rarely straightforward. Equally, their anthropological work was often in the service of the mission and always influenced by their Christianity; their contributions to ethnography were never purely scientific.

Note

1 Helen Bethea Gardner revealed this relationship in 'Practising Christianity, Writing Anthropology: Missionary Anthropologists and their Informants', in *Missionaries, Indigenous Peoples and Cultural Exchange*, ed. by Patricia Grimshaw and Andrew May (Eastbourne: Sussex Academic Press, 2010), pp. 110–22 (pp. 113–117).

10

ROBERT MOFFAT, *MISSIONARY LABOURS AND SCENES IN SOUTHERN AFRICA*

(London: John Snow, 1843), pp. 1–15 [abridged]

Chapter I

The continent of Africa, though probably the most ancient field of geographical enterprise, still is, and there is reason to believe that it will long continue to be, the least explored portion of our earth. Though once the nursery of science and literature, the emporium of commerce, and the seat of an empire which contended with Rome for the sovereignty of the world,—the cradle of the ancient church, and the asylum of the infant Saviour, yet Africa still presents a comparative blank on the map, as well as in the history of the world. [...]

[...] Africa had once her churches, her colleges, her repositories of science and learning, her Cyprians and bishops of apostolic renown, and her noble army of martyrs; but now the funeral pall hangs over her wide-spread domains, while her millions, exposed to tenfold horrors, descend like a vast funereal mass to the regions of woe. Christendom has been enriched by her gold, her drugs, her ivory, and bodies and souls of men—and what has been her recompense? A few crucifixes planted around her shores, guarded by the military fort and the roar of cannon. Had it not been for British power and British sympathy under the favour of Heaven, Africa to this day, with scarcely one exception, might have had the tricoloured flag waving on her bosom, bearing the ensigns of the mystery of Babylon, the crescent of the false prophet, and the emblems of pagan darkness, from the shores of the Mediterranean to the colony of the Cape of Good Hope.

"The countries extending throughout by far the greater portion of the vast surface just mentioned, are, as regards soil and capabilities, among the finest in the world; but the population of the whole, with the exception of Egypt in ancient times, and the population of the shores of the Mediterranean when under the Carthaginian, the Roman, and the brighter days of Arab sway, have been, through every age, and are still, sunk into the lowest depths of ignorance, superstition, disorganization, and debasement; the glimmer of civilization, which for a time appeared in Nubia and Abyssinia, compared with the whole, scarcely forming an exception."[1]

83

Before entering into a detail of Missionary operations, it may be proper to glance briefly at the position, extent, and character of some of the fields which have been occupied.

The bold and mountainous promontory of the Cape, was first discovered by Bartholomew Diaz, the Portuguese navigator, and was taken possession of by the Dutch, in 1652. At that period the whole of what is now designated the Colony, was inhabited by Hottentots proper, whose history and origin, from their physical appearance, language, and customs, continue involved in profound mystery. They resemble none of the Kafir, Bechuana and Damara nations, which bound the different tribes of that remarkable people, extending from Angra, Pequena Bay on the west, to the great Fish-river on the east. The whole race are distinct from all others with which we are acquainted. Taking the Hottentots, Corannas, Namaquas, and Bushmen, as a whole, they are not swarthy or black, but rather of a sallow colour, and in some cases so light, that a tinge of red in the cheek is perceptible, especially among the Bushmen. They are generally smaller in stature than their neighbours of the interior; their visage and form very distinct, and in general the top of the head broad and flat; their faces tapering to the chin, with high cheek bones, flat noses and large lips. Since the writer has had opportunities of seeing men, women, and children, from China, he feels strongly inclined to think, with Barrow, that they approach nearest in the colour and in the construction of their features, to that people than to any other nation. Since his arrival in England, this supposition has been strengthened by seeing two blind Chinese children whom, had he not been previously informed, he would have taken for Hottentots; and if they had had their eyesight, the resemblance would have been much more striking. It is well known that the Hottentots inhabit the southern point of Africa, and spread northward, while the Bushmen, the most northerly, exist among the inhabited regions, where they continue perfectly distinct, and, which is very remarkable, do not become darker in their complexion, as is the case with all the other tribes that inhabit, or have inhabited the Torrid Zone. If they had been gipsies from Egypt, as some have thought, it is another singular circumstance, that they should not, during the successive ages which they must have required slowly to advance through nearly 5000 miles of territory, have adopted one word of the language of the myriads with whom they came in contact, or one of their customs of any description, not even that of sowing seed in the earth. It may not be considered chimerical to suppose that when the sons of Ham entered Africa, by Egypt, and the Arabians, by the Red Sea, that the Hottentot progenitors took the lead, and gradually advanced in proportion as they were urged forward by an increasing population in their rear, until they reached the ends of the earth. It may also be easily conceived of by those acquainted with the emigration of tribes, that during their progress to the south, parties remained behind, in the more sequestered and isolated spots, where they had located while the nation moved onward, and research may yet prove that that remarkable people originally came from Egypt.[2] At all events, it is evident that they have arisen from a race distinct from that of their neighbours, and extended inland, inhabiting the most fertile spots, till their course was arrested on the east by the bold and warlike Kafirs, and on the north by the Bechuana and Damara. [...]

[...] The Bushmen are the most remarkable portion of the Hottentot nation. Various opinions have been offered on the origin and state of the Hottentots, among which is that of Gibbon, that "they were the connecting link between the rational and irrational creation." If he had been acquainted with the Bushmen, who are unquestionably inferior to the Hottentots, he would have felt more confidence in this strange and long exploded theory. Some say they are the progenitors of the nation; others, that they are an entirely distinct race; and others, again, that they are Hottentots, who have been directly or indirectly plundered of their cattle by the Dutch farmers. That the Bushmen are the people from whom the Hottentot tribes have descended, is irreconcilable with existing facts; that they are a distinct race, is still farther from probability; and that they are plundered Hottentots, is, in my humble opinion, a preposterous notion, resulting from limited information on the subject. If this were to be admitted, then we must also admit that the Hottentots, in being deprived of their cattle, and becoming Bushmen, were deprived of their language also; for it is well known, from the earliest records that can be obtained on the subject of their language,—which has, in addition to the klick of the Hottentot, a croaking in the throat,—that they never understood each other without interpreters.

Another fact is, that the Bushmen are to be found scattered, though thinly, among all the Bechuana tribes of the interior with which we are acquainted, even as far as the Mampoor lake, about eight hundred miles north of Lattakoo. The Marosa, or Baroa Bushmen, are found of the same description as those just beyond the boundaries of the colony; and from the oldest traditions we can find among the Corannas and Namaquas, who are the unmixed Hottentots, as also from the Bechuanas, it may be demonstrated, that they existed a wandering people without homes, or cattle, or even nationality of character. That they descended from Hottentots, requires little argument to prove. Probably there are connected with all the tribes of Africa numbers of a nomadic character, whose origin will throw light on the history of the Bushmen. A parallel is furnished by the following facts of the case, which have hundreds of times come under my own observation, during a residence of more than twenty years among the Bechuana tribes. Connected with each of the towns among that people, there are great numbers of what are called "Balala," poor ones, who stand in the same relation to the Bechuanas in which the Bushmen formerly stood to the Hottentots, and whose origin doubtless was of the same nature. These Balala were once inhabitants of the towns, and have been permitted or appointed to live in country places for the purpose of procuring skins of wild animals, wild honey, and roots, for their respective chiefs. The number of these country residents was increased, by the innate love of liberty, and the scarcity of food in towns, or within the boundaries to which they were confined by water and pasture. These again formed themselves into small communities, though of the most temporary character, their calling requiring migration, having no cattle of any description. [...]

[…] From the famishing life to which they are exposed, their external appearance and stature are precisely to the Bechuanas, what the Bushmen are to the Hottentots. Those, however, who live in places which afford a better supply of food, are generally of equal stature with those who live in towns. The natives I have observed throughout southern Africa are like plants on a sterile soil and bleak aspect, stunted in growth, while in a more genial situation the same species are trees instead of shrubs.

The next problem is the variety of languages spoken by the Bushmen, even when nothing but a range of hills or a river intervenes between the tribes, and none of these dialects is understood by the Hottentots. This may be solved with still greater ease, by again referring to the Balala. The dialects of the Sechuana as spoken by these people, especially in districts remote from the towns, is so different from that spoken by the nation generally, that interpreters are frequently required. In order to account for this, it is necessary to become acquainted with their habits. In the towns the purity and harmony of the language is kept up by their pitchos or public meetings, at which the finest language is spoken, by their festivals and ceremonies, as well as by their songs and their constant intercourse; for, like the Athenians of old, they are ever telling or hearing some "new thing," and the first question a person who has come from a neighbouring village is asked will be, "Lo yélang gona?" What do you eat there? or, "'Mpuléla mahuku." Tell me the news. There is no end to conversation, excepting when sleep overcomes or pinching hunger prevails. With the isolated villages of the desert, it is far otherwise. They have no such meetings, no festivals, no cattle, nor any kind of manufactures to keep their energies alive; riches they have none, their sole care being to keep body and soul together; to accomplish this, is with them their "chief end;" they are compelled to traverse the wilds often to a great distance from their native village. On such occasions, fathers and mothers and all who can bear a burden, often set out for weeks at a time, and leave their children to the care of two or more infirm old people. The infant progeny, some of whom are beginning to lisp, while others can just master a whole sentence, and those still farther advanced, romping and playing together, the children of nature, through the livelong day, become habituated to a language of their own. The more voluble condescend to the less precocious, and thus from this infant Babel proceeds a dialect composed of a host of mongrel words and phrases joined together without rule, and in the course of a generation the entire character of the language is changed. Their servile state, their scanty clothing, their exposure to the inclemency of the weather, and their extreme poverty, have, as may be easily conceived, a deteriorating influence on their character and condition. They are generally less in stature, and though not deficient in intellect, the life they lead gives a melancholy cast to their features, and from constant intercourse with beasts of prey and serpents in their path, as well as exposure to harsh treatment, they appear shy, and have a wild and frequently quick suspicious look. Nor can this be wondered at, when it is remembered that they associate with savage beasts, from the lion that roams abroad by night and day, to the deadly serpent which infests their path, keeping them always on the alert during their perambulations. All this and much more which might be said of the Balala, may also with the strictest propriety be affirmed of the Bushmen. [...]

[...] North of Kafir-land, between the Winterberg mountains and the higher branches of the Yellow River, lies the country inhabited by the Basutos, a tribe of Bechuanas. Since the days of Chaka, the tyrant of the Zoolus, who oppressed them from the east, while the Bergenaars on the west were exercising dreadful barbarities, and reduced most of the tribes to extreme poverty; they have risen again in a fertile country, to comparative affluence. The commencement of missions among them by the brethren of the Evangelical Missionary Society at Paris, and subsequently by the Wesleyans, is the cause of this improvement in their circumstances.

Notes

1 McQueen's Geographical Survey of Africa.
2 A few evenings ago I was in the company of a Syrian who lately came from Egypt. On giving him a specimen and a description of the Hottentot language, he remarked that he had seen slaves in the market at Cairo, brought a great distance from the interior, who spoke a similar language, and were not near so dark coloured as slaves in general. This corroborates the statements of ancient authors, whose description of a people inhabiting the interior regions of Northern Africa, answer to that of the Hottentot and Bushmen.

11

GEORGE TAPLIN [AND JAMES NGUNAITPONI], *THE NARRINYERI*

In Woods (ed.), *The Native Tribes of South Australia*
(Adelaide: Wigg and Son, 1879),
pp. 1–2, 34–36, 48–51, 128–129

The Narrinyeri, or Tribes of Aborigines inhabiting the Lakes Alexandrina and Albert and Lower Murray

The people who are described in the following pages call themselves "Narrinyeri." The name is evidently an abbreviation of Kornarrinyeri (from *kornar,* men, and *inyeri,* belonging to), and means "belonging to men." They take great pride in this designation, and call other nations of Aborigines wild black-fellows, while they say, "we are *men.*" These Narrinyeri occupy a tract of country which would be included within lines drawn from Cape Jervis to a point about thirty miles above the place where the River Murray discharges itself into Lake Alexandrina, and from thence to Lacepede Bay. They are divided into eighteen tribes, and each is regarded by them as a family, every member of which is a blood relation, and therefore between individuals of the same tribe no marriage can take place. Every tribe has its *ngaitye* or tutelary genius or tribal symbol in the shape of some bird, beast, fish, reptile, insect or substance. The reader who is not sufficiently interested may skip the following names of the tribes[1] of an obscure race of savages. Some, however, may like to know them, and for such I write them.

Name of tribe.	Locality.	Ngaitye.
1 Welinyeri	River Murray	Black duck, and black snake with red belly.
2 Lathinyeri	River Murray	Black swan, teal, and black snake with grey belly.
3 Wunyakulde	River Murray	Black duck.
4 Piltinyeri	North-eastern shore of Lake Alexandrina	Leeches, catfish (native pomery).

Name of tribe.	Locality.	Ngaitye.
5 Korowalle	North shore of Lake Alexandrina	Whip snake.
6 Karatinyeri	Point Malcolm, entrance to Lake Albert	Wild dog, light colour.
7 Rangulinyeri	Lake Albert River	Wild dog, dark colour.
8 Mungulinyeri	Lake Albert	Mountain duck (chocolate sheldrake).
9 Kanmerarorn	McGrath's Flat, on the Coorong	Mullet called Kanmeri.
10 Ngrangatari	Lacepede Bay	Kangaroo rat.
11 Pankinyeri	Lake Coorong	Butter fish (native Kungulde).
12 Turarorn	Mundoo Island, Lake Alexandrina	A kind of coot called Turi.
13 Lungundi	Sea-mouth of the River Murray, south side	Tern, a small kind of gull.
14 Kaikalabinyeri	Lake Albert, south shore	Bull Ant; a kind of water weed called by the natives Pinggi.
15 Kondolinyeri	Peninsula on the north-west side of sea-mouth of the River Murray	Whale (native Kondarli).
16 Tanganarin	Goolwa	Pelican.
17 Raminyeri	Encounter Bay	Wattle Gum.
18 Punguratpular	Milang	Musk duck.

Chapter II

The Tendi

The form of government amongst the Narrinyeri was much more complete and regular than would have been expected amongst such a barbarous people. They actually have an institution which is extremely like our trial by jury, and they have had it from time immemorial.

This they call the Tendi. It is the judgment council of the elders of the clan. Every clan has its tendi. The number of the tendi is not fixed; it appears to be regulated by the size of the clan; but it always consists of experienced elderly men. When any member of the tendi dies, the surviving members select a suitable man from the clan to succeed him. This council is presided over by the chief or rupulle of the clan. He is generally chosen for his ready speech, temper, and capacity for authority. The office is not hereditary but elective in the council itself. A seat in the tendi is called "tendi lewurmi," the *judgment seat*. All offenders are brought to this tribunal for trial. In case of the slaying by a person or persons of one clan of the member of another clan in time of peace, the fellow-clansmen of the murdered man will send to the friends of the murderer and invite them to bring him to trial before the united tendies. If, after full inquiry, he is found to have committed the crime, he will be punished according to the degree of guilt. If it were a case of murder, with malice aforethought, he would be handed over to his own clan to be put to death by spearing. If it should be what we call manslaughter, he would receive a good thrashing, or be banished from his clan, or compelled to go to his mother's relations.

All cases of infraction of law or custom were tried thus. A common sentence for any public offence was so many blows on the head. A man was compelled to hold his head down to receive the stroke of the waddy, and would be felled like a bullock; then get up and take another and another, until it was a wonder how it was that his skull was not fractured.

It is this tendi which so often causes natives to leave work suddenly and mysteriously, and go off to some meeting of their people. An interesting trial is to come off, in which, perhaps, they are witnesses, or, at any rate, concerned. I have been at the tendi. I find the following entry in my journal:—

I went to the camp to-day. They were holding the tendi. There are about 200 natives here, and they were nearly all present. It appeared to be a united tendi of two clans which had met to settle some dispute. There were forty-six men present, who took part in the talking, either as councillors or witnesses, I suppose. The tendi took place at a distance from the camp, and was arranged in two parties all decently seated on the ground, opposite each other. On one side was our clan, with King Peter sitting in a very dignified manner at their head as president, and on the other was the Coorong clan, over whom old Minora presided. Several men of the Murray and Mundoo clans sat at the side, between the two parties, and joined in the discussion, apparently as *amici curiæ*. The matter under consideration was a case of suspected murder. The Point Malcolm clan were accusers, and the Coorong clan defendants. A young man had died under suspicious circumstances; the latter clan asserted the death to have been purely accidental, while the former brought forward witnesses who deposed to reasons for suspecting that certain men of the Coorong had been guilty of foul play. I cannot give the natives credit for much order in their method of conducting business. There was a tremendous amount of talk. Sometimes one would speak, then half-a-dozen would all speak together in an excited and vociferous manner, then some friend would interject an exclamation. I could not make out the drift of the discussion. If it had been English it would have been bad enough, but in Native it was incomprehensible. I afterwards heard that the tendi broke up without any decision being arrived at.

I was told by a very trustworthy native a remarkable circumstance connected with the tendi, and the ideas of these people on the subject:—"An old man, the uncle of my informant, who was then a boy about ten years old, was very ill. This was some thirty-five years ago, and before the clan to which he belonged had any intercourse at all with Europeans. During the old man's illness he was assiduously attended by his friends, for he was much beloved. His nephew was continually at his bedside. At last death was manifestly approaching, and the sufferer was being supported in the arms of his friends, who expected every minute to be his last. As he lay there he pointed upwards to heaven and said in the Potauwallin dialect, 'Tand an amb Kiathangk waiithamb,'[2] which is to say, 'My tendi—or judgment— is up there.' It was a remarkable recognition of a judgment to come, by one in heathen darkness. My informant, who is a believer in Jesus, said the words of the old man ever after stuck in his memory. He also said it was not uncommon to hear the aged men say that there was a tendi in the heavens for the spirits of those who died."

I am rather sorry that the tendi is not so potent as it used to be amongst the natives. It is still resorted to as an excellent means of discussing and disposing of difficulties, but its penalties cannot always be carried out.

Chapter VI

Relationships

For many years I had been aware that the system of relationships amongst the Aborigines was different from ours, and had prepared a table of degrees of kinship. [...]

[...] The following is the system of relationship amongst the Narrinyeri:—

1   I being male, the children of my brothers are my sons and daughters, the same as my own children are; while the children of my sisters are my nephews and nieces. The grandchildren of my brothers are called maiyarare; while the grandchildren of my sisters are called mutthari.
2   I being female, the children of my sisters are my sons and daughters, the same as my own sons and daughters are; while the children of my brothers are my nephews and nieces; consequently it is common to hear a native address as nanghy, or my father, the man who is his father's brother, as well as his own father; and as nainkowa, or my mother, the woman who is his mother's sister, as well as his own mother.
3   All my father's brothers are my fathers, but all my father's sisters are my aunts. But my father's elder brothers have the distinguishing title of ngoppano, and his younger have the title wyatte. These terms would be used in the presence of my own father. The name for aunt is barno.
4   All my mother's sisters are my mothers, but all my mother's brothers are my uncles. Wanowe is the word for uncle.
5   The children of my father's brothers are my brothers and sisters, and so are the children of my mother's sisters; but the children of my father's sisters,

and those of my mother's brothers, are my cousins. The word for cousin is nguyanowe.

6   I being male, the children of my male and female cousins are called by the same name as the grandchildren of my sisters, mutthari.

7   The brothers of my grandfathers, and those of my grandmothers, and also their sisters, are my grandfathers and mothers. Whatever title my father's father has, his brothers have; and so of the sisters of my mother's mother.

8   My elder brother is called gelanowe, and my younger brother is called tarte. My elder sister is called maranowe, and my younger sister is called tarte. There is no collective term by which I can designate all my brothers and sisters, whether older or younger than myself.

9   The Narrinyeri make a difference in the termination of relationships, according as they are used in the first, second, or third person. Thus:—

Nanghai, is my father.	Gelanowe, my elder brother.
Ngaiowe, your father.	Gelauwe, your elder brother.
Yikowalle, his father.	Gelauwalle, his elder brother.
Nainkowa, my mother.	Maranowe, my elder sister.
Ninkuwe, your mother.	Marauwe, your elder sister.
Narkowalle, his mother.	Marauwalle, his elder sister.

Generally the difference in the terminations is nowe for my, auwe for your, and walle for his or hers.

A father and child, when spoken of together, are called retulengk; mother and child, ratulengk.

10   The Narrinyeri have words which signify bereaved persons answering to our words widow and widower.

A widower, is Randi.	Fatherless, Kukathe.
A widow, Yortangi.	Motherless, Kulgutye.
One bereaved of a child, Main-maiyari.	One bereaved of a brother or sister, Muntyuli.

These particulars may not be very interesting, but they are important as indications of the race to which the Aborigines belong. They are also proofs of the precision and nicety of expression to be found in their language.

The general scheme of relationship being the same as the Tamil and Telugu races in Southern India would go far to make us believe that the Australian Aborigines originally came from India. There seems a probability that their original seats were the East India Islands and the Malayan peninsula, and that they were dispossessed and driven southwards by the Malays; even as the Aboriginal races of India were dispossessed by the invasion of the Aryan tribes.

Chapter X

Language

[…] As might be expected, the Australian dialects are almost destitute of abstract terms and generic words. I cannot discover in any of the languages which I have examined any traces of figurative expressions. Among the Narrinyeri the poetical kind of speech so much admired by the Maori is not to be found. I do not know a single phrase worthy to be called a metaphor.

The languages of the Aborigines of this continent divide themselves into two classes. These are distinguished from each other principally by their pronouns. One class has monosyllabic or dissyllabic pronouns, while those of the other are polysyllabic. […]

[…] This indication of their being *two* races of Aborigines is supported by other facts. A kind of caste distinction has been found to exist among some which does not exist in others. The Kamilaroi and Dippil tribes, on the Upper Darling and its tributaries, were the Aborigines amongst whom this was discovered. The Rev. W. Ridley was the first to make this known.

Amongst the nations of Aborigines a system of relationship prevails similar to the Tamilian; but it is not universal, and it appears that it is modified by some tribes having originally had a different system. Again, there is a remarkable difference in colour and cast of features. Sir George Grey noticed this in Western Australia. Some natives have light complexions, straight hair, and a Malay countenance; while others have curly hair, are very black, and have the features of the Papuan or Melanesian. It is therefore probable that there are two races of Aborigines; and, most likely, while some tribes are purely of one race or the other, there are tribes consisting of a mixture of both races.

Before closing this chapter on native languages I should like to say that I do not think it would be possible to translate the whole Bible into the Aboriginal tongue without importing into it a great number of foreign words. At the same time, the simple truths of the Gospel can be expressed in it. We can say "Pornir an amb itye, Jesuse ngurn ambe;" that is, "Jesus died instead of us."

Notes

1 I have used the word "tribe" as that which is most intelligible to the reader. We may either consider the Narrinyeri as a nation divided into tribes, or as a tribe of Aborigines divided into clans. The native word for tribe or clan is Lakalinyeri.
2 This in the Point Malcolm dialect would be "Tand in amb kerau waiirrangk."

1.6

Biblical History, Geography and Travel Writing

1.6 Biblical History, Geography and Travel Writing

Evangelicals encountered the world through a Biblical lens, and their travels – both real and imaginary – were influenced by the missionary movement (see also Volume I, Evangelical Religion). The Holy Land was especially significant for missionary supporters. Not only was it the site of Christianity's birth, but a number of evangelicals also believed that the Jews needed to be returned to their homeland and converted to Christianity before the second coming could be realised. (A specific mission to the Jews was founded for this reason, see this volume, Mission to the Jews.) Information about missionaries' activities in these countries and others filled the religious press, just as news of military campaigns filled more mainstream newspapers.

In the same way that anthropological observations about other races were sometimes understood in the context of the religious theory of the Lost Tribes of Israel (see this volume, Ethnography and Anthropology), poets and travel writers often explained geographical features of foreign lands with reference to Biblical history. Charlotte Elizabeth Tonna's poem, 'Palestine', and the *Sunday at Home*'s article on Lebanon depict these lands as being denuded and fruitless because of the historical actions of the Jewish race that lived there.

Charlotte Elizabeth Tonna (1790–1846) was a politically conservative, staunchly anti-Catholic evangelical writer. She first began writing for the Dublin Tract Society and became founder editor of the *Christian Lady's Magazine* in 1834. She also wrote popular novels such as *Helen Fleetwood*. Her poem 'Palestine' appeared in the collection, *Osric: A Missionary Tale, with The Garden and Other Poems*. Tonna states that the poem was inspired by the Jewish Christian missionary Joseph Wolff, who, in his missionary journal (published 1824), described how he met Jews who had travelled to Israel so they could die there. In her poem, Tonna portrays Palestine's landscape as 'barren' both because the Jews did not accept Christ ('no ripening fruit repaid my patient skill') and as a result of the race being scattered, with 'Pagan foes' taking their place. However, ventriloquising God and Christ, Tonna prophesies that the desert will 'blossom as the rose' should they convert ('turn') and submit to be forgiven. Past, present and future are compacted in this poem, as Tonna suggests that Biblical history is still being played out and that the Holy Land's current landscape is only a temporary perversion of that described in the Bible, which will one day be corrected.

The *Sunday at Home* was a publication explicitly designed to provide entertaining reading that was suitably Christian in its subject matter for families to read on Sundays, when many other forms of entertainment were frowned upon. The piece reproduced here, 'Lebanon and its Cedars', was typical of a certain type of natural history non-fiction article that the periodical ran – others included 'The Fig Tree', 'The Almond Tree' and 'The Olive Tree'. These articles refer to the representation of these plants in scripture, poetry, and Classical texts, alongside the more scientific, contemporary descriptions by missionaries. This mixing of scientific and religious discourse shows that evangelicals did not see the domains as separate and were confident in their ability to reconcile the findings of natural science with Christianity (see Volume IV, Scientific Approaches).

By the late nineteenth century, religious tourism had become popular, with Americans and Europeans guided around the missionary field by indigenous converts. Whereas in the early nineteenth century missionaries travelling to their mission posts often assumed they would never see home or relatives again, by the later years of the Victorian period missionary enthusiasts could visit missions for their holidays. Constance Maynard's pieces of travel writing outline the experience of this sort of missionary tourism, including the disappointment many Christians felt at the disparity between the Holy Land they had imagined from reading the Bible and that which they encountered in reality.

Constance Maynard (1849–1935) was the first principal of Westfield College – a women's higher education college associated with the University of London, which aimed to turn out highly educated women missionaries to lead schools, colleges and other institutions. The texts reproduced here were published in Westfield College's magazine *Hermes*, but versions were also privately circulated by Maynard to particular groups of students with whom she regularly corresponded. The first article (published in two parts) describes her experience accompanying one of her graduates to her new missionary post at Lovedale Mission in South Africa, while the second details part of her holiday in the Holy Land. From her position of authority she depicts these countries as places in which her students have a role to play in the imperial and religious mission – a role in Christian history – following in the footsteps of such missionary 'warriors' as Dr Stewart of Lovedale and Robert Moffat (see this volume, Ethnography and Anthropology).

In their imagined and reported depictions of missionary lands, whether they purported to be scientific or poetic in nature, these texts from across the nineteenth century contribute to the same ideology of non-Christian countries as fallen – emerging from this fallen nature only through the agency of British-imperial missionary activity.

12

CHARLOTTE ELIZABETH TONNA, 'PALESTINE' [1826]

In *Osric: A Missionary Tale, with The Garden and Other Poems* (Dublin: Curry, [n.d.]), pp. 43–48

The Missionary, WOLFF, met at Jerusalem with some aged Jews, who came from Poland to die there. One of them said to him, "It is not pleasant now to *live* in Palestine, but it is pleasant to *die* in this land, and all of us here have come *to die in the land of Israel.*"

> Returning from a stranger land,
> We come, a feeble, aged band,
> To linger out life's fading hours
> Beside our ruined Salem's towers;
> Where once exulting myriads trod
> To throng the fane of Judah's God;
> With trembling pace her exiles creep,
> Lean on the way-worn staff, and weep.
>
> The spicy breath of Lebanon
> Our welcome sighs, and passes on;
> We stand on Olivet's ascent,
> Where royal David weeping went,
> Behold yon spot, profaned by foes,
> 'Twas there our beauteous Temple rose;
> But not a vestige, not a stone,
> Tells where Jehovah's dwelling shone!
>
> Unmeet it were for us to dwell
> Where Pagan hymns through Zion swell;
> And day by day, with callous eye,
> Gaze on her faded majesty;
> And view the gorgeous Mosque arise,

THE FOREIGN MISSION MOVEMENT

Where blaz'd her holiest sacrifice.
Beneath the Crescent's impious pride
It is not meet that we abide.

But oh, how pleasant 'tis *to die*
Where Israel's ruin'd glories lie!
How sweet to bid her children's bones
Blend with the dust of Salem's stones!
Her's is the mould beneath them spread,
And her's the sod above their head.
E'en the cold worm with slimy coil,
Is welcome, bred in Judah's soil.

Soon shall these weary frames of ours
Dissolve like Salem's crumbling towers;
Her outcast tribes no longer come
To greet her as their hallowed home;
But sadly joy to lay their head
Beneath her foes' insulting tread;
To fall by her they could not save;
Their glory once, and now their grave!
Say, Christian, can'st thou hear that plaintive strain
Breathe o'er Judea's desolated plain;
While the sad Exiles, worn with age and woe,
With faultering step, and swelling bosom go;
Where erst, descending from the Olive steep,
One mightier far than David paus'd to weep?
O can'st thou hear nor ask an eagle's wing,
An angel's tongue, the tale of peace to bring?
From the high mount to send the joyful word,
"O comfort ye my people," saith the Lord.
Say not, thou trembling one, that I am gone,
That all my loving mercies are withdrawn.
What mother can forget the infant, prest
In helplessness to her supporting breast?
She *may* forget him, smiling on her knee,
But I, the Lord, will yet remember thee!
Still in my sight the mighty Bulwark stands,
And still thy name is graven on my hands.
What though from age to age the bitter draught
Of wrath unmix'd thy quivering lip hath quaff'd,
'Twas Sin expos'd thee to that wrath divine—
My ways are straight—but how unequal thine!
Draw near, my people, with your Maker plead;

CHARLOTTE ELIZABETH TONNA, 'PALESTINE'

Produce your cause, and vindicate the deed;
Retrace the gloomy wilderness of time,
Raise the dim veil, and contemplate your crime.
Lo! in the centre of yon scoffing crew,
Say what Majestic Victim meets the view?
O fools and blind! ye raise the murd'rous knife
Against the Son of God, the Lord of Life;
The promis'd Prince, the Saviour of your line,
The Branch of Jesse's root, Messiah, King Divine!
A Man of woes, rejected and unknown,
Press'd by a weight of sins, but not his own;
Guiltless and uncondemn'd the Suff'rer stands,
Mute as the sheep beneath her spoiler's hands.
Turn to the record of your ancient Seer,
The shadow there behold—the substance here.
In vain—the heart is harden'd, clos'd the eye,
And He—the very Paschal Lamb—must die!
Hark to the import of that fearful strain,—
"On us and on our race His blood remain!"
The word is past—the awful doom is given!
And Israel stands accurs'd before the God of Heav'n!

O thou afflicted, worn, and tempest-toss'd,
How hath my thund'ring scourge thy path-way cross'd!
Hungry and weary, desolate and sad,
Fed with my fury, by my vengeance clad;
Victim of mocking hope and fruitless toil,
The scorn of nations and the people's spoil;
Where'er thy wand'ring feet assay to pass,
The field is iron, and the sky is brass.
The beauteous land, thy glory and delight,
Devour'd by Pagan foes before thy sight!
But deeper woes thy tainted soul hath known.
Thy conscience sear'd with fire, thy heart a stone.
Thine eye is dark beneath the day-beam's blaze;
Thine ear is deafen'd to the song of praise;
Thy back is bowed, thy table is a snare;
Thy piety a sin, thy hope despair!
"And will the Lord of Mercy ne'er forgive?"
Oh turn to me, my people, turn and live!
My Israel, turn! thy murder'd Lord survey,
I rend the veil, and wash thy guilt away.
My own, my ransom'd Judah, doomed to prove
A moment's wrath, and everlasting love!

I, even I, will wipe thy streaming tears,
And raise thy drooping head, and dissipate thy fears.
I am thy God—thy Husband—thou art mine;
Thy glory shall return—arise, and shine!
From burning flames thy life do I redeem,
My hand upholds thee through the swelling stream.
Thy darkest night with noontide splendour glows,
Thy howling desert blossoms as the rose;
Thanksgiving, and the voice of melody,
Burst from thy lip, and echo through the sky;
As, Zion-bound, thy homeward footsteps tread,
With everlasting joy upon thy head!
Thou wert a chosen Vine, supremely fair,
Placed by my hand and nourished by my care.
With watchful love I built a fortress round,
Beam'd on thy head, and fertiliz'd the ground;
But barren, wild, unprofitable still,
No ripening fruit repaid my patient skill.
In wrath I turned, and smote thy spreading boughs,
Gave the wild cattle on thy leaves to browse;
On thy bare trunk my storms and tempests hurled,
A monument of vengeance to the world!
But I will graft thee with a nobler shoot,
And with heaven's dews revive the fainting root;
The wondering nations in thy shade shall meet.
To quaff the streams that murmur at thy feet;
Thy Moon the brightness of the Sun display,
While sevenfold lustre gilds the solar ray;
And thou, far lovelier, dearer than before,
Beneath Jehovah's smile shalt bloom for evermore."

13

'LEBANON AND ITS CEDARS'

Sunday at Home, 1 (May 1854), pp. 6–7

Lebanon and its Cedars

Some of the most elegant scripture imagery is derived from this mountain, or rather, range of mountains, and its scenery. Its trees, its fruits, its fragrance, its cattle, its snows, and its cooling streams, have furnished the sacred writers with abundant material for the exhibition of whatever is august, dignified, or sublime. The strength, beauty, and prosperity of the church have been shadowed forth from these magnificent heights, not only over Syria, but throughout all lands.

This range of mountains forms the northern boundary of the Holy Land, stretching from Sidon on the west, to the vicinity of Damascus on the east. There are two ridges running parallel, in a crescent form, and pursuing nearly the course of the Mediterranean—the one called Libanus (or White Mountain); the other, Anti-Libanus. The sublime elevation, the steep ascent, and the gigantic masses which shoot into the clouds, excite in the mind of the traveller feelings of reverence and astonishment; and should he reach the highest point of Lebanon, the immensity of space which expands around him becomes a fresh subject of admiration.

The general appearance of Lebanon as it now exists, may be thus briefly described:—"Around its base is a girdle of terraced hills; higher up is a zone of oak and cedar; next comes a belt of green pastures and flowery herbs; and above, the barren, craggy, and snow-covered heights of the upper Lebanon." Streams, fed by the snows and ice, descend from the rocks in many places, forming beautiful cascades, and diffusing a fertilizing influence on every side.

"But Lebanon," as another writer observes, "so renowned for its extensive forests of cedar, 'coeval with the sky-crowned mountain's self,' is now almost entirely unclothed, only here and there presenting to the traveller a solitary specimen of its former glory."

Various accounts have from time to time been given of the exact number of cedars to be found on Lebanon. They differ considerably, since some counted the younger trees and others did not:—

In 1565, Furer counted	25	In 1696, Maundrell	15
1575, Rauwolf	24	1738, Pococke	15
1583, Radzivil	24	1810, Burckhardt	11 or 12
1600, Biddulph	24	1818, Richardson	8
1605, De Breves	24	1832, Lamartine	7
1612, Lithgow	24	1836, Lord Lindsay	7
1630, Fermenel	22	1816, Buckingham	20
1633, Rodger	22	large and single, 200 altogether.	
1688, La Roque	20		

While Dr. Kitto also remarks that more cedars are now growing in England than in the whole of Mount Lebanon.

Robinson, referring to the somewhat secluded position of the ancient cedars now remaining, says, "They stand in a hollow, as if ashamed," verifying the prophetic allusion, (Isa. xxxiii. 9,) "Lebanon is ashamed." And Elliot informs us that the modern cedars are never allowed to attain any considerable size, the mountaineers cutting them down for the sake of the charcoal and tar. (See Isaiah x. 16, 18.) The present comparative desolation of this once glorious region has been thus celebrated in song:—

> Where are the goodly cedars now,
> That from the stately mountain's brow
> Look'd once upon a land of glory?
> How thinly scattered now they stand,
> A small and melancholy band,
> Recorders of their own sad story!
>
> They tell us of those pillar'd domes,
> Where princes had their costly homes,
> With gems, and gold, and ivory,
> Wrought by the famed artificer;
> Alas! they only live to stir
> The bitter thought, the fruitless sigh!
>
> For who can look on Lebanon,
> Nor sigh to see its glory gone?
> Or see unmov'd that front of snow,
> That wont to wear a verdant crown,
> Dart through the misty air its frown
> Upon the howling scene below?
>
> Mourner of Israel! take thy stand
> Upon that height, and there command

'LEBANON AND ITS CEDARS'

All Sharon's vale and Bashan's plain,
Where once a blooming surface smil'd,
And Summer spread his banquet wild,
And Autumn stretched his golden reign.

There from those cedars might be seen
Unnumbered rills and forests green,
And cities in the distant blue,
With terrac'd Tabor's beamy crest,
And Carmel for her vintage drest,
All bursting on the conscious view.

What hand hath laid that circuit bare,
And scattered thorns and thistles there,
Apostate Earth's too natural dress?
What spell upon that scenery
Hath made it interdicted lie,
Mock'd by its claim to fruitfulness?

The dread anathema of God
Hath struck the vales and cursed the clod;
They lie in blank astonishment;
Ages of barrenness attest
The sentence which has all unblest
The blessings to his chosen sent.

Mourner of Israel! turn thine eye
To that prophetic mystery
Which offers comfort to the soul;
See, in the treasure of God's word
For thee, e'en thee, rich blessings stor'd,
And healing grace that "maketh whole."

Again shall Sharon's roses bloom,
And Salem rise amid the gloom,
More great and glorious to behold;
When God shall make his promise good.
And give the conquest of his blood
To the lost sheep of Israel's fold.

14

CONSTANCE MAYNARD, CONTRIBUTIONS TO *HERMES* (WESTFIELD COLLEGE NEWSLETTER), 1898–1900

(i) 'A Few Pages from a Diary', *Hermes*, 12 (1898), Queen Mary Archives, WFD/23/3, pp. 8–10; (ii) 'A Few Pages from a Diary (Continued)', *Hermes*, 13 (1899), Queen Mary Archives, WFD/23/3, pp. 13–15; (iii) 'Letter from the Mistress', *Hermes*, 17 (1900), Queen Mary Archives, WFD/23/3, pp. 10–12.

i
A Few Pages from a Diary

By the Mistress

My journey to South Africa was of such real living interest that I feel a desire to share some of it with you, my friends. No time shall be wasted on the preliminaries, but I will plunge at once into the part that I think will interest you, so you will take the voyage for granted, and the landing at Cape Town, and the fortnight spent in its neighbourhood, and the long train journey of two consecutive days and nights, and imagine J. C. Bewes and myself in a hotel at Grahamstown going to start on our first drive in a real Cape "post-cart."

We had already enjoyed what little we have seen of the wilder country; the great Karroo desert with its ridges and layers of barren hills, the scrub of Mimosa looking like a silvery network of cruel gray thorns, the scarlet aloes standing up like stiff candles here and there, the enclosures with herds of ostriches feeding, and now and then a Dutch farm looking trim and tidy and fresh amid the desert waste, surrounded by its folds for cattle or mohair sheep; everything was of interest, especially our first sight of Kaffir kraals, which give one a general impression of round huts and naked children running, but which were not near enough to see clearly. So it had been thus far, but now we were going to see everything close at hand, and the prospect was delightful of the long drive across the hills

C. MAYNARD, CONTRIBUTIONS TO *HERMES*

from Grahamstown to *Lovedale,* the great Kaffir school and college and mission, the oldest and best of the kind that is founded and supported mainly by the Free Church of Scotland. On account of its excellent work in providing interpreters and teachers for elementary schools, it receives a Government grant of some £2,000 a year; in consequence it has to keep up with the Government requirements, the ludicrous side of which struck me pretty forcibly, as you will hear. But it is a noble institution, and Dr. Stewart, the principal, has been there nearly forty years. In his youth he was a long time with Livingstone, and he knew Moffat also, and he looks the very pattern of a brave and scarred old veteran of the African missionary warfare. Disheartening truly, it has been, and still is in many ways, on account of the excessive childishness and instability of the race he has to deal with, but he is one of those who is laying the foundation-stones deep down, and others later will build upon them.

The morning of Friday, August 6th, was glorious and cloudless. Being the middle of their winter it was not oppressively hot, but was brilliant all the way through. We rose early, for there was some uncertainty as to when the post-cart started; a friend who had drawn up our plan of travel said 5.30, the time-table in the hotel said 6.30, our landlord said 7.30, but that it wouldn't really be *off* till 8.30; and it was exactly 10.5 when we rattled out of the hotel yard. Such a strapping and unstrapping of luggage and great mail-bags to get the balance just right, but at last the dusty gaunt old cart seemed to satisfy its critics, the four bony horses were put in, and we jolted and clattered down the wide, stony street and out into the open country, and away, away into the very heart of the hills. Everything wants water badly, the road was white and dusty, and each side was endless parched-up bush, with euphorbias like giant candelabra, and prickly-pears and bare mimosas, and endless dwarf thorny shrubs, and all close-matted together with ivy-leaved geranium, with its strong green leaves and narrow, pale, pink flowers. As we reached the top of this first hill what a sight met our views—line beyond line of blue hills fading away into soft, hazy distance, and folds on folds of nearer moorland, a maze without ending. There was the whole range of the Katsbergs and the Winterberg, and the three pointed hills where King Williamstown lies. Never did Africa seem so *big*! And down we bumped and clattered and jolted, down to a deep valley where the great Fish river runs, now a series of muddy pools in a wide, stony bed, but to be traced all along by the taller trees interspersed with the tender green of beautiful willows that grow beside it; then up again to the top of a cliff one might well think inaccessible to wheels, and then down again to the Kat river, and then a toil of several miles to a still higher ridge with another phase of the magnificent view, and so on.

Our driver was full of gruesome and awful stories, and he told them graphically and well, whether of the upsets of post-carts and mistakes of drunken drivers; or of the deadly rush for gold in the early days of Johannesburg, where three acres of cemetery was filled full and over full in nine months, and people died everywhere and anywhere; or of the overturning of a whole ox-waggon down a precipice, killing a steady young fellow and his bride, whom he had seen married three days before; or of the terrible shiftlessness and criminal laziness of the Kaffirs. Really, he seemed to think a horse the higher and better animal of the two, and that to educate them was to condemn them to be worthless forever. "And Dr. Stewart knows all this as well as I do myself," he added sententiously.

Twice we stopped for a while and had tea and very nice bread and butter in a gay little drawing-room, and wondered much how the piano, the mirror, and the cheap glass ornaments had come over these rough roads. In one room a large clean, white hen was sitting on a down cushion in the armchair, and was reported to be laying eggs. At another station an ostrich chick, two days old, was brought out for us to look at, a nice little beast, the size of a large fowl, with a back like a hedgehog, but softer, and a downy, grey neck and large eyes with eyelashes, and large, clean, padded feet.

After the last stop it was about 4.30, and we started at an immense altitude, with a view all round one could hardly take in for mere size. Our driver told me I must learn to drive four-in-hand, and put the reins rightly between my fingers. "Off, near, near, off," is the right order. But I had to take both hands to it at once, and even then, *how* my hands ached. Yet this was level ground, with only the weight of the reins to bear, and what it must be to hold them up on these steep gradients I do not venture to think. After a mile or more the road began to descend, and I said, "The responsibility is too great," and gave them back, and he took them laughing, and began again with his gruesome tales. But the beauty of it all for the next two hours would be hard to tell. The level sun struck the dry landscape into a beautiful bloom of russet and red and plum colour, and the huge rolling hills and moorlands lay around us for untold miles and miles. Golden and brown, and with depths of indigo shadow in the winding valleys, and not one sign of human habitation anywhere.

And then the sun set, and in the west "a heap of gold lay burning," and all the mountain ranges changed to a deep cobalt blue, and rose up like a cup all round us, and we felt ringed by the whole world. This was not for long, for again they faded into dim and hazy distance, and down, down, down we jolted and rattled, and the moon (exactly at the half) stood right in the zenith, and the planets came out in the purple sky, and then the stars, and the wind went down with the sun, and soon we were driving in the still night. I could not but admire the sharp senses of our driver—in the utter loneliness he would blow his post-horn. "Why?" I asked. "Why do you not smell the dust not yet settled?" he replied, "That *may* be an ox-waggon." Sure enough, in half a mile more one could *see* the white dust like a circle of mist in the moonlight, and when we reached it we could hear the shouts of the Kaffir drivers as they tugged their long teams out of the way. This occurred five or six times, as these waggons only travel at night. At last the road became smoother and better, and we saw a light or two ahead, and at 7 p.m. we sailed into the wide street of little Beaufort, with fifty miles behind us.

ii
A Few Pages from a Diary (Continued)

The next morning a drive of sixteen miles more brought us to the hills above Lovedale. There it lay below us in a wide shallow valley, with the barren hay-coloured hills all around it, and itself an oasis of life and freshness. The space was dotted with white houses, and crowded with trees, eucalyptus and cypress and deodar and willow, and surrounded with green fields of springing wheat, and plantations of young walnut trees, and of osiers for basket-making. There is no lack of water in beautiful Lovedale, and all around stand the brown slopes dotted with Kaffir kraals, and beyond again the bare mountains, looking hazy and desolate in the silent noontide heat. But we clattered down the hill side, splashed through the shallow river at the foot, bowled up a long avenue of giant eucalyptus trees, as smooth and well kept as a nobleman's approach, passing building after building belonging to the Institution, and stopped at last before a comfortable house in the centre. Out came Dr. and Mrs. Stewart to welcome us, and fairly made us at home with their kindness. Dusty and gritty and travel worn we arrived, and soon under their care we became clean and rested and comfortable. It was amusing to see one's well-known luggage going upstairs balanced on the house-maid's head, and amusing to hear the bare feet, pad, pad, padding, as the maids waited at table. I had a lovely room that looked toward the sunrising and was all coloured in shades of yellow, so that when at six o'clock "up leaped of a sudden the sun," I used to wake in a blaze of gold and lie and be happy. There are a great many young Stewarts, two being grown up and at home, and two more being St. Andrew's School girls, and there are a good many more besides, and it is a happy home-like home set like a jewel in this huge land. And the best part of it all is Dr. Stewart himself, the true old warrior who has held that post for so long, and has seen it grow from small beginnings to its present heavy responsibilities, and bears it all with a complete modesty and self-forgetfulness that sometimes verges on discouragement.

It is a difficult problem this of the education of native races. They are so bright, so imitative, that our language and the arts of our civilised life are picked up rapidly, and then to your dismay you often may discover that this is but a shallow veneer, and that scarcely the most elementary conceptions of morality lie behind it. Both the Moravian and the French Missions feel the point so strongly, that I understand they teach their Kaffirs only religion and handicrafts, even the art of learning to read their own language being reserved as a prize for the best and most promising, who have done well in other respects. But the "Government Requirements" stand as a huge shadow over Lovedale, and subordinates the life there to its iron rule. And what is one to do? It is better surely that these "requirements" should be in the hands of the Missionaries, for the rewards that success brings are a great inducement to learning, and the most promising young men crowd in from the kraals around and even come from long distances up the country. The handicrafts taught are capital, and the inspectors say the work done is "unique" in its quality. We saw a huge carpenter's shop with forty complete sets of tools, and doors and windows and wheelbarrows and school-desks are made there by the score, and even a splendid great solid ox-waggon was standing in the stud complete and shining, and ready for use. Then there was a forge in good working order, and wheel-tyres and horse shoes being made in plenty, also a basket-making and boot-making, and a very fine printing establishment. After correcting and re-correcting, the Kaffir dictionary is thought for the present to be complete, and I watched the stereotyping of some of its pages, and was surprised to see the boiling lead poured into a matrix of mere brown paper. Every book in the Kaffir language, whether hymn-books or grammars, is printed at Lovedale.

The religious side of the education I cannot enter into here, but I can truly say it was simple and earnest and good, and that the spirit in which all the work was carried on, seemed to me admirable, Dr. Stewart's many helpers working well in a line with him, and treating the strange material they have to manage, with true gentleness and kindness. Such material! People that have never slept in a bed, or ate with a spoon, or sat at a table (or had a wash, or combed their hair), in their lives, presenting themselves with the small sum needful in their hands gained by selling an ox or a few sheep, and asking vaguely "to be taught." They are docile as children, and in a few days acquire a code of manners that would not disgrace any simple standard. In dress they differ a good deal, from the light summer suit and spotless collar of the would-be European, to the frayed canvas shirt and trousers of the true nigger of literature, yet all look well content and smiling.

But you must hear finally about the "Government requirements," and you shall see them in full working order. Imagine a fine lofty airy room, a black-board with an energetic Scotchman standing at it, and before him five or six rows of round woolly heads, all with still faces and gentle troubled expression anxiously eyeing their teacher. This class is at Algebra, a long sum in fractions with lots of brackets in it, and on he goes at the board as fast as ever his fingers can write, answering to the soft bass voices of his pupils as they rapidly chant in chorus the figures he is to put down. This is not so bad, but the next room is doing "The Merchant of Venice," and going on there is the analysis of curious sentences, the explaining of archaic terms, and the Shakespearean use of adverbial clauses. When one looked at the flock of black heads, the round shoulders studiously bent over the books, and the pathetically bewildered faces that looked up now and then, and when one guessed at the utter blank of a Kaffir's mind, the force of irony can no further go! Where is Venice? and what is a merchant? What is a Jew? What is a lawyer, a surety, a balance?—the simplest elements of the background of knowledge all are wanting in such a mind. No one complains of this more loudly than the teachers themselves, but there stand the "requirements," and if they want a career as teachers or interpreters, they must pass. Their verbal memory is extraordinarily good, and by sheer force of using it they somehow *do* pass, and get most satisfactory places, and are highly valued by their employers,—but I pray you just to think a minute of the ground plan and cubic contents of a Kaffir's mind, after this process!

In another room the class was repeating twenty-four lines out of Goldsmith's *Deserted Village* (another of the set books), but the most fiery energy of the teacher could only produce a soft monotone with the consonants at the end of words curiously slurred over. Other rooms were passed of Algebra and arithmetic, and reading aloud, till the lowest Class was reached, and this was doing simultaneous reading. They all went on sing-song together, some of the pupils having but the most scanty idea of what reading was, some looking anxiously to see which line had been reached, and some giving up altogether and rolling their eyes around, while they never ceased chanting, following by ear. This was the lowest College class, but in the school among the children it was touching to see here and there a heavy grown man with his face lined and anxious, and his great rough finger following word by word. They had a man and his grandson sitting together in the Infants' Class. There are many proofs of this kind of how sincerely they value education, yet the more I saw of the working details of it all, the more emphatically confused does my judgment become. Religion has its grand victories and trophies among this curious and childish race, and apparently intellect has its wonderful conquests also, but the two things, which Lovedale so bravely and perseveringly tries to unite, do not always go together, and then the effect is always strange and sometimes disastrous. The "blameless Ethiopians" are indeed a problem, and will remain so for many years to come.

But I must end here for this time, my friends. The day to leave came only too soon; I was called in pitch darkness, got myself and my small luggage soon ready, had breakfast by lamplight, and drove away in the ever-brightening dawn of a cloudless day, away alone to more new experiences. J. C. Bewes had been cordially welcomed as a valuable ally for the Girls' Department, and believed she found there her true sphere of work, and the last sight of Lovedale was that of a long white dusty road, and she standing beside the tall figure of Dr. Stewart waving her hands, while I was carried away into the distance.

iii
Letter from the Mistress

My Dear Students,—

Another number of *Hermes* must not see the light without a page or two from me in these distant lands. This is the great holiday of my life, and I must make the most of it all round, as I should like never to take another holiday away from Westfield till the end comes. Seventeen-and-a-half years is a long while to sit on one nest, precious though the eggs may be, and now for the first time the whole current of thought is changed, and news from the College is only one element in a show of surpassing interest that has been continually moving before my eyes.

On February 8th, I left the crowd of dear faces on the College steps, and started off, stretching so tight behind me the threads of affection, that for a short time, at any rate, it seemed almost more than I could bear, and at Charing Cross Station, I should have been heartily glad if I might have hailed a cab and calmly driven home again. But, suffice it to say, I went after all, and went straight to Egypt, missing out the Spring, and plunging from bitter cold straight into the roses and carnations, and fierce July heat of Cairo. If I give you a description of this part of the town, it must be another time. It had indeed its own vivid interests, and strange and splendid pictures are left on my mind that never will be obliterated, but this time I want to give my actual first impression of the Holy Land itself. My opinion may have been to some extent coloured by the fact that fully half my time was spent in being ill with influenza and acute bronchitis, but I confess I do *not* like Egypt, neither the land nor the climate nor the people, nor anything save the magnificent relics of their past history and religion. The babies' faces are black with flies, and they are pitiable objects of neglect; the land itself has neither of the two *smiles* of Nature, wild-flowers and singing birds, and dust and glare are everywhere; Cairo is brilliant, gay and careless, and the rest of the country is bare and hard-worked, and it is hard to say which to me is the most depressing; worst of all is the condition of the women in a Mohammedan country such as this, for they are simply not there to be seen at all in ordinary life, and one only catches side glimpses, as it were, of the semi-idiotic existence that is theirs behind the picturesque lattice windows that adorn the streets. This mass of feeble unhappiness and emptiness made a silent background to everything, and when you add a foreground of an endless whining cry for Backsheesh from men old and young, from blind beggars and moony school-boys, of insatiable greed in the eyes of everybody, of a hungry looking at you as a thing to squeeze something out of, of pestering and complaining combined with insolent looks from black eyes, I am sure you will see that the picture is a sad one. Poor Egypt, I do not wish to draw her in colours too dark, and we English are doing wonders there, and she is lifting her head slowly from the mud and dust of her degradation, and those who know say that everything has changed and improved with the most extraordinary rapidity during the last fifteen years, and that the outlook is one of clear hope and encouragement, so you must only take my picture as the snap-shot of a single observer, who was six weeks on her soil.

But I confess I was glad, heartily glad to leave, and when on the quite early morning of March 30th, I ran up on the deck of the *Caledonian,* I felt a new and better world was opening out before me. Yes! yes, there were the hills of the Holy Land full in view, and looking wondrously barren in the bright morning sun; sand hills in front, plain, soft, yellow sand hills, and a long line of visionary blue heights behind. "The hill country of Judea," I said to myself. The crowded roofs of Jaffa drew nearer and nearer, a little packed up town amid the sand and rocks. A gentleman lent me his field-glass and there printed right across a modern house was the single word "Tannerie," and most appropriate I thought it. But what a barren coast! Where are the famous orange groves? We soon had evidence of our senses, for the delicious scent of orange blossom came wafted in great gusts out to sea, like an offering and welcome of bridal perfume. Then came the famous "landing" where people sometimes wait days and days to pass between the teeth of jagged rock that adorn the harbour. But this day a mill pond wasn't in it, and we were gently rowed ashore between the perilous neighbours. One of them is the sea-beast that came to eat up Andromeda, and was turned to stone by the Gorgon's head, but which one it was, I could not well make out. The rock where she was exposed stands near, and is not at all high. Well, we landed into a swarm of ragged Syrians in dirty striped garments, and passive Turkish officials, and the Customs and all else was about as badly managed as such things can be, the third-class passengers with their wretched baggage being all bundled in with us to await inspection. But we were through at last and walked up to the little German Hotel, and there carriages awaited us, and we tripped off to see the house of Simon the Tanner. As Jaffa has been razed to the ground two or three times in the subsequent course of its history, of course it is *not* the same house, but it pleased me perfectly for all that! The tanning business was a very modest affair, for a deep cool well, and beside it a stone trough about the size of a coffin, but deeper, were the whole of the "plant," but there were the old worn steps, there was the stalwart fig-tree growing over them with her branches yet tender and putting forth leaves of exquisite transparent greenness, and there was the flat roof where that wonderful lesson was learned for ever in the world's history, "Thou shalt call no man common or unclean." Yes it *was* here! There were the same limestone houses, with the same flat ungainly roofs all around, the same vines and figs peeping up here and there over garden walls, the same hot sunshine and cool wind, the same cloudless blue sky overhead and the same beautiful sapphire curve of the sea, "the marriage-ring of the land." I don't even *wish* to come nearer than this, and am quite content!

Thence we drove away to see Dorcas's house, the heavy scent of the orange and lemon groves following us all the way. Oh, the joy and the beauty of being once more in a natural land, a land that drinketh of the rain of heaven! The common hedges of prickly pear, which were crowded underneath common fumitory and nettles, were a treat, and the tender little maidenhair ferns growing in long fringes out of a damp stone wall were a charm I cannot forget. Six weeks in an artificial land where all is dead dry save the fields of barley and lucerne, where every drop of water is the result of toil, and none is a free gift, and the delight of these least little spontaneous growths is known and felt. No, no; the House of Bondage is not for me from the greatest things even to the least!

Dorcas's house is now a Greek Church, full of eikons and tawdry gold and silver pictures, and her grave—for she did die in time really and permanently—is a satisfactory dark cavern, with a flooring of mosaic work by the Crusaders, and all the path to her tomb was carpeted with sweet blue veronica and corn marigold, and small poppies of intensest scarlet, a lovely blaze of the three primitive colours in the hot sunshine. But this was the first time we, the "Cooli's Party,"

113

were herded together, and I confess to having been filled with sore dismay at the ignorance of some of our members! It is past belief. It began after we left Simon's house. The Dragoman, in his laborious English, began slowly, "Now we will go see de House of Dorcas; Dorcas, she was raise from de dead." "It's Lazarus you mean," interrupted an American gentleman of our party; "Lazarus, you know, he *was* raised from the dead." The Dragoman started again: "Dorcas was vera good woman, and she was raise from de dead. I show you her grave." "Lazarus, *Lazarus*" said the American; "it was he who was in the grave, and was raised up again; we all know that." Once more the patient Dragoman began: "Dorcas, she vera good woman, and she make clothes for the poor peoples," and then he slowly toiled through the whole story, ending triumphantly with, "And I tell you true, for you will find it all in Acts de nine chapter and de thirty-six verse!" "Is that *so?*" said the American. "Well, do you know as you tell it us like that I begin to recollect something about it?"

That very afternoon we went on to Jerusalem, but the description of that, the City of the Great King, I must leave for another time. I wish I could let you all have a share in my great holiday!

Your affectionate Mistress,
C. L. Maynard.

Part 2

HOME MISSIONS

2.1

Unitarian Home Missionary Board

2.1 Unitarian Home Missionary Board

The Unitarian Home Missionary Board was an educational organisation set up in Manchester in 1854 to train working-class men to become Unitarian domestic missionaries and ministers of rural congregations. At this point the Board had only two tutors: the Reverend John Relly Beard (1800–1876), who was theological tutor and principal, and William Gaskell (1805–1884), who fulfilled the role of 'literary tutor' (for an example of William Gaskell's didactic literary work, see this volume, Temperance). As can be seen from the source, in addition to theology and pastoral care, the Board's curriculum included study of English language, literature and composition as well as study of the Bible within a global literary history. Good quality preaching, based on an understanding of composition and rhetorical devices, was considered important to ensure missionaries and ministers could transmit the truths of Christianity with sufficient force.

This circular was originally drawn up by Beard for private circulation in 1853, but was later published in the *Inquirer* (18 November 1854) as part of Beard's response to critics of the new education body. Some Unitarians objected that the new ministers would not be learned enough, while others thought the scheme proposed would over-educate men intended to be simple missionaries of spiritual Christianity – rather than proponents of Unitarian orthodoxy (for more information see Volume I, Forms of Dissent). By May 1854, however, sufficient support, including donations and subscriptions, had been received to establish the Board. Much of the material from the original circular was used in the published document that introduced the establishment of the Board, although this document placed even more emphasis on the need for domestic missionaries carrying out home visits.

In addition to setting out the particulars and rules of the new institution, the circular sets out the need for the new body using powerful rhetoric. Beard warns that the country is moving towards 'Atheistic secularism' as the less intellectual Christian faiths are unable to counter the competing ideologies of an advanced civilisation, such as science or political economy (see Volume IV, Scientific Approaches). This slipping into sin and misery he characterises as an urgent 'call' – a term he repeats three times as he pleads 'Will not Unitarians give heed to that call?' Beard suggests that Unitarians have been remiss in not using their talents to carry out missionary work, and stresses that there is an urgent need to train more members of the lower classes to take on the less well-paid positions of rural ministers and urban missionaries. He uses the familiar religious imagery of fields requiring harvesting to represent unsaved souls, and identifies potential working-class Unitarian men as a supply of labourers as yet not utilised in the same way that women were identified by missionary movements (see this volume, Women and authority in the mission field).

Significantly, Unitarians' anxiety for the future of their congregations and society in general, especially the rural and urban poor, led to the inclusion of another group – working-class men – in the missionary movement and in further education. The work of the Board in Manchester also began to systematise the practice of missionary home visiting.

15

[JOHN RELLY BEARD], 'UNITARIAN HOME MISSIONARY BOARD'

Privately circulated, 1853, University of Manchester Library, Unitarian College Collection, UCC 1/6/2/3

The necessity of a learned ministry was never more apparent than in the actual state of society. Scarcely less forcible is the call for a class of religious teachers, who, from the special nature of their office, may be called Home Missionaries. Christianity itself is a mission. It was a mission that Christ gave his Apostles. The duty of preaching the gospel to every creature is not completed until every creature has received the gospel. That duty pertains to every member of the Christian Church. Specially does the duty pertain to those whose gifts and attainments fit them in any way to take oversight of the flock of the family of God (*I. Peter,* v. 2, *Ephes.* iii. 14, 15). It may be doubted whether the Unitarians of England have performed their share of that solemn duty. Certain, however, it is that there is not only a scope but a demand for the best efforts they can put forth. The field offers itself under three aspects. In the first place, the old and inveterate evils of man, namely, sin, ignorance, and misery, call for the remedy—the only safe and sufficient remedy—which God has provided in the Gospel of his Son;—will not Unitarians give heed to that call? In the second place, the call daily becomes more urgent, because the popular forms of Christianity are either loosing their hold on the mind of the nation, or are wearing away under the decomposing influences of a progressive civilisation. In both tendencies, Unitarians may recognize a duty and an opportunity. The rather, because in the third place, the result of these movements is toward the rejection of Christianity, and the adoption of an Atheistic Secularism—the grave of all religion, and the birth-place of personal impotency, and social disorder.

In this field of labour there are one or two points of immediate interest to the Unitarian body. Under the Providence of God, and as a consequence of free inquiry, some three hundred societies, holding Unitarian opinions, have come down to us from the past, and ought, with due increase, to be transmitted by us to the future. The ministry is the hand by which the transmission has to be made. The present supply of ministers is insufficient. At this moment there are some thirty societies in want of ministers. If the existing disproportion between the supply and the demand is allowed to continue, in ten years more the deficiency will be doubled, and before the century is out, very many of the present Unitarian places of worship will be closed. The want, however, under which our churches are suffering, is not one of numbers merely—*a different class* of religious teachers is required. If the average stipend of Unitarian ministers now occupying pulpits, is less than a hundred a year, it is very clear that either a learned ministry will not be formed, or if learned men are prepared for the ministry, they will either in part or wholly find resources, and spend their energies in pursuits not immediately connected with their pastoral charge. But in more than one half of the congregations now without a minister, the average salary does not exceed fifty pounds a year. At least one third of existing Unitarian Churches are in a not much better condition. What but extinction is before these congregations, unless means for their revival are speedily taken? There appears but one alternative, and that is that those which have endowments fall into the hands of unprepared and needy men. While such is the state of the less prosperous of Unitarian congregations, the benevolent efforts of the body in general are cramped for the want of a sufficient supply of suitable ministers. The Domestic Mission has been restricted in its expansion by that want. Still more has the same cause narrowed and checked Unitarian Missionary operations. At the present moment, fields "white unto harvest" remain unreaped, simply because there are no labourers. And yet candidates for the office of Unitarian Missionary are not wanting, and would, there is reason to think, be found in sufficient numbers, if provision was made to train and form them for the work.

It is, therefore, proposed to make the necessary arrangements in the city of Manchester, which, as a sphere of earnest thought and active benevolence, and as a centre of liberal and specially of Unitarian influence, offers opportunities and advantages of peculiar importance. With a view to secure the ends contemplated in the preparation of a succession of earnest, well-informed, benevolent, laborious and pious men, whose special duty, in imitation of the great Master, shall be to "go about doing good," the following plan has been adopted:—

Rules

Government

The Government of the Unitarian Home Missionary Board is in the hands of its members.

The Members

Of the Institution are—

1   *Life Members;* every person making a donation of not less than Twenty Pounds, in one sum, is a Life Member.
2   *Honorary Members;* every minister settled with a Unitarian congregation in Great Britain, may become an Honorary Member by signifying, in writing, his willingness to promote the objects of the Institution.

HOME MISSIONS

3   *Representative Members;* the Trustees or Managers of any fund from which a subscription of not less than Five Pounds per annum is made to the Institution, may appoint one of their body as their Representative; also, every Congregation subscribing annually not less than Two Pounds, is entitled to elect from its own body a layman as a Representative member.

4   *Subscribing Members;* being all who annually subscribe Ten Shillings or upwards.

Meetings of the Members

A General Meeting of the Members shall be held at the end of the second term every year, at which shall be read a full Report of the proceedings of the Institution during the year preceding; a Board and other officers shall be chosen; and all other necessary business shall be transacted.

The President shall call a Special Meeting of the Members whenever he is requested so to do by five members of the Board, or by twenty members of the Institution, provided always the request is signed by each of the members; provided also that it sets forth the specific business for which the meeting is convened, and that the request be in the President's hands one calendar month before the day on which the meeting is held.

The Board

The Board shall consist of at least twenty persons besides the President, the Vice-Presidents, the Treasurer, the Deputy-Treasurers, the Secretaries, and the Examiners, who shall be members of the Board in virtue of their office. The Board, subject to the fundamental rules, and under the direction of the members, in annual or special meeting assembled, shall have in their hands the entire management of the Institution.

Examinations

There shall be an examination of the Students near the end of each term, the result of which shall be reported to the Tutors and to the Board, attested by the signature of the Examiner or Examiners. At the same time the Tutors shall present, in writing, to the Board, a report minutely describing the diligence, regularity, and proficiency of each of the Students; also his tone of mind and general demeanour, with an opinion as to his fitness for the office of a Unitarian Home-Missionary, as well as to the desirableness or otherwise of renewing his admission. The Tutors' report shall also recommend meritorious Students (if any) for pecuniary aid and encouragement.

The Tutors

One Theological Tutor and one Literary Tutor shall be appointed, to whom shall be entrusted the instruction of the Students. Either Tutor may suspend a Student for misconduct, and the allowance of such Student shall cease from the day of his suspension, provided that such suspension shall be forthwith reported to the Board, who shall act in the case as they may judge desirable. A Superintendent Missionary also shall be appointed, whose business it shall be to initiate the Students in their practical duties,—that is to say, in teaching, preaching, and visiting,—and who shall present to the Board, every month, a full report of the conduct of the Students.

The Terms

The first term shall extend from March 25th to August 25th The second term shall extend from October 25th to March 20th.

The Object

The object is to assist in the education of young men for the work of preaching and diffusing the gospel among the people, especially the poor, the untaught, and the neglected, in towns, villages, and districts where there is no place of Unitarian worship, or where Unitarian Churches, already in existence, may either be unable to support a learned ministry, or wish to extend their influence by missionary labours.

Means

In order to effect this object, aid shall be given to young men who are desirous and fit to engage in Home-Missionary labours. The aid shall be of two kinds,—first, pecuniary, and secondly, instructional. The pecuniary aid shall not exceed ten shillings a week; but the Board shall have a discretionary power to reward merit in special cases. The instruction shall comprise a course so laid out as to supply, in a simple but systematic form, the results of sound scholarship in the following

Subjects of Study

1   —The English Language and Literature, including Composition.
2   —The Greek of the New Testament.
3   —The History of the World, with special reference to the History of Civilization.
4   —The Qualities, Laws, and Relations of the Human Mind, with special reference to secularistic doctrines and tendencies.
5   —The History of Religious Systems and Opinions in their substance and in their influence, comprising the History and including the Evidences of Revealed Religion.
6   —The literary History of the Bible—its position in the literatures of the world—and its specific and genuine value.

7   —A Course of Scriptural Interpretation, founded on the Development of the Religious Ideas of the Bible, with a view to the application of the doctrines hence deduced to the permanent interests of mankind, and the special interests and controversies of the present age.

8   —Instructions in the Pastoral Care, specially designed to form the students for active usefulness, and to assist them to attain ease and efficiency in public speaking.

The Period of Instruction

Shall extend over six terms, each of five months' duration, to be completed in about three years.

Terms of Admission

1   —No person shall be admitted for more than one term at a time.

2   —Persons found, on examination, duly qualified, may be admitted at the commencement of any one of the six terms.

3   —No person shall be admitted unless he has attained the full age of eighteen years—is of an unblemished character, a benevolent disposition, and respectable talents,—proves himself to the satisfaction of the Board, to be both willing and able to promote the religious improvement of his fellow men—and has signed the following declaration;—

"I (A. B.) hereby declare that with the aid and blessing of 'the only true God,' *(John* xvii. 3) the Father of our Lord Jesus Christ, I solemnly intend to devote my life to the work of preaching and extending the gospel, specially among the poor, and during the period of my preparatory studies will, to the best of my ability, assist in Sunday School teaching, in visiting the poor at their own homes, and in such other means of usefulness as the Board may direct." *(Signed)* A.B.

2.2

University Settlements

2.2 University Settlements

In the late nineteenth century, many students from the university colleges of Oxford, Cambridge and London were inspired to take up opportunities for social service in the London slums through a 'settlement' movement. More or less distinct from city missions, settlements were places where young university graduates lived alongside the London poor, socialising with and learning from the local residents rather than preaching to them. Some settlements, like Toynbee Hall or the University Women's Settlement, were non-denominational, while others, like the Lady Margaret Hall Settlement in Vauxhall, adhered to the tenets of High Anglicanism (see Volume I, Anglican Developments). By focusing on friendship between the classes as a means for 'purifying' humanity and curing the social ills represented by the slums, the settlement movement transformed social welfare work.

The first source reproduced here is a paper by Frederick Rogers (1846–1915), the honorary secretary of the Whitechapel branch of the London Society for the Extension of University Teaching. In this capacity he presents himself as someone already living and working alongside the artisans of the East End, and therefore well-placed to give advice to university students who would become settlers. Rogers particularly emphasises the power of friendship for breaking down barriers between classes. He portrays the difference between university men and artisans as an artificial one by describing them in very similar terms – they are both 'the youth' of England, though one group has been educated by public schools and universities and the other by Board schools and apprenticeships. In Rogers' rhetorical conclusion, the East End artisans are also referred to as the college men's 'fellows' – as much possessors of the 'English character' as the upper classes – and members of humanity in which the settler is enjoined to have 'faith'. Rogers argues convincingly that the majority of East End men should not be seen as secularists or atheists, but simply as non-religious, with an abiding respect for religion in the abstract. He also suggests that many who call themselves secular in fact only claim to be, and actually live according to religious principles. Significantly, moral principles, such as integrity and sincerity, are conflated with masculine traits in Rogers' text, and are attributed to both classes equally. While he stresses the self-resignation that will be important for a settler – they must 'lose sight of self' – this sort of sacrifice that could be associated with femininity (see this volume, Women and Authority in the Mission Field) is described alongside references to 'chivalrous manhood'. The work of a settler is characterised as a noble calling, contributing to the English imperial mission to cure social disease and advance human progress.

Lady Margaret Hall's (LMH) *Old Students' Association Newsletter* exemplifies the social work of members of the new women's colleges. Current and old members saw themselves as part of the same community, in fellowship with women from other colleges, and newsletters attempted to nurture this feeling of connection. Indeed, writings in the newsletter about settlement work focus far more on the connections between women of the colleges than they do on connections between the classes. Work carried out with the Women's University Settlement is described almost as a hobby for old students with 'leisure time' and 'inclination'. And the founding of their own, Anglican settlement under the supervision of the Bishop of Rochester is championed for its potential to strengthen the 'esprit de corps' of the college and the connections between current and old students. Once the settlement was founded it was mildly criticised for being possibly too comfortable, and praised mostly for the positive impact it had on the conditions of the middle-class agents of the Charity Organisation Society (COS) working in the area. However, this impression is probably a result of the form of the newsletter – it was meant to appeal to all members of the college, whether they were devout or not. The address of the Bishop of Rochester that was made at the opening of the new LMH buildings in 1896, and reported in full in the newsletter, reflects a more religious view of the Settlement. His address focuses on the connection of the activist alumnae of LMH to the Anglican establishment and Oxford as a whole; the power of LMH to create such women activists; and the influence that such alumnae as the recently deceased Mary Eleanor Benson, daughter of the Archbishop of Canterbury, could have on other Oxford students as well as the poor of Lambeth. Many of the alumnae of LMH and other women's colleges who devoted their energies to settlements went on to work in the charitable and social welfare sectors, such as Eglantyne Jebb who founded the Save the Children charity.

16

FREDERICK ROGERS, *THE NEW MOVEMENT AT THE UNIVERSITIES AND WHAT MAY COME OF IT, BY A WHITECHAPEL MAN*

([n.p.]: [n.p.], [1886])

The object of the movement which was championed by Mr. Gell at Cambridge is to endeavour to bring the direct influence of young University men of education and leisure to bear upon the lives of the poor in the East of London. The originator of the scheme is the Rev. S. A. Barnett of St. Jude's, Whitechapel. It proposes to achieve its ends by the foundation of University Settlements, that is to say, of houses where young men may live, for such time as they choose after leaving the University, and devote themselves to social, educational, or religious work.

The question which practical men will ask themselves about the movement will almost certainly be, not "Is it good?" but "Has it practical ideas at the back of it, will it work?" It will certainly bring no credit to those who are interested in the social well-being of East London if, when they have in their midst such a powerful force as is the generous enthusiasm of high-principled youths, they fail to turn it to some practical purpose.

There is plenty of work that such a scheme might do in East London; though if they look around on other parts of the Metropolis they will find that the conditions they deplore exist elsewhere as well. The movement, however, if it would succeed, must justify its existence by what it does, and its best justification will be found when it can show that it supplies some public need which would not be supplied, or would only be inadequately supplied, without it.

Mr. Gell's idea of bringing into East London a "leisured residential class" who shall devote themselves to public work is hardly likely to be realised in the early stages of the movement. If, however, it succeeds, this is almost certain to be one of its results. The most important question is, "What is it that young men can do who come from the Universities and go and dwell among the workers of London?" As young men, they must not go there as teachers but as learners. Men who

129

have been living under differing conditions cannot be brought in close contact without each learning something from the other. It will be a good thing for the youth who has been educated at the Public School, and who has graduated at the University, to know something of the youth who has been educated at the Board School, and who has finished his education at the workman's bench. One of the most noticeable tendencies of the present day is the tendency to take a man at his true value, and not at the value which caste or class distinction gives him. Young men with the generous warmheartedness that belongs to early manhood will not be slow to break through artificial divisions, and to sympathise with, and after a time understand, the hopes and aspirations, the hardships and difficulties, of the artizan's life. If this movement were to do no more than lead people who belong to different sections of society to understand each other it would deserve all our sympathy and support. But those who believe in it believe that far more than this is to be done by its agency.

Proceeding on practical lines, it may be well to indicate a few of the methods whereby they may reach the social life they seek to understand and to benefit. Let them, if they would find out how the people look at political movements, join the local parliaments. To those who only see the grotesque side of playing at government this suggestion will seem fanciful enough. Nevertheless, it is not to be denied that the education that comes of a couple of years' membership of a local parliament is quite worth any man's getting. He will obtain a very much more accurate notion how politics are regarded by men who know little or nothing of political theories, than he will gather from many years' membership of University debating societies. Let him also take his share in local political organization. In these days when organization reigns supreme in politics, he will not lack opportunity for this. There is also room for work in workmen's clubs, whether they be social or political. Working men are by no means exclusive in their club arrangements, and a man who wishes to understand something of them will not experience much difficulty in doing so. They are always willing to welcome outside help, and a man who has anything to tell there is always sure of being listened to; but they are quite as quick as other people to find him out if he has not.

There is also work to be done among the various religious organizations, though work of this kind will not bring those who do it very much into connexion with working men. This need be no reason why it should be neglected. There are religious people, and not a few of them artizans, who are chiefly to be found in the various nonconforming churches. The average artizan, however, usually leaves religion to his wife. It is often thought that secularism is the coming creed of the working man. Those who think so make a great mistake. Secularism, when organized, is very vigorous, and sometimes very noisy: its votaries are mostly working men, but, as a system, it has almost no influence even on the non-religious artizan. If it were possible to obtain accurate information on the subject, it would probably be found that the non-religious workman has a sort of respect for religion, even though he considers it none of his business.

Secularism is not strong in East London, but it exists. If young men are brought into contact with it they will find it, as a system, narrow and dogmatic, and often intolerant. They will also find, however, that in that denomination, as in every other, there are men who are better than their creed. They will find Secularists with as high an ideal of life as Christians. They will find some narrow enough; but they will find others who live quiet, unobtrusive, self-denying lives, and who, claiming to be without religion, act in every way as religious men.

For those who are fitted for educational work much may be found to do. This, however, should hardly be attempted by the younger men. It may be that a man fresh from the University has a fund of special knowledge to impart to the non-University man. He, however, can hardly be expected to have things which are quite as important to the successful teacher, a knowledge of the world and a knowledge of men.

Let those who take part in this work lose sight of self if they would do it successfully. They will find many among the artizans who, by their sincerity of purpose and integrity of character, are worthy of the friendship of any man. If they seek to make friends among their poorer neighbours they will find the same differences of temperament and character as exist among their own class. They will find high and noble lives, lives as full of chivalrous manhood as the life of any knight of old. They will find others whose thoughts never rise above the commonplace, and whose lives have little enough of the ideal in them.

The type of man who is most likely to succeed is the man who does not hope to achieve miracles, who is willing to work and learn while he works, in the faith that no sincere and wise effort for human good was ever in vain. He must forget class and think only of humanity. He must forget creeds and think of that, which in the last result is the inspiration of all creeds, the desire to purify and ennoble this human life. He must not think that social diseases are to be cured in a moment, any more than physical diseases. He will find dull heads sometimes; but he will find, too, that they often have warm hearts to balance them. He must have faith in the power of high principle, in the force of noble example, faith in his fellows, faith in the English character, belief that in the majority of human hearts there will be an answering echo to every inspiring cry. With these things, and with steadiness of purpose that is not turned aside by difficulties or failures, those who cast in their lot with this scheme may help forward the march of human progress.

Frederick Rogers

Hon. Sec. London Society for the Extension of University Teaching (Whitechapel Branch).

17

LADY MARGARET HALL NEWSLETTER

(i)'The Women's University Settlement', *Old Students' Association Newsletter* (Oxford: Lady Margaret Hall, 1894), pp. 10–13; (ii) 'Opening of the Lady Margaret Hall New Buildings' and (iii) 'Proposed LMH Settlement', *Old Students' Association Newsletter* (Oxford: Lady Margaret Hall, 1896), pp. 12–18, 19–23; (iv) 'The Settlement', *Old Students' Association Newsletter* (Oxford: Lady Margaret Hall, 1897), pp. 10–11

i
Women's University Settlement

Several past students help in various ways in the work at the Settlement in Southwark [...] Those who attended the Extraordinary Meeting in the spring were told of the acquisition of the three adjoining houses in Nelson Square, these are now being turned into one and undergoing very necessary repairs and alterations. [...]

[...] Residents look forward with great pleasure to the day when there will be sitting room for all at meals, an entrance-hall large enough to allow of one person passing another, a quiet room for writing and working, and perhaps above all, a room, or rooms, for classes, meetings and interviews, which have hitherto been held in most unexpected and unsuitable places. It is expected that 17 or 18 residents will be accommodated when all the rooms are ready for use, the present number being 14. The need of help from outside increases proportionately with the increase of residents.

Any Lady Margaret living in or near London with leisure time, and any inclination for this sort of work, would no doubt find a place to fill there. Those interested in work among children would perhaps be specially welcomed just now, as this is being much considered and extended at the present time in various ways as visiting and attending the invalid children, teaching those able to learn but unfit for school, visiting the homes of truants, conducting evening classes for those who have left school, but are too young for the Polytechnic and technical institutes, and helping those in need of work to find suitable places. Present Students at the Hall are good enough to get up a Christmas Entertainment in the Autumn Term, and to come down in the vacation to perform before appreciative and enthusiastic audiences, who remember and talk of it for many months, the audience being composed of school children, benefit societies, working girls, tenants of Miss OCTAVIA HILL'S, and (perhaps these enjoy the entertainments most of all) the residents and workers themselves.

ii
Opening of the Lady Margaret Hall New Buildings

The great event of the year at L. M. H. is the completion of the first part of its new buildings. [...]

[...] At 4 p.m. a short service, conducted by the Bishop of Rochester, was held in the New Buildings, at which the members of the Council of L. M. H. and nearly fifty old students were present; tea followed, and then the Bishop gave a most interesting address of which he has kindly allowed us to print the subjoined report.

Address by the Bishop of Rochester

"In speaking on this occasion, when we meet to celebrate the opening of these New Buildings, I must go back in thought to the first beginnings of this Hall, and what was in the minds of all of us at its origin.

I remember, just before Lady Margaret Hall was started, paying a visit to Cambridge, and seeing the great buildings at Cambridge and Girton, and how one felt what a new stage and start of educational and intellectual life this meant in England. One's academic sympathy and one's Christian sympathy went out to it, but there was one matter which gave occasion to some sad reflection.

Here were new institutions springing up side by side with the old colleges and the old system; and that old University system, despite the great changes which have passed over it, and despite its greatly modified form, still retained its old religious character—chapels, worship still offered in its ancient chapels as a part of the day's order, and some order of religious teaching. But here on the other side were large Women's Colleges, with no Chapels and no definitely religious basis. Looking at the future there seemed one great flaw which caused a saddening feeling; and yet not altogether sad, for why should not the Church do with the new what she had already done with the old; why should not the Church have her own place, and speak her mind to those who would welcome it? That was the beginning of Lady Margaret Hall. Let us hope that with God's blessing these thoughts and hopes have been in some degree realized in the work of the past years. [...]

[...] I have had the pleasure of knowing several of the students and of having personal friends among them, and one in especial comes to my mind. As an example of what such a place should have been desired to train none fitter to represent it could be imagined than Mary Eleanor Benson. Modern to her finger tips, full of all the dash, I might say the mental smartness of modern life, with an understanding so quick as to be able to hold her own anywhere; but how much more there was, warm deep affections, a power of glorifying her friends, and of seeing the best, developing the best, and bringing out the best of everybody; deep and large thoughts of what the time required; and a fund of strong and wide charity for its people and their needs. Oxford knew one part of her, Lambeth knew another; it is not Lambeth the Palace of which I am speaking, but the streets and lanes of the "Great City." If L. M. H. helped to form in a century ten souls such as hers it would I think be worth the doing.

And this leads me on to another subject. We are meeting under the shadow of a great sorrow, illuminated by glory and peace. But it is a happiness to remember that that great ruler, guide, and friend who has been taken from us, set the mark of his approval on this place by sending his two daughters to it; and it is a blessing to think that in their training L. M. H. was able to give back something to Lambeth. Therefore I felt sure, on receiving the sad news, that our gathering here must still be continued. Mrs. Benson I knew would wish it, and I felt that anything to help towards advancing the work of L. M. H. would be a carrying out of his wishes and desires.

There is one more question I wish to touch. We used to talk very much of what would happen to the Students after leaving the Hall; I don't know that this problem agitates anyone very much at the present time; they go their different ways, and, let us hope, make the world better wherever they go. But, among other things which we learn here in Oxford, one is the habit of looking on life with far-reaching eyes, with hearts open to the needs of others in less happy parts of Society. Old Students have already done good work among the poor in East and South London, but there are ambitions now stirring amongst us, we are thinking of a possible L. M. H. Settlement. I have one very strong wish, nay, I have an intention, on this subject, and that is, that the L. M. House should settle down in South London, and if it may be, in Lambeth, near to the Palace, and carrying on the memory of the work done from there.

Oxford House has, I know, been an important factor in the life of many at Oxford; its effect has been bracing and stimulating on those living here; and I feel strongly that in the same way such a work connected with the Hall would be a real influence on the Students, and would help to make it what we desire in its own educational and intellectual sphere. It is not so much the gain to Lambeth of which we think, though that would be great, but the gain to L. M. H. itself.

I end by praying God's Blessing on the present and future of all L. M. H. students."

After the Meeting the Bishop and Mrs. Talbot discussed with some of the past students the proposed L. M. H. Settlement in which they take a deep interest, and advised that the work should be begun as soon as may be practicable.

iii
Proposed Lady Margaret Hall Settlement

A Meeting was held at the Hall during the Gaudy last July to consider the subject of a Lady Margaret Hall Settlement, notice of the Meeting having previously been sent to all past and present students.

Miss WORDSWORTH took the chair, and the following Resolutions were carried:—

I   That in the opinion of this Meeting, a time has come when the Hall might endeavour to found a Settlement on Church lines for the promotion of charitable work in or near London. [...]

II That the house of the Settlement be in the Rochester Diocese, and preferably in Lambeth, and that the residents work in with parochial and other charitable organisations of the district, according to the discretion of the Council to be hereafter nominated; the Bishop of the Diocese to be invited to act as Visitor. [...]

[...] The need of the Rochester Diocese for Settlements of this nature was shown to be great, as comparatively little work of this kind has been done in South London. Lambeth was preferred, as affording a suitable area of work for a new Settlement; as a convenient locality for outside workers living in London; as the central point of a large and poor district having few resident workers; as being in a healthy situation, with houses likely to be suitable for the Settlement; and as having good means of communication with the district and other parts of London.

III That a Provisional Committee be nominated and elected. [...]

IV That the decision of this meeting be communicated to the Women's University Settlement. [...]

V   That the Provisional Committee be instructed to communicate the results of this meeting to the past and present students of Lady Margaret Hall, and to consider the ways and means of carrying the project into effect. [...]

iv
The Settlement

Since the last O.S.A. report the Lady Margaret Hall Settlement has been permanently established in South London.

At present it may be looked upon by some as almost too comfortable to be ideal; the idea of life in a slum with only a crust to eat is rather lost sight of in the comfortable quarters of 129, Kennington Road, and there is a somewhat prosaic healthiness in the appearance of the residents as a whole; however, one good work is done in supplying a comfortable lunch in a warm room for the members of the C.O.S. Committees on this side the water, who leave the office in a state of exhaustion, and who formerly could not obtain a respectable penny bun nearer than the other side of Westminster Bridge.

An important change has recently been made in the appointment of Miss Langridge as head of the Settlement; all who know her will be delighted to hear that she is thus identified with the Settlement, and her friends wish her every success in her new office.

The present students of the Hall have rendered valuable assistance by unfailing sympathy and interest, and also by considerable financial aid; they are always interested to hear about the work, and always willing to do their best to help.

At present there are four residents, there are also many who come for a week, a night, or even for a meal; anyone who can come even only for a meal is heartily welcomed, and offers of assistance of any kind will be gratefully received by Miss Langridge, who will also supply any information which may be desired.

2.3

Revivalism

2.3 Revivalism

The nineteenth century saw a number of religious revivals. Early in the nineteenth century the Methodist revival begun by John Wesley in the previous century was widely influential, feeding into broad-church evangelicalism. In the 1830s, at the other extreme, the Oxford Movement sought to renew the Anglican Church by reviving doctrines and rituals from Roman Catholicism (see Volume I, Evangelical Religion, and Anglican Developments). The texts chosen for this section, however, deal with revivals of the mid- to late nineteenth century. In the 1850s and 1860s North America's 'Third Great Awakening' spawned the Holiness Movement, which spread around the world. American Holiness preachers such as Phoebe Palmer (1807–1874) and her husband travelled to England as missionaries, taking the revival into all the British Isles. Meanwhile, the Oxford Movement was succeeded among High Church congregations in the 1860s by an Anglo-Catholic Mission, associated with the international Society of the Holy Cross and an Anglican religious order for men, the Society of St John the Evangelist, which was founded in Oxford by a group known as the 'Cowley Fathers'.

Phoebe Palmer emerges from her book of the Primitive Methodist revival in Britain as something of a religious celebrity. A letter from a clergyman, that she includes in *Four Years in the Old World*, refers to how her earlier book, *The Way to Holiness*, has saved souls, and describes how his congregation are eagerly awaiting her arrival. Significantly, his sermons in preparation for Palmer's visit focused on the importance of 'female influence' in religious work, and he refers to preaching from Acts 17 to justify this. However, the clergyman criticises his own veneration of Palmer as verging on idolatrous, interpreting his inability to be present at her services when she visits Newcastle as punishment for 'thinking more of the instrument than of the agent'. Palmer presents the success of her mission in terms that are consistent with her Primitive Methodism. It is the Holy Spirit that is working its power in the chapels, and the conversions are 'manifestations' of this Spirit. She is an instrument of God, like the mechanic or 'salvation smith', whose vignette appears near the end of the extract. In Palmer's theology, God intervenes in the world frequently, and she tells a story of such 'divine interpositions' as the background for the clergyman who is her host in the north. The experience of the mission service itself, she presents evocatively, as being in the presence of God's grace, holy fire, and the spirits of those recently departed to Heaven. This spiritual language contrasts with what was also a physical experience: she describes people in the chapels crowding into the aisles and struggling through the mass of bodies to the communion rail.

Charles Maurice Davies (1828–1910) was a High Church clergyman who, in the 1850s, was associated with the Catholic Society of the Holy Cross. In the 1870s, however, rather than take part in the 'Twelve Days' Mission' of the Societies of the Holy Cross and St John the Evangelist, he instead reported on the mission for the daily paper, the 'Broad Churchman'. As part of this reporting he depicts scenes similar to those described by Palmer. An hour before a particular service was due to start, he found 'fifty people' waiting to enter the church. And on another day, he likens their rush into the Church when the gates were opened to theatre-goers thronging in for 'a Jenny Lind night … at the Opera'. He continues to stress the theatricality of the service, comparing the weeping of men and women in the congregation to that of audiences at powerful dramas, and is struck by the 'sensation' produced by the powerful and 'fascinating' eloquence of the preacher. However, he insists that he himself is merely fascinated by the phenomenon he is witnessing, remaining detached, analytical and critical, as befits a professional journalist. He also draws a distinction between the power of this particular preacher of the movement, and the lacklustre experiences in other churches following the same service composed for the mission. He suggests that much in the practice of ritualism is awkward, embarrassed and forced, and that the idea of Confession is too alien and threatening to English masculinity to be successfully introduced.

The final extract in this section is from one of the 'little penny books with the big crosses outside', that Davies references in his article. These were the books of the service that was to be followed at churches taking part in the 'Twelve Days' Mission', compiled and printed by the Society of St John the Evangelist. In addition to the mission-specific material extracted here, the book contained twelve hymns and litanies, including 'Onward Christian Soldiers' and 'Rock of Ages'. Notable in this extract are the detailed instructions for Confession, which, as Davies notes, was unfamiliar to English congregations. But it is the opening of the Mission service that bears most resemblance to revivalist rhetoric. The mission in London is linked with the Biblical missions to Nineveh and Sodom, collapsing the distinction between Biblical times and modernity. And the repeated exhortation, 'Why not you?' draws attention to the mass movement taking place around the world, and encourages the congregant to be carried away by this current.

18

PHOEBE PALMER, *FOUR YEARS IN THE OLD WORLD: COMPRISING THE TRAVELS, INCIDENTS, AND EVANGELICAL LABORS OF DR AND MRS PALMER IN ENGLAND, IRELAND, SCOTLAND AND WALES*

(New York: [n.p], 1866), pp. v, 84–85, 90–98, 106–107, 110–112

Preface

[...] We did not visit the Old World in anticipation of making a book on our return, but solely in view of religious profit, and in answer to repeated solicitations of earnestly pious friends, and also in faithfulness to our own solemn convictions that the Lord of the harvest called us to that portion of the vineyard. If the result as here set forth has proved to the hearts of the multitude that we have not run or labored in vain, the pious will unite with us in ascribing all the praise to the Triune Deity.

Chapter IV

[...] We are now in the north of England. We are here by the affectionate solicitation of our beloved friend Mrs. J. M. K—. As guests, we have divided our time between Mrs. K—and her brother C. B—, Esq. Special meetings were held each evening during the week. A few of the Lord's people were, we trust, sanctified wholly, and several born into the kingdom of grace; how many, I do not know, as the names were not taken: but I trust that the Book of Life will bear some enduring records of this visitation in the increased activities of Zion's hosts, and the enlargement of her borders. Here we remained a few days. Our last Sabbath in Weardale was spent at St. John's Chapel. The meetings on Sabbath and Monday evening were blessed with manifestations of the Saviour's presence and power. We were the guests of brother J. Dawson, a Wesleyan local preacher: he is a man of the Bramwell spirit, and, though in humble life, is mighty in word and deed.

Some divine interpositions in his behalf prove that the God of Elijah still lives. He formerly was a school-teacher in this place. Though as fully patronized as he could reasonably expect, he was just able to meet the daily demands on his purse, and unable to lay up as much as five pounds; and it having been decided that there should be a British school, aided by government funds, commenced, he saw no way to provide for himself and family.

He began to plead with the Lord to open some way of support, and thought, if he could get but five pounds, he might obtain a few goods, open a shop, and get in a small way of trade. He might have borrowed the sum; but he preferred not to risk the debt, and therefore did not speak to others of his want, but prayed, if it could consist with the divine will, that he might in some providential way receive the needed amount.

One day, after pleading thus, on retiring from his closet, he saw a letter awaiting him. He felt sure, even before he opened it, that faith had prevailed; and, on breaking the seal, was not surprised to read a nameless letter, presenting the sum asked, with the words, *"From a friend of Jesus to a lover of Jesus."* [...]

[...] We are in reception of letters from our valued correspondent, Rev. R. Young, chairman of the Newcastle district. He has been a champion in the ranks of God's Israel, and one of the most eminent revivalists of his day. He is the author of several valuable works bearing on the extension of the Redeemer's kingdom; and long since was my heart divinely aided and inspired while reading his "Suggestions for the World's Conversion." Would it might be read by every Christian in England and America!

He is now in a low state of health, and unable as formerly to lead forth the sacramental hosts to conquest. But the fast-failing energies of the outer man do not dampen the fires of his ardent spirit. The letters just received are in anticipation of our visit to his district. I hardly know whether tears or smiles would predominate, could you read his letters. I could not but weep as I read portions of them. He says,—

"My medical attendant has ordered me to the seaside for a month. I have delayed for two weeks, hoping to have the very great pleasure of seeing you amongst us, and partaking more fully of that spirit which so manifestly influences you; but the privilege at present is not to be mine, as I am obliged to leave home on Monday next. Should you, however, find it convenient to visit Newcastle in my absence, my colleagues will be glad to see you. But how strange is this! Few things in my history I have anticipated with so much *warmth* and *pleasure* as I have your visit to us; and now it would seem that I am not to enjoy it. I may have erred in this, and possibly thought more of the instrument than of the agent. I fear I have done so, and feel now rebuked. 'And they lifted up their eyes, and saw Jesus only.'" [...]

[...] About the time Rev. R. Young was writing the above, we were engaged in penning a line to say that we would be in Newcastle on Wednesday of the present week. In reply to this, he says, "I feel delighted at the prospect of your being so soon in Newcastle. I have, in conjunction with our leaders, arranged for a meeting on Wednesday evening in Brunswick Chapel, and published the same in all our chapels in the town. I hope, therefore, to have a good gathering. I preached this morning in Brunswick Chapel, to a large congregation, from '*She hath done what she could.*' I spoke of female influence, and what that influence might accomplish if fully sanctified to God. I believe the good ladies were pleased with their position, and I know some have resolved to be more active in the Lord's work. When we previously expected you, I preached from 'Some believed and consorted with Paul and Silas; of devout Greeks a great multitude, and of the *chief women* not a few.' It was then said that I was preparing the way for Mrs. P——; and, after this morning's service, the saying has been extensively repeated, and it is true. I have, in my humble way, been preparing the people to receive with joy your visit; and I believe they will do so. It is my intention to come up from the seaside, and be present at your meeting on Wednesday evening. One of my colleagues, who has just arrived in the circuit, tells me that he some time ago received the blessing of full salvation as the result of reading your 'Way of Holiness.' This, I am sure, will gladden your heart."

Chapter V

[...] The God of the armies of Israel has commenced to display his all-conquering power here in the north of England. A work is progressing, which, my heart seems to assure me, is destined to spread over England, provided human limitations do not obstruct, and the ministry and laity, as workers together with God, unite in spreading the flame.

We have been engaged in many revivals in America, and more recently in Ireland, and have seen thousands saved, but never remember to have witnessed a more glorious work than has been going on here within the last few days. We came last Wednesday evening. You are aware of the long-standing solicitations of the Rev. R. Young, that we should make an early visit to this place; but little did we know what an outpouring of the Spirit was awaiting us. We now apprehend the meaning of the inspiring assurance, "Call unto Me, and I will answer thee, and show thee great and mighty things which thou knowest not."

You will remember we told you how signally the Lord gave us this promise when we first set our feet on British soil, repeating it again and again in a most memorable manner. Oh! if you could only be here for a few hours, you would see how wonderfully the Lord is fulfilling the word on which he hath caused us to hope. Between three and four hundred souls, we have reason to believe, have been gathered out of the world, and translated into the kingdom of God's dear Son, during the last few days. Every day and hour, the work is increasing in power. Last

HOME MISSIONS

night, I presume there were not less than seventy forward for prayers, and probably not less than fifty received pardon. The secretaries of the meeting recorded the names of forty-two. They took as many as they could; but the seekers were so scattered, and the interests of the meeting were otherwise so varied and engrossing, that they were not able to get all. Others also were blessed in the afternoon meeting, whose names, I believe, were not recorded. We are having four meetings per day. Here is one of the bills which are posted throughout the town:—

" 'Seek ye the Lord while he may be may be found; call upon him while he is near.' Revival services will be held every day during the present week in the Brunswick-place Chapel. Meetings will be held every day from twelve to one o'clock. Afternoon services in the chapel will commence at three o'clock. Meetings of a more social character, for serious-minded persons, who may desire to inquire, 'What must I do to be saved?' will be held from six to seven o'clock. Public evening service in the chapel will commence at seven o'clock. Persons of all denominations are invited to attend. Dr. and Mrs. P—, from America, will be present, and assist in the services. 'And the inhabitants of one city shall go to another, saying, Let us go speedily to pray before the Lord, and to seek the Lord of hosts: I will go also' (Zechariah). 'The Spirit and the Bride say, Come; and let him that heareth say, Come' (St. John)."

Hundreds are coming out to the meetings. Have you ever been in the spacious Brunswick Chapel? Would that you could witness the multitudes which nightly congregate there! The place seems filled with the awful presence of God. Solemnity, deep and impressive as eternity, is depicted on every countenance. The expression of every face, young and old, professors and non-professors, ministers and laymen, seems to say, "Surely God is in this place." Again and again have we heard the solemn annunciation going from one lip to another, "The place whereon thou standest is holy."

Our first meeting was held on Wednesday evening, in the Brunswick Chapel. This is the largest dissenting place of worship in Newcastle, and is considered the most commodious in the north of England. A large number of the people of the town and its surroundings were present. Our message was to the Church. Dr. P—gave out the hymn [...]

[...] We talked about the endowment of power, the full baptism of the Holy Ghost, as the indispensable, ay, *absolute,* necessity of all the disciples of Jesus, if they would be answerable to the duties of their high and holy calling in bringing this redeemed, revolted world back to the world's Redeemer. Many, by their intensely earnest, longing looks, manifested the absorption of their desires for the reception of the grace; and not a few, by most decisive action, signified before the assembled multitude their resolve not to wait till the morrow, but to seek the endowment of power *now*. A local preacher was the first to hasten to the communion-rail, and was the first to receive "the tongue of fire." Would that you could have heard his clear, unequivocal testimony, as with a holy boldness, which perhaps scarcely was more than equalled on the day when the holy flame first descended on the Pentecostal morn, he spake as the Spirit gave utterance. Several other witnesses, principally interesting young men, who looked as though they were destined to be valiant in pulling down the strongholds of Satan, were raised up that night.

This, as you may observe, was the first meeting; and surely now, as in the early days of the Spirit's dispensation, Pentecostal blessings bring Pentecostal power. The next afternoon, we had a meeting of remarkable interest in the lecture-room. I cannot describe it. The Rev. R. Young, chairman of this district, speaks of it as exceeding in interest any meeting he ever attended. Surely there was One in our midst who "baptizeth" with the Holy Ghost and with fire; and many felt the penetrating influence of the baptismal flame to a degree, which, I trust, may be as far-reaching as life. When we sung, at the close,—

"Glory to the Lamb! glory to the Lamb!
For I have overcome through the blood of the Lamb!"—

it did seem as if the spirits of the just made perfect around the throne were blending with us in holy song; and the influence was indescribably glorious. Since this time the afternoon meetings have been held in the commodious chapel, and are numerously attended. The power of the Lord is gloriously and most manifestly present in all our assemblies.

We do not say this only from what our own feelings suggest, but from the outspoken indications in the countenance, action, and words of the congregated multitudes. All seem ready to say, "Surely God is in this place." Not only as the God of Sinai, before whom the mountains melted, but "the Man of Calvary," who walked the streets of Jerusalem,—the Redeemer and Saviour of the world,—is here inwrapping sinners in his crimson vest, and making known his unspeakable name. The numbers in attendance are daily on the increase. Last night, I presume, there could not have been less than from fourteen to fifteen hundred present. The crowd in the lower part of the chapel was so great, that there seemed to be danger of retarding the work: the aisles were so crowded as to make egress from the pews to the communion-rail difficult on the part of those who were wounded by the sword of the Spirit.

You will wish to hear of the number that have received the full baptism. Of this I cannot tell you as accurately as I would. For the glory of God, and the promotion of important truth, I thought it might have been well if the secretaries of the meetings had taken some note of the number who have sought and obtained the blessing of entire sanctification. Scores have surrounded the communion-rail, especially during the afternoon services, seeking the blessing of heart purity. Not a few of these are persons distinguished for their position in the community and in the church. They have come, laying all upon Heaven's altar; and the holy fire has fallen upon the sacrifice; and many scores have been able to testify that the consuming, purifying fires of the Spirit have energized their whole being as never before, and, by the manifestation of their lives, are declaring, "The zeal of Thine house has eaten me up." The ministers are all in the work; and heaven and earth seem to conspire in assuring us that this is but the beginning of a mighty flame which is to spread all over this region. "Alleluia! the Lord God omnipotent reigneth;" and let all the people say, "Amen!" [...]

HOME MISSIONS

[...] World-loving and worldly-conformed professors are apprehending, as never before, that the God of the Scriptures means just what he says when he enjoins separation from the world. "Come out from among them, and be ye separate, saith the Lord, and touch not the unclean thing," has become an obvious and experimental realization. A minister once said to us, "Mrs. P——, how do you get people to believe so easily?" Our answer was, "Because we never attempt to persuade any one to appropriate a promise until we have reason to conclude they are on *promised ground*." The promise, "I will receive you," is only applicable to those who, through the enabling grace of God, separate themselves from the spirit of the world. This done, and the obedient disciple is on promised ground; and he has only to lay hold upon the promise at once, and cleanse himself from all filthiness of the flesh and spirit. I must confess I have felt some solicitude, since I have been in England, in regard to the general conformity of professors to the world, which I have witnessed well-nigh everywhere. But the gracious change is being produced. Said a lady of influential position and wealth—who has not heretofore felt the full import of the command, "Be not conformed to the world,"—about thus: "I care not how public you make my renunciation of worldly adornments; my brooches, &c., are at your disposal; the avails may go to the cause of missions, or anything else you suggest; I find I cannot wear them to the glory of God." And thus it is that jewelry and costly array are being renounced, and we are having a revival, not only of primitive power, but primitive principles.

The revival is the absorbing theme of the place, and it is most significant and heart-cheering to observe how this resuscitation of primitive Christianity and primitive Methodism seems to be appreciated by all Christians of every name and sect. At our afternoon meetings, "Holiness to the Lord," or, in other words, the full baptism of the Holy Spirit, as received by the one hundred and twenty disciples on the day of Pentecost, is set forth as the absolute necessity of all believers of every name. Hundreds, composed of various sects, and from miles distant, crowd to these meetings; and, when Dr. P——gives the invitation to all who are resolved with unyielding faith to claim the grace at once, the communion-rail, which will accommodate about sixty persons, is generally surrounded. [...]

[...] Another man, who is a mechanic, residing about four miles distant, is in the habit of daily attendance on the afternoon and evening meetings. As he walks to and from the chapel, he literally obeys the command, "Go ye out into the highways and hedges, and compel them to come in, that my house may be filled." It is estimated that as many as two or three hundred have, through his agency, been brought more or less under the influence of this visitation of the Spirit. The reception given to this truly Christian man, while thus urging the gospel invitation, is worthy of note. Said one, "Are you a blacksmith?" "I am a *salvation smith*," rejoined the earnest Christian, and, producing his Bible, said, "I have a *hammer* that can break the hardest heart in pieces." The zealous man then went on using the hammer of the Word so truly in the demonstration of the Spirit, that the questioner began to weep and tremble under the power of God. So completely was the heart of this hardened sinner broken, that he who so dexterously wielded the hammer of the Word said to us that he thought he might have witnessed the healing power of Christ on the man at once, could he only have found a place to take him aside for prayer. The same power attending the labor of this man, and of the weavers of Connor, might be seen all around us, if men would be alike filled with the power of the Spirit, and sacrifice that which costs them something, by way of making every earthly consideration subservient to the salvation of souls. [...]

[...] I presume you wonder how our physical ability can be answerable to such a long-continued series of services. We are, and have been for years past, a wonder to ourselves; but, while we would with much carefulness give God all the glory for spiritual and physical ability, we feel it our duty to acknowledge the affection-ate and considerate assiduities of our beloved Christian friends. The people do not generally disperse from the three-o'clock service till about five o'clock, and not a few of them linger and remain till after the evening service. Between five and six o'clock, tea is furnished in the vestry. Ladies in turn take this upon them-selves, and, in generous, loving solicitude, seem to vie with each other which may best serve the convenience of the multitude by providing for the greatest possible number. Last night, I think fifty at least took tea with us; and those that could not be seated in the vestry were supplied in the chapel. In view of the many ministers and people who come from abroad to participate in the work, this is as the Master of the feast would have it. Surely Jesus is now passing by. Even men of the world, and the community at large, are acknowledging his visitation; and, through the invitations of his Spirit, multitudes are gathered from "the regions round about;" and, in the "beauty of holiness," the friends of Jesus in Newcastle seem to meet the emergency. To God be all the glory! and to this your ever-attuned heart will, I am sure, say, "Amen, AMEN!"

19

MAURICE DAVIES, 'THE "TWELVE DAYS' MISSION"'

In *Orthodox London: Or Phases of Religious Life in the Church of England*, 2nd edn (London: Tinsley Brothers, 1874), pp. 267, 269–271, 274–278, 279–282

The "Twelve Days' Mission"

A Broad-Church clergyman, at that time in easy harness, I was honestly anxious to discover whether the sudden "special attack on sin and Satan" on the part of the Church of England, organized some years ago, was simply spasmodic or a sign of real vitality. I had no preconceived ideas on the subject, though I may say frankly I did not like the idea of the Confessional grafted on the originally colourless scheme so innocently sanctioned by the Bishop of London. Still, if a good end be gained, it is the extreme of folly to quarrel about the means. The question to be settled was whether this *"Guerre de Douze Jours"* will do Satan any harm. If it did not do him harm it would do him good in its recoil. I propose to chronicle diary-wise my experiences of as many of these mission-services as a somewhat busy life enabled me to attend. [...]

[...] My first effort at witnessing a mission-service was infructuous, and Satan scored one, I suppose. This, of course, was a mere hitch in the working of machinery new to the Church of England, which the tact and courtesy of the incumbent of St. Mary Magdalene's would soon remedy by drilling the gentlemen in the cassocks. In point of fact nothing can be more un-Catholic or offensive to the poor than thus picking out the well-dressed; as much as to say, "You do not want saving from sin or Satan, only those poor folks." The very essence of Catholic worship, or of a mission-service, surely is that rich and poor shall meet without distinction. The Roman Catholics realize this. The Anglo-Catholics will learn it when they get a little more *au fait* at their new work.

A second remark which it occurs to me to make is that the "bowing to the altar" is not yet satisfactory at this church. If it be done at all, it should be properly done. At present it looks as though the genuflectors were ashamed of themselves. It put me exactly in mind of the awkwardness of my countrymen in lifting their hats to the lady at the *comptoir* in a French restaurant. Contrast this awkwardness with the inimitable grace of the thorough-bred Parisian diner, and you know the difference between the genuflexion at St. Mary Magdalene's and St. Mary of the Angels. The fact is I know from a poor parishioner, who appealed in the most honest ignorance for the *rationale* of the proceeding, the poor people fancy they are bowing to the magnificent brazen eagle which serves as a lectern. This I know is literally and simply true. The question was put to a member of my household by a poor woman, "Why do they bow to the brass eagle?" In point of fact, until the reservation of the sacrament is allowed, there is nothing else to bow to. The genuflexion of the Romanist means something—that of the Anglo-Catholic can mean nothing as yet, for devoutly as he may believe in the Real Presence in the consecrated elements, there are simply no consecrated elements there, and I venture to presume the most advanced Ritualist does not hold a special presence in the chancel more than in the body of the church. These, however, as we have said, are merest details, about which it would be unwise and wicked to quarrel, if the great end is attained of diminishing sin, and so diminishing sorrow and suffering.

Wednesday

Attended the five o'clock service at All Saints', Margaret Street. There seemed no doubt that this mission was doing good in the way of calling out the preaching power of the Church of England. The old objection (true enough in its degree) of clinging to the MS. sermon will probably not attach to us much longer. All praise to those who help to make us natural. The method will probably be by running violently into the opposite extreme for a little while. A sharp bend in a contrary direction will straighten the crooked stick. I got to All Saints' ("sicut meus est mos") half an hour before service, and found myself in the thick of a sermon. It was a sermon, and no mistake. A young man, whose name I could not ascertain (but whom I afterwards found to be Mr. Body), was habited simply in a cassock, and occupied a chair in the middle of the chancel—that is, there was a chair there for him, but he ran about, fell on his knees, &c.—in fact, was everywhere but in the chair, and poured forth a torrent of fervid words with the voice of a Stentor. He was thoroughly in earnest, thoroughly practical, and certainly very striking. There was nothing to offend the most sensitive; yet still there was no doubt that his sermon came under the popular denomination of "rant." [...]

Saturday

Attended the 5 p.m. service at St. Paul's, Wilton Place, Knightsbridge, where the Rev. W. J. E. Bennett, of Frome, was preaching a course of sermons. It was amusing to notice how the former generation of so-called "Puseyites" represented by such men as Messrs. Liddell and Bennett, was completely distanced by the modern Ritualists. They cannot get out of their old habits of rigidity and formalism, which these young Titans have thrown to the winds. The sermon was exceedingly dry, and not preached, but read from a MS. In fact, both time and place lifted it out of the category of "Mission" sermons. It was a Belgravian discourse *pur et simple,* and even made distinct reference to the sins of the London "season." The only symptom of the Mission was a collection introduced into the service, and a certain jaunty, not to say rollicking air about the hymn tunes, which is always assumed to be a characteristic of a Revival. "O Paradise" was thus sung to a jumpy measure in six-eight time, about as alien from the spirit of the words as could well be imagined.

Eight p.m.—"*On revient toujours,*" &c. To All Saints', Margaret Street, again. I found at least fifty people waiting outside the gate at seven o'clock for a service which was to commence at eight. Mr. Body preached on the Magdalene at the house of Simon, though he was so nearly voiceless as to be obliged to forego his Bible-class. His subject naturally led him to speak much of the "social evil," *par excellence,* and he was just enough to address his sharpest remarks to the men's side of the congregation. He told a somewhat sensational story of a poor creature from the streets who the evening before had been attracted to St. Alban's simply by seeing the large cross at the head of the Mission bill outside, and went in to ascertain its meaning. The "priest" saw her and spoke to her; the result being that she left her course of life, and "that night, instead of sleeping in a haunt of sin, slept in a house of penitence." He truly said, if no other result than this came of the Mission—supposing this to be permanent—that Mission had not been in vain. After the sermon the men were again invited to stop to confession. "Do stop now. Wont you stop?" But alas! they didn't stop. It was rather too much for our English reserve just yet to expect one or two individuals to come out in the face of that congregation, and undergo the unaccustomed ordeal of confession. I do not think the preacher expected it; for he was so very urgent in his invitation. He said he had no difficulty with the women, but he wanted the stronger sex. I fear it will require a great deal of Mission work before any of the stronger sex, really deserving the name, will be up to confession point.

Monday

Attended the Mission service at St. Alban's, Holborn, where for the first time I found the form of service followed out as it stands in the little penny books with the big crosses outside. It was very doleful. The Penitential Psalms were chanted slowly to the most unmitigated Gregorians, and the prayers monotoned very low down in the gamut. One cannot help wondering whether a little cheerful music written in round notes on five lines would not suit these simple folk as well as the dreadful square-headed notes on four lines. Why must we go back to imperfect musical notation when we want to sing about religion? The hymns, however, were more lively, and "There is a fountain," followed by its refrain of "I do believe, I will believe," &c., put one in mind of the meeting-house. In fact, the whole affair is a wonderful congeries of the Roman and Ranter elements grafted on the stock of "the Church of England as by law established." By all means let us be eclectic. We cannot afford to neglect any means for "evangelizing the masses," as the phrase goes. The sermon of the Rev. "Father" O'Neil was on the Sacrament of Penance! Think of that and weep, ye orthodox, who teach your little children to answer the question, "How many Sacraments?" "Two only." The "Rev. Father" preached on "the Sacrament of Penance." He was a little stiff and unnatural, labouring under a conscious effort to popularize an unpopular and unpalatable subject. It failed utterly, because it was unnatural; and the congregation, not large at the beginning, dribbled away perceptibly on the women's side. It was surmised that the second week of the Mission would prove more attractive than the first; but one fails to see much sign of it here. There were a dozen or two of outsiders, evidently, like myself, come to see what it was all about, who had to be plied with little mission-books by an attentive priest in a long cassock, who walked about all service and sermon time for the purpose. I kept looking back, around, and about me, in real curiosity, but I could not see the faintest trace of enthusiasm, or anything suggestive of a revival service. In fact, to my mind the characteristic of the service was listlessness; of the sermon, effort—and effort unsuccessful in attaining its end. In plain words, the whole affair at St. Alban's on Monday night hung fire. [...]

[...] So, then, the much-talked-of Twelve Days' Mission was at an end, and became matter of history. As it does so, we cannot but pause for a moment, and, with the experiences fresh upon us, inquire—will it prove to have been only a violent spasm, or a real epoch in Church history? Happy—on the *suave mari magno* principle—those whose lot it is to stand, like myself, on the bank, watching the current of events, without danger of being carried away by it. Seeing at the end of the Mission-book a form of service for the "Renewal of Baptismal Vows," I sallied forth on Wednesday evening, prepared to renew mine; though I had never formally renounced them, and fancied they were renewed once for all at confirmation. I must look up my theology. However, the difficulty did not occur, for the service was ignored. My last Mission evening was spent—shall I own the soft impeachment?—still at the shrine of Mr. Body at All Saints', Margaret Street. Perhaps no stronger proof of the fascination exercised by mere fluency of speech and earnestness of purpose could be adduced than this man's power to bring me thither evening after evening at the sacrifice of so much valuable time, and amid influences not altogether congenial. If I, who could sit there coldly criticising even his most telling "bits," felt this fascination, what of the sensitive females, and men more impressionable than myself, whom I saw there with the tears they tried to conceal actually bursting through the hands with which they covered their faces! I certainly never saw such a sight outside or inside the walls of a church as I have seen at All Saints'. One hour and a quarter before sermon-time there was a crowd in Margaret Street. At ten minutes past seven, when the outer gates were opened, the rush resembled a Jenny Lind night in olden time at the Opera. The church was filled in a few minutes; for many persons—members of the regular congregations we will presume—were admitted through the clergy-house. Then ensued a time of conversation; not light flippant talk—I witnessed no one single instance of that—but, both before the service and also between the sermon and Bible-class, there was deep, earnest conversation of men on religious topics. The sermon, to my thinking, was Mr. Body's *chef d'œuvre*. Its subject was Perseverance; its text the suggestive one, "Let us run with patience the race that is set before us, looking unto Jesus, the author and finisher of our Faith." It was a discourse not to be forgotten; more quietly delivered, and truer to its logical divisions, than any that had preceded it. Its subject was characteristically summarized by the preacher as "Christian *Pluck*." The Bible-study that succeeded was an eloquent picture of the condition of the Departed in Paradise, and an appeal by that softest of all sanctions to perseverance. When the mother was pointed to the arms of her dead baby-boy beckoning her forward, or the young man urged by the love of a lost mother, one can well understand the sensation (I wrote that word unadvisedly, and not with its new meaning) produced. Looking round analytically, I could not but confess I had seen as much feeling evoked by a powerful drama. I have seen grey-headed men weeping at Mrs. Mellon's impersonation of the mother at the foot of the guillotine where her son is to be executed, in Mr. Watts Phillips' "Dead Heart." Will this prove more lasting? I believe each does good; but one, we know, is ephemeral. I am only echoing the preacher's own anxious and often-expressed doubt. Will this "sensation" prove more permanent?

The experiment of this Mission has been cleverly elaborated and successfully worked out as far as immediate result goes. I saw strict Roman Catholics and ultra-Evangelicals, in whose nostrils All Saints' has been hitherto unsavoury, gathered in last night's congregation. Will the cohesive power last?

Whatever else be the upshot of all this, it proved we had at least one Boanerges amongst us, the Rev. Mr. Body, "of Wolverhampton." I felt a little like Iscariot, I must confess, when, passing out by the side door, I found Mr. Body, arrayed in priest's cloak, standing there to shake hands with members of the congregation as they passed. I thought I might get by unobserved; but no, he insisted on a shake, and said in a cheery tone, "Good-bye, your face is very familiar to me at this Mission, though I don't know your name. Are you working in London?" I did not tell him my name; I only told him half my work; and omitted to mention that I was doing the Mission for a Daily Paper. I wonder whether, had you known my mission, you would have felt as I did, that I was grasping the hand of an honest man, at all events.

20

SOCIETY OF ST JOHN THE EVANGELIST (THE HOLY CROSS), *THE BOOK OF THE MISSION*

(London: [n.p.], [1870]), pp. iv–v, 17–19

What is a Mission?

1 A Mission is a special call from God

It is a call to the *sinner,* "Awake, thou that sleepest!" "Repent, for the kingdom of heaven is at hand."

It is a call to the righteous, "Prepare to meet thy God;" "Judge yourselves, that ye be not judged of the LORD."

Jonah preached a Mission to Nineveh, and the whole city repented and was saved.

Lot preached one night to Sodom, but they would not hearken, and were destroyed by fire.

2 A Mission is a time of special grace

Thousands are praying for your soul. JESUS opens his arms to you. Angels watch anxiously to see what you will do—whether you will cast yourself before Him or turn away. The churches are open. Hundreds of sinners are weeping for their sins. *Why do not you?*

Hundreds are crying to JESUS for help. *Why do not you?*

Hundreds are resolving to give up sin. *Why do not you?*

Hundreds are cleansed in JESUS' Blood to-day. *Why not you?*

Hundreds are happier than they ever were before. *Why not you?*

Hundreds are set free to-day. *Why not you?*

Hundreds are joining the pilgrims—bound to Heaven. *Why not you?*

HOME MISSIONS

Prayers for the Mission

ALMIGHTY God, we beseech Thee graciously to behold this Thy Family, for which our LORD JESUS CHRIST was contented to be betrayed, and given up into the hands of wicked men, and to suffer death upon the cross, who now liveth and reigneth with Thee and the HOLY GHOST, ever one GOD, world without end. Amen.

O LORD JESU CHRIST, who at Thy first coming didst send Thy messenger to prepare Thy way before Thee; Grant that the ministers and stewards of Thy mysteries may likewise so prepare and make ready Thy way, by turning the hearts of the disobedient to the wisdom of the just, that at Thy second coming to judge the world we may be found an acceptable people in Thy sight, who livest and reignest with the FATHER and the HOLY SPIRIT, ever one GOD, world without end. Amen.

O MERCIFUL GOD, who has made all men, and hatest nothing that Thou hast made, nor wouldest the death of a sinner, but rather that he should be converted and live; Have mercy upon all Jews, Turks, Infidels, and Hereticks, and take from them all ignorance, hardness of heart, and contempt of Thy Word; and so fetch them home, Blessed LORD, to Thy flock, that they may be saved among the remnant of the true Israelites, and be made one fold under one Shepherd, JESUS CHRIST our LORD, who liveth and reigneth with Thee and the HOLY SPIRIT, one GOD, world without end Amen.

Confession

"Be not ashamed to confess thy sins" (Ecclus. iv. 26). "If we confess our sins, He is faithful and just to forgive us our sins, and to cleanse us from all unrighteousness" (1 S. John i. 9).

A Mission is a time for a fresh start. By going to Confession you cast the burden of your sins at the foot of the Cross, and are enabled to go on your pilgrimage to Heaven rejoicing.

By Confession you purge your soul of the sins which obstruct and pain it, and are prepared to receive the Heavenly Food of the Body and Blood of CHRIST.

Are you sorry for your sins?

If so, you will determine never again to commit them.

If so, you will flee from temptation, you will give up the company of those who tempt you to sin, you will avoid the places where temptation comes.

If so, you will make up for the evil you have done by doing good. You will not keep what you have got unjustly. You will restore the good name of him whom you have falsely accused.

If so, you will forgive those who have injured you, and pray for them.

SOCIETY OF ST JOHN THE EVANGELIST

How to make a good Confession

1 Ask God to help you, for you cannot do it without his grace.
2 Determine not to keep back anything.
3 Take care to be plain and simple; and if you find it difficult, ask the Priest to help you.
4 If you doubt whether anything you have done was sinful, ask the Priest.
5 Keep to the point, and remember you have to confess *your own* sins, not the sins of other people.
6 Make your confession as if it were your last, and you were going to die to-night.

A form of Confession

In the Name of the Father, and of the Son, and of the Holy Ghost.

I confess to GOD Almighty, and to our LORD JESUS CHRIST, before all the company of Heaven, and to you my Father, that I have sinned very much in thought, word, and deed, through my own great fault.

[Then tell the Priest your sins]

I am truly sorry for these and all my other sins, which I cannot now remember, and I pray GOD to pardon me, and you my Father to give me penance, counsel, and absolution.

Some Prayers before and after Confession

A Prayer before Confession

Help me, O GOD, to know my sins, and to confess them truly and with penitence, that so they may be blotted out of Thy Book, and I may be saved at the Judgment Day.

Thanksgiving after Absolution

At Thy feet I fall, O merciful JESUS, and thank Thee for cleansing me from sin. Grant me to follow Thee in holiness here, that I may reign with Thee forever hereafter.

An Act of Contrition

I am deeply sorry that I have offended Thee, O my GOD. I hate the sins which have offended Thee, especially my.... Never again will I commit them. I will fly from temptation as from a serpent. Help me, O merciful JESU, to keep my firm resolve!

HOME MISSIONS

If you have injured anyone

O LORD forgive me that I have wickedly injured..... I am resolved to make amends by doing good to him. Help me, O GOD!

If anyone has injured you

Forgive me, O LORD, all my sins, for I forgive..... and pray for him, that we may both be saved, and meet in heaven.

Pray for the Mission

All the faithful should pray earnestly, not only for their own souls, but for the souls of others.

1   Come to Church every morning, and pray whilst the Priest is offering the Holy Sacrifice. For this is the *best* time.
2   Pray in your heart often during the day.
3   Pray, when you can, upon your knees.

O MOST merciful JESU, Who hast said, "I came not to call the righteous, but sinners to Repentance," we beseech Thee to look graciously upon this Parish: subdue and convert the hearts of all careless and godless sinners, that they whom the subtlety of sin has deceived, or darkness of ignorance has blinded, may at length find Light and Truth in Thee, the Sun of Righteousness, Who, with the FATHER and the HOLY GHOST, liveth and reigneth, one GOD, world without end. Amen.

2.4

The Salvation Army

2.4 The Salvation Army

The Salvation Army began in 1865 as the East London Christian Mission, run by William Booth (1829–1912) and his wife Catherine. From the beginning, women were as active in the Army as men, and were able to be ordained and continue religious work after marriage. William Booth was known for a somewhat dictatorial style, which found full expression in his designation of the religious organisation as an Army, and himself as the General. The army structure of the organisation also formalised adherents' membership and training, and kept the organisation separate from the communities in which they lived; one of the General's rules was that officers could only marry other officers.

The first extract in this section comes from the General's rule book, *Orders and Regulations for Field Officers*. In addition to rules there are also instructions for how to run the various meetings for which the Salvation Army was known. The 'Free and Easy' described here is reminiscent of revival meetings, containing testimony and 'plentiful singing'. However, Booth insists that the meeting requires the control of the officer, and attempts to manage the sorts of testimony to be given by members of the congregation. There is a need for control because 'Roughs' might be present, who must be entertained and interested enough so that they do not cause 'mischief'. Booth instructs that testimonies should interest people as much as singing, especially if they tell a story, which is 'seen, felt or known by the speaker'. Women's words are stated to have a special power – a 'moving influence' – so Booth urges officers to induce women to speak, especially as, he says, they have a 'right' to do so.

The *War Cry* was the Army's main publication, and in 1895 it reviewed 'Quenched', the Army's annual report of the rescue work carried out by women officers. The review extracts sections of the report that display all the techniques of its writing: combining statistics and narratives, factual interviews and sentimental flourishes to convince readers to donate to the cause. The story of Maggie, the 'well-saved scrubber', presents the saved girl as a sort of Cinderella, desperate to escape her wicked and worldly stepmother, who had brought 'the element of drink with all its fearful accompaniments' into her home. Her tears are presented in an exaggeratedly sentimental manner – as a trail visible on the stairs after she has scrubbed them – to create sympathy. Statistics serve to evoke the scale of the social and rescue work carried out by the Army's women officers, but also to stand in for what cannot be said. Women saved from prostituting themselves are referred to as 'fallen' and tabulated as 'Night attendances'. And Captain Sowden falls back on reporting how many babies have been born at Ivy House maternity hospital, as 'So much of our work can't be put into print'.

In the *War Cry*'s series of officer profiles, titled inconsistently 'Women Warriors' and 'Married Women Warriors', rescue work is shown to be only part of the work of women officers. There is little difference between these portraits – the one not titled a 'married' officer became a married woman when she was posted to Australia, but continued to work as an officer, opening a rescue home in

Sydney. In this sort of work the women are presented chasing down girls who are 'going wrong', being depicted almost like mother hens chasing after their chicks. Alongside the rescue work and leading meetings, their domestic work as wives and mothers is emphasised. They are admired when they manage these responsibilities while remaining committed to the work, and for minimising the level of challenge this presents with phrases like 'where there's a will there's a way'. Conversely, their feminine physical weakness is almost fetishised, as it makes plain God's power in working through such weak instruments. As all the sources in this section show, while women were treated with a semblance of equality, Salvation Army rhetoric was riven with contradictions when it came to its female officers.

21

WILLIAM BOOTH,
ORDERS AND REGULATIONS FOR FIELD OFFICERS

(London: Salvation Army, 1886), pp. 322–323

The Free-and-Easy

1   The form of meeting which goes by this name has been very useful in The Army from the beginning, and if managed with care and conducted with spirit, no class of gathering is calculated to produce better results.

2   There is some danger of this meeting, from its very freedom, degenerating into license and levity, but this can be guarded against by any thoughtful F.O. who rightly appreciates the solemnity of his position and is himself under the leading of the Holy Spirit.

3   Such an Officer will never allow the atmosphere of any meeting under his command to become such as will make it seem out of season at any moment to invite sinners to the penitent-form, or to kneel down and speak to God in prayer.

4   In conducting a Free-and-Easy, let the following directions be attended to.

   (*a*) Open with a Salvation song—one well known for words and tune.
   (*b*) Let there be prayer and singing—kneeling.
   (*c*) Then a solo.
   (*d*) A few general remarks by the leader with the reading of a few verses from the Bible, closing the reading by giving his own experience.
   (*e*) Then the meeting should be thrown open, making it plain that all truly saved people will be welcome to speak in any part of the building and encouraged to do so.

5   The testimonies calculated to make a good Free-and-Easy should be:—

   (*a*) *Short,* that is to say, not exceeding two or three minutes, and yet long enough to contain something worth hearing. If the speaker is too long the leader must not hesitate to strike up singing. All properly saved speakers will take this in good part, and rather enjoy it than otherwise.
   (*b*) They should be *varied,* either about the speaker's own conversion, or as to the possession of a clean heart.

(*c*) Some remarkable Salvation *incident,* that is, describing somebody else's conversion.

(*d*) They may tell of some triumphant death-bed.

(*e*) Some special *supernatural* dealings of God with the speaker, such as being healed by faith.

(*f*) Or perhaps the most effectual of all is some Divine present time experience.

(*g*) To be effectual, these experiences should always be something *seen,* or *felt, or known* by the speaker.

(*h*) There should be plenty of *united singing.* Long solos will spoil any meeting, unless the songs are of extraordinary interest.

(*i*) The people must be made to *speak up.* It is cruel to have them muttering or whispering what cannot be heard by those on the other side of the building. To keep the roughs from getting into mischief, let them hear what is being said. Therefore, no Soldier or anyone else should be allowed to talk on if they cannot be heard. If new converts or feeble women or anybody else, say anything which cannot be heard all over the building, if it is worth repeating, let the F. O. say it over again; tell the people that "this woman says so-and-so and so-and-so."

(*j*) When there is a great crowd the speaking is by far the most effective from the platform. Everyone who wants to speak should be urged to sit there beforehand.

(*k*) The women should be induced to speak. As a rule they hang back, and the F.O. may go through the meeting with scarcely a testimony from a woman; yet no one has a greater right to speak, or will speak with a more blessed, melting, moving influence upon an audience than a woman.

(*l*) Testimonies, to be effectual, should generally refer to the speaker. Hearsay is of very little concern to a big meeting. Speakers should stick to the present time, what is happening in their hearts, and lives, and circumstances to-day. What has been said in a sermon or read in a book will not be cared for by a crowd. But when a speaker sticks to what he has heard, seen, felt, and known himself, everybody will listen.

22

THE WAR CRY, 1895–1896

(i) '*Quenched*: Rescue Report for 1895', *The War Cry*, 23 November 1895, p. 4; (ii) 'Married Women Warriors' *The War Cry*, 26 January 1895, p. 7; (iii) 'Married Women Warriors' *The War Cry*, 13 April 1895, p. 13; (iv) 'Women Warriors' *The War Cry*, 11 April 1896, p. 5.

i
"Quenched": Rescue Report for 1895

"I claim that the purpose of this work is equal with the value and noble-ness of human life itself.
"And I also claim that the work is a success."

With these two statements Mrs. Bramwell Booth launches her Annual Rescue Report.

"Quenched," a well-dressed pamphlet of some forty pages, is divided into read-able chapters, in which the purpose referred to is never lost sight of, whilst both incidents and statistics do more to prove the success which has attended this noble effort to save our perishing sisters than any sentiments which might be expressed within the limits of a short review.

Take, for instance, the following figures, culled from a chapter dealing chiefly with the inner working of the various Rescue Homes.

In so far as it is possible to reduce soul-saving work to the terms of arithmetic, the following figures show what has been done in our thirteen Rescue Homes dur-ing the past year, the proportion of satisfactory cases being about eighty percent.

Sent to situations	741
Sent home to friends	279
Sent to hospitals or otherwise assisted	195
Sent to trades	57
Married	2
Died (while under our care)	1
Unsatisfactory	281
Total number dealt with	1,556

HOME MISSIONS

One thousand five hundred and fifty-six souls for whom "nobody cared," dealt with in the course of the twelve short months! Just how many tears, how many heartaches, how many sleepless nights these figures represent, can only be known to Him who never slumbers nor sleeps.

The following case will, we feel sure, make those who read want to know more of this divinely begotten work:—

"The door-bell rang at one of the provincial Rescue Homes, and three weary, bedraggled, foot-sore girls were brought before the Captain. They were all under sixteen, and stated that they all had run away from thoroughly bad homes, having tramped about twenty-five miles to reach the Home. They were taken in temporarily, to allow of their story being investigated, and a few days later, there being no apparent reason against it, were accepted as regular cases. However, before long, the other two acknowledged that their homes were not so bad as they had made out, and decided to return to their friends.

Not so, Maggie. The mere mention of "home" brought terror to her mind, though she told the officers of a time when the word had been a synonym for all that was happy and good. But her own mother had died; the father, once a respectable, hard-working man, had married again, and the step-mother brought into the little home the element of drink, with all its fearful accompaniments. Maggie saw no reason to desire a return to that life.

But the step-mother evidently had her sane moments, in her intervals of debauchery, and she knew Maggie's good points of physical strength and willingness to work; so she sent a demand that the girl should return at once.

Everything possible was done to enable Maggie to stay, but all to no purpose. The father had a legal right to his daughter of fifteen, and he was the tool of the step-mother. So Maggie was finally told that in two days she must return to her own home.

These were days of misery for Maggie, and of real sympathy on the part of her companions. It was quite pitiful to see the girl, for though she tried to be brave, the sobs would come. When she was given scrubbing to do, her tears fell into the bucket, and when she swept the stairs they marked her progress downward. Poor child! she had to go, but she went with the promise not to forget what she had learned, and to try in God's strength to keep good.

One afternoon, about six weeks later, the officers had just finished tea and were praying, when the door-bell rang again. It was Maggie, triumphant, who pulled it. "I passed my sixteenth birthday last week, and I've come home," she said.

The Captain looked at her hair. "You have cut a fringe," she said solemnly and in a grieved tone.

"Oh, no, I didn't; *she* did it," responded Maggie with a reference miles back to the wicked step-mother, who no longer had any legal claim.

Maggie, like Louise, can give an up-to-date testimony, for she is doing well today. She is still her own merry, mischievous self, but she is kind, affectionate and earnest. Best of all, she is truly grateful to the One Who is leading her in what are to her "green pastures."

THE WAR CRY

Women's Shelter

So far as any line of distinction can be drawn among institutions which work for the one common purpose, and whose methods are in a large degree similar, the Women's Shelters and Metropoles may be considered as belonging to the Social branch rather than to that which is more generally known as the Rescue Work. Still, the line of demarcation is almost an imaginary one, for the Homes do their full share for women who are not "fallen," while the Shelters and Metropoles are able to accomplish a great deal in the way of direct preventive work. During the past year, the Whitechapel Shelter alone has passed thirty-six girls into our various London Homes; has been the means of restoring twenty to their parents or friends, who had either been anxiously searching or who had given them up for dead; and also arranged in four cases for the reconciliation of wife with husband.

"I can't starve and I can't find any work, so there's nothing left for me to do but to live on the streets," is the excuse very often given to our officers when they are dealing with girls who seem to know what they are doing, and yet not to care. Up to the limit of our Metropole accommodation, this position is no longer tenable, for though the promise to find work on the following morning is not written in the bond of a fourpenny ticket for a night's lodging, yet no pains are spared to find suitable employment for all who are willing to undertake it and to do their best. The "pound of cure" is a veritable God-send for those who have passed beyond the stage where they can be helped by the "ounce of prevention," but our various Shelters have constant contact with many women who are just beginning to sink under the force of sin and the force of circumstances, so that the ability to offer work to these means keeping them from the so-called necessity of sin. This isn't the place for a lengthy appeal—but will you remember our women the next time you want some extra scrubbing done?

Number of Night Attendances	155,701
Number of Meals Served	93,315
Number of Meetings held	794

Ivy House

Two Interviews on Maternity Work

"'Tis an awkward thing to play with souls,
And matter enough to save one's own."

The first interview took place most appropriately so far as the where and the when were concerned.

Capt. Sowdon hardly knew at first what would be of interest. "So much of our work can't be put into print," she said, "but it goes on, for all that, and we have more applications for outside nursing than we can supply. Is that the sort of thing you want to know?"

165

"Yes, that too, but more about the work of the hospital itself. Has it grown during the past year? How many babies have been born there?"

"We have had one hundred and twenty," she said, "against eighty of the year before. That means that we have been able to help forty more mothers, so you can see that the work *is* growing; there is no question about that. Of course, most of the girls pay something, the expenses are so heavy here that we have to insist upon that, and in many cases the affiliation department sees to it that the man pays up, but we rarely have anyone in who is able to give full value for what she receives, and occasionally we feel obliged to take a case for nothing, though we really cannot afford to do this."

SLUM MATERNITY STATISTICS.

Births attended	179
Visits to same	1,801
Other diseases nursed	104
General visits	7,012
Hours actual visiting	6,858
Prayed with	4,318

Police Court Work

Eight o'clock in the morning, is for the two Rescue Officers who are on Prison-Gate duty, the signal, not for breakfast, but for work. Breakfast they have had already, and the work cannot wait, for just at eight the men are discharged, and ten minutes after the women will follow; of course, the Sisters must be there to offer them a helping hand. This Police-court work for women is a comparatively recent development, and has not had a fair chance for growth because of the lack of officers to do the work; but this can at least be said, that wherever the work exists, no excuse remains for any woman to say "I got down, and I couldn't get up again." The Rescue Officer stands at the prison gate in full view of all those who receive their discharge, stands there to offer tea, or counsel, or both. Many a time have the few words of kindness and of warning spoken over the cup of steaming tea or coffee been the means, through God, of bringing back to her senses some poor girl who once knew what it meant to be innocently good, but who has since wandered far along the path of sin and crime.

The most important part of the Police-court work is the dealing with the women in their cells previous to their being tried before the magistrates. In this there is, indeed, no telling what a day may bring forth, or what sort of a mood the prisoners may be in; always respectful toward the Army uniform, they seem to realise the fact that the Salvationist is there simply for the purpose of helping them, and they appreciate the willingness even when they postpone the offer.

Friends will do well to secure copies of "Quenched" as early as possible. It will help them to decide the very important question of Christmas offerings. They can then pass the Report on to their friends, instead of the played-out Christmas card. The International Rescue Headquarters is at 259, Mare Street, Hackney, London, N.E.

THE WAR CRY

ii
Married Women Warriors

Mrs. Major Orsborn

Our chat was rather an unfinished one, but it gave us an idea of the full heart of love and full hands of help that Mrs. Orsborn must have. She was in the midst of the anxieties and perplexities of a Rescue case when we reached the little officer-like home at Bedford.

"To begin at the beginning, how and when did you come to be an officer in The Army?" we asked.

"Twelve years ago I entered the Clapton Training Home, which had then only been opened a few months. My salvation was at Tunstall six months before. I was saved through my husband at his first corps. I professed to dislike The Army, but I knew each time I opened the 'War Cry' that some day I must be an officer. When a child I thought I should like to be a Christian, and went out to an enquiry room. An old man talked to me for a very long time, and then he prayed a very long prayer and asked me if I believed on Jesus Christ. I said, 'Yes,' and he told me 'Then you're saved!' I said, 'Am I?' and went away trying to believe that I was for a time. Growing older I gave it all up, and became very fond of fashion and theatre-going. When The Salvation Army came, my sister got converted, and lived such a beautiful life at home that I began to get convicted, too. I was brought to the point on Christmas Day by my husband's singing of 'Over the line,' and on Boxing night, in my own room, God saved my soul. My sister said, 'If you're saved, you'll come on the platform and put my shield on!'

"When I became a Salvationist I felt I ought to speak, but—I had such a dreadful temper. Five weeks after, God delivered me from it, and it has never troubled me since. Then I was free to speak, and the first time I spoke, though the barracks was full, I saw no one, and they tell me I talked for twenty minutes.

"When I volunteered for the Work, mother said I wasn't strong enough."

"A usual remark of mothers," we ventured to interpolate.

"I don't think Headquarters thought I should make an officer, and I couldn't go to Birmingham to see the Major of the Division, for mother wouldn't pay my travelling. When Mr. Ballington Booth came for a week-end, all the Candidates were to speak before him, and on the Saturday night my voice went, a thing unheard of either before or since. However, I did see the Major at last, and I suppose he backed me, for I was accepted. Mother was very sorrowful. I loved my training days. As to the lectures—I can remember them now, and the impression they made on me. I was Soldier, Sergeant, Cadet and Captain in twelve months.

"After marriage I had about five years more Field work, and then we went to Norway, and now, after various changes, we are in charge of the Herts and Beds Division."

The Major's entrance arrested our talk for a moment.

"Is it Women's Rights you're discussing?" he asked.

We turned to Mrs. Orsborn for an explanation.

167

HOME MISSIONS

"That's the name I give to some special meetings of mine—'Women's Rights' to preach the Gospel. I try to show that a woman's life need not be filled up with making antimacassars.

"My work here is not in the office. When I am out for the week-end two of the children always accompany me. Yes, I do some visiting, and the various girls who come to me for help keep me very busy. Last Saturday a servant-girl sought me, whose master had hit her with the poker, and I had to see after her box and money."

"It's beautiful to feel that they come to you in their distress. But you want to hear what I do all day? Here is a sample. I got up at four o'clock (my usual hour on washing day) and helped the girl to do all the washing—there are between twelve and fourteen dozen clothes every week—before breakfast. Then I went out visiting with my Rescue goods—a good stock of which I keep here—and sold nearly £1 worth. After dinner I walked nearly all over the town to find out a lassie who was going wrong, and then after tea I folded the clothes and mangled them. What else do I do? I make all the children's clothes and do all the ironing. My writing is done when the little ones are at school or in bed."

Mrs. Orsborn would have told us more had not a knock summoned her attention to some friendless lassie.

"I'm afraid you wouldn't like to interview people like me every day," said Mrs. Orsborn.

"Our interview, with its interruption so significant of your labour of love, has been only typical of you and your work," we answered.

iii
Married Women Warriors

Mrs. Keegan is a 'Derry Boy! or, to be quite within the mark, worth two of the ordinary braves of our old North-Irish corps! We say so with deliberation, and are prepared to combat it at the point of the bayonet, if necessary, either inside or outside the walls, always provided, of course, that the bayonet is nothing more dangerous than a quill pen!

A Field officer's wife should be qualified to lead an indoor or outdoor meeting, visit the sick, interest herself in the young and keep the corps books straight. [Mem.—F.O's who are candidates for matrimony, please jot down!—ED.] Mrs. Keegan answers to all these qualifications, and adds a few more, such as a readiness to sing a solo without a book and to stop in the middle of a line, press home the truth of it, and then resume; and also, in a special degree, take up her Bible, which she almost worships, and discharge red-hot, salvation-artillery shot.

She has her weak points of course; one of them is a shrinkage from publicity in "The War Cry," and the other is not a weakness—to perpetrate a paradox—every drop of her blood is Irish!

THE WAR CRY

Talking with her, the other day, upon some of her experiences as a Field officer's help-meet, she said to our representative that one thing she determined to do when entering the Work with her husband, and that was to take a full share of responsibility for everything connected with his corps, and to go in for the salvation of souls with just as much zeal as if she had been called to the War as a single woman.

Our man took up both of these points and asked her several questions upon them.

"How far have you been able to adhere to that resolution, Mrs. Keegan?"

"I have not once departed from it!"

"But your family—have they not stood in the way?"

Mrs. Keegan saw what was passing in our man's mind, and after a moment's reflection, she replied, "No, sir; my family have not. I should be ashamed to go on to a platform and talk to soldiers' wives about turning up to the open-airs if I felt that they could point, with justice, to my inconsistency. Excepting in the case of sickness, and an illness which kept me for two months in retirement, I've scarcely missed a meeting since we left 'Derry, seven years ago."

"Does that include open-airs?"

"Yes—and I lead many of them myself. I always take the Sunday afternoon's open-air."

"Why?"

"The Captain is then doing the Juniors."

"But what about the baby and the children meantime?"

"Well, in some corps the children are a difficulty, especially if the quarters is far from the barracks. But I do the best I can. Sometimes I take them to the barracks, sometimes a soldier will help me; but, as a rule, I get someone to look after them. Where there's a will there's a way. The children are a difficulty at nights; but there's more put on the children's backs than they are responsible for."

There was no need for our man to put the next question, as to health. Mrs. Keegan is the pink of strength and good spirits.

"But even if the open-airs and meetings were hard upon me," said Mrs. Keegan, voluntarily, "we didn't come into the War expecting an easy path."

"What do you consider is the principal difficulty that an F.O. has to fight—money?"

"No."

"Backsliders?"

"No."

"What then?"

"Making converts into fighting, believing, conquering soldiers."

"I think you are right, Mrs. Keegan. How do you account for it?"

"There is not one thing in particular. There are many things. But I should say—Fear of reproach and humiliation ranks first. I generally find that behind the so-called objections to the jersey and the bonnet and The Army's methods and doctrines, pride is the greatest thing we have to fight. We can't afford to compromise as other people do, or we should sell our power to the enemy."

"Is there any other cause you would name?"

"The small love of principle that exists about Divine realities, I think, springs from superficial reading of the Bible and poor training of children."

"Any others?"

"The world. We are a separate people, and unless our converts are instructed in the sense and teaching of our separation, we can't keep them very long."

Mrs. Keegan has the root of the matter in her.

iv
Women Warriors

ALTHOUGH born under the sound of "Bow bells," all the school-days of Clarissa Lewis were spent at Cheshunt, Herts. Her father dying when she was quite young, her mother was left with three little ones, and being anxious to shield her only girl from the snares of the world, did her part well by creating a Christlike home influence and making little Clarissa a special matter of prayer, which the Lord in a wonderful way answered.

Returning to London while yet in her teens, there were strong desires in her young heart for worldly pleasures. Not being able to have them gratified, she thought it hard, and inwardly rebelled; but the Holy Spirit was doing its work even then.

For the second time she felt her terrible sinful condition in His sight, and attended some revival services, hoping to get that pardon and peace that her soul longed for. To a certain extent she was helped in the right direction, but was Far from Satisfied.

The General was at the same chapel one Bank Holiday, and led some real Holy Ghost meetings in it; but she could only sit, watch and wonder at the earnestness and enthusiasm of those Salvation soldiers. Oh, how they prayed! No one-knee business, but flat on their faces they besieged the Throne of Grace.

There was no getting away from it—she was not living up to her privileges, and from that time felt more than ever dissatisfied with herself. Then, with one of her brothers, she began to attend the historical Whitechapel Corps and in one of Mr. Bramwell Booth's Friday night meetings she gave soul and body unreservedly to God. This was in February, '81.

From that hour she was a different girl. All desire for things of the world were completely gone. Selfishness was lost in love. Now her whole heart was filled with a compassionate love for sinners.

Capt. Baugh was in charge at that time, and, with his permission, she would go with two or three others, directly the Sunday's morning meeting was over, and hold an open-air service in the neighbourhood, dinner being a Very Secondary

THE WAR CRY

Piece of Business. The crowds generally were tremendous, while the uproar was awful, but the brave lasses stood to their guns and the Spirit germinated in many hearts to life everlasting.

Clarissa Lewis and Lucy Read had the honour of being the first two tambourine players in the corps. The latter is now well-known as Mrs. Major Unsworth. Says our comrade: "If it did nothing else it attracted many of our old friends to the barracks who never before had been in a Salvation Army meeting."

It was when the Maréchale farewelled for France in the St. James' Hall that she decided to become an officer. Shortly after she paid a visit to Miss Emma Booth, at Gore Road, when she received Candidate's papers. For nearly twelve months these were kept, to be read, re-read and prayed over.

She felt the importance of taking the step, yet God had called, she dare not refuse; so the battle was bravely fought, and the victory won.

Her Cadet days, spent at Clapton, were helpful and happy. In that same place of renown the late Mrs. Cooke, Mrs. Keetch, and Mrs. Harding were also taking their degrees.

In the beginning of '83 she was commissioned for Glasgow IV., and here she well proved that "His strength is made perfect in weakness." God sealed her first command by saving souls from the beginning of the seven months' stay to the end, and she is assured that many bright, sparkling gems from Cowcaddens will decorate the Saviour's crown who were saved from the depths of sin.

Then came a blessed soul-saving stay at Paisley I., where she followed Capt. Hannah Franks, now in Heaven. Here also the Great Physician cleansed and healed, making many aching, desolate hearts rejoice. Subsequently she did some specialling, and while holding on at Battersea I. orders came for the sunny shores of Australia. In a short time she set sail for Sydney, at which memorable place Her Name was Changed from Lewis to Lindsay. The first meetings here were held in the Exhibition Building, which seated about ten thousand people, and crowds of all sorts and conditions of men were converted to God every Sunday night for seven months.

In travelling throughout the Colonies of New South Wales, South Australia, and the Ballarat Division, she was privileged to help many hundreds into the Kingdom of Christ.

While in Australasia God gave her three children, but one of these sweet flowers He transplanted to blossom more profusely in the Eden above, filling her place by another, who was born in England.

Midnight meetings were held in Adelaide, for to Mrs. Lindsay the Rescue Work was a great delight, while a Home was opened in Sydney. Many a successful chase has she had after some poor, deluded girl, and many are living good lives to-day.

The last five years have been spent in England, where she has been a blessing and inspiration to thousands, and the means in His hands of leading many precious souls to the feet of the Master. "How Is It," said a lassie Captain to us once, at the close of an officers' meeting, "that I get more lasting good from Mrs. Lindsay's words than from anyone else?" We think the secret is this: She is a woman of prayer, her words are heartfelt; no talk for the sake of talking with her, but with a burning desire to help and be of practical service, and He who knows us through and through gives His own the desire of her heart.

Physical weakness has been, and still is, a great drawback to her fighting spirit, and one has only to look upon the fragile-looking figure and pale, thin face, to feel this fact.

"Ah!" she says, "it's a trial, because I feel so keenly the terrible state of the unsaved and the shortness and uncertainty of time; my heart is all aflame for the salvation of the lost."

2.5

The Mission to the Jews

2.5 The Mission to the Jews

The Mission to the Jews was both a foreign and a home mission. Many Christians believed that the salvation of the world, and the second coming of Christ, were events dependent on the restoration of the Jews to Israel and their conversion to Christianity (see the poem on this theme by Charlotte Tonna in this volume, Biblical History, Geography and Travel Writing). The London Society for Promoting Christianity Among the Jews (LSPCJ) refers to this millenarian reason for missionary work at the end of its report of 1835, when it suggests that all 'who seriously study the Word of God, and attentively mark the character of passing events' will understand the urgency of this mission. As well as the LSPCJ's *Jewish Intelligence,* a number of periodicals focused on the mission to the Jews, and *The Christian Lady's Friend* included the mission alongside other domestic Christian issues (see this volume, Fidelity in the Upper Classes, for another article from this magazine). As with the foreign mission movement, biography was an important tool for the mission to the Jews, and this is how Osborn Trenery Heighway styled his narrative of a Jewish convert, *Leila Ada*.

Jewish Intelligence was an official publication of the LSPCJ, and communicated news of both the home and foreign mission. The abstract of the society's Annual Report extracted here details some of the activities being carried out in England, especially schools for the young, and conferences for the adult population. In some ways, their missionary activities are reported in a similar way to those of foreign missions. The main incident stressed in the operation of the schools is the death of a young convert. Though this is not characteristic of domestic mission life, it is described in the same way as the death of a foreign convert would be, and the hope is that such a deathbed scene will have an effect in Bethnal Green as it would elsewhere in the mission field. However, the way that conferences are described highlights the different character of a domestic from a foreign mission, in that the mission to London's East End Jews is being carried out among a people who can not only speak the same language as the missionaries, but also have the knowledge and education to argue against Christianity. Not to be discouraged, the society suggests that the opposition and 'hostility' they encounter in fact demonstrate how seriously the Jewish community takes the mission.

The evangelical periodical, *The Christian Lady's Friend*, regularly took up the cause of Jewish conversion. The piece extracted here is a report, written by a convert, of a visit to a chapel of Jewish Christian converts. The visit takes place at a highly symbolic time – the Passover – so that as the writer witnesses the converts celebrating the Last Supper, they can imagine other Jews still blindly celebrating an out-of-date 'dispensation' at synagogue. The author reveals that it is not only converts who attend this chapel, but also unconverted Jews and gentiles, swelling the numbers of the congregation so that they have outgrown the chapel and require new premises. The author is inspired by this example of inclusion and sees it as a particularly Christian phenomenon: the breaking down of barriers is attributed to Christ's atonement; it is the Redeemer's goodness that recalls the unconverted Jews – the stray sheep – to the fold; and it is Christianity alone that seems to have the ability to unite the 'whole church' in a mysterious spirituality, which the author insists 'Christians only know'.

Despite its claims of authenticity, Heighway's narrative of a Jewish convert, Leila Ada, is most likely fiction. In his introduction, Heighway problematises evangelicals' strict adherence to truth as he argues the necessity of depicting conversion narratives as poetically sublime. Heighway insists on the physical beauty of his heroine, as well as the beauty of her exemplary life and all-important death. Not only does he claim that this beauty stems from God, and that it is therefore correctly Christian to appreciate it, but he also argues that deathbed scenes should be drawn poetically in order to 'allure the heart and soothe and exalt the soul'. This expected effect on readers suggests the utility of the deathbed scene – whether authentic or fictional – in prompting readers to a more religious life, and to support the mission. In a similar way to the biographers of the Indian and African converts, Ramabai and Crowther (see this volume, Women and Authority in the Mission Field, and Masculinity and Leadership), Heighway emphasises Ada's humility, to suggest the unimportance of the individual life in comparison with the cause for which it is used. Like the British women missionaries, or the unlikely African Bishop, Ada is cast as an instrument of God, her human frailty only underscoring the supernatural power of Christianity to convert all nations – even the 'House of Israel'.

23

LONDON SOCIETY FOR PROMOTING CHRISTIANITY AMONGST THE JEWS, 'ABSTRACT OF THE 27TH REPORT'

Jewish Intelligence, 1835,
pp. 6–8, 15–16

[...] Schools.—Your Committee have to report with much satisfaction and thankfulness to God, the continued prosperity of your Schools for Jewish children, although the number is not so large at present as at some former periods. There are now thirty-one boys and thirty-two girls in the Schools. Since the last Anniversary seven boys have been admitted, three have been apprenticed to very eligible situations, and one has died. The occurrence of a death in your Schools has been very rare, and your Committee venture to hope that the following particulars of this recent instance may not be uninteresting:—

On Friday, January 30, after a long and lingering illness, died Jonathan Delevante, aged nine years and eight months. His mind and body were both too much enfeebled for a considerable time to permit him to enter into a lengthened conversion; but he had been early instructed in the knowledge of the Gospel, and he was continually reminded of the love of that Saviour who is the only hope of dying sinners, and who said, "Suffer little children to come unto me."

As it respects the state of his mind during his illness, he was at all times patient, and willingly took any medicine, or submitted to anything proposed for his recovery. When spoken to on the subject of his eternal interests, he said but little; and, on being informed of the prospect of dissolution, he evinced much uneasiness, and said, he should not like to die. Eventually, however, he became quite resigned, and said, he should like to be with Jesus. When spoken to on the subject of prayer, and asked if he ever prayed to Jesus, he replied, "Yes, often," and being asked what he prayed for, he replied, "That God would forgive all his sins, and when he died take him up to heaven to dwell with Him." The last few days he was incapable of speaking much, but still very patient and thankful for what was done for him: he manifested signs of consciousness to the last, and died without a struggle. We doubt not that he fell asleep in Jesus, and departed hence to be with Christ, which is far better.

On the following Wednesday afternoon, Feb. 4, he was buried at the parish church of St. Matthew, Bethnal Green. His parents and brothers followed as mourners, and the children of the Hebrew Schools attended the funeral. As the procession moved along, it seemed to excite much interest, and some hundreds of persons, children and adults, followed to the church and the grave. The same evening a funeral sermon, particularly addressed to children, was preached in the Episcopal Jews' Chapel by the Rev. M. S. Alexander, and the attendance of a large congregation again showed the interest which was felt on this occasion.

Your Committee are accustomed to keep a watchful eye over the children for some time after they have left the Schools. In the case of the boys who are put apprentice, they make regular inquiries into their conduct and progress during the whole period of their apprenticeship. They regularly appear with their masters before a Sub-Committee at the Schools at least once a-year, when, if their conduct is approved, small rewards are assigned to them, a moiety of which is always retained in the hands of your Committee, to be given to them at the termination of their engagement. At this time twenty-one boys are serving their apprenticeships to various trades with satisfaction to their masters; and of seventy-two boys who have left the Schools during the last thirteen years, your Committee, after particular inquiry, are only acquainted with eight cases in which they are not conducting themselves in a creditable manner, and even of these none have relapsed into Judaism. Amongst the many who in their general conduct give satisfaction, there are several who are affording pleasing evidence of their genuine piety.

Conferences.—On Saturday, the 11th of November, the Conferences at No. 18, Aldermanbury, were resumed, and continued to the 21st of March. At first attendance of Jews was small, and there seemed on their part no inclination to speak. The number, however, gradually increased, and some of the speakers at the former conferences appeared to advocate Judaism, or to offer their objections against Christianity. It had been the intention of the Christian speakers to go regularly through the objections advanced by Rabbi Isaac, in his famous book called the Chizzuk Emunah, and a great number of these objections were actually brought forward and replied to; one Christian speaker taking the objections derived from the Old Testament, and another those directed against the New Testament, as they are found in the first and second parts of the above-named book. It was not possible, however, to adhere strictly to this plan, as the Jewish speakers brought forward many independent arguments. One speaker, for instance, attacked the authenticity and genuineness of the Gospels. Another adopted the Socinian line of argumentation, and endeavoured to show that the doctrines of the Trinity, and divinity of the Lord Jesus Christ, are not to be found in the New Testament. A third Jewish speaker endeavoured to show that the New Testament was invented and written by persons who did not understand Hebrew, but had been misled by the Septuagint version. These objections all required distinct answers, and this interfered with the plan originally proposed, at the same time that it afforded an opportunity of exhibiting the great variety and power of the evidences of the truth of Christianity.

Some of the speakers seemed to think, that an attack upon the London Society was more easy and more profitable than a discussion of the arguments upon which Christianity rests. They therefore endeavoured to show that it is not an efficient instrument in promoting Christianity amongst the Jews, and gravely marked out a different line of operations, which, as they thought, the Committee ought to adopt. All such attacks are, in one point of view, regarded with pleasure by your Committee, and hailed as a token of the efficiency of those means which they employ. Systematic opposition proves two important facts; first, that the Jewish nation is awake and sensible of the efforts that are making to spread the knowledge of Christ amongst them. Secondly, that they do not disregard them as powerless or contemptible, but think it quite worth their while to attempt to put them down. Hostility on the part of the Jews to the London Society is one of the most decided testimonies to its efficiency, and this testimony is now abundantly given. But your Committee does not need evidence of this sort. Believing the New Testament, they are convinced that the Gospel is the power of God unto salvation, and therefore rejoice that at these conferences of the past season, all the leading and saving truths of this Gospel have been faithfully and uncompromisingly proclaimed to many Jews, who would otherwise, perhaps, have had no opportunity of hearing them. The whole Jewish congregation have thus had a public testimony to the fact, that there are some at least in the Christian Church who are deeply interested in their temporal and eternal welfare; and even those who have never been present, have had a weekly admonition to repent and believe in the Lord Jesus Christ. Your Committee rejoice to add, that the conferences closed in a most kindly spirit on both sides, and that many Christians have been led to feel a deeper interest in the spiritual welfare of Israel. [...]

[...] In closing this Report, your Committee would earnestly press upon you the necessity for increased exertion. They have lately received most encouraging proofs of a growing attachment to the cause in which they are engaged. Yet, notwithstanding the increase of funds which they have this day thankfully announced, the means at their disposal are still inadequate to the demands made upon them. There is a pressing call for a large and liberal diffusion of the Word of God among His ancient people; there are openings for Jewish schools; there is a great want of tracts, and other suitable publications, in Hebrew and other languages, to meet the inquiring spirit of the Jews; there is a demand for Missionary labourers, especially clergymen of the Church of England, to occupy some of the most important posts in the Jewish Missionary field.

Your Committee cannot but see, in common with many pious and distinguished friends of the Jewish cause, and, they may almost add, in common with all who seriously study the Word of God, and attentively mark the character of passing events, that this is peculiarly the time for active exertion amongst the Jews. The history, condition, and prospects of the Jews are exciting increased attention in the world at large—great changes are taking place in the Jewish mind—and the eyes of serious Christians are opening more and more to the great purposes of Jehovah respecting this wonderful people, as revealed in the Scriptures.

For themselves, they desire the Divine influences of the Holy Spirit, to awaken a more lively sense of the obligations and privileges connected with this great cause. The Word of Truth declares that the Lord Jesus Christ is to be the glory of His people Israel. That He has not cast away His people, but that with everlasting kindness will he gather them, saith the Lord, their Redeemer. Almighty God himself has given us a solemn charge to hear his Word, and to declare it in the isles afar off, and to say, "He that scattered Israel will gather him, and keep him as a shepherd doth his flock." Your undertaking rests upon the most scriptural warrant; your hope is founded upon the undeniable promises of the Eternal God; the very details of your duty are thus minutely set forth in his Word, "Prepare ye the way of the people; cast up, cast up the highway; gather out the stones; lift up a standard for the people." Nor would it be possible to enforce the universal obligation to join in this work of promoting Christianity among the Jews in stronger and clearer language than that Word employs—"Behold! the Lord hath proclaimed unto the end of the world, Say ye to the daughter of Zion, Behold, thy salvation cometh!"

24

'A VISIT TO THE CHAPEL OF THE HEBREW CHRISTIAN BRETHREN IN LONDON BY A CONVERTED ISRAELITE'

The Christian Lady's Friend and Family Repository, May 1832, pp. 421–423

The best interests of Israel lay very near my heart, and the true peace of Jerusalem is inexpressibly dear to me. I have the privilege of knowing personally several of the Hebrew Christian brethren and sisters of the above community, and love them in the Lord, giving thanks to his holy name for the grace vouchsafed to them. May they increase daily in all spiritual wisdom and knowledge, abound in good works, flowing from that faith which is the gift of God and worketh by love, and prosper before the Lord, until the little one is become a thousand! Even so, if it be thy will, Lord Jesus!

I have been privileged to know, love, and worship a covenant God in Christ many years, and having so much love to my brethren, it appears strange to say, this is my first visit to their chapel. But Providence has so cast my lot, that never before could I have this gratification. Nevertheless, by that mysterious but real communion of spirit, which unites the whole church in one indissoluble bond of love, joy, and peace, in the Holy Ghost, I have joined them more than once, at their "hour of prayer." Wonderful union! Christians only know the blissful privilege of meeting in spirit at the throne of grace!

In the evening of April the fourteenth, the Jewish nation celebrated the passover. Consequently, Sunday, the fifteenth, was the first day of that festival with the Jews. It was therefore a memorable period of time, and feelings of mingled joy and awe stole over my mind, as I entered the very small chapel in which a little band of converted Israelites were assembled to worship the true Paschal Lamb— the Lord Jesus Christ;—while their benighted brethren were also assembled in their synagogues to celebrate, with veiled hearts, and eyes holden from discerning truth, the shadowy type of a shadowy dispensation, long since fulfilled and passed away. Such an exhibition of omnipotent power, such a visible manifestation of sovereign grace, on the one hand, and the other, could not but mingle profound

HOME MISSIONS

reverence with the most ardent thanksgivings, as I took my seat amidst this gracious earnest of a more abundant harvest, these few berries from the topmost bough. Self-abasement at my own station among this little flock, gave a needful counterpoise to feelings that else had been too ecstatic.

But the service has commenced. The children of Israel are singing the praises of Jesus the Messiah—*their* Messiah! If ever I was privileged to taste a feeling of pure happiness, wholly unmixed with the base alloy of self, it was at this moment. What! the children of those who cried "Crucify him," called by grace and enabled to worship and sing praises to that Jesus whom their fathers pierced! With heart and eyes overflowing I could not but exclaim, mentally, "O the depth of the riches both of the wisdom and knowledge of God! how unsearchable are his judgments, and his ways past finding out."

The Jewish brother whom the Lord has been pleased to place over this little band, delivered a good and scriptural discourse from these heart-reviving words, "I am the Lord that healeth thee." Exod. xv. 26. The text was given in Hebrew and English.

It was a word in season at this time of extraordinary sickness, but the chief aim of this son of Abraham was to glorify Jehovah, Father, Son, and Spirit, Israel's one God, which he did with a degree of energy evidently heartfelt. I could not but remark that the manner in which our dear brother illustrated his text, was peculiarly adapted to a Jewish auditory; by which term I more especially mean an assembly of *unconverted* Jews, and many of them are in the habit of coming to this chapel; for, in the course of the sermon, he bore a noble testimony to "the truth as it is in Jesus," in a manner unbelievers *might* scoff at, but *could not* gainsay.

The afternoon service was devoted to the administration of the Lord's supper. Never did I see the condescending goodness of the great Redeemer more powerfully displayed than in thus calling to the feast of incarnate love, these stray sheep of the Jewish fold. It was truly a time of refreshing from the presence of the Lord. And there, too, was set before us the partition wall evidently broken down by the atonement; for Gentiles have joined themselves to these believing Jews; and in one holy bond of christian love and unity, did they partake the blessed symbols of dying love and grace ineffable. This little church has lately received an accession of twenty Gentiles and three Jews to its number. A Jewess was baptized by them a fortnight since, and more are expected to come forward. There are now, I believe, about sixty members. Their chapel is so small that numbers cannot obtain admittance; and as the lease of it expires at Christmas, and it is much out of repair, they intend to hire or build a place of worship as soon as sufficient funds are collected for that purpose. May the Lord, in whose hands are all hearts, incline affluence to give of its stores in aid of their pious endeavour to preach Jesus among their brethren.

On the whole, I have had much spiritual enjoyment in this visit to my beloved brethren. May the blessing of our covenant God be upon them! May He make them strong in Christ Jesus, rich in faith, and zealous for good works!

25

OSBORN W. TRENERY HEIGHWAY, *LEILA ADA: THE JEWISH CONVERT, AN AUTHENTIC MEMOIR* [1852]

(London: Partridge, Oakey and Co., 1854),
pp. vii–xiii, 88–96

Introductory Remarks on the Third Edition

The young lady who is the subject of this memoir was, as its title indicates, a Jewess by birth. The majestic beauty of the religion of Jesus has, in all ages, obtained its finest representatives from the house of Israel: and among the many lovely examples of sublime attainment in the Divine life made by Hebrew Christians, Leila Ada is not one of the least conspicuous. What she appears in the record of her now presented that she was in real life, a pure, holy, humble Christian—a Christian hallowed, sublimed, etherealized by the influences of the Holy Spirit.

Leila is a character of undoubted loveliness: but she is not in the *very least* degree an ideal. We have been scrupulously exact in our descriptions and comments throughout. We have written from knowledge obtained through personal acquaintance of the dearest kind.

Leila was one of those fair and flower-like natures, which at intervals rise to cheer us along the dusty highways of life; but she was a plant which flourished in the shade, and her real worth was known to very few. Her natural abilities were of the highest order, and she had cultivated them with the strictest care; so that had God seen it fitting to spare her life and call her to a more public situation, she would have occupied no humble position among those noble-souled and intellectual women who are an honour to our country. She was one of the loveliest flowers that ever gleamed in the cold atmosphere of a world of sin; a flower fragile in its pensile form, delicate in its tender purity, spiritual in its beauty; too frail to live amidst these tempestuous clouds of earth, and only at home in the kindlier soil and among the stormless skies of "the better land."

All Leila's papers are given *verbatim et literatim*. Write incorrectly she could not. A thoughtful, reflective mind she always had. Although her language is in some places diffuse and inartificial, we could not feel at liberty to alter it. We felt (and perhaps our feeling may be smiled at—let it be even so,) that Leila would never have consented to any similiar mode of procedure while she lived; to be truthfully exact was always the rule of her conduct; and that if she were cognisant of our occupations now that she were in the skies, she would regard such disguise with even less allowance still. It is almost unnecessary for us to say that she never expected anything she wrote would be given to the world.

We have written, we trust, with a single heart—with a pure intention that God may be glorified. To Him Leila was indebted for whatever she was. That in every respect she fully realized the picture of her which we have drawn, we are assured. We say this from a calm, unprejudiced, deliberative judgment. Were we to speak as we *feel,* we should be at once inclined to say, that her sweet Christianity could be estimated at its proper value only in the hearts of those who knew her while she was upon earth—that any attempt to give in writing an adequate idea of her character must of necessity fall short.

It is very possible that, after all, some right-hearted people may object to the way in which we have written some parts of her memoir. Before they say a single word we would beg them kindly to pause and think WHY they object. Is it because of our references to personal appearance? We are clear in this matter. We believe it to be one of the noblest, and one of the most proper employments of the Christian, to trace out and thankfully admire the beauty of the Creator in all His works. And is the human form—most beautiful of all beauties—to be *the* thing which must neither be thought nor spoken of? If so—why? Why did God make it beautiful—"very good," as He Himself pronounced? In His own blessed word the descriptions of human beauty are neither few nor sparing. Is it because we have allowed to imaginative feeling rather more license than the stereotype forms of religious biography permit? In this matter also we humbly think that our gracious Redeemer will approve our conduct. It is high time, indeed, that Christian biographies were cast in a new mould. It is a false and a cruel law which compels us to have recourse to fiction, if we would obtain pictures of dying scenes, &c., drawn with all those soft poetic touches which insensibly allure the heart and soothe and exalt the soul. Is it not true, that the love of Jesus shed abroad in the heart, has moulded characters which in fineness, consistence, sublimity, far exceed any of the creations of imagination? Father!—mother, bereaved! we beg you to vindicate us in this matter. Is it possible for the liveliest imagination to depicture any beauty which will surpass the peculiar graces, the tender charms, the dying moments of your loved one who is not? Oh, no! The last hours of those who have lived wholly devoted to Jesus, are surrounded by a loveliness so celestial, a radiance so divinely beautiful, that the most glowing pencil can but faintly shadow it forth.

In David's beautiful lament over Saul and Jonathan, did he think it proper to embellish with his imagination? or did he confine himself to a mere iteration of cold matter-of-fact?

In these popular days we must have popularized thinking, popularized feeling, popularized writing, popularized preaching; and rapidly are we approaching a state in which we must have a popularized Christianity—a popularized Gospel! May the Spirit of God interpose: or Christianity will soon mean little more than one of the fine arts,—a system of moral requirements and observances, to be always accommodated to time, circumstances, and national peculiarities of character.

The Spirit of Christ is love—all love—nothing else but love. In this Spirit His disciples are commanded to clothe themselves. When will it be?

If only twenty of His followers would this hour resolve henceforth to exhibit the spirit—the whole spirit, of the Gospel, what a heaven would be introduced into our country before the present generation has passed away!

It is under the influence of such feelings as these, that we have made our sketches of Leila Ada.

For when we had indulged our fancy and feeling to the utmost, we should still fail in depicting the sweet hush, and the celestial peace and love, which surrounded her as she sunk into the tomb. In her short Christian course, she walked with God; and her dying weeks were lived upon the very verge of heaven.

Finally, we again repeat that we have nowhere written one word, look, or expression which is not most exact to the truth. Our dear relative, Miss H. (*the* Miss H. whose friendship with Leila is noticed in the Memoir itself), once said to us—*"Such* a life, and *such* a death. You cannot possibly give it a beauty which it did not really possess."

Osborn W. Trenery Heighway

Chapter VII

Leila's conversion

We are now brought to the most interesting portion of Leila's life—her conversion to Christianity.

It has already appeared that her belief in the tenets of Judaism had received an irremediable shake; the absurd fables of the Talmud were cast aside as unworthy of a thought, and the trammels of rabbinical authority completely burst asunder. On her return to England she was only waiting for more instruction in the articles of the Christian belief, to dispose her to embrace it with all her heart. One of her first objects, therefore, was, she says, "to find a company of simple, earnest Christians."

At a small village, distant about three miles from her residence, there was a chapel in which was exercised such a ministry as she desired. This was the nearest place of Christian worship which presented itself, and it was here she began to attend. Being aware that a knowledge of this would call down the severest displeasure of her father, her visits to it were by stealth, and, chiefly indeed, except in one or two instances, solely by night; and she always sat closely veiled. The way to the chapel was through a long, dreary, and solitary lane; but, at all hours, when it was possible for her to be present at the services, Leila might be found, unattended, wending her way among the gloomy trees. Her natural timidity was painful, and her dread of walking alone at night unconquerable, until now that an earnest desire for the salvation of her soul made her superior to any bodily fear she might entertain. In her own pleasing way, she says, "I was dreadfully frightened during my first essays in the dark, I usually ran the very utmost of the distance that I could; my agitation and terror of mind being, during the whole time, indescribable. Hurrying in this manner, the whole distance from our house to the chapel was frequently done in a few minutes over half-an-hour; but, by prayer, all my terror was removed, and although I continued to be just as fearful of going anywhere else, yet I could always go to, and return from, my dear chapel without the slightest perturbation of mind, feeling quite sure that my Father would give me His protection."

We have said that, during the first part of her attendance, she kept herself strictly secret, even from the congregation; but, as the influence of the Holy Spirit applied each discourse more and more powerfully to her mind, this fear subsided, and, in proportion, she felt an increased desire to unbosom herself to some Christian friend, who would sympathize with, and still further instruct her in that glorious cause to which she had now engaged her whole heart. Being assured that this would assist her to the attainment of that peace she so ardently desired, she conferred not with flesh and blood, but, with that fearless decision in favour of duty which ever characterized her, she resolved to seek an interview with her minister. This was easily obtained; and she describes it as "a blessed season:" and says, further, "It has stirred me up to seek the Lord fully—to agonize with a determination not to rest till I am accepted in the Saviour—till my mourning is turned into joy." And, again, "O, for that earnest, child-like simplicity and faith of which Mr. —— [her minister] told me. I want to take the Word of God simply, just as it is. This is the faith of the New Testament: this is the faith God requires, and will have, in order to my salvation. Lord, save me! increase my faith; increase it largely—mightily; confirm my hope, and fan my love for Thee into a mighty flame!"

She was an earnest and humble seeker of the truth as it is in Jesus. Her heart had now become intent upon one great business—the salvation of her soul, and to this end she used every means, and every effort, regardless of personal consequences. This we think, is abundantly set forth in the entries made in her diary at this important period. We make a scanty extract:—

"O, that I could express half that I feel of love to that gracious Being who has kept me hitherto, and led me from my deep darkness into spiritual light. I have not yet the evidence that He has pardoned my sins through the blood of the Atonement—through my Jesus, but I earnestly pray for it; I am determined to agonize for it in simple faith. I know, I believe—oh, yes! *I do believe*—that Jesus died for me. I thirst, I pant for the Spirit of adoption, whereby I shall be enabled to cry, 'Abba, Father.'

"O, my Father, I thank thee; I adore and praise Thy holy name, that Thou hast removed from my heart that dark, impervious veil which so long separated between me and Thyself, and so between me and the source of all happiness. Now through Thine infinite mercy, I behold Thy glory, who art full of grace and truth, and the form and comeliness of Him who is altogether lovely, even the Saviour and Preserver of my soul." [...]

[...] And in a very little time after this she was enabled to rejoice in the God of her salvation; her heart was filled with joy and gladness, and her mouth with praise. This delightful change took place while receiving the sacrament of the Lord's Supper, after having been dedicated to God in baptism. In her diary she thus refers to it:—

"Bless the Lord, O my soul, and never forget this day's benefits! I have sealed the covenant—have enlisted under the banners of the cross, by receiving the ordinances of baptism and the Lord's supper—but, let me write while my eyes overflow with tears of joy—*my gracious Redeemer has manifested His presence to my soul, has filled me with the joy and peace of believing.* That blood which the Jews have imprecated upon themselves and their children, has been showered upon me, in the most abundant and unspeakable mercies; I am happy beyond expression; I do, indeed, rejoice with a joy that is unspeakable and full of glory. I feel on the very verge of heaven; I have experienced a glorious elevation of soul—*Christ is mine and I am His.* Unspeakably happy conviction! Come unto me all ye that fear God, and I will tell you what He hath done for my soul! Bless the Lord, O my soul, and never forget this day's benefits.

"It is a solemn season, a day to be held in everlasting remembrance. When the cup was held to me and the solemn words were pronounced—'The blood of Jesus Christ, which was shed for thee, preserve thy soul and body unto everlasting life! Drink this in remembrance that Christ's blood was shed for thee, and be thankful—I felt that my God was reconciled through my Saviour's death, and I was enabled to feed upon Christ in my heart through faith, and with thanksgiving.

"O, my Jesus, help me now to *persevere!* There are heights and depths in religion which I long to experience: my soul is on fire with the Divine love. Help me to tell to all what a gracious, what a mighty Saviour Thou art. May no motives of personal comfort induce me to swerve from the character of an Israelite indeed, in whom is no guile. O, that Thou wouldst give me Thine assistance, and direct me by Thy Holy Spirit, *while I make it known to my dear father!* Do, O my Saviour, hear my prayer for this, and to Thee I will give all the glory, now and through endless ages. Amen.

"I bless and adore Thee—Father, Son, and Holy Ghost, that all have united to deliver me from my guilt and bondage. And now, O God, my heart is fixed: my heart is fixed to *live* in Christ. Nothing but the *constant* indwelling of Thyself will satisfy my soul. O, for that mysterious and incomprehensible union with my God which shall produce in me mighty faith, ardent love, lively hope, and active obedience. Blessed be God, all this is promised! I believe it. Who shall circumscribe the Holy One? He can so touch the heart as to extirpate sin, and save with this full salvation; for it shall be my never-ceasing prayer. Lord enable me to feel myself as nothing, and Thou my all. Keep me in the hollow of Thy hand. Prepare me for all Thy righteous will, for I have given up all my soul and body's powers fully and unreservedly to Thee. O, accept my sacrifice; enter into covenant with me and ratify it in Heaven. Amen."

Leila's baptism was an interesting—a singularly lovely scene. We do not expect ever to witness another equally affecting on earth. It was our privilege to be one of four friends who at her request waited near her during the performance of the solemn ceremony. Arrangements had been made to prevent the gaze of inquisitive and idle curiosity, by ensuring that none but regular members of the congregation should be present. At the appointed time Leila was led from the vestry, her pure countenance having in its expression more of heaven than of earth. Her answers to the questions were made in a calm and decided, but weak and tremulous tone; for she was bathed in tears. Indeed, we think all present wept with deep emotion. The solemn act of baptizing her in the name of the Triune Jehovah having been performed, the minister delivered an exquisitely touching and beautiful address. This finished, the sacrament of the Lord's supper was administered to all present, which concluded a season of hallowed and holy influence never to be forgotten.

Having herself become acquainted with the truth as it is in Jesus, she wept as she thought of the darkness which still surrounded her dear father; she felt that her Christianity, and, indeed, every natural feeling was involved, if she made no effort to induce him to renounce Judaism. But how was she to proceed? To obtain an answer to this question cost her much mental agony. To her father she was tenderly devoted, and she knew that he was a strict believer in the faith of his fathers; and, therefore, all the prejudices of his mind would be strongly against her Christianity. To the present period in her life he had never once spoken to her with a look or tone of displeasure, and she had at no time crossed his will, nor done anything to which he would not give permission; but God was with her, and through the fortitude of Christian principle, she was enabled to dare the worst. And unquestionably, if we reflect a moment upon the Jewish character, we shall perceive that she had *cause* to fear this would not be a little.

Part 3

REFORMING PRIVATE LIFE

3.1

Temperance

3.1 Temperance

The Temperance movement had its origins in the evangelicalism of the early nineteenth century, along with other campaigns to reform the manners and everyday lives of citizens so that they were more compatible with Christian life (see Volume I, Evangelical Religion). Religious societies promoted the use of tracts and other literature to influence the working classes in particular to change their ways, and temperance literature became an important genre of the early and mid-century. Temperance became associated with radical social groups such as the Chartists, who mobilised a growing working-class consciousness of sober respectability to emphasise that they deserved the vote as much as the often intemperate upper classes.

William Gaskell (1805–1884) was a Unitarian minister and the husband of the novelist Elizabeth Gaskell. His *Temperance Rhymes* are explicitly didactic, which is made clear in his dedication to the 'Working Men of Manchester', among whom he worked. The first section is devoted to poems which show the negative effects of intemperance on working-class domestic relations, and the second to poems about temperate and moral domestic life in the same class, as a contrasting ideal for his readers to emulate. The poems extracted here from the first section of the work present the evils of intemperance in ways that became common in temperance literature from the 1840s onwards. For example, both poems present the male drunk as a debased figure whose intemperance has starved his family; the causal relation between drunkenness and poverty is made plain. Although not explicitly presented, violence and ill-treatment are hinted at in the anguished, 'martyred', and forgiving wives. Sentimentality characterises all the poems, especially in the form of innocent 'little Jane', in her 'tiny shroud/Like a snow-drop crushed'. Interestingly, the first two poems of the second section appear to refer to Scottish or Welsh working-class families, suggesting that William Gaskell believed intemperance to be a particular evil of the English city.

It is probable that Elizabeth Gaskell assisted William in writing *Temperance Rhymes*, as she supported his work with the Manchester poor, and as he assisted with her writing. The depiction of the working-class domestic relationships in *Rhymes* is not dissimilar to that drawn in Elizabeth's novel *Mary Barton*, and the Welsh tradition of exclaiming 'Nefoedd iddo' – 'Heaven to him' – that inspires the second of the more positive poems was most likely known to the Gaskells through Elizabeth's Welsh connections. (For a discussion of religion in Elizabeth Gaskell's literary work, see Volume III, Shame.)

The typical RTS temperance tract reproduced in this section begins with a story from the Classics. While the Classical story suggests that complete abstinence is best – Cyrus the Great does not drink from the cup of his drunken grandfather – the tract, like much of the movement at this time, recommends temperance instead, criticising only *excessive* drinking. This alarming phenomenon it paints in vivid colours. The scenes depicted of intemperance among the poor are the most dramatic: there are the usual images of a drunken man's family suffering his anger, living lives of abject poverty, but the tract also highlights the 'hideous' spectacle of 'mothers staggering with infants in their arms'. Young men and women from more affluent homes are also warned of what they will sacrifice by indulging too frequently: young women are reminded of the importance of reputation, delicacy, 'loveliness', and both sexes are warned of the degradation and degeneration that a habit of drunkenness can lead to, and the psychological suffering it can cause. Interestingly, the tract employs scientific, medical language to describe the course of addiction that some of its readers might recognise, and refers to drunkenness as an infectious disease in families. Its final threat though is spiritual, in that drunkards will suffer eternal damnation.

26

WILLIAM GASKELL, 'DREAD MEMORIES!', 'A MOTHER'S DEATH-SONG FOR HER CHILD', 'PARTING WORDS' AND 'HEAVEN TO THEE!'

In *Temperance Rhymes* (London: Simpkin, Marshall and Co., 1839), pp. 15–17, 23, 67–69, 70–71

To the Working-Men of Manchester these rhymes are inscribed; in the hope that they may act as another small weight on the right end of that lever which is to raise them in the scale of humanity

Dread Memories!

Though no blood is on my hand,
    There is murder on my soul;
And a pale, pale spectre-band
    Round my pillow nightly roll!

First there comes my martyred wife,
    With her gentle face of woe,
As it looked, when out of life
    Faintly sighed she, 'I must go';
When so tenderly she told me,
    The past was all forgiven;
And she prayed she might behold me,
    In the happy homes of heaven!

Next there comes my little Jane,
    With her wan and shadowy face,
Whereon the hands of pinching pain,
    And want have left their trace;

195

Just so as in her tiny shroud,
    Like a snow-drop crushed, she lay;
When, sobbing, Neddy cried aloud,
    'Not take poor Jane away.'

With a sterner look, too, he
    By his little sister stands;
(Him they sent across the sea,
    And he died in distant lands;)
'Tis the look he had that day,
    When before the judge he said,
'Father drinks my wage away,
    Hunger made me steal the bread.'

Never now comes round to me
    Night with pleasant slumbers blest;
Still these phantom-shapes I see,
    Still they trouble all my rest.

Oh! for once but let me sleep
    Sleep like that my childhood knew;
Once these burning eye-lids steep
    In its soft refreshing dew!

See! they come, they come again!
    Whither, whither shall I flee?
Flee? alas! 'tis all in vain,
    Till I flee from memory!

A Mother's Death Song for her Child

Though I weep for thee, my baby,
    'Twas well that thou shouldst go;
And not thy father's guiltiness,
    Thy mother's anguish know:
Yes; happy, happy is thy doom,
    To sleep so early in the tomb!

Though I long shall miss thee, darling,
    'Tis well that thou art gone;
Mine might have been thy destiny,
    Hadst thou to woman grown:
Yes! better far to fill the grave,
    Than live a brutal drunkard's slave!

The following are added, by way of contrast with one or two of the foregoing.

Parting Words

Ye'll mind me when I'm gane, Jamie,
    Ye'll aften think o' me,
An' saft will be the tear, Jamie,
    That gathers in your e'e;
For there's nae thought o' bitterness,
    Nae memory o' strife,
Can make it sair for ye to turn
    To your ain blessed wife.

Ye aye were leal an' kind, Jamie;
    An' like a heavenly light,
Your love came beaming forth, Jamie,
    To make bright days mair bright;
An' when the clouds o' sorrow lowered,
    It only shone mair true;
An' still as mirkier fell the night,
    It still the brighter grew.

Ye ken the time is come, Jamie,
    For this puir frame to die,
But then ye'll no forget, Jamie,
    The spirit will go free;
An' ye're sure in thae blest mansions,
    Where we hope its place shall be,
Ye canna be forgotten lang,
    Or grow less dear to me.

Ye've watched by my bed-side, Jamie,
    When sickness brought me low;
Ye've whispered soothing hopes, Jamie,
    When I've been sunk in woe;
Ye've cherished me wi' love through life,
    It comforts me in death,
An' I bless you, bless you, Jamie,
    Wi' this my latest breath!

Heaven to Thee!

In Wales, formerly, on the Sunday after a funeral, each relation of the deceased knelt on his grave, exclaiming, "*Nefoedd iddo,*" i.e. "Heaven to him."

My son! my son! I scarce can think,
    That I never more shall see
Thy noble face, thy matchless grace,
    Thy step so bold and free.
Thy presence made my labours light;
    Ah! strength and joy were in thy sight:
Heaven, heaven, my son, to thee!

Thou wast a dear and blessed child,
    When an infant on my knee;
And when thou grew to manhood too,
    Thou wast the same to me;
Ne'er didst thou grieve thy mother's heart,
    Ne'er cause one bitter tear to start:
Heaven, heaven, my child, to thee!

My brother! by whose side I played,
    In the days of infancy;
Who, through long hours, wouldst gather flowers,
    To bind sweet wreaths for me;
How often hast thou dried my tears!
    How often stilled my throbbing fears!
Heaven, brother dear, to thee!

Thou wast the loved of many hearts,
    But of none like mine couldst be,
For I was blest above the rest—
    Thine own, thou calledst me!
Ah! treasured safe, most dear, most kind,
    What memories hast thou left behind!
Heaven, heaven, my love, to thee!

27

THE IMPORTANCE OF SOBRIETY ILLUSTRATED BY THE EVILS OF INTEMPERANCE

(London: RTS, *c.* 1850), pp. 1–7

Cyrus, when quite a youth, at the court of his grandfather, Astyages, undertook one day to perform the office of cup-bearer. He delivered the cup very gracefully, but omitted the usual custom of first tasting it himself. The king reminded him of it, supposing he had forgotten it. "No, sir," replied Cyrus; "I was afraid there might be poison in it; for I have observed that the lords of your court, after drinking, became noisy, quarrelsome, and frantic; and that even you, sir, seem to have forgotten that you were a king."—"Does not the same thing," inquired Astyages, "happen to your father?"—"Never," answered Cyrus.—"How then?"—"Why, when he has taken what wine he chooses, he is no longer thirsty; that is all."

Happy the man who shall live in those days in which the practice of excessive drinking shall be universally laid aside and detested! At present we can scarcely name a vice more common, or that is carried to a more alarming height. It prevails in the city, in the town, in the village, in the hamlet; among gentlemen, who ought to blush for its vulgarity, and among labourers, who can ill bear the expense. Are there not intemperate young men, intemperate old men, intemperate parents, intemperate magistrates, intemperate professors of religion, intemperate preachers of the gospel? Oh! could we view the scenes which intemperance creates in the alehouse, the tavern, and the festive parlour; what grief what indignation, would stir within us! "There is woe, there is sorrow, there is contention, there is babbling, there is redness of eyes, there are wounds without cause."

To mark exactly the line which separates sobriety from excess is not easy. While a man preserves his eye and his understanding clear, while he speaks without faltering, while his passions are undisturbed, and his step firm, who shall accuse him? Yet, with all these favourable appearances he may be guilty. There may be excess, where there is no discovery of it: it is well for those who abhor the former as much as they would dread the latter. To them conscience is a better guide than a thousand rules. Every one knows when he has quenched his thirst, diluted his food, refreshed his spirits; what does a man want more? He claims a cheerful glass; we fear it will prove one too many; and such assuredly it is, when it becomes questionable to a man's own mind whether he is intoxicated or still sober.

There are two sorts of intemperate persons: some are flushed with liquor, or, it may be, drowned in riot, but it is not often; others exceed more frequently, but the symptoms are not so visible and gross. The first plead their general sobriety; the last challenge you to mention a single instance of brutal excess. They are both deceived, they are both slaves of appetite; the difference between them must be sought for in their palates, in the measure of their prudence, in the cast of their associates, in any thing rather than in their principles. Such difference, we may easily suppose, will, in many cases, subside, and we shall see the same man reel through life, the constant tippler and the downright drunkard.

Let him that would guard against all approaches of this habit, consider the evils which attend it.

Excessive drinking is imprudent. It brings dimness and decay over the faculties of the soul; it has made the rich poor, and the condition of the poor intolerable; it robs a man of his real friends, and gathers round him designing knaves and empty fools; it destroys the taste for innocent and solid pleasure; it arms reflection with a sting; it sows the seed of innumerable disorders; it has brought millions to a premature grave.

Excessive drinking is sinful. Usually it suspends the exercise of sound reason, and thus levels the noblest distinction between men and brutes; it is an ungrateful waste of the Creator's bounty; it is disobedience—our Lord having expressly commanded his disciples to take heed, lest at any time their hearts should be overcharged with surfeiting and drunkenness; it is a practice of which the natural effect is to stupify conscience; then vice rushes in like a flood, confidence is betrayed, anger storms, the defiled heart meditates fornication and adultery, the robber is wrought up to the ruffian pitch, duty and anger are equally despised. Go to the drunkard's residence: what injustice, what barbarity, what wretchedness are exemplified there! Imagine the offender to be poor, and you complete the picture. He who should be the counsellor, the comfort, the ornament of his family, is its tempter, its trouble, its reproach. His wife and children, when alone, enjoy a respite, and begin to brighten up: he returns; they tremble, and are again distracted. He has spent their money, he has quarrelled, he has met with mischief; sometimes he forgets it, and then he only disgusts them with buffoonery and nonsense; more frequently he remembers it, and then he wreaks upon them the spite and fury collected and inflamed amidst a drunken crew: and they must bear it; they must be stunned by his stupid roar; they must weather the tempest of blasphemy; they must be sickened by the approach of his loathsome person; they, for his prodigality, must appear half naked, and live half-starved.

Intemperance (we observe with pain) is not confined to men; there are women, who, by "adding drunkenness to thirst," supply a spectacle still more hideous and mortifying. We have beheld mothers staggering with infants in their arms; and we have heard that in situations of comfort, and of affluence too, this degrading practice obtains to a wide extent. Should any of our female readers, by their sedentary

THE IMPORTANCE OF SOBRIETY

habits, by the pressure of grief, and by the perpetual recurrence of opportunity, be tempted to indulge, we entreat them by every thing that is important in reputation and delicate in sentiment, by the loveliness which they would sacrifice, and by the horrors which they would feel and inspire, we entreat them to beware, to start from the rising purpose, and thus to preserve a character both unsullied and unsuspected.

Excessive drinking is a habit soon formed, rapid in its growth, and hard to root up. At first a man drinks for refreshment; he then takes a larger draught for pleasure; he still adds a little and a little, till he can never leave his cups without taking a little too much. His appetite increases as it is indulged; the quantity which once intoxicated, now does but just cheer him; he feels a craving, he removes it by excess; he craves again, and becomes miserable, if he does not again receive an extravagant supply. Thus he degenerates into the finished sot; and then, whatever intervals of remorse disturb him, whatever tears flow, whatever promises and vows are uttered, he generally relapses, grows worse and worse, and—dies. It may be easy, O young man, to refrain in these thy sober days; but intemperance when perfected into a habit, defies the powers of a warning voice, and would in every instance lead us to withdraw our counsels in despair, but that we recollect, a dying thief has been converted; God is able of stones to raise up children unto Abraham; with God all things are possible!

Excessive drinking is contagious. One drunkard makes many; he is generally what the world calls a social fellow; he secures a companion of the same stamp; they meet; they are joined first by one, and then by another; the circle enlarges, they call for the flowing bowl; they feel their spirits elevated; they raise them higher by songs, and jokes, and peals of laughter; they persuade the unthinking that it is happiness; they tell the young it is manly; they allure the frugal by treating them; and when they part, they swear they will meet again. Each of these influences some other connexion. If the husband drinks abroad, the wife may take a similar liberty at home. The son asks, "What harm is there in doing as my parents do?" Thus the disease infects neighbours and relatives; and who can say where it will stop? Let him who spreads it, remember that he is responsible for all its consequences. "Although the waste of time and money," as Dr. Paley observes, "may be of small importance to you, it may be of the utmost to some one or other, whom your society corrupts; repeated or long continued excesses, which hurt not your health, may be fatal to your companion; although you have neither wife, nor child, nor parent to lament your absence from home, or expect your return to it with terror, other families whose husbands and fathers have been invited to share your inebriety, or encouraged to imitate it, may possibly lay their misery or ruin at your door."

Excessive drinking, persisted in, ruins for ever. It is written, "Neither fornicators, nor drunkards shall inherit the kingdom of God." Is it any wonder that God has published such a threatening? What would a drunkard do in heaven? The spirits of the just are there, an innumerable company of angels, and God himself, a Being "glorious in holiness." It is all a scene of purity, a scene the reverse of all that the intemperate can love or enjoy. And what reason has the reveller to hope that the moment he leaves the world he shall acquire a new character, and a relish for those things which he now dislikes? It is surely far more probable that the moral habits of the future state bear a relation to those of the present. When the heirs of heaven are described, we hear of "adding to knowledge temperance," of "keeping under the body," of "crucifying the flesh with its affections and lusts," of "being made meet for the inheritance of the saints in light." The reveller heeds not this, but despises those who do. Not so, when he shall witness their confidence and joy at the appearing of Jesus Christ: not so, when in hell he shall lift up his eyes, and in vain solicit one drop of water to cool his tormented tongue! What will it profit him in that day that here he drank himself into mirth, and was saluted as "the happy rake." Oh! dreadful result! Tremble, ye victims of intemperance, and hasten, while yet you may from the horrors of such a precipice!

Excessive drinking appears, from every view of it, to be a vice against which we cannot plead too strongly. It should be avoided and abhorred in all its stages. Unnumbered evils compose its train, and eternal vengeance is its reward. The young, for they are our chief hope, will permit us to put them on their guard, and to recommend suitable precautions.

Let them beware of false complaisance, that easy compliant temper, which yields to every pressure; that chameleon character, which varies its colour with its company. There is a point of indulgence beyond which invitation is criminal, and acceptance contemptible. Think what dignity belongs to the happy youth, who can say, in a decided tone, "I love to oblige you, but I cannot do it at the expense of offending God."

Let the young consider beforehand the chief occasions of excess. Are they destined to some laborious employ, or exposed to the midnight air? They will be tempted to think no supply of liquor too liberal. Are they disappointed in their projects? They will hear that sorrow is best drowned in a jovial cup. Invited to a feast, they are surrounded by a luxurious variety, they are reminded that such seasons seldom return, and that the deeper their draughts the warmer will be their welcome. If they, on the other hand, are the providers, they will be in danger of circulating the glass too freely, lest they should be charged with the want of hospitality. How many are there who, when they began to travel as men of business, when they first resorted to the market and the fair, enjoyed an unblemished name! but now they are quarrelsome, and vulgar, and debauched, and callous; now they lie as upon the top of a mast, while winds and billows roar around them.

Let the choice of friends be a subject deeply regarded. Failure here is often the prelude to entire destruction. We dread the consequence of a single hour spent in the company of profligates. There the forces of temptation meet; there the sober, if not seduced into guilty compliances, learn to palliate what they may refuse to practise, and are considered as giving a silent sanction to all they see and all they hear. What has a virtuous man to do at the convivial club, and the noisy revel? And why should the public-house, adapted, we allow, for the weary stranger and for the occasional transaction of public business, why should it be so

THE IMPORTANCE OF SOBRIETY

much frequented by its nearest neighbours? The wise and good are pursuing their useful labours, or conveying instruction and entertainment round an attentive and affectionate circle.

Let the mind form a true estimate of pleasure. If there were no gratification in excessive drinking, it had never been practised; but will you call it pleasure? No; pleasure is associated with duty and dignity; it is durable, and it leads to God.

> "Live while you live," the epicure would say,
> "And seize the pleasures of the present day;"
> "Live while you live," the sacred preacher cries,
> "And give to God each moment as it flies:"
> Lord, in my views, let both united be;
> I live in pleasure when I live to thee.
> Doddridge.

Let the young, and the aged too, add to temperance, godliness. Godliness includes faith, repentance, love, and obedience; and as it is the very soul of character in general, so, in a particular manner, does it fortify a man against the charms of sensuality. It constitutes a living principle, which reaches to the whole behaviour, and extends from youth to age, from time to eternity. It is indeed the likeness of God, as the word signifies, wrought in man by the power of His grace in the heart. In this state a man is sober and temperate, not by constraint merely, and to avoid the consequences of excess, but because it is become natural to him; for he loves holiness because he loves God, who commands it, and enables him to obey his word. This is a great change indeed for a man to undergo; but all must experience it, or be for ever lost; for all have sinned, and come short of the glory of God. All the world is become guilty before God. What a mercy that we are not wholly abandoned! "God so loved the world that he gave his only begotten Son, that whosoever believeth on him might not perish, but have everlasting life." The Divine nature, in thousands of happy instances, has been restored by the washing of regeneration, and renewing of the Holy Ghost. Wherever the gospel sounds, sinners receive an invitation, and are assured that Jesus Christ "is able to save to the uttermost all that come unto God by him." Oh that our readers would make the trial!

We shall be well rewarded, if by means of this paper, one person hitherto ignorant and insensible, be led to the Saviour. He will blush and mourn for the past; but his future conduct will be honourable and holy, and his prospects will open into a glorious immortality. Disgusted with the pollutions of the world, and with the excess of riot to which he himself may have run, he will henceforth keep under his body, and bring it into subjection; he will abstain from all fleshly lusts, which war against the soul, in one word, he will live under the influence of this apostolic and most important exhortation: "Whether ye eat, or drink, or whatsoever ye do, do all to the glory of God."

3.2

Sabbatarianism

3.2 Sabbatarianism

Like Temperance (see this volume, Temperance), Sabbatarianism was part of the evangelical movement's reformation of lives and manners. Christians were enjoined, as in the Bible, to keep the Sabbath holy, and to refrain from profane activities on that day. Even reading was controlled on Sundays, with fiction discouraged in favour of more serious or improving literatures, such as biographies, tracts and religious magazines (for an example of Sunday reading matter, see the *Sunday at Home* extracted in this volume, Biblical History, Geography and Travel Writing). Ideally, Sundays were to be spent in church and in private Bible study. Like Temperance, Sabbatarianism obtained a radical social flavour when it was used by groups such as the Chartists to argue for regulations on working hours, especially for factory workers, so that they could enjoy a day of rest and, if they pleased, worship.

The RTS tract reproduced here reminds its readers of the Biblical roots of Sabbatarianism, and uses allusions to the Old Testament to warn those breaking the Sabbath that this sin will be punishable in hell. While the religious beliefs and language contained within this tract suggest it was probably written in the very early nineteenth century, tracts had long lives, as they were circulated throughout the century. The God of this tract is seen to be very much involved in people's day to day lives, able to bless families with health and wealth if they live according to their religion, and able to curse with sickness and death if they sin. Significantly, the tract criticises employers and those who break the Sabbath as they embrace capitalism. It also criticises the upper classes for setting a bad example, but makes the potentially radical suggestion that the lower classes should not look to them as their 'betters' in terms of conduct. When it comes to describing ideal Sabbath occupations the tract is more conservative, recommending that staple of Victorian domesticity, family prayers, as well as family attendance at a place of worship and Sunday school for children.

Edward Capern (1819–1894) was a working-class Methodist from Devon who wrote poetry while he worked as a postman. His poems were first published in the *North Devon Journal* and then collected and published by subscription. His poem, 'The Rural Postman', reveals its Wordsworthian influence, as the postman is depicted delighting in nature in the same way that his spirit honours and loves the 'good'. Nature was seen as God's other book, to be studied alongside the Bible. However, as Capern's poem makes clear, nature could not be a substitute for proper Bible study and Christian worship, and the postman criticises modern, capitalist Britain for not having laws to restrict working hours so that workers can attend church – as in 'olden times'. He accuses Britain of hypocrisy with his question 'alack-a-day/where's Britain's piety?', and the poem ends with an emphatic denial that anyone prays for the postman, who is 'robb'd of his Sabbath'. This radical criticism again suggests that true piety lies with the respectable working classes, rather than the rulers of the land.

207

28

SABBATH OCCUPATIONS

(London: Religious Tract Society, *c.* 1820), pp. 1–8

Friend

Allow me to ask, what are you engaged in, or whither are you going? Are you preparing to join in the public worship of God? Or are you following your worldly business, or seeking for amusement on this day? If one of the latter is your object, do you not recollect that this is the day which God has marked as his own, by the fourth commandment? But lest you should have forgotten it, permit me to refresh your memory: it is thus written in the xxth chapter of Exodus, "Remember the sabbath-day to keep it holy. Six days shalt thou labour, and do all thy work; but the seventh day is the sabbath of the Lord thy God: in it thou shalt not do any work; thou, nor thy son, nor thy daughter, thy man-servant, nor thy maidservant, nor thy cattle, nor the stranger that is within thy gates: for in six days the Lord made heaven and earth, the sea, and all that in them is, and rested the seventh day: wherefore the Lord blessed the seventh day, and hallowed it."

What excuse can you now make for profaning this day, which God has pronounced holy? If you did not know it before, you can now plead ignorance no longer. But, in truth, I strongly suspect, that this is not the first, nor the second time, you have broken this commandment, by working, travelling, drinking, or other idle practices: your own conscience will tell you whether I am right in what I suspect or not.

Perhaps you will say, "It is not often I break this commandment." Show me any one authority from the bible, which permits you to break it at any time. I am certain you cannot. It does not appear that the man who was stoned in the wilderness, for gathering sticks on the sabbath-day, had ever done so before: and yet he was stoned to death, God himself being the judge who tried the cause, passed the sentence, and ordered Moses to see it executed. See Numb. xv. 32. Were you, and all who are at this moment breaking the sabbath, to be struck dead by the visitation of God, what a dreadful spectacle would this country exhibit! there would hardly be a house, a street, or a road, where there would not be some dead! It is only by the patience and long-suffering of God that you are spared, that you may repent and not perish: and will you despise this mercy, and continue to insult your God, sabbath after sabbath? If you will do so, beware lest he cut you off suddenly, and

SABBATH OCCUPATIONS

deliver you over to everlasting torments. Or, if sudden judgment should not over-take you, as you know it has others, in very awful and recent cases, be sure your repeated and aggravated sins will find you out at death, at judgment, and in hell, where your mispent, abused sabbath-hours will be followed with ages of useless repentance.

But, perhaps you will say, "I see those who are my betters, and who ought to know what is right, travelling, driving about in their carriages, and follow-ing their amusements, as much on the sabbath as on any other day." I allow you may, and they will have to answer for it at the dreadful day of judgment; but their conduct, my friend, is no rule for you. The bible, which ought to be your rule of life, directs you "not to follow the multitude to do evil," Exod. xxiii. 2. It declares that "though hand join in hand, the wicked shall not be unpunished," Prov. xi. 21. Perhaps you may say, "I am a poor man, or have a large family, and cannot afford to be idle; besides, I can make more by working or letting my cattle work on this day, than on any other, and you know I should disoblige my employers and cus-tomers were I to refuse their orders." O friend! reflect for a moment on the folly, as well as sinfulness of these excuses; so far from excusing, they add to your sins. Can you not trust to God for such a blessing on your six days' labour, as will sup-ply the wants of your family? By working on the sabbath-day, you plainly declare that you will not trust him. And if so, how can you expect that He will bless any thing you do? Is it not God, whose day you are breaking, who gives you health and ability to earn the food that you eat, and the clothes that you wear? Can all your wages do you good, if he puts his curse upon them? The little that is got in the fear of God, goes much farther than the rewards of sin. How many are there who have all their earnings poisoned by their greediness in working on the sabbath! God can send sickness to take away what is sinfully gotten. Look around among your neighbours, and if you know any one that fears God, and keeps his sabbaths, I will venture to say that you find that man more happy and comfortable, than those who work, or take their pleasure on those days. "Godliness hath the promise of the life that now is, as well as of that which is to come." Poor unhappy creatures, who are toiling at your labours, keeping open your shops, sitting at your stalls, when you ought to be employed in worshipping God, and seeking for the salvation of your souls by Jesus Christ his Son, how much do I pity you, how much do I blame you! I will suppose, that by working on the sabbath you gained six times as much as on any other day, but let me ask you in the words of our Lord Jesus Christ, "What would it profit you, if you gained the whole world, and lost your own soul?" If you fear disobliging your master or employers, it plainly shows, that you fear man more than GOD. But let me ask you, Are you to obey GOD or man, or which ought you to seek to please? Oh! my friend, remember that Jesus Christ hath said "Seek ye first the kingdom of God and his righteousness, and all these things shall be added unto you," Matt. vi. 33.

Perhaps you may say that you do keep the sabbath-day holy, for you go to church, and when going on business, or on a journey, you attend prayers in the way, and that, after you have done your duty, you think there is no harm in

REFORMING PRIVATE LIFE

working, travelling, or entertaining yourself with your friends for the remainder of the day! But be assured, my friend, whatever you may think, there is much harm in it, though you may have been at prayers! observing the day in one part will no more excuse you for profaning the remainder, than having hitherto kept the whole law, will excuse you for committing murder. The sabbath-day consists of as many hours as any other day, and it is the day, and not a particular part, that God commands to be kept holy. Suppose you hire a labourer for a day, do you not consider him as bound to work for you the whole of that day, except during the time allowed for his meals; or would you pay him the day's wages, if he only worked for one hour and a half? I am very certain you would not; and do you suppose that the great God will allow you to despise his day, and put him off with a formal service of an hour or two? Be assured he will not; he will require it of you.

Had the laws of your country enacted, that every sabbath-breaker should lose his property and substance, and also be confined in prison for life, would you then dare to break it, when you knew the consequence? It is true you are not subject to such punishments here; but permit me to assure you that, by the laws of God, you are exposed to much more dreadful judgments hereafter. The wilful breach of any one of God's commandments subjects you to the loss of both soul and body, when they will be cast into a prison from whence there is no escape, even into that bottomless pit, "where there is weeping, and wailing, and gnashing of teeth; where the worm dieth not, and the fire is not quenched." Will you therefore fear the power of man, and yet pay no regard to the laws of that God, who can destroy both soul and body in hell fire? Consider, that at this moment you are exposing yourself to his just vengeance; this very night your soul may be required of you, and you may be summoned before the bar of that dreadful Judge, whose laws you are now breaking, and whose judgments you seem at present to despise.

Ah! could one of those miserable and tormented spirits, which are at this moment suffering the agonies of eternal despair, tell you what he feels, and what he would give for one hour of this sacred day, which you are trampling under foot for pleasure or for gain, so as to have the offers of pardon and eternal life made to him but once more; how would you tremble to hear his language, and fear lest this sabbath should pass away before you were delivered from that curse under which he suffers! Be assured that unless you repent, a few more broken sabbaths will make you his companion and fellow-sufferer. Some are now in hell, who were on earth breaking with you, perhaps, the last sabbath. Do you not know some one who spent the last Lord's day with you at work, or in idleness, if not in the public-house, who is now dead? Be sure, that if he did not truly repent, he is a wretched soul, in the fire that can never be quenched. And, as surely as you follow his sins, shall you suffer his punishment. You cannot tell but this may be the last warning you may ever have, and therefore, I beseech you, for the sake of your never-dying soul, to consider what I now lay before you, and to read it over and over again, till it pleases God to bring you to a sense of your guilt, and work

SABBATH OCCUPATIONS

in you true repentance, living faith in Jesus Christ, and a firm resolution of paying respect and obedience to all his commandments in future.

Should you ask me how you ought to keep this day holy, I shall feel great pleasure in directing you. You are to consider the sabbath as a day on which you are to rest from labour, not that you may be idle, or that you may have time to amuse yourself with sports, but that you may have leisure to attend to "the one thing needful," the salvation of your soul. How often have I heard persons complain, that they were so occupied by business as to have no time for reading the bible, or regarding religious things? If such persons had considered, that the sabbath was given for this very purpose, and had they spent it in reading the scriptures, in prayer, hearing the gospel preached, joining in public worship, and in conversation with pious persons, they would have had no reason to complain of ignorance, and might now have been Christians in reality, as well as in profession.

Hoping that you have some desire to improve this holy season, I will give you a few plain directions concerning it.

If you are sensible of the blessings which the sabbath affords, you will hail its returning dawn with praise and thanksgiving—you will pray to God to free your heart from worldly thoughts and cares, and enable you to profit by the means of grace which he has afforded you. You should employ the early part of the morning in prayer, and reading the bible, or hearing it read, and thinking upon it. This will prepare your mind for joining in the prayers and praises of the congregation, and for hearing that gospel preached, which will direct you in the way of life, and is able to make you wise unto salvation.

After worship, you should return home, thinking of what you had heard, and talking with your family or friends about it, seeking to apply it to yourself, and praying to God to make it profitable to you. If you are a husband and a father, you must be careful that all your family attend the worship of God with you. Suffer not trifling excuses to keep your wife and children away from the house of God. But you must also worship God in your own house as well as in public. Call your family together, in the morning and evening, read the bible to them, pray with them, and for them, and teach them, as far as you are able, the things of salvation. If you cannot instruct your children yourself, send them to a neighbouring Sunday school, where they may be taught to read God's word, and to know their duty to God and man. Be careful that no one belonging to you is suffered to mix in the company of those who break the sabbath, lest their example should tempt him to do the same; nor, under pretence of needful recreation, to loiter about the streets or fields, in the hours between and after public worship. The remainder of the day you should seek to improve in such a way as will be most profitable to your soul, and those of your family; for if you are determined to keep the sabbath-day holy, you will no longer keep company with those who profane it.

If you have no bible, or cannot read yourself, seek out, among your neighbours, for some religious persons who observe the sabbath; they will be glad to receive you among them: there you will hear the bible read, and you may derive more

REFORMING PRIVATE LIFE

benefit than you can conceive at present, from their experience and conversation. They will perhaps tell you, that formerly they were in the same blind and unconcerned state as yourself; how they were awakened to a sense of their lost condition, and brought to seek the Lord; how they sought him by fervent prayer; how they found peace with him, through the blood of his dear Son Jesus Christ, which "cleanseth from all sin;" how he has given them not only the pardon of their sins, but the assurance of his favour; and taught them by his Holy Spirit to see that, although they are guilty in themselves, they are accounted righteous before God for the sake of Jesus; that they shall never more come into condemnation, but are passed from death unto life. They will bring you to those ministers from whom they have derived comfort and instruction in righteousness, and they will all pray for you, which thing is a greater blessing than you may be aware of; for "the effectual fervent prayer of a righteous man availeth much." James v. 16.

If you will spend the sabbath in such a manner as this, I hope you will soon find the comfort of it; you will no longer look upon it as a restraint or drudgery but will esteem one such day better than a thousand spent in idleness and folly; and if so, you will be prepared to conclude it as you began, with prayer and thanksgiving. After such a sabbath, you will be able to enter on the business of the following week with cheerfulness, and with a lively hope that God will abundantly bless your labours. I shall conclude this, by requesting that you will keep it by you, that you will consider it over and over again, and also lend it to those of your neighbours who have been your companions in this sinful course, recollecting that you and I must soon meet at the judgment-seat of Christ; where we must give an account of all the advice we have received and refused to attend to, and all the opportunities we have neglected to improve. Farewell.

29

EDWARD CAPERN,
'THE RURAL POSTMAN'

In *Poems* (London: W. Kent and Co., 1859), pp. 9–13

O' the postman's is as pleasant a life
    As any one's, I trow;
For day by day he wendeth his way,
    Where a thousand wildlings grow.
He marketh the date of the snowdrop's birth,
    And knows when the time is near
For white scented violets to gladden the earth,
    And sweet primrose groups t'appear.
He can show you the spot where the hyacinth wild
    Hangs out her bell blossoms o' blue;
And tell where the celandine's bright-eyed child
    Fills her chalice with honey dew.
The purple-dyed violet, the hawthorn, and sloe,
    The creepers that trail in the lane,
The dragon, the daisy, and clover-rose, too,
    And buttercups gilding the plain;
The foxglove, the robert, the gorse, and the thyme,
    The heather and broom on the moor,
And the sweet honey-suckle that loveth to climb
    The arch of the cottager's door.
He knoweth them all, and he loveth them well,
    And others not honour'd with fame,
For they hang round his life like a beautiful spell,
    And light up his path with their flame.
O, a pleasant life is the postman's life
    And a fine cheerful soul is he,
For he'll shout and sing like a forest king,
    On the crown of an ancient tree.

Heigho! I come and go,
Where the Lent lily, speedwell, and dog-rose blow,
Heigho! and merry, O!
Where hawkweeds, and trefoils, and wild peas grow.
Heigho! Heigho!
As pleasant as May-time, and light as a roe.

O, the postman's is as happy a life
    As any one's, I trow;
Wand'ring away where dragon-flies play,
    And brooks sing soft and slow;
And watching the lark as he soars on high,
    To carol in yonder cloud,
"He sings in his labour, and why not I?"
    The postman sings aloud.
And many a brace of humble rhymes
    His pleasant soul hath made,
Of birds, and flowers, and happy times,
    In sunshine and in shade.

The harvester, smiling, sees him pass,
    "How goes the war?" quoth he;
And he stayeth his scythe in the corn or grass,
    To learn what the news may be.
He honours the good, both rich and poor,
    And jokes with each rosy-faced maid;
He nods at the aged dame at the door,
    And patteth each urchin's head.
And little he thinks as he whistling goes,
    To the march of some popular tune,
That beauty grows pale at the tramp of his shoes,
    And sometimes as rosy as June.

O, a happy lad is the rural post,
    And a right loyal servant, I ween;
For let a proud foe but threaten a blow,
    He shouteth "Hurrah for the Queen!"
Heigho! I come and go,
Where the mountain ash and the alder grow.
Heigho! I come and go,
With a smile on my cheeks and a ruddy glow.

O, the postman's is as merry a life
    As any one's, I trow;

EDWARD CAPERN, 'THE RURAL POSTMAN'

Waking the hill with his musical trill,
    From its crown to the base below.

For he windeth his horn where the blushing morn
    First kisseth the green earth wide,
And snuffeth the breeze where the nodding trees
    Stand strong in their forest pride.
He heareth the bee in the broad oak tree,
    In quest of its honey-clad leaves,
And marks with delight when swallows alight
    To build 'neath the cottager's eaves.
When forest tribes sing till green valleys ring
    With the soul-stirring music they make,
His spirit as free as the fetterless sea,
    Chaunts out o'er the meadow and brake.
When making his call at a nobleman's hall,
    In garments bespattered and rude,
He thinks that sound health is the best of all wealth,
    With a spirit in love with the good.
Full many a heart with a paper-wing'd dart,
    Hath he wounded in Cupid's employ;
And trumpet-tongued Fame says that Hymen's bright flame
    Is fed by the honest old boy.
I'm welcome, he singeth, whenever I go,
    When buds or bright blossoms appear,
At autumn-tide too, when golden tints glow,
    And *most* when old Christmas is near.
Heigho! I come and go,
With the black seal of DEATH, and young LOVE's bow;
Heigho! I come and go,
With a smile for each joy and a tear for each woe.

O, the postman's is as blessed a life
    As any one's, I trow,
If leaping the stile, o'er many a mile,
    Can blessedness bestow.

If tearing your way through a tangled wood,
    Or dragging your limbs through a lawn—
If wading knee-deep through an angry flood,
    Or a plough'd field newly sown,—
If sweating big drops 'neath a burning sun,
    And shiv'ring 'mid sleet and snow;

REFORMING PRIVATE LIFE

If drench'd to the skin with rain, be fun,
    And can a joy bestow!

If toiling away through a weary week
    (No *six-day* week, but *seven*),
Without one holy hour to seek
    A resting place in heaven,—
If hearing the bells ring Sabbath chimes,
    To bid us all repair
To church (as in the olden times),
    And bend the knee in prayer,—
If in those bells he hears a voice,
    "To thy delivery,
"God says to every soul, 'Rejoice,'
    "But, postman, not to thee."
O, the postman's *is* a blessed life,
    And, sighing heavily,
"Ha, ha!" he'll say, "alack-a-day,
    "Where's Britain's piety?"

Heigho! I come and go,
Through the muck and miry slough;
Heigho! I come and go,
Heavy at heart, and weary O.
Heigho! Heigho!
Does any one pray for the postman?—*No*.
No! no! no! no!
Or he would not be robb'd of his Sabbath so.

3.3

Fidelity in the Upper Classes

3.3 Fidelity in the Upper Classes

As the previous sections have suggested, the evangelical movement of the first half of the nineteenth century was often critical of the behaviour of the English upper classes. Leaders in the movement also understood that evangelicalism would only be truly influential if it could gain a foothold in the upper echelons of society. This was shown by the huge influence in favour of Christianity that William Wilberforce wielded as Prime Minister, as, for example, he threw England's support behind abolitionism and opened India to missionaries. Wilberforce had been influenced in his youth by an evangelical nursemaid, and Christian groups sought to have a similar influence on other members of the upper classes, through education (see this volume, Education), but also through literature and magazines. Their message to their converts in the upper classes was to be faithful in their religion and to demonstrate this fidelity to their acquaintances, rather than hiding it for fear of ridicule or losing status.

The Christian Lady's Friend aimed at interesting its readers, many of whom would have been from the upper-middle and upper classes, in a number of religious causes, including the mission to the Jews and abolitionism (see this volume, Mission to the Jews and Abolitionism). A cause even closer at home, however, was the mission to the upper classes, and in this article, 'Letter to a Friend' the magazine exhorts its reader to become a missionary to her friends and family. The friend is portrayed in a similar manner to converts of other missions – like Heighway's *Leila Ada* (see this volume, Mission to the Jews), or the African Bishop Crowther (see this volume, Masculinity and Leadership) – as closer to the writer of *The Christian Lady's Friend* than to her family: a member of the converted, bound for heaven, and separated from her unconverted family, bound for hell. The methods she is instructed to use in her attempts at conversion are described in language that alludes to upper-class femininity. For example, it is her 'deportment' and temper that are imagined will have an influence, and she is told that it is her duty to make Christianity 'inviting'. Though encouraged to give friends and family appropriate books as well as continuously including references to religion in conversation and letters, she is instructed not to weary her audience with her piety. Interestingly, the Letter suggests that the upper classes are less advantaged than the lower when it comes to religion: they do not have access to many of the means by which the poor are converted, they are assailed by the temptations of fashion and dissipation, and those that think themselves already Christians neglect their souls. When the Letter encourages the reader to take her relatives somewhere 'where the gospel is *faithfully* preached', it is implying that, for many of the upper classes, Church had become just another place for fashionable visiting on a Sunday.

The Church is a significant presence in *The Young Governess* by Arthur Selous, more so because of its initial absence. When the young governess, Martha Smith, arrives at her new situation of Clereton Manor, the Church has been shut for renovation, and she reflects on how much she will miss attending daily service.

219

Midway through the novel, the rector appears with the news that the Church will be re-opening and to encourage Lady Clere and her household to attend, partly as an example to the people in the village. Lady Clere's reluctance to attend church, largely because it would disrupt her upper-class routines – especially dinnertime – and the rector's attempts to overcome her opposition make for an amusing dialogue (which can be compared with the RTS's dialogue 'concerning the Church Missionary Society', this volume, Gaining Support). Lady Clere is characterised as one of the unfaithful upper classes, more worried about being snubbed in society than about her soul. *The Young Governess* can be seen as a novel of the conservative silver fork genre, popular among those who wanted to know about how the upper classes lived. In this example of the genre a certain type of upper class is criticised for its lack of religious fidelity, but ultimately the class as a whole is redeemed, because the faithful governess Martha is revealed to be of genteel birth and, according to the romantic tropes of the genre, ends by being rightfully restored to her position through marriage. The story ends with evidence that, while a governess, she was able to religiously influence the idle Eleanor Clere, in the same manner as Wilberforce's nursery maid, or the imagined 'Friend' in the *Christian Lady's Friend*.

30

'LETTER TO A FRIEND IN THE HIGHER CIRCLES OF SOCIETY'

Christian Lady's Friend and Family Repository, November 1831, pp. 101–105

On the Duty of personal Effort for the Salvation of Relatives and Acquaintances.

Dear Christian Friend,

I rejoice to think that the mercy of the Lord has "called you out of darkness into his marvellous light;" that you are, as the first-fruits of a large family, called to be a witness for the truth, "a new creature in Christ Jesus." My earnest prayer for you all is, that you may *each* be saved; that your conversion may not be a solitary one; that not one of your dear family may be left in ignorance of God and his great salvation. This I am assured must be your *own* earnest desire; and I now write to offer you a few hints of affectionate exhortation and encouragement on the subject. You will, doubtless, have deep and sorrowful feelings at seeing so many dear to you, still ignorant of the ways of peace, of the only path to real happiness; and while you pray for their conversion, you must bear in mind you have a large *share of responsibility* attached to your *example* and efforts on their behalf. Yes, while *you pray* that they may be saved, you are to use the most likely and persevering efforts to lead them to the Saviour. While you tell them of the blessedness of the righteous, and of the joys of religion, you are daily to shew forth, in your life and conduct, the fruits of righteousness. While you invite them to the Saviour, you are to make religion appear *inviting*, by its lovely effects, fruits and tempers. Let the peace of God rule your own heart, and the grace of God influence all your actions: then there will be a holy uniformity in what you do, and say, and recommend to them. Thus by consistency of deportment, by "walking in wisdom towards them that are without," religion will appear to be a transforming reality: not in precept only excellent, but in deed and in truth will you be known as a partaker of it; a witness for the truth, "a new creature in Christ Jesus."

The condition of your unconverted relatives must be continually and deeply impressed on your mind, as that of great and *imminent danger*. Yes, they are each of them, dear as they are to you, under the curse of God, being "enemies to him by wicked works," unreconciled, "dead in trespasses and sins," and, as such, on the brink of everlasting woe: and when you connect with it the uncertainty of their lives, it should draw forth your tenderest sympathy and unceasing diligence, to use every means in your power to point them to the Saviour—to entreat them to "flee from the wrath to come." Never take leave of them but with the utmost affection, and entreaty that they would remember your words, follow your advice, and "seek the Lord while he may be found;" and when your visit is renewed, your persuasions must be also, reminding them of the suddenness with which death may make an eternal separation between you, and still urging them to remember how freely salvation is promised to the renewed in heart. You must never dare close a letter to them when absent, without recurring to the same subject; your letters should be a faithful record of the best desires of your heart for their salvation: "let them bespeak the earnestness you feel for their salvation; thus will they not rise to condemn you at the judgment day."[1] And O, never, never forget, above and with all other means, to unite *a praying Spirit;* to pray, yes, to *agonize* in prayer at a throne of grace, that your efforts may be availing, that your dear kindred may be saved.

But these are not all the means you can adopt in drawing the attention of your dear friends to the worth of their souls, and the importance of salvation; others may be used, in dependence on divine help, to promote their everlasting welfare. Lend and give them suitable books; this has been a means much owned and blessed: Mr. Richmond, the excellent author of many useful works, was led to the Saviour, by a friend lending him Wilberforce's Practical View of Christianity. Booth's Reign of Grace was similarly blessed to a lady I lately read of; and Doddridge's Rise and Progress, and Pike's Persuasives, have been lent, and given, and made alike useful. Invite your dear relatives also to go with you where the gospel is *faithfully* preached; introduce them to the society of truly converted judicious friends; and carefully watch your own conversation, that it may be seasoned with such good things, and rendered so pleasantly profitable, that they may *not be weary* of it. There need be nothing impertinent or intrusive in the *most persevering* efforts of this kind. Be much in prayer for divine help, when about to speak or write, or recommend any thing to them; that you may do it in a right and acceptable manner; always uniting melting kindness with your words, that no offence may be taken at any fancied superiority, of your own attainments, but with kindness, affection and simplicity, speak and act for the welfare of their souls.

Moving in a superior station in society, your dear relatives are excluded from various benefits which the poorer classes are favoured with: hence the salvation of the great and wealthy, generally speaking, is an object far less hopeful than that of the poor; the round of gay pleasures with which they are encircled adds also to the snares with which the God of this world has bound and led them captive. It follows then, as the almost alone hope that can be entertained of the salvation of such, that it may be accomplished by the instrumentality of domestic influence and relative affection, where divine grace happily exists in the heart of a friend

'LETTER TO A FRIEND IN THE HIGHER CIRCLES'

and relative: hence, the obligation you are under, my christian friend, is so *much the greater,* to do all in your power to promote this glorious object. The larger part of the higher circles either already think themselves Christians, and therefore neglect to seek a Saviour, or are unbelievers plunged in the vortex of fashion and dissipation, whence the sound of the gospel, the terrors of the law, and the invitations of mercy are altogether excluded. How hopeless is the prospect on their behalf! What is to be done for their deliverance, if it be not by *personal influence,* under the divine blessing, from those who have themselves been delivered from the same snares? O, do not forget this, my christian friend: you were once walking with them the downward road; and, now you are in mercy delivered, forget not those who are hasting to perdition, walking in "a way right in their own eyes, but the end thereof is death," The gospel must be pressed home upon the consciences of those who *go not* to hear it; and all with whom you are connected, although they may not wish you to do it, have a claim *upon you* for this faithful act. I wish you to feel *this deeply,* as if put in *trust,* as it were, with the *souls* of your *relatives;* and that on your use or neglect of the affection and influence you possess on their judgment and hearts, so your conscience will accuse or acquit you at the great day. Tremble you well may, lest either of them should reproach you, in the day of final account, for not having done *your utmost* in warning them of danger, exhorting them to turn unto the Lord, urging the suitableness of the gospel to their lost condition, and inviting them to their Saviour, *with assurance* that he will not reject the penitent sinner. Do not fail to seek grace from above, to make you equal to this self-denying duty: it shall be given you if you ask it. Do not withhold the endearing expressions and promises of the gospel; or through a false shame forbear to be a witness for God unto them.

And not only with your relatives, but your acquaintances, should you labour to be faithful; particularly with such that you had your conversation with in times past, with whom you travelled in the broad road to destruction: perhaps there are some now farther advanced in the ways of misery, who were formerly led on by *your example* and influence prior to your conversion. O, consider such; *they have a double claim* upon your prayers and efforts for their good. Pity them, pray for them, *labour to save* them. I press this particularly on you, for you must not be content to go to heaven alone; and those with whom you associated in the downward road should be the especial objects of your desire, to travel with you the way to heaven. If you do not faithfully labour and lay yourself out in *this way,* to promote the divine glory and good of souls, you will most likely have to lament over coldness of heart, and want of enjoyment in the divine life. It is the diligent soul that shall be made fat; it is "those who water others, shall themselves be watered;" and to such the promise is made, that having turned "many to righteousness, they shall shine as the stars for ever and ever." O that your labours may be blessed and directed to the conversion of such as I have named! Think of them all, make a list of their names, and rest not satisfied, till to each you have presented a suitable book, accompanied with a faithful, affectionate letter. Commend the attempt to the Lord in earnest prayer, that the Holy Spirit may make it effectual to their salvation. I subjoin a list of books: many of them have been much blessed, to my personal knowledge.[2] It is my prayer that you may be found faithful to the grace given to you, and the opportunities put into your hands to do good. May you meet many on the right hand of the Judge, won by your faithful labours and consistent example to the knowledge of the Saviour.

Affectionately I bid you farewell.
Z. Z.

Notes

1 Dr. Raffles' Lectures on Practical Duties.
2 Vital Christianity;—Jesus shewing Mercy;—Sermons to the Aged;—Boston's Fourfold State;—Owen on the 130th Psalm;—Orton on Eternity;—Divine Origin of Christianity;—Doddridge on Regeneration;—Wilson's Youthful Memoirs.

31

ARTHUR SELOUS, *THE YOUNG GOVERNESS: A TALE FOR GIRLS*

(London: Griffith, Farran, Okeden and Welsh, *c.* 1870–9), pp. 17–18, 26, 28–29, 39, 106–114

[...] The door had not been quite shut; and as Annie entered with the packages, she saw tears in Martha's eyes. 'Poor thing! it hurted her, I daresay,' she thought; and moved with compassion, she offered in a kind manner to uncord the boxes. 'You're tired, Miss,' she said, looking at the pale, drooping figure seated on the bed.

Martha was quite deformed: a fall in childhood had been the cause, from the effects of which she had never recovered; it had injured her health materially, and she was a constant though silent sufferer.

'Yes,' she answered, 'a long journey is always tiring.'

The school-room bell rang violently at this moment.

'That's Miss Eleanor, for me,' said Annie; 'I must run, she don't like waiting.'

'Thank you, quite as much,' replied Martha, 'but I can do the rest myself; I will not keep you.'

Annie departed; and Martha closing the door, sank on her knees beside the bed, and resting her tired head against it, lifted her heart for a few moments to One whom she had long since found to be her only Rest. None but He knew the sorrows of that heart; none, well-nigh, but He cared for them. Alone, homeless, poor, despised, afflicted; thrown upon strangers, who considered it a condescension and a charity to employ her for the sake of her talents; keenly, indeed, she felt it all. But trial had taught her to go 'to the Strong for strength;' that strength which is 'made perfect in weakness' she had sought and found. Martha had learnt the secret of inward peace. She lifted her heart, now, not in complaint, but in thankfulness; for dreary as her lot promised to be, she looked at the blessings in it, only. She thanked God for providing for her; for giving her work to do for Him; for her safe journey; for Annie's kindness. She asked His blessing on the duties before her, and His guidance in the fulfilment of them; and rose from her knees with the helpful thought, 'I can do all things through Christ which strengtheneth me.' [...]

[...] It was half-past nine before Eleanor made her appearance in the school-room, where Martha had already been for two hours. Her breakfast had been cleared away, and Eleanor's succeeded, and ten o'clock struck before there was any prospect of lessons.

'My dear, these are not good habits,' said Martha gently, as she laid aside her book when Eleanor had finished her breakfast. 'Are you accustomed to rise so late, or is it an accident?'

'I have no particular time for rising,' Eleanor answered carelessly. 'Miss Budd, my last governess, was not strong, and did not rise early.'

'I shall be able to do so. I have always been used to it,' replied Martha. 'I think, my dear, you must try to get into the way of rising earlier, it is better both for body and mind. You have good health, I think?'

'Yes,' answered Eleanor sulkily.

'You should turn it to account while it is given you,' said Martha. [...]

[...] 'You do not seem to have been in the habit of giving much of the day to study,' said Martha, who thought this a very idle life, compared with her own in the school-room at the same age.

Eleanor knew it was, but did not see fit to acquiesce. She answered, 'Oh, it is quite enough in the country! I make up for it when we go to London in the spring. I have masters then, and am obliged to work.'

'You do not consider that you are obliged to work with your governess?'

'Not in the same sort of way. Now, am I?' half apologetically.

'Don't you think so?' inquired Martha. 'It is the first thing you have to learn, then.' She spoke so archly, and with such a pleasant smile, that Eleanor could not feel angry, though dignity whispered that she ought. She was obliged unwillingly to own that there was something superior in Martha; and though determined not to like her, or to agree with her in anything, she felt that Martha was a person not to be resisted. An examination followed, into Eleanor's progress in various branches of learning and accomplishments. Martha thought that the latter had been allowed to usurp too large a share of her pupil's attention; she, however, refrained from making any comment, knowing that it is generally better to make reforms gradually. The morning passed in looking over books, and arranging future plans of study. Eleanor foresaw a much stricter rule than any she had been used to. She did not like the prospect, but she felt there was no redress. Her mother would not listen to complaints on this head; for it was Lady Clere's ambition that Eleanor should be highly educated and accomplished, and the governess was to do it. . . .

[...] Taking her Bible and Prayer Book, Martha rested herself on the bed to read the Psalms and Lessons for the day. 'How I shall miss the daily service!' she thought with a sigh, as she finished, 'it was so happy at Elverton!' The next moment the half-repining thought was checked, and she blamed herself for selfishness. 'To lose self; that is the great lesson before you in your daily life now,' had been some of the words in her letter; and Martha had resolved over them, that she would seize every opportunity of learning how to do so.

'It is the lesson of all others we are slowest to learn,' she thought, 'and I especially. I have been thirty years in coming to the knowledge that I am selfish; how unwilling one is to see it in one's self!' Poor Martha! of all beings apparently the most unselfish and lowly; but she did not see herself 'as others' saw 'her.' Daily careful self-examination had long been her habit; and nothing but earnest perseverance in this shows us what we really are. [...]

[...] Gerty had a general invitation to the Manor; she could come and go as she liked. She was a great favourite there; partly, it might be, on account of her musical talent, which delighted Colonel Clere, and which Lady Clere thought an advantage to Eleanor. Gerty was quite Eleanor's equal in point of cultivation, and in much her superior, though with fewer outward accomplishments. Mr Leyton had himself had some share in her education; the little time he could spare from his parochial duties being divided between nursing his sick child and teaching Gerty. She called with her father at the Manor the next morning, and Eleanor kept her for the rest of the day.

Mr Leyton came to announce to Lady Clere that the church would be opened for daily service the week following. He said he hoped some of the household from the Manor would be able to attend, as it would set the example to the Clereton people.

Lady Clere listened, and answered, that it was very desirable, but she really did not know who could be spared. As for herself and Colonel Clere, it was out of the question, of course, so early.

'There is the evening service, at seven, also,' observed Mr Leyton.

'Ah, true; that would be more reasonable, but, unfortunately, seven is our dinner hour,' Lady Clere replied; 'I am afraid it will be quite impossible for us.'

Mr Leyton glanced at Eleanor.

'Oh, Eleanor certainly cannot! It would be too great a break upon the school-room duties,' said Lady Clere, smiling.

The Rector did not smile, he replied:

'Do not you think the daily service might help on the studies? It is only half an hour, or three-quarters at most. Gerty will attend it always.'

'Gerty is rather different,' said Lady Clere.

'You see, Eleanor has not much more time in the school-room, and it is of importance that she should make the most of it.'

'My dearest mamma,' said Eleanor, 'seven o'clock is the very time I am free from lessons. I could quite well go in the evening.' This was said in the spirit of opposition, for the moment before, when it was proposed, she had been thinking how she should hate being 'dragged to church' every day.

'Yes, and what would your papa say?' answered Lady Clere.

'By all means, my darling, if you like!' replied Eleanor, laughing. They all laughed; and Eleanor added, 'And he will come too, if I like!'

Lady Clere knew very well that he would. She did not want it to be the fashion at the Manor to attend daily service. She said:

'It is such a break in upon one's evening to have some of the family absent at church! It could not be a regular thing,' determining in her own mind that it should not be at all.

REFORMING PRIVATE LIFE

'I had forgotten that seven was your dinner hour,' said Mr Leyton. 'Of course I wish to arrange what best suits all. Six would do just as well for Clereton, perhaps better. It has not been given out yet.'

'Oh, pray do not think of altering the time for us,' said Lady Clere.

'We will see what Colonel Clere says,' replied Mr Leyton.

'The Lord of the Manor!' said Eleanor, laughing. She carried off Gerty upstairs, leaving them to discuss it.

Lady Clere immediately began to remark on Eleanor's love of opposition, saying:

'It would be much better for her to learn to yield to her mother's wishes, than to go to church a dozen times a day.'

'I quite agree with you,' said the Rector, 'but I also regret that your wishes are opposed to those of the Church.'

Lady Clere coloured. She was used, however, to sharp speeches from the Rector. She smiled and answered:

'We will not quarrel! You know, I do not see the good of going to church so often. It does not make people better or pleasanter.'

'Does it not?' replied Mr Leyton. 'Whose fault is that, then, if it is so?'

'Besides which,' said Lady Clere, getting out of his question, 'it is very inconvenient often, and puts people out of the way.'

'People will put themselves a great deal more out of the way to go to a ball or a dinner-party,' answered Mr Leyton. 'What is your next objection?'

'Why, a serious one; not personal, recollect. But I don't want Eleanor to be a Puseyite. She is too young to take up that sort of thing. I cannot have it.'

'Excuse me,' said the Rector. 'May I ask what you mean by a Puseyite?'

'Everybody knows what a Puseyite is!' said Lady Clere. 'You know what I mean perfectly.'

'I have heard different definitions of the term,' replied Mr Leyton. 'They vary. Some describe it to be "a horrid subtle thing;" others, again, pronounce it to be "a dull dry prig," "a formalist," or as some have it,

> "An Anglican angular,
>   Stiff and particular."

Is that yours?'

'Not exactly,' answered Lady Clere, laughing heartily.

'What *is* yours?' asked the Rector. 'I should like to hear.'

'Oh, what I mean by a Puseyite,' replied Lady Clere, 'is a person who goes to daily service in all weathers, thinks it necessary to affect a dismal dress, eats no meat on Fridays, and that sort of thing; people who make themselves ill of religion, in fact. I can't have Eleanor's health or complexion spoilt. It is all very well for people of a certain age who like to do it, but it is not the thing for her. Those ways unfit people for society. I mean such society as we move in,' she added, recollecting that Mr Leyton himself was supposed to be guilty of something of the kind.

'Your argument is only equalled by your definition,' he replied gravely. 'Those ways, as you call them, do not suit the world, it is true. Have you no thought for yourself and those you love beyond this world?'

'Of course I have,' she replied. 'But one has a position in society to keep up, and cannot make one's self singular.'

'Rather, that very position should be the reason for setting an example,' said Mr Leyton. 'I hope that it will, when you come to think it over. I do not speak of yourself. One does not expect an invalid to attend daily service; but it plainly is your duty to encourage, or at least allow it, in your household. Whether it makes people better and pleasanter, or not, or subjects them to party names or inconvenience, or anything else which is disagreeable, is not the question. There can be no doubt that it is the duty of every member of the Church who can do so to attend her appointed services; and you incur a very great responsibility if you forbid it.'

Lady Clere was silent. She valued the Rector's friendship, and was desirous of his good opinion, but she did not know how to get over his plain, strong words, sometimes. She dreaded a *tête-à-tête* with him, almost as much as Eleanor could have done, because he said things which made her think; and she did not like reflection on some subjects.

'Come,' he said, 'I shall hope that you will think over it, and do what is right. Recollect, you set Eleanor an example of undutifulness in yourself refusing to favour her attendance at the daily service; and though one would not for a moment encourage opposition in her, you could hardly complain if she did oppose you in that matter.'

'It would not be from principle if she did,' answered Lady Clere, 'but self-love.'

'Now you will hardly forgive me, I suppose,' replied the Rector, 'if I apply the same remark to yourself. It is not from principle that you object to her attending the daily service. Your objections centre in the supposed detriment to her health or her complexion;—only supposed, observe, because it would be neither necessary nor right for her to go out in all weathers.'

'Oh, well, she can go occasionally, I do not mind that; but you know how one thing leads to another, and, if she once takes it into her head to adopt extreme views, she will follow them out, and I shall have her end in being a Sister of Mercy, or something of that sort. You know her headlong disposition.'

'I think,' answered Mr Leyton, 'that with such dispositions, opposition fosters the very evil it is intended to counteract. I do not, at present, see any tendency in Eleanor to that which you predict; she has too little sense of religion, I grieve to say. You ought to be thankful for any means which might lead her to a better knowledge of her duty.'

'She does not want for knowledge,' answered Lady Clere, 'she knows well enough.'

'Alas! we all know better than we do,' replied the Rector. 'I should have said, to a better practice of her duty; and practical religion alone will do this.'

Lady Clere was silenced but not persuaded, and feeling herself unequal to argue the point, changed the subject.

Mr Leyton left the Manor, as he always did, disappointed and troubled at heart. What more disheartening to one who has the care of souls, than that cold, calculating worldliness, which will go just as far with religion as is necessary for its own convenience and respectability, and no further!

'I shall go, see if I don't, whenever I choose,' was Eleanor's laughing remark to Gerty, as the latter took off her bonnet and shawl in Eleanor's room.

'Well, I shall like it very much if you can, you may be sure, dear, if Lady Clere gives you leave. You won't go against her wishes, Eleanor?'

'Do you think she ought to forbid it, Gerty?'

'I don't know,' answered Gerty. 'There may be reasons. We cannot be the judges of what our parents do.'

'*No* one has a right to forbid what the Church commands,' said Eleanor decidedly; 'and if it were only for the sake of proving that to mamma, I should go.'

'The Church commands obedience to the powers that be,' returned Gerty, smiling, 'doesn't she?'

'The *higher* powers,' retorted Eleanor; 'which are the higher, the natural or the spiritual?'

'Now, I shall not argue with you, because you are as perverse as you can be: all the quips and quibbles in the world will not prove to me that you are right.'

'Well, there are exceptions to every rule.'

'Yes, that is what people say when they have no other argument; a nice get-off!'

Eleanor laughed. 'If I were not so much afraid of your father, Gerty, I should ask him about it,' she said.

'I wish you would,' answered Gerty earnestly.

3.4

Education

EDUCATION

3.4 Education

It was not only the education of the young upper classes that preoccupied evangelicals. As the middle class grew, and the number of women employed as governesses from all sections of the middle class increased, commentators became exercised about the moral standards, as well as the education, of these women who were to mould the next generation of Victorian society. These concerns led to philanthropic efforts to improve the status of governesses. Colleges such as Bedford College looked to improve education and training, and the Governesses' Benevolent Institution – for which Dinah Craik (1826–1887) wrote her novella *Bread upon the Waters*, and which published the work in 1852 – provided an economic safety net to preserve them from falling into disrespectful poverty between situations or in their old age.

Craik's *Bread upon the Waters* presents as its central protagonist the ideal, religiously self-denying governess, Felicia Lyne. Originally of noble birth, Felicia and her brothers are displaced from their home when their mother dies and their father remarries. As their stepmother makes their home unbearable for faithful Christians, Felicia believes it is her duty to leave home, taking her brothers with her, and to support herself by becoming a governess. The novel is written in the first person, so that Craik can provide the reader with a candid view of how Felicia experiences her sacrifices: how she initially endures and later glories in these sacrifices, supported by her faith. The hardest thing to relinquish is her love for her friend Sir Godfrey Redwood. For, in Craik's novella, unlike in romances such as *The Young Governess* (see this volume, Fidelity in the Upper Classes), Felicia is not restored to her correct place in the social hierarchy through marriage. However, Felicia is shown to have her own kind of nobility, equivalent to that of the middle-class gentleman who earns his 'own bread honourably and usefully'. She and Sir Godfrey stress that this is just one way that governesses can be noble, true Christian women, and that, if they wish, they can make themselves 'reverenced' as those who form 'the whole mind and character' of their charges.

While writers and activists aimed to reform the teachers of the middle and upper classes, organisations such as the Society for Promoting Christian Knowledge (SPCK) and the Sunday School movement targeted the young working class en masse with tracts, hymns, lessons and religiously themed entertainments.

The SPCK's tract, *Charlie Brame: or What Came of Loitering*, is highly typical of this genre of moral tracts for children, and, as the subtitle reveals, it is a didactic warning to children to avoid the particular sin of loitering. Charlie, bored by spending all day helping his mother with the baby, is tempted while running errands to loiter with his friends and, in doing so, disobeys his mother's direct instruction. When Charlie falls in the pond, losing the soap he was sent out to buy, he expresses his regret at the consequences of his actions in the simple direct speech of a child: 'Oh I will never, never disobey mother again'. The tract emphasises the importance of emotional domestic relations as a precursor to a correct relationship with God: Charlie's sadness at disappointing his mother and sister is redirected by his mother, as she reminds him 'to ask God to forgive him too'. As part of the tract's didactic form, the author uses direct address at two key points in the tract. At the point of temptation, the author breaks off to remind Charlie of 'the One who is always watching' and quotes the hymn that his Sunday school teacher had explained to him. And, at the end of the story, the author assures readers that Charlie is now 'a better boy', while explicitly enjoining them to remember the lesson of 'poor Charlie Brame'.

The skit (or 'concerted recitation') 'The Missionary Meeting', was written for Sunday schools providing week evening entertainment for young people. This emphasis on providing wholesome entertainment alongside religion may have been inspired by the activities of the Salvation Army (see this volume, the Salvation Army). The children are given the roles of young mission advocates to act out, which is only really an extension of the way they were already seen as contributors to the missionary cause as Sunday school students (see this volume, Children). As such, it is a highly appropriate theatrical performance, and could be seen as preparing the students for future lives as mission supporters, fundraisers, and visitors. The verse recited by the character 'Lizzie' emphasises the usual message of how lucky Sunday school students are to know about God, in comparison with their brothers and sisters in the non-Christian world (again, see this volume, Children). Meanwhile, the other characters tell stories of fundraising that range from the satirical, in the depiction of those who do not give, to the pathetic, in the generosity of the old and lame. The young missionaries are also painted as bold, storming 'the enemy's fortress' in the shape of 'Mr Cross'. Their success, both in collecting money and winning Mr Cross's respect, encourages the audience to see the role of 'lady collector' as one of influence and one to aspire to, showing the distance travelled since the early century (see this volume, Gaining Support).

32

DINAH CRAIK, *BREAD UPON THE WATERS* [1852]

In *Bread upon the Waters; A Family in Love; A Low Marriage; The Double House* (Leipzig: Bernhard Tauchnitz, 1865), pp. 50–59, 70–72

[...] After a day or two, I have leisure and quietness to write down the circumstance which has made such a change in the boys' future, and consequently in mine.

It was the day of the prize-distribution at King's College; and Henry had taken his younger brother with him "to see the fun," as he boldly called it,—poor Harry! though I noticed how pale he was all breakfast-time—aware that his own fate hung upon the balance. Since, till their names are called out, none of the boys know who are the winners of prizes.

I could not go, for pleasure must always yield to duty, in my profession; and I had two music lessons to give that afternoon.

Returning home I found to my surprise that the lads were not come in; I should have been foolishly restless, only I knew Aleck's good sense, and how, had any disappointment befallen his brother, no one could calm him better than Aleck could. So I employed myself in seeing that dinner was all ready, and in making the room neat—a weary business where there are two growing boys. And I am getting such a fidgetty particular old maid,—as Harry often tells me; though he always kisses me afterwards, lest I should be vexed.

—How long I am in coming to my story!

It was six in the evening, and I was growing thoroughly wretched and frightened, when I heard a knock, and a foot that could be none but Harry's, leaping up stairs (we live on the drawing-room floor now). In a minute, the lad burst in, all delight, and Aleck after him.

"Oh! sister, sister, only guess!" they both cried.

"No! don't let her guess," said a third voice; and then I saw that a gentleman was with my boys. One—than whom I would sooner have expected to see an angel of heaven standing in our room!

"I should have known your face any where, Miss Lyne, though I fear you have forgotten mine."—He was mistaken in both these things; but it did not signify.

235

Very soon we had shaken hands cordially, and partly from Harry, partly from Aleck, I began to hear how my brothers had met with Sir Godfrey Redwood.

He, now a man of consideration, had been invited to the distribution; there in the College Hall, he had heard called out the name of Henry Trevethlan Lyne; and seeing my boy walk up to receive his well-earned prize, had made sure it was his old favourite. Afterwards he had spoken to the lads, and they had told him our whole story. It was very different from the one my step-mother had given him concerning us, some eight years ago. No wonder he had suffered us gradually to drop out of his memory, unworthy a good man's thought.

He dined with us that day, though the proud boys were rather shocked that he should see our humble board. And all that evening, with the June sun slanting in upon his face,—in which the former boyish likeness gleamed strangely at times, though he is much changed by the thick moustache and beard he wears, foreign fashion,—Sir Godfrey Redwood sat talking, sometimes gaily, sometimes thoughtfully, with "Miss Lyne the governess," and her brothers.

I saw in the first ten minutes, that despite his kind courtesy about knowing my face, he, too, was struck by the change which I so clearly perceive in myself; and that if the old "Felicia" had not been long swept out from what could have been at best a mere boyish memory, the sight of "Miss Lyne" had now made it, and all belonging to it, irrevocably *the past*. It was well for me that I had discernment and strength of mind enough at once to assure myself of this, so that our future intercourse may be, as indeed it is, perfectly free and unembarrassed on either side.

Sir Godfrey told us much of what had happened to himself since the days when he used to visit at the Square. It was the ordinary life of a young man of fortune, filled up with many extravagances and follies, all of which he owned so freely, that one could plainly discern—even if his whole countenance, bearing, and the accidental nothings by which we judge of character, had not confirmed the fact— that there had been in him no vice; that the son of his proud and virtuous mother was, as I had long learnt from other sources, the stay and glory of the Redwood house.

His "wild oats," he said, had been sown early, abroad and at home, and he was now in the midst of manhood's grave and earnest career,—the career of one who deeply felt, that as regarded talents, influence, and the power of doing good, to him much had been given, and of him much would surely be required.

Harry asked him if he was married? to which he laughingly answered, "No, nor engaged either, though he had been in love and out of love at least a dozen times, as Master Harry would himself ere long."

Then, turning to me, he changed his tone to seriousness, and spoke of all the cares he had had with his younger brothers and sisters, and what a happy and noble mistress his mother made at Redwood Hall. "It would be long ere I should find a Lady Redwood like her," added he, smiling; and then the conversation died.

But now comes that act of generosity, which I find my brother Henry and he had settled entirely between themselves before ever the matter was confided to me, though of course my nominal consent was to be asked as a seal to the bond.

DINAH CRAIK, *BREAD UPON THE WATERS*

Sir Godfrey is about to proceed abroad as *chargé d'affaires* at—. He wishes to take with him Henry, who at seventeen—nay sixteen, for it wants three months to his birthday—is as manly-looking and manly-minded as many a youth of twenty. He said, the boy should be his secretary, or *attaché,*—some nominal office, through which I see clearly his generous purpose of taking all care for Harry's future entirely upon himself.

And Harry must go. It would break the lad's heart did I refuse. I have no right to let any foolish scruple stand in the light of this, the sole chance that may ever offer of my darling brother's earning his bread and making his way in the world in the sole manner that his proud nature would ever thoroughly bend to—as a gentleman. Besides, as Sir Godfrey reminded me, this change in fortune only replaces Harry in the sphere where he was born; since—like water, the pure blood of the Trevethlans and the Lynes will always find its own level.

When he said so, I smiled, and in my turn reminded him that I was still "the governess."

"Well!" he answered, "and what is more honourable than a governess, when she is a lady by birth, or at least by education, as all governesses ought to be? What more noble than a woman who devotes her whole life to the sowing of good seed, the fruitage of which she may never see? If I ever have a wife and children," here his eyes smiled with some dim, dawning thought, "I will teach them, that after father and mother there is no one on earth to whom they owe such reverence as to her on whom depends the formation not only of their intellect, but of their whole mind and character. But, accordingly, I will take care that this model governess is worthy of the trust,—a true lady, and more, a true *woman,*—in fact, just such a woman as you are yourself, Miss Lyne."

I had no answer to that. I—*his* children's governess!

Still, it gives me comfort to think he should so honour the sisterhood to which I belong—unto which I had joined myself in humiliated despair, until at last I began to wear my heavy chains as the badge of a worthy service, and to discover that every governess has it in her power to make herself, and with herself all her fraternity, reverenced and honourable in the sight of the world.

***

Henry is gone away—Henry, my noble, handsome boy! my right hand and strong-hold in the bitter days of adversity, which hardly seemed adversity when borne for him! But, please God! there is only prosperity in store for him now.—Also, for me and little Aleck, still *little*, gentle, and pale. But Aleck shall go to college, if he likes, nevertheless; for he too must be well educated, as is his brother. My mother's sons shall not be inferior in any way to the children who, I hear, cluster round my father's hearth, and will inherit his property. Well! we envy them not. May they prove a comfort to his old age!

To-night Aleck and I have sat for the last time in our old lodgings, from which we are now removing nearer town. I cannot walk so well as I used to do, and we need better rooms, since the situation I have now obtained through Sir Godfrey Redwood, and which I have promised him to hold until he and Harry return home, is one of a higher class and higher salary than any I have hitherto had. Think of my teaching a little Lady Anne!

She is the youngest daughter of a poor earl—I see he is poor for an earl; but he lives in honest retirement, keeping within his means; which is doubtless the reason why Sir Godfrey honours him so much. I honour him too, and his three fair daughters, as cordially as if they had not "a handle" to their pretty Christian names.

A quiet yet somewhat dull tea we had, Aleck and I; and then we sat in the twilight, talking, and watching the shadows in the room, which now seems mean yet once appeared to us magnificent, compared to the former back-parlour. The poor old room, which has seen so much! We almost grew sad to think we should no more watch the street-lamp's glimmer creeping in along the wall, so pleasant and dim—besides often saving us an hour or two of candle-light, in times when every small saving was of pathetic value. Ah! the poor old room!

Soon we broke off talking of the past to speculate on the dawning future, and to wonder whether it would be two years, three, or four ere Harry came back! and if so, what a man he would be!—Especially when in the constant society of such a perfect gentleman as Sir Godfrey Redwood. Aleck quite envied him that; for Aleck, with all his quietness, has an exquisite taste for the refinements of life. Nay, coming one day to fetch me home, he has quite fallen in love with my little Lady Anne, and I hear of nothing else from morning till night. The foolish boy! Sixteen and five feet four to adore eleven and four feet nothing! But Aleck is a young poet, and so, as I tell him, must fain begin the usual destiny of poets—to be *always* in love!

Love!—Have I, even I, begun lightly to use that solemn word?

Aleck is at last gone to bed, and I have taken away his candle, lest he should set the house on fire through reading novels, which would be a pretty climax to our long abiding here.

I go up to my own room, and in its solitary silence think of many things—chiefly, of the steamer which, under this same midnight moon, is floating down the broad Thames, and bearing with it my best treasures in this world,—bearing them to a future, in which as regards neither, shall I have in time to come any share or claim. Both will ere long have taken to their hearts much nearer ties. To-night Aleck made me laugh, by prophesying that it would not be very many years before I dandled on my knees Harry's children:—and Sir Godfrey Redwood gaily promised I should be governess to his! All these jests will one day come true; and then I,—this one solitary I—

No matter!—May'st Thou, O God, receive the life-sacrifice on which, year by year, I have thrown all that was lovely and precious in my eyes, and so make the offering—worthless of itself—sweet and acceptable in Thine! [...]

[...] This morning, after breakfast, Sir Godfrey Redwood asked me to walk with him, that he might show me the conservatories; and there, sitting down under a fair orange-tree, with the sun shining in upon all sorts of gorgeous flowers he has brought home from abroad, he talked with me long and seriously of the future—of my brother's future.

He says, that he intends entering public life under the new ministry, and that Harry, now more than twenty years old, shall be his secretary, or have a government appointment, as may be. The boy is able and willing to carve out his own fortunes now; and will be placed where he need not dread that one word—which Sir Godfrey never uses—*patronage*. He will be independent, too, though not rich; and, as I said, Henry and I between us can give Aleck what he desires—a college-education, to fit him for the Church; so that, in every way, the path before us is straight.

And here came in Sir Godfrey's generosity, which I can hardly think of without tears.

He asked me about my health,—if I were happy,—if I should not be lonely when Aleck was at Cambridge,—and if, as my younger brother's college expenses could easily be managed, (ah! I knew how!) I would consent to give up teaching, and, just till Harry wanted me to keep his house, settle in a pretty little cottage there was near Redwood Hall? He said all this with some confusion and hesitation; but,—let me quite assure myself of that fact,—only the hesitation of a delicate generosity, to which the mere act of seeming to bestow favours is a pain.

For me, if I were somewhat agitated, he would easily attribute it to a similar cause.

I answered, that I had always lived independent, and wished it to be so to the end;—that it was much better I should still remain a governess. Only, as I had rather be with those I loved than with strangers, perhaps he would use his influence that I might stay permanently with little Lady Anne.

When I said "use his influence," he half smiled; then looked sad, and said gravely, that he had no influence in the Airlie family except as an ordinary friend.

(Then, things are not yet quite as I imagined!) Sir Godfrey, after a pause, continued the conversation. With true delicacy, he did not oppose my wish; and I shall still earn my own bread honourably and usefully. It is far the best: an idle life would kill me. Work, constant work, is the sustainer, cheerer, and physician of the soul.

But that fact alters not the noble kindness of this most noble man, kindness of which I can hardly write or speak, but which I shall remember while I live.

After our talk we joined the others, until I came up softly into my own room, to be quiet and rest.

Henry provided for, placed where his career through life lies, humanly speaking, in his own hands; Aleck given his heart's desire:—how happy my two boys will be! And how thankful, solemnly and deeply thankful, am I!

Sitting at my little Gothic window, I can see him,—I mean Sir Godfrey,—walking on the lawn, with Lady Dorothy and little Lady Anne. How happy he looks; happy as a man must be who diffuses happiness wherever he sets his foot. Such a man I knew he would become! God bless him—God evermore bless him! And what does it signify how far off one stands from great treasures, eternally set aside, when one knows of a certainty that the gold has not become dim, that the fine gold will never change!

33

G. F. B., *CHARLIE BRAME: OR WHAT CAME OF LOITERING*

(London: Society for Promoting Christian Knowledge, 1870), pp. 5–15

"Charlie," said Mrs. Brame to her little boy, "put on your hat and go and get me a pen'orth of soap at the shop; I find I have hardly any left, and I must wash Ada's frock to-night, that she may have a decent one to go to the school-feast to-morrow."

Charlie, who had been nursing baby nearly all day, gladly put her down in her cradle, and taking up his cap ran off to the village.

"Mind you don't loiter, Charlie. If you don't come straight home I shan't have time to do the washing."

"All right, mother," he answered; and, to prove his readiness to execute her commission, he ran off so quickly that in a minute he was out of sight.

Mrs. Brame's house stood halfway up a hill, at the foot of which lay the village. Charlie soon reached the shop, and, after buying the soap, started on his homeward path. But he had not gone far before he was stopped by a group of little boys who were standing at a gate through which he had to pass.

"Oh, here's Charlie!" cried one of them. "Charlie, we've found such a jolly place to float Ted Smith's boat in. Do come with us and see it."

"No, I can't," he replied; "mother told me to come straight home."

"Oh, but it is on your way home. It is a pool by the river side where some water was left after the floods; and you can't think how beautifully the boat sails."

"Yes, come along," cried the others. "You need not stay more than a minute."

Charlie hesitated. He had been nursing that cross baby all the day. Why shouldn't he have a little pleasure like other boys? He would not stay more than a minute, and it was on the way home. Mother would never know that he had been loitering, because he had run so quickly that, even if he waited five minutes, he would be home earlier than she would expect him.

Ah Charlie, but have you never heard of One who is always watching us, and knows all we do, even if mother does not?

Yes, Charlie knew it. Only the Sunday before he had learnt the hymn beginning—

"God sees all I do,
  He hears all I say,
He knows my thoughts, too,
  And my every way."

And his Sunday-school teacher had explained it to him; but Charlie was fonder of looking out of the window and thinking of his play, than attending to what was told him, unless, indeed, it were an interesting story, and so he did not remember it.

"I will come," he said; "only let us be quick, for I do want to see the boat very much."

They scampered off. Soon the boat was launched into the pool, and Charlie and the boys, regardless of the mud, knelt round it, absorbed in the exciting amusement.

Many minutes passed away, and still Charlie stayed, throwing stones to make waves, and loading the boat with fir cones. At last they loaded it too heavily, and, when halfway across the pool, it began to sink.

"Save it, Charlie," cried the owner to the little boy who was nearest to the boat. "The flag will be quite spoilt if it gets wet."

Charlie stretched forward—his feet slipped down the wet clay bank, and splash! he fell into the water. The pool was only a few feet deep, so he easily got out; but what a sad plight he was in! His clothes were dripping with wet, his cap was fished out soaked and muddy, and he stood shivering on the grass, half-inclined to cry, and afraid to go home. However, the boys could not help him—some, indeed, almost laughed when they saw the miserable picture that he presented,—so he walked sulkily up the hill, heartily wishing that he had never loitered.

His mother, who was standing at the door looking out for him, held up her hands in silent astonishment when she saw that the wretched, forlorn-looking child whom she had seen in the distance was her own little boy. She was not silent long, however; but when she had heard his story sent him at once to bed.

"Give me the soap before you go upstairs," she added; "I shall hardly have time to wash Ada's frock as it is, so don't keep me waiting any longer."

Charlie put his hand into his dripping pocket, but the soap was not there.

"What can I have done with it? I know I put it here," he cried, growing very red.

"What! lost the soap, too," cried Mrs. Brame, quite out of patience. "Charlie, I am ashamed of you; you have been both careless and disobedient. Go to bed at once. I wonder what father will say to you. Poor Ada won't be able to go to the school feast. It is getting too dark for me to go back to the village and leave the house with only you children in it. Well, I hope you are ashamed of yourself!"

Charlie crept off to bed, feeling very unhappy. He loved little Ada very dearly, and knew that she would cry her eyes out when she heard that she must stay at home, while all the other children went gaily up to the hall to have tea and games in the park.

"Oh," said he to himself, "I will never, never disobey mother again, and then, perhaps, she will forgive me this time." And when his mother came to fetch his clothes to dry he told her so, and she said that she hoped he would never forget the lesson he had been taught by such sad experience, and that she would forgive him, but that he must not forget to ask God to forgive him, too, and help him to remember his good resolution, and, as he did so, I have no doubt that he is now a better boy.

One of the young ladies at the house, when she heard why little Ada Brame could not come to the school feast, sent her a pretty china doll which pleased her so much that she quite forgot her sad disappointment.

If any little children who read this story are in the habit of loitering about when sent on an errand, let them remember poor Charlie Brame.

34

MARY B. G. SLADE, 'THE MISSIONARY MEETING'

In *For Week Evening Entertainment* (London: Sunday School Union, 1887), pp. 1–4

A Concerted Recitation for Several Girls

[*Persons:—Several young ladies, representing a missionary meeting; one very little girl; three girls acting as advocates for the mission cause.*]

Miss A. The business before the meeting is simply to wait till our young advocates bring in their report.

Miss B. I hope they will have done well. I think it is quite time we older persons transferred some of our work to younger hands.

Miss C. While we are waiting, let us hear if little Lizzie has her verses nicely learned for the next mission day.

Miss A. (lifting Lizzie up into the chair). Now, Lizzie, dear; speak slowly and clearly, so that all can hear.

All Lizzie Knows

Lizzie. I am a very little thing,
    As you can plainly see;
But then I know who came to bring
    God's gift of love to me.

When I am well, I know who makes
    My life so sweet and bright;
When I am sick, I know who takes
    Care of me day and night.

And when I die, I know whose hand
    Will lead my soul away,
Through Death's dark valley, to the land
    Of bright, eternal day.

REFORMING PRIVATE LIFE

Just such dear little girls as I
    Live o'er the ocean wave;
They do not know who came to die
    A sinful world to save.

Poor little heathen! Friends, I pray
    That you will quickly go,
Or send somebody straight away!
    To teach them—*all I know!*

Miss B. (taking Lizzie down). That is Lizzie's mission offering. I think if Jesus were here, He would say she hath done what she could.

Miss C. Here come our young advocates, Alice, Carrie, and Susie. Good morning, girls.

Girls. Good morning, ladies.

Miss C. I hope you bring us plenty of money, and that you have enjoyed making the visits, too.

Alice. We really have enjoyed it, though in various ways. Shall we tell our experience?

Miss D. Yes, if you please.

Carrie. First, we called on Mrs. Brisk. That call was finished in a hurry, I assure you. "Missionary offering?" said she. "Yes, indeed! Walk right in; it's all counted out! Thought you'd be here soon. Here it is. Can't say I wish 'twas more, because it's just according to my means, and the Lord has the regulating of them. I won't ask you to sit down, for I suppose you've ever so many places to go to; besides, I'm as busy as a bee myself!" So off she flew, and we walked off, having obtained the money in less time than we have taken to tell of it.

Miss A. Where next?

Susie. We went to Mrs. Kindly's, Mrs, Allright's, and Mrs. Ready's. They all had a pleasant word for us, and cheerfully gave their contribution. Mrs. Kindly said it was very good in us to go round so, and save people the trouble of sending in their money. Here are their gifts. Now, Alice, you tell the next story.

Alice. Well, then, our next visit was to Mrs. Splendid. "*Mission*-school money," said she. "What mission-school?" So I told about the mission-school we support in India, how hopeful we were of the good it was doing, and how glad we were of the good it had done. I thought I was making such a moving speech!

Carrie. It proved so; for Mrs. Splendid stiffly said, "I have many calls for my money, young ladies; I have nothing for you to-day." And she moved in, and we moved out. Just think of it! Such lots of money as Mrs. Splendid has!

Miss C. Here, girls, is a lesson for you: when you meet such rebuffs, take them in a gentle spirit. Judge not, but try to feel kindly toward the selfish and ungenerous, and then dismiss them from your thoughts, as quickly as Mrs. Splendid dismissed you from her door.

Susie. Can't we call her shabby?

MARY B. G. SLADE, 'THE MISSIONARY MEETING'

Miss D. "Not a bit of it!" as you girls say. Just say nothing about her.

Alice. Then we went to see lame Jenny. We didn't think she ought to give anything, she is so very poor; but Susie said we would go in and tell her what we were doing.

Miss A. Poor patient sufferer! What did she say to you?

Carrie. She clapped her little thin hands, and said she was so glad we had come! She had been thinking so much, since she cannot go to church and Sunday-school, of the heathen children, who never had a church or Sunday-school, and who know nothing about the Heavenly Father's Book.

Miss B. But, of course, you didn't ask her to give anything?

Susie. Ask her! We hadn't the chance! She said at once, "you must have my mission-offering, only you will have to wait while I go to the bank for it."

Miss C. Go to the bank, when she cannot walk a step!

Alice. Yes. She took her little tin savings-bank, and made believe knock at the door. "Any money for me, to-day?" said she.

"How much do you want?" she made believe answer from within.

"All you have," said she. "What for?" "For my mission-offering," said Jenny.

"Yes! here it is. Come down the chimney and get it!" You know they have to turn the pennies out at the chimney-top; so she counted them out, and made us take them.

Carrie. I asked if she wouldn't need it for something. She said no; it was given her to buy sweets with; but if missionary sweets tasted better to her than any others, she ought to have her choice.

Miss D. Oh! girls, I don't need to tell you to learn a lesson from her sweet self-denying spirit!

Susie. I think we did. We were intending to buy us each a new ribbon on our way home; we had been choosing between blue and pink. When we left Jenny's, Alice said, "Girls, how would you like *missionary* colour for our ribbons?" We took the hint, and all decided to have that colour.

Alice. Only, ladies, as we are indebted to Jenny for the plan, we think the money ought to go against her name, and we have put it so.

Miss A. That's right! She will be so happy when she knows her humble example has influenced you in the right way.

Miss B. Did you go to Mrs. Dillydally's?

Carrie. Yes. She said, "Well, she'd see; she didn't know. How much did the deacons' wives give? How much did the pastor's wife give? For her part, it seemed as if there was always something coming. We might call again; she'd see about it."

Miss C. And Mrs. Sharpe?

Susie. Oh! she said Mr. Sharpe gave enough already! *She* couldn't be bothered! And she said good morning as quickly as Mrs. Brisk; but oh, in such a different tone!

Miss D. Here is more money than your list of names accounts for; how is that?

Alice. I'll tell you. It was so funny! We saw Mr. Cross coming down the street. You know he is as rich as can be, but doesn't believe in missions, nor

Sunday-schools, nor anything of the kind. Carrie said, "Let's storm the enemy's fortress, and see what we can get."

Carrie. So I told him our mission-work, and politely asked for a contribution.

Miss A. What did he say?

Carrie. He lifted both hands and rolled up his eyes and said, "The *beggars* are coming to town!" That roused me! I told him we were not beggars; that the mission cause was God's cause; that we were very young, but we meant to try to do all we could for the cause, and for God; and, if he pleased, I preferred he would never call us beggars again!

Miss B. I hope you did not make him vexed.

Alice. I rather think not. He looked steadily at Carrie as if he were thinking of what she had said. Then the queer man said, "Hold out your hands!" We did so, and he dropped a penny into every one, saying, *"that's* for your mission!" Then he made a low bow to Carrie, and said, laying a sovereign in her hand, "respected madam, *that* is for your *preach!*"

Miss C. Well done, Carrie! I never knew a mission "preach" have any effect on him before. I hope it may be lasting.

Miss D. You had Mrs. Flutter's name; what did she say?

Susie. She said, "Deary-me, no! She just couldn't. Everything was so high! Bad as war-times! Elizabeth Eliza was taking music-lessons, and deary-me, it cost so much! And Elizabeth Eliza must have a new silk dress, and 'charity begins at home,' and deary-me, she just couldn't!" So she didn't.

Alice. Oh! but the last place was so different! Dear Grandmother Eld gave her money, with her poor, trembling fingers, and then she talked to us so sweetly!

Carrie. Yes. She told us how glad she was, we were beginning so young to work in the dear Lord's vineyard. Then she showed us a little ivory box on her shelf, in which she had kept her mission fund for forty years.

Susie. And she said, "Next year, when you come, I don't think I shall be here. I think I shall be in the beautiful city, whose gates are of pearl. But my offering," said she, "I shall leave in the box, and you may open it, and find it, and take it." Then she prayed God to bless us, and we came away.

Miss A. Young ladies, we are highly gratified at your report. You have not only brought us a good large sum of money, but your experience has been both useful to yourselves and pleasant to us. And we shall certainly move at our next meeting that you all be reappointed as young lady collectors for the coming year.

Part 4

SOCIAL AND POLITICAL REFORM

4.1

Abolitionism

4.1 Abolitionism

From its very beginnings, the anti-slavery movement in Britain was associated with the Quakers and evangelical groups (see Volume I, Forms of Dissent). John Wesley and Hannah More wrote against the slave trade, William Wilberforce spearheaded the Parliamentary campaign against the trade, and members of Quaker anti-slavery societies started economic boycotts of sugar and other goods produced by slave labour. In 1807 the slave trade was abolished by law in the British Empire, and eventually slave owning in the Empire was outlawed completely in 1833. However, England still imported goods such as cotton from the United States, which continued to use slave labour until 1865, and societies in England campaigned for the complete abolition of slavery.

Anti-slavery activity was not confined to Parliament. Local campaigns were essential to the success of the movement, and the network of women's anti-slavery societies came to be highly valued by abolitionist leaders for, among other things, their ability to increase public interest. The Quaker, Elizabeth Heyrick (1769–1831), and her friend Susanna Watts (d. 1842) led the Leicester branch of the Female Society for the Abolition of Slavery and co-produced the anti-slavery periodical, *The Humming Bird*. In the article from this periodical extracted in this section, the author takes on the persona of 'Common Sense' in order to respond to a recently published text by a member of the Christian clergy ('The House of Bondage' by Reverend B. Bailey). The writer criticises Bailey for making an argument in favour of slavery, and aims to discredit his thesis by attacking its premises through logic and reasoning. She displays intellectual confidence as she uses the Bible to refute Bailey's argument that Africans were doomed to be slaves because, as the descendants of Ham, they were cursed. She also uses anthropological knowledge to ridicule Bailey for the sheer number of peoples he is asserting are doomed to slavery (see this volume, Ethnography and Anthropology). Insisting that the only argument remaining for slavery is that of economic interest, the writer calls on Bailey to accept that the arguments against slavery – 'Justice, Truth' and 'Christian Feeling' – outweigh this. Her description of the anti-slavery movement is reminiscent of women's mission writing; she expresses gratitude that she and other abolitionists were born in England with its freedom and Christianity, and she uses military metaphors, calling for Christian heroes to join the movement, which is characterised as an army (see this volume, Women and Authority in the Mission Field). She also connects national feeling with abolitionism: she references an English love of common sense, English sympathy, and likens the movement's determination to the firmly rooted 'native oak'.

Isaac Nelson (1809–1888) was an Irish Nationalist and a Presbyterian minister (see Volume I, Scottish Presbyterianism). Like the writer of the *Hummingbird* article, his lecture to the Free Church Anti-Slavery Society draws on nationalism, among other discourses, to criticise one of its leaders, Thomas Chalmers, for making an argument in favour of the continuance of slavery. Nelson reminds the society that the British state has acted to outlaw slavery, that the British constitution would not tolerate it and that – it follows – Britain's soil is therefore too sacred for 'the foot of the slave master'. In contrast, he alleges that the men of Scotland, despite being descended from heroic Scottish rebels, are now associated with the defence of slavery and with allowing the death of a leading American abolitionist. Like Heyrick and Watts, Nelson highlights the economic argument that is being advanced by supporters of slavery – that they should not have to give up their property – and he uses Biblical quotation to argue that slave owners will need to sacrifice their slaves before they can be worthy of God or received by the Church. Nelson also ridicules Chalmers' argument that allowances must be made for the slaveholders' culture, in which slaveholding has been engrained by 'custom'. His most powerful criticism is saved for the American Churches however, as he details how they teach that slavery is not condemned in the Bible, and how they allow slaves to be treated, in what he describes as a 'perversion' and 'pollution' of the gospel.

35

[SUSANNA WATTS AND ELIZABETH HEYRICK], 'REMARKS ON THE DESCENT OF THE AFRICANS FROM HAM'

The Humming Bird, or Morsels of Information on the Subject of Slavery, 1, January 1825, pp. 35–38, 39–45

Remarks on the Descent of the Africans from Ham

In a Letter, addressed to the Rev. B. Bailey, A. M., Curate of Burton-upon-Trent

Rev. Sir,—As *my* sentiments upon subjects of importance (I wish to speak this with gratitude for such distinction) have long been honored with peculiar notice in this nation, one of whose distinguishing characteristics is a *sound understanding*, I request your candid perusal of the following thoughts. They were suggested by two passages in your late publication upon the subject of Slavery, intitled "The House of Bondage," &c. The passages I allude to are these.—

"*The whole continent of Africa, which was peopled by the descendants of Ham*, has been successively galled by the relentless oppression of the Romans and the Saracens, and is now chiefly under the dominion of the Turks.[1]—But by what nations have not the miserable Negroes been enslaved? The very cattle of our markets have not been bought and sold in more cold-blooded traffic, more publicly and universally, and with less sense of shame, than these wretched outcasts of society. What nation of Europe, what nation of the earth is there that hath not dealt in the blood of *these denounced children of the wicked Ham?* Had not God's providence for the punishment of vice, been visible to the eye of religious *faith;* did we not look upon them as the victims of the crimes of others, and mysteriously fulfilling ancient prophecies for wise, though to us, inscrutable purposes; did we not behold them as living evidences of the earliest ages of the world; did we not contemplate this wretched people as an awful warning of the wrath of God, and believe, that, in another state, they will be placed in a condition of progressive, moral and intellectual advancement;[2] did we not, I say, regard the sufferings of this ignorant and servile race, with feelings chastened by religious *faith,* we could hardly endure the reflection of their sufferings without *indefinable sensations of horror."*—pp. 22, 23.

Again—"We have seen that, according to the course of Divine Providence, this wretched race hath been prostrated in subjection to their fellow-creatures from the earliest ages. We must not arraign God's Providence, neither can we divert its course. To do the one, or attempt the other, were equally *presumptuous"*—p. 34.

Here we have an argument in favor of Slavery, *new, singular* and *striking.* Allow me, Sir, to try it by the test of *sound reasoning;* not the bewildering logic of the schools, but the logic upon which I always establish my plain rules of argumentation, viz. that whatever premises are laid down, the conclusions which *naturally* and clearly follow from them, must be admitted. This, you will readily grant, and now let us see what conclusions naturally follow the premises you have, in the foregoing passages, laid down. These premises are, that *the whole Continent of Africa, as being peopled by the descendants of Ham, is under a curse, and therefore it is presumptuous to attempt to rescue the Africans from Slavery.*

Alas! poor Africa!—it is not enough that thou shouldest have thy sons and daughters stolen by other nations, bought and sold and chained and flogged, and made drudges to the luxuries of their fellow-men, but thou must be blotted out of thy place on the terraqueous globe!—be no longer a part of the visible creation!— no longer have any claim upon the compassion of more favoured nations!—no longer any title to the common mercies of a superintending Providence!—no longer any share in the fatherly goodness of HIM whose *"mercies are over all his works!"*—Thou who art so sacrificed and abandoned, and from a *Slave* art become *a Castaway*—it is *presumption* to pity and redress thy injuries!—That word being thus *engaged,* where shall we find another to express what it is, thus to denounce upon thee *an everlasting curse?*—No word can be found—"expressive silence must muse the rest."

Let us examine the Scripture authority for this tremendous denunciation against the *descendants of Ham.* The first notice of a curse upon Canaan, the youngest son of Ham, (for Ham himself is not mentioned) stands thus. "And he (Noah) said, Cursed be Canaan; a servant of servants shall he be to his brethren. And he said, Blessed be the Lord God of Shem, and Canaan shall be his servant. God shall enlarge Japheth, and he shall dwell in the tents of Shem; and Canaan shall be his servant."[3]

Noah here, agreeably to the custom of the Patriarchal fathers of families, denounces blessings and curses upon his children, according as their conduct was good or bad. The words may probably be rather prophetic than maledictory; and if so, they were awfully accomplished in the degradation and extermination of the Canaanites. But it is very remarkable that Ham is not mentioned either in the foregoing denunciation, or ever afterwards. Canaan, not Ham, stands as the head of this race. Let it be remembered, that this denunciation is not prefaced with the divine sanction of "Thus saith the Lord;"—and that in the positive command given by God to Moses and Joshua, utterly to extirpate the Canaanites, the reason expressly assigned for this punishment is *their own wickedness* alone, and no allusion whatever is made to the curse of Noah.—"Understand, therefore, this day, that the Lord thy God is he which goeth over before thee as a consuming fire: he shall destroy them, and he shall bring them down before thy face: so shalt thou drive them out, and destroy them quickly, as the Lord hath said unto thee. Speak not thou in thine heart, after that the Lord thy God hath cast them out from before thee, saying, For my righteousness the Lord hath brought me in to possess this land: *but for the wickedness of these nations* the Lord doth drive them out from before thee. Not for thy righteousness, or for the uprightness of thine heart dost thou go to possess their land: but for *the wickedness of these nations*, the Lord thy God doth drive them out from before thee, and that he may perform the word which the Lord sware unto thy fathers, Abraham, Isaac and Jacob."[4] [...]

[...] But supposing, for an instant, that you could prove your position, let us enquire, who are *"these denounced descendants of the wicked Ham?"*—You are not, perhaps, aware of the *extensiveness* of this imaginary curse.—The descendants of Ham, as you allow, include all the inhabitants of one whole quarter of the globe, a tract of country 4,300 miles long and 3,500 broad. It is twice the size of Europe, more than twice that of North America, and more than eighty-five times that of Great Britain and Ireland.[5]

The giants of the poets performed wonderful feats, when they tore up the islands to throw them at the Gods; as did Milton's angels, who

> "———pluck'd the seated hills with all their load,
> Rocks, waters, woods; and by the shaggy tops
> Uplifting, bore them in their hands.—"

But you have far outdone them; for with a stroke of your pen, you have cut through the isthmus of Suez, and torn away the vast peninsula of Africa from all union with the rest of the earth!

But this is not all by a great deal—you have done *more;* let us look at the opinion of a man, whose authority in matters of ancient research, you will, doubtless, acknowledge to stand very high; and I fear, we shall find the posterity of Ham to have extended farther than Africa. What will you do now?—Will you next sever *India* from the earth?—let us hear Sir William Jones.—

"Three sons of the just and virtuous man, whose lineage was preserved from the general inundation, travelled, we are told, as they began to multiply, in *three* large divisions, variously subdivided. The children of YA'FET (Japheth) seem, from the traces of *Sklavonian* names, and the mention of their being *enlarged,* to have spread themselves far and wide, and to have produced the race which, for want of a correct appellation, we call *Tartarean;* the colonies formed by the sons of HAM and SHEM appear to have been nearly simultaneous; and among those of the latter branch, we find so many names incontestibly preserved at this hour in *Arabia,* that we cannot hesitate in pronouncing them the same people, whom hitherto we have denominated *Arabs;* while the former branch, (Ham) the most powerful and adventurous of whom were the progeny of CUSH, MISR and RAMA,[6] (names remaining unchanged in *Sanscrit,* and highly revered by the Hindus) were, in all probability, the race which I call *Indian,* and to which we may now give any other name that may seem more proper and comprehensive."[7]

Again, in the same discourse, this profound Orientalist draws a strong argument from the etymology of names, to prove that Cush was an ancestor of the Indian race. [...]

[...] Now, Sir, you are bound, by the simplest rules of logic, to reason fairly from your own premises.—*The descendants of Ham*, you believe, are under the doom of an inevitable decree. In this position *all* his descendants are included—that is a clear consequence, which no reasoning can evade.—Therefore not only the *Africans,* but the Indians, and not only the Indians, but the *Cushean Arabians,*[8] and all the *Hamians,* who have mingled with other nations, must likewise be *outlawed* and *excommunicated.* Take them all, trace them throughout the world—but see that thou touch not one descendant of Shem or Japheth!

> ——"nor cut thou less, nor more,
> But just a pound of flesh: if thou tak'st more
> Or less than a just pound, be't but so much
> As makes it light or heavy in the substance,
> On the division of the twentieth part
> Of a poor scruple————thou diest!"

There is another *inevitable* consequence attached to your position.—If there exists in this world of probationary sufferings, *any one* calamity which it is *not* our duty to relieve, it follows that it is not our duty to relieve *any;* because no human understanding can comprehend that the Great and Good Creator would command us to assist some of our afflicted fellow-creatures, and not *all.*—Therefore, if it is *presumption* to rescue the Africans, now labouring as they are, under a more accumulated burden of calamity than ever afflicted any other race of men, it must be as great presumption to relieve other evils.—The *Priest* and the *Levite* were, *consequently,* humble and pious men; and the *good Samaritan,* acted like a presumptuous Fanatic, in pouring oil and wine into wounds which were never meant to be healed.—We may surely be spared the trouble and expence of erecting Hospitals.—The vast Lazar House of bodily tortures may remain unvisited, and "*Despair may tend the sick, busy from couch to couch!*"—Nay, does not it also follow that it is *presumptuous* to relieve our own sufferings?—Certainly it does.—Why, then, take medicine when we are sick?—Why eat when we feel hunger?—Why sleep when we are weary?—This conclusion cannot be avoided, but by resorting to the monstrous absurdity of maintaining that the vast aggregate of calamities endured by the slaves, is *remediless,* but that all other natural, physical and moral evils may and ought to be relieved.

Thus, my good Sir, you see whither you have conducted yourself, for want of my *clue*, which is at your service whenever you will condescend to use it.—The natural course of an argument is a strait line, a wide *avenue*—the reasons stand bold and prominent on each side, like the upright, unbending trunks of the trees.— Each keeps its place in exact and measured regularity, and as we advance, becomes clear and distinct. The moment we enter, we behold the termination, in a perspective that is true to immutable rules, consequently we know where we shall find ourselves at the end.—But you, upon the subject in question, have, at the onset, rushed into a *Forest,* and, I verily believe, an *enchanted* one; for you have been scared, by horrible phantoms, from lending the help of your valour to the CONFEDERATE ARMY, which now stands much in need of the vigorous arm of every CHRISTIAN HERO. But to be serious.—You see, Sir, that your argument in favour of African Slavery, upon the ground of *a supposed curse,* is *fallen down,* a thousand fathom deep!—*Interest* is the only leading champion on your side of the question, who, with his "helmet of brass, and his spear like a weaver's beam," boldly defies "the armies of the living God."—Long established custom, for centuries, has blinded the eyes of men to the enormities of Slavery. The Negroes have been as necessary appendages to the plantations, as horses to an English Farm. Even Locke, that enlightened Metaphysician and firm believer in Christianity, could observe, "The Negroes are very advantageous to the American Plantations."—We can all feel the mighty power of habits, which throw their imperceptible, yet fatal and entangling, chains around mortals in every path of human existence. Private and political advantages have, in this debate, assumed more room in the field than justly belongs to them—they do not allow a fair vantage ground to justice, humanity, and plain reason.—Nay, they do not even listen to the argument, that "*Free labour is the most productive,*"[9] which is proved by our most acute political economists. The Colonies are of importance to the Kingdom, and the Planters have laid out their money in the purchase of Slaves, therefore their rights must be secured. All this is alledged strongly, and let it have a full, free and liberal discussion. Let the subject be fairly investigated with that earnestness and justice which its most awful importance demands;—and when every argument is honestly and accurately weighed in the even balance of immutable justice, then, but not till then, let it be decided by the English nation, whether Slavery ought or ought not, to be abolished.

Now, Sir, as there is *one* point which the closest reasoner is bound to *assume,* though it be not mathematically demonstrable. I mean *the good intentions* of its adversaries. I take it for granted that you are a man of honour and sincerity. You observe, that without *Faith* (that is, without a most *irrational,* I had almost said an *impious* belief, that one whole race of men lie under an *interminable* curse, and it is *presumptuous* to relieve them) "*we could hardly endure the reflection of their sufferings, without indefinable sensations of horror.*" And though to *my plain understanding*, the best evidence we can give of our *Faith* is to shew it by our *Works;* and the best way of consoling ourselves for the miseries of others is to endeavour to relieve them, I yet think that you have a portion in your composition of *the milk of human kindness.*

257

SOCIAL AND POLITICAL REFORM

There is something in you *impressible* by compassion. Call in, then, your better judgment, and listen to right reason.—Among the numerous arguments *against* Slavery, every one of them built upon pillars of adamant, upon the immutable basis of the moral attributes of the Supreme Father of all his creatures, there is one, which though only collateral, is of irresistible force. I mean the inconclusiveness, the futility, and the glaring absurdity of the arguments of our opponents. When they say, the Slave-trade is profitable to the Planters, and very convenient for the purpose of supplying us with the luxuries of Rum and Sugar, such an argument is, at least, *clear,* and the lowest understanding can comprehend it. But when they alledge, that the Negroes are an inferior race, a link of the chain between a monkey and a man, and with Mr. Lawrence, the Professor of Anatomy,[10] doubt whether they have capacities to learn that there is a Creator and a Redeemer of mankind;—when you, Sir, maintain that the whole race is *accursed;*—satisfying your feelings, by the strength of their *faith;* what shall we say of the *rationality* of such reasoners?—

We can only meet these firework bombardments of our fortresses, by a little playful fire in return, while the cool calculations of interest, expediency, &c. we shall answer, with like cool calculations, hereafter. Opposition, fairly conducted, is of the greatest use to any cause. Without it, reasons cannot be weighed, nor truth established.—When once this kingdom is divided, upon this cause, into *two* Parties, viz. *Friends* and *Enemies,* there will be good hope that it may be *decided.*—It is the numerous class of the *neutrals,* the *sleepers,* that are the most to be dreaded; because if *they* were once to be awakened, they would either join us, or be, in the end, defeated by our powers.—We speak *confidently,* you will say. We do;—with confidence in Almighty assistance.—"We go forth in the *strength* of the Lord God." In the behalf of his suffering creatures—to *restore* them to the rank of *men,* to *elevate* them to the rank of *Christians.* And, in this confidence, we say, while there remains, in the English bosom, any particle of commiseration for the miseries of others, any sense of the invaluable blessings of our own free laws, any gratitude for the "unspeakable gift" of the Gospel, our firmness in the cause of the degraded negroes will be rooted, like our native oak; adverse winds will only make it shoot the deeper, and not a *Jamaica* hurricane will be able to bend it.

Condescend then, I conjure you, to weigh well the arguments of your opponents.—We wish not to oppose with violent and headstrong zeal, but to *convince,* to *persuade.* Remember that it is *fairly* proved there is no argument *for* Slavery, but INTEREST, *that* includes policy, and private and public advantage.—You cannot muster any other reasons whatsoever.—There are, *against* it, JUSTICE, TRUTH, CHRISTIAN FEELING, I will not add *Mercy*; mercy is only extended to *criminals,* and the African slaves, being not in the rank of *men,* not *responsible beings,* having no will of their own, no civil or political existence, cannot, in any sense, be objects of *Mercy,* but of *Justice.*

Notes

1 The Turks have only possession of PART of Egypt; the Barbary states are tributary to them;—they have no dominion in the vast tracts of Caffraria, the Guinea and Gold Coasts, nor in Abyssinia. Therefore Africa is NOT CHIEFLY in the power of the Turks.
2 Where proofs of any other probationary state for man, except the present world, are to be found, I know not.
3 Genesis, ix.—25, 26, 27.
4 Deuteronomy, IX c—3 to 5 v.
5 See Campbell's Survey.
6 And the sons of Ham; CUSH, and MISRAIM, and Phut, and Canaan, and the sons of Cush; Seba, and Havilah, and Sabtah, and RAAMAH," &c.—Genesis, x c—6 and 7 v.
7 Sir W. Jones's Discourse on the Origin and Families of Nations; delivered to the Asiatic Society, Feb. 23, 1792.
8 A tribe of the Arabians, living near to the Sabeans. See Lowth's Isaiah, vol. 2. p. 272.
9 "It appears from the experience of all ages and nations, I believe, that the work done by free men comes much cheaper, in the end, than that done by Slaves. It is found to do so even at Boston, New-York and Philadelphia, where the wages of common labour are so very high."—Adam Smith's Wealth of Nations, vol. 1, p. 109.
10 "The retreating forehead," says this Anatomist, "and the depressed vertex, of the dark-coloured varieties of man, make me strongly doubt whether they are susceptible of these high destinies; (i. e. mental culture and pure religion) whether they are capable of understanding and appreciating the doctrines and the mysteries of our religion."—

36

ISAAC NELSON, *SLAVERY SUPPORTED BY THE AMERICAN CHURCHES AND COUNTENANCED BY RECENT PROCEEDINGS IN THE FREE CHURCH OF SCOTLAND*

(Edinburgh: Charles Ziegler, 1847),
pp. 2–7 [abridged]

Christian Friends

At the request of the Free Church Anti-Slavery Society, I come before you without hesitation, conscious, as I am, that to entertain the same sense of duty, to hold the same views of any great question, and earnestly to labour for the same consummation, is bond enough to unite our hearts, whose moral emotions are happily not modified by climate nor bounded by geographical limits. Neither do I come to complain to you. No feeling of depression weighs on my spirits relative to the ultimate success of the measures we advocate. As sure as there is a God who hates oppression and avenges the oppressed, slavery must perish, and for ever. As sure as a saviour appeared in our nature to open the prison doors and proclaim liberty to the captive, our cause is his.

I come to address you concerning the sins and the duty of the professed followers of the Lord Jesus Christ; as I believe that multitudes of simple-minded, unsuspecting Church members remain aloof from this work, because they have not studied the subject; they do not understand the enormities of slavery nor the relation which the Church holds to it; they do not perceive that it is Christian countenance which makes slavery strong and slaveholding respectable. The Churches of America, and the friends of these Churches who repeat their stale and feeble reasonings, on them lies the responsibility,—they alone are the bulwarks of slavery. Bring then, dear friends, the subject near to you; let not the distance lend enchantment to the sin. Remember you are men, and every thing human concerns you, especially that you are Christians, and every thing which dishonours Christ concerns you. The midnight robber is not respectable, because men agree to denounce his sin, and no Church opens its doors to receive him. The assassin is execrated, because civilized man loathes blood. The pirate is not treated as a respectable Christian member of society, but the slaveholder is received into society; is received, did I say, into society? he is welcomed into the Church of Christ, and sits down at the table of the Saviour, though his crime embraces within it the concentrated essence of all sin—the sin of the robber, the sin of the pirate, the sin of the murderer, embraces within it what John Wesley called *"the sum of human villany."* How long, O Lord, ere thy people awake to examine their condition, and see that the blood of innocents is in their skirts!

Do not suppose that our object is to heap blame, much less abuse, on any one party or Church,—we have all been guilty concerning our brother. But at this particular time, and owing to certain events, there is a spirit of examination on this topic gone abroad among the people, and the startling and appalling fact meets our view, presents itself to us at every turn, that those are most guilty who ought to be the lights of the world, the salt of the earth. How is the gold become dim, and the most fine gold changed! Slavery finds an asylum within the temple of the king of righteousness,—the house of our God has been made a den of thieves,—the pulpit and the press employed by Christians in consecrating the crime, and hallowing the sin, yea, unblushingly proclaiming the heaven-derived right of man to hold property in man, *salva fide et salva ecclesia.* Statesmen have discarded the guilty phantasy. Our nation, in the exercise of a righteous jurisprudence, would not now venture to assert the accursed principle; but what the enlightened statesman has ceased to do—would blush to do,—is done by whom? Tell it not in Gath, publish it not in Ascalon, lest the enemy rejoice, and the infidel triumph. What the statesman would not do Christian ministers are found attempting. Theologians assert that the bible does tolerate, is silent upon, utters no condemnatory word against that accursed thing, which the British constitution would not tolerate. England does not permit any of her subjects to buy, sell, or hold a fellow man in bonds, but Christ and his apostles, say these divines, did not condemn men for so doing, nay, enjoined upon the poor degraded slave to return to and obey his owner, and be content with his doom. The soil of Britain is too sacred for the foot of the slave-master, and when he touches it the fetters fall from the limbs of the slave; yet these grave expounders of the oracles of truth tell us, and expect us to believe it too, that the apostle Paul would have dishonoured our soil by sending back the fugitive; for, say they, he did send back a slave to his master, thereby recognising the body of Onesimus as the property of Philemon. Surely the public papers must have misrepresented the reasonings I have read as delivered in the Scottish capital. Surely I must be mistaken. It cannot be that the men who are so jealous of their own liberty would join in palliating or extenuating the sin of the man-owner in any circumstances. Surely the descendants of the men who fought at Bannockburn and Bothwell brig, can never pollute their hands by clasping those of the slaveholder. It cannot be that a Scottish deputation trod the American soil at the time Charles T. Torrey was tried and condemned; yes, a pious, devoted, laborious, evangelical minister was condemned for the crime of assisting three

SOCIAL AND POLITICAL REFORM

slaves to escape, and not a word uttered in his defence by the strangers from the Church and land of the free. Aye, Charles T. Torrey was judicially murdered, and his persecutors, the men who stoned him, have laid down their garments at the feet of some Churches in Britain, and they have found among these Churches defenders of their Christianity, piety, and usefulness, as devoted ministers of the Lord Jesus from that hour to this. It is asserted by American ministers that a man ought not to be compelled to give up his property, and the sentiment has been re-echoed in Scotland. Ministers of the Free Church assert that a man may hold property in man—that slaveholders are not in all circumstances sinners—that you may stand in that unhappy relation and yet be a genuine disciple of the Lord Jesus—that Christianity does not require of you in all circumstances to relax your grasp of your neighbour's throat, in order to be a respectable and useful Church member. You may hold the slave fast if you treat him well; you may still hold him as a slave if you treat him as a Christian brother. Can you treat me as a man (I will not dishonour Christianity by saying *Christian brother)* while you deny me the pursuit of happiness under the direction of those reasoning powers God has given me? Can you treat me well so long as you withhold from me liberty,—the birthright of heaven: "disguise thyself as thou wilt, still slavery thou art a bitter draught," or, as the American reading is, oppression, thou art a bitter draught. You may feed the slave well, and call him Christian brother, you may even allow him a seat in the evangelical alliance, (if his master will only allow him to come,) yet so long as the chain is kept on him the iron enters his soul, and, till you can reduce the man to the brute—till you can alter the laws of our moral constitution, you can never treat a fellow creature as a man, much less a Christian brother, while you retain him in chains. The whole talk about treating a slave well, whether uttered in New York or Edinburgh, is only adding insult and mockery to sin; and yet one of your most remarkable ministers, and one whom I was accustomed from my youth to admire, has said: "*We must not,*" says Dr Chalmers, "*we must not say of every man, who, by inheritance is himself the owner of slaves, we are not to say of him, that unless, by an act of violence on all those possessory and proprietary feelings which exist in such strength within every bosom, he make the resolute sacrifice of these, and renouncing his property in slaves, renounce the all which belongs to him, we are not to say that, unless this surrender is made, he therefore is not a Christian, and should be treated as an outcast from all the distinctions or the privileges of a Christian society. The truth is, that according to all the laws and the likelihoods of human nature, the very men who are now looking at the object* ab extra, *and in the character, it may be, of zealous abolitionists, would, if placed from infancy in the condition, and exposed through life to all the besetting influences which operate on the mind of the slaveholder, have been those very slaveholders themselves."—* See Dr Chalmers' Letter to Editor of *Witness.*

I can hardly persuade myself that the two statements contained in this paragraph were intended for arguments. Had I been born—had I grown up and been educated in the doctrines and dogmas of the Koran, I would have been a Mahommedan, does this make Mahommedanism the less sinful, or my condition the more

262

innocent? that I would, if born at Constantinople, have been a Mahommedan, is a poor defence to set up for the possible innocence of my position, except among those who deny the necessity of revelation. Had I been born in the family of a Brahmin, I would, in all probability, have lived and died a believer in the divinity of Brahma; yet this, I thought, would have been one argument, and a powerful one to the Christian missionary, to leave his home that I might not perish for ever. This argument would make sad havoc of missions, and yet, weak as it is, it does not apply; for no American minister, or Scottish professor of divinity, has a right, with the bible in his hand, to urge ignorance and the force of habit as a palliation of slavery. Dr Chalmers tells us, besides, that it is too much to ask a man to resign his property in slaves. Is it, then, too much to demand that the slave owner shall resign his property in man—his ill-gotten gain—to which earth can give no title and heaven no sanction; and because, too, it is his all,—I do not now speak of what nations ought to do who once legalized the traffic, I only speak of Churches and Christians. I remember one who said, If any man love father, or mother, or houses, or lands, more than me, he is not worthy of me, and the last persons from whom I would have expected such reasonings, are the men who called upon each other to resign what some might have regarded their all for freedom and truth. Members of the Free Church, to you I address myself; you who have established the Free Church Anti-Slavery Society, by which you have proved yourselves no recreants to the cause of liberty, be firm, be temperate in your resistances, but tell your ministers—those men who have the management of this matter, that the pulse of Scotland still beats faithful to the cause of righteousness and truth,—that the public voice is with you if it could be heard amid the din of metaphysical distinctions, if it were not stifled by the cobwebs of sophistry. Tell these men you do not think it too much to ask from a professed follower of him who came to break every yoke, that he should do violence to his proprietary and possessory feelings; for he ought never to have had property or possession there. He has no title, he can have none. Earth's laws cannot give it—heaven's laws will not. Tell them that it is the duty of every Christian to offer freedom, liberty at once to his slaves; the longer they have been kept the greater wrong has been done them. Tell them, in words of Christian firmness and of Christian power, what the lamented Dr Andrew Thomson enunciated in thunder tones, till the nations of Europe heard the duty of immediate emancipation, No law can make you either *slaveholders* or *slavehavers*. If unconditional, immediate emancipation has been offered to your bondmen, then if the coloured man stays as a servant in your employment, receiving your wages, you treat him as a man; if he goes elsewhere to seek a master, you can enter the sanctuary of your God, and bend before his altar, with your hands washed in innocence. The territorial antipathy to slavery is too strong on the soil of Scotland for the sentiment ever to take root, that we are asking too much from the Christian when we ask the immediate emancipation of the too long oppressed slave. The atmosphere is too keen and pure up here, in the neighbourhood of the Grampians, where the Roman eagle had to stoop from his quarry, for the assertion ever to live and move and have a being, that the bones, and flesh, and rational moral nature of immortal man were ever intended to be the property of his fellow man, to be treated as a vested right—to be counted on in the ledger—to be bought up when the market suits, and sold again to serve the profit of the owner. Tell these theologians, man can make out no title deed to man—God never transfers him, for he is the coin of heaven stamped with the features of a king. Will the day not soon come when these reasoners shall frankly admit their mistake? 'Tis not disgraceful to err in judgment, but, oh, it is disgraceful to persist in error. [...]

[...] Before adverting to the influence of the American Churches in perpetuating slavery, permit me for a moment to direct your attention to the nature of slavery itself. [...]

To treat a man as a slave is to hold him entirely subject to the will of another, a master to whom he belongs. Slavery is an invasion, a denial of the obligation which lies on man to obey God: it is a denial of moral obligations; for to subject man as a chattel, as a thing, to the will of his fellow man, is to treat him as if there were no claims of conscience, no heaven to be won, no hell to be avoided. God could never delegate to man the right to treat his fellow man as a chattel; for this is virtually to treat him as not accountable to his maker, his creator. To treat a man as a chattel, that is, as a slave, is to treat him as having no right to the development of his powers, as having no interest in the present preparation for a future state, as having no share in the glories of man as redeemed by the atonement of Christ, and sanctified by the Holy Spirit. To reduce man to the rank of a chattel is not to give him bad food, is not to overwork and overtax his strength, but it is to deny his heaven-descended claim to be treated as a rational accountable being; it is to make his affections a marketable article; it is to make his mind a thing to be improved, not for his own but his master's profit; it is to make his moral emotions a means of commercial benefit to his owner. [...]

[...] A silly attempt was made by a Free Church court to distinguish between slavery and holding man as a chattel. The court would not undertake to say that slavery was in all circumstances sinful, or a just and valid reason for excluding a Christian from Church fellowship; but the court would undertake to say that all who treated man as a chattel were acting contrary to Christianity. The distinction must have afforded great amusement to the slaveholders; for they know full well that if you deny the chattel principle, you deny slavery—they are one and the same thing. If you grant to the slave any claim, any privilege, any right, above the brute, you cease to make him property, that is, you cease to regard him as a slave. You may educate him as you would a pointer dog, for your profit; you may keep him comfortable as you would your horse, because it is your interest; you may tell him of heaven or hell, but it is to make him more patient, enduring, and obedient here; but the moment you bid the master cease to treat him as a piece of chattel property, (sentient, moving, speaking, intelligent chattels, I admit), that moment you destroy the claim of the owner, the right of the proprietor; that moment you give the lie to American legislative enactments; that moment you condemn American decisions in reference to their living chattels. Do not treat him as a chattel, says the Church court, that is, set him free, treat him as a man accountable to God and not to you. Hold him as a slave, says the same Court; for in some cases and circumstances it is no sin; yet you must not treat him as a chattel—how contradictory, impossible, and absurd. There was a purpose to serve, or we would never have heard of such suicidal Church utterances. To hold man, then, as a chattel, is not merely to violate all those rights which, among civilized nations, are regarded as inalienable, namely, life, liberty, and the pursuit of hapiness, responsible only to God, but it is to invade, to deny, abrogate, and annihilate the claims of Deity. You have heard much in this country of invading the crown rights of Messiah; I will tell you what it is to invade the crown rights of Deity, not only as creator, but as reconciling the world to himself by the death of Christ. Look at that poor, weeping, broken-hearted husband and father dragged out as a piece of property to be sold in America, the land of the free, the home of the brave. The dealer in human flesh comes forward to inspect his limbs and feel his muscles,—he must not resist the indignity, he is but a chattel. He is a man of robust and powerful frame, and therefore his price is high. Again, his mind becomes valuable, and his owner will have all his value, mortal and immortal; the buyers are told he is a skilful workman, a good tradesman or mechanic, his price goes higher on this account. His wife—I need not say his wife—a slave has no wife; the mother of his children—I need not say his children—the mother of the children which are his master's property, stands weeping by. One other effort is made by the owner to raise the value of the article in the market,—it is announced to the buyers,—and listen to it Christians, and be horribly affraid,—it is announced that the slave is a converted man. Yes, Christ is formed in him, the hope of glory, and therefore this enhances the price; the re-created features of the heavenly Father are marketable commodities, bought and sold in the land of revivals. Is this invading the crown rights of heaven's King? Is this doing violence to God manifest in the flesh? Is this crucifying Christ afresh in the person of his little ones? Answer, ye Churches of America, who support that giant iniquity, and betake yourselves to the Bible for arguments to support the system. Though ye climb up to heaven, to the heaven of God's word, to hide, yet hence will he bring you down. The converted man of the auction block has been told of a Saviour; you dare not let him read for himself; you keep men to tell him some truth and many lies, pretending to be out of God's word,—for the unadulterated word of the Lord you have vowed not to let into his hands,—he may be converted even under American religion; but woe to the seller and the sold, if they have both been deceived, when they meet at the tribunal of a righteous God. This is slavery, this is the accursed thing for which earth has no parallel, and Christianity, as preached in America, has hitherto had no cure. Her slaves have encreased in the ratio of population, under the preaching of the gospel. The pulpit, the Church, the gospel, as preached in that wretched land, have given their strength to the beast. Let the Church withdraw its countenance and support from slavery, and that moment it falls to the ground.

4.2

Prison Reform

4.2 Prison Reform

Many Christians believed early Victorian prisons, and penal policy more widely, required reform. Punishment was often seen as unjust, conditions in prisons were bad, prisoners were not being reformed and the threat of custodial sentences was not preventing crime. This led to campaigns for prison reform, especially concerning the conditions of women prisoners, and the incarceration of children. Prison reform campaigns were not solely restricted to England: after her experiences with British prisons and reformatory schools, Mary Carpenter (1807–1877) visited prisons in India and presented the Indian government with her proposals for reform.

Mary Carpenter was highly influential in the prison reform movement. A Unitarian, she began campaigning for better treatment of young offenders after working with children in the slums of Bristol, where she ran a ragged school. Between 1851 and 1852 she published *Reformatory Schools for the Children of the Perishing and Dangerous Classes* and *Juvenile Delinquents, their Condition and Treatment*, and established her own reformatory school in Bristol. The paper extracted here was written for a collection of papers on prison reform. Carpenter presents the Reverend Sydney Turner's 'Redhill' as the main example of her short history of reformatory schools in England, associating her newer venture with this established institution. Carpenter criticises the government for not supporting reformatory schools or bringing them into the formal penal system until 1854, suggesting that they allowed fear of public opinion to prevent them from tackling an obvious social ill. Beyond referencing the emotion of 'disgust and righteous indignation' at the root of prison reform, Carpenter maintains a factual tone in her paper, leaving out 'deeply touching illustrated cases', ostensibly due to a lack of space. She is clear, though, that those employed in reformatory schools need to be inspired by love and faith, and that they are doing the Lord's work. Moreover, she uses the common religious metaphors of sowing good seed and labouring in the vineyard to describe reformatory school teachers.

In the preface to his memoir of his father, John Clay, a prison chaplain, Walter Lowe Clay acknowledges Mary Carpenter for allowing him access to her correspondence with his father. On the subject of young offenders, Clay notes that his father had campaigned for an early reform of the system to ensure children were kept separately from the general prison population, and that, in his experience, only severely hardened young offenders required the influence of reformatory schools – for others a few months isolated in cells would suffice to prevent recidivism. Clay's main theme, though, in the section extracted here, is more philosophical. While admitting that there was a case for reform of the penal system – that the laissez faire state fostered crime, and the severe, un-Christian treatment of criminals was not effective – Clay argues that philanthropists have gone too far in removing Godly punishment from the theory of reforming criminals. He criticises them for substituting 'moral hospitals' for prisons, which he argues goes against the tenets of Christianity. Instead, he argues that his father found 'righteous

269

retribution', 'guilt', and 'Godly sorrow' to be important tools and emotions for the atonement and reformation of sinners (see Volume IV, Shame).

Although *Female Life in Prison* was purportedly written by 'The Prison Matron', the author was in fact the male writer of popular fiction, Frederick Robinson (1830–1901). This knowledge renders the truth claims in the introduction to *Female Life in Prison* highly problematic, and forces us to read the author's disavowal of 'mere book-making' ironically. The author's defence of truth telling in the form of an entertaining narrative – that it is in the aid of social reform, and to encourage others to become involved in the cause – is characteristic of evangelical writing, and can be compared to Heighway's writing about Jewish converts (see this volume, Mission to the Jews). Robinson's narrator eschews romance, and sets her work against that of Charles Dickens, denying his suggestion that all imprisoned women retain shreds of innocence from their youth, and stressing instead the ignorance of religion that characterises most inmates. Further than this, in his description of their 'mad defiance, rage and blasphemy', Robinson relegates his women prisoners to another class, or even another race, suggesting that, however hard prison chaplains or philanthropists try to reform them, only a minority can be helped.

37

MARY CARPENTER, 'ON REFORMATORY SCHOOLS AND THEIR PRESENT POSITION'

In Jelinger Symons (ed.), *On the Reformation of Young Offenders: A Collection of Pamphlets, Papers and Speeches on Reformatories and the Various Views Held on the Subject of Juvenile Crime and its Treatment* (London: G. Routledge and Co., 1855), pp. 131–135, 138

Three years ago the public were almost entirely unacquainted with the mere existence of schools especially intended for the rescue and reformation of young persons who had fallen into crime. The idea of the establishment of such schools was not indeed a new one, even in England; and seed had long been silently, and almost secretly, germinating, which, when the appointed time was come, would spring up and bring forth unexpected fruits; but of this people in general knew nothing, and if the unhappy boys and girls, who had fallen within the iron grasp of the law, excited any but a passing emotion of disgust and righteous indignation that those so young should be so depraved, it was only one of hopeless compassion or despairing apathy, for it appeared as if nothing *could* be done, since the law *must* take its course; and, as the gaol was well known to be entirely inefficient as a cure in the case of erring children, they must be left to their sad fate.

But though the public knew it not, the way had been long preparing for a better state of things. "In the year 1788," says the Report of the Philanthropic Farm School for 1850, "the attention of several earnest and enlightened men was directed to the increasing numbers of depraved and vagrant children infesting the metropolis and its neighbouring districts, living, and trained to live, by begging and dishonesty." A single child was the first commencement of what was gradually extended to be a large institution for both boys and girls of the criminal class; but though it continued under the watchful care of benevolent persons of intelligence and energy, and under the patronage of men of high rank, the public were little acquainted with its operations, even when, in 1849, a new impulse was given to it by the adoption of that agricultural system of training which has been found so beneficial in the continental schools; and also by its being placed under the devoted care of one admirably calculated to carry out the object,—the Rev. Sydney Turner; under his management the small seed which was sown nearly seventy years ago, is spreading far and wide;—about 200 criminal boys are now receiving, at Redhill, a training which is calculated to prepare them to be useful members of society. [...]

[...] While the public was as yet quite ignorant of the existence of these schools, or of the principles on which they are founded, and while members of the Government said to those who urged the subject on their attention, "We perceive the evil, we approve of your views, but the public mind is as yet unprepared, we do not see our way clear to do anything;" a few earnest and devoted persons, in different parts of England, and quite independently of each other, determined, quietly and unostentatiously, to prove that the thing could be done, *by doing it*. [...]

[...] The difficulties to be encountered were extreme, and such as would have daunted any but those who had their hearts in the work. There was of course no legal detention of the children; this could not be supplied by the delegation of parental control, for in such cases this seldom existed. The school could not take the place of the prison, in the actual state of the law, and young persons who have been accustomed to a wild, lawless, and independent life, enjoying the feastings they had procured by unlawful means, and regardless of the frequent fastings which their mode of life rendered but comparatively small privations,—such as these are not often ready to resign their free and exciting mode of life for regular work and discipline, or, if they do crave admission to the school when they have been recently smarting under the penalty of the law, will be ready to consider that if they have come of their own free will, they may go whenever the fancy moved them, or restraint became irksome. Hence, those who were commencing these schools, had to contend not only with the vicious habits and ungoverned passions of these poor children, but with their frequent attempts to escape from a control which could not but be irksome to them, however reasonable or salutary it might be. But all these difficulties the conductors of these schools perseveringly encountered, certain that their principle was a right one; and, gathering experience and new courage from every failure and mistake, they have satisfied themselves, and proved to the public that the work can be done.

In all the schools the system which alone has been found efficacious, has been, in the first place, to inspire the child with a confidence in the kind intentions of those under whose care he is placed, and gradually, as opportunities occur, or still more by the influence of the daily life of the school, to awaken the spiritual life, and train the conscience. To carry out the objects of the school, industrial training, especially agricultural labour, has been found indispensable, with an ordinary amount of school instruction. A steady, firm, yet kind discipline, with method, regularity, and order in the daily routine, such as would be found in every well-ordered family or school, are of course important auxiliaries. The success which has attended each of these schools has fully answered all reasonable expectations. Some few refused to remain in the schools, and, as was to be expected, at once plunged into a criminal course; others were impatient to leave it before a sufficient time for reformation had elapsed,—and even these have generally shown a decided improvement; while a large proportion are giving every hope of becoming honest and useful members of society. In the Kingswood school, out of about sixty boys who have been or are in the school, not one has absconded so as to be entirely lost sight of; some who absconded shortly after they came to the school, and soon fell into crime, begged permission to return after their discharge from prison; while only two who stayed but a few weeks, plunged completely into a vicious course. On the other hand, many can be pointed out now doing well and earning a livelihood, who, without the intervention of the school, must have hopelessly sunk into the dangerous classes. Deeply touching illustrated cases might be cited, but space will not permit. [...]

[...] We must not, however, close our eyes to one great obstacle in this work, which will always throw serious difficulties in the way of its successful operation,—that of finding masters adapted for the work. Peculiar qualifications must be possessed by individuals successfully engaging in it, and though no government criterion of fitness, no gauge of knowledge can test their powers, yet, in addition to natural adaptation, they ought to have such experience in the training of young persons as will enable them to avail themselves of the important aids of order and regularity. As the work proceeds, those fitted for it will present themselves, and experience will be the great teacher;—but besides, those whose souls are deeply imbued with the work, must by their sympathy and co-operation, kindle the hearts of those teachers more actively engaged in it. It is thus that at the Rauhe-haus, the instruction and influence of M. Wichern have sent forth a body of zealous teachers into different parts of Europe. Thus at Mettraye there is no lack of *chefs* and *sous-chefs de famille,* who cheerfully undergo privations, and share with the scholars the hard fare and strict discipline of the school, who love the colony, and will not be induced by even advantageous offers to quit it. M. De Metz "had kindled them with the fire which burnt in his own breast," as he lately expressed himself to a visitor. This great difficulty, like all others, may and has been subdued; and if we go forth in faith, and hope, and love, sparing no effort, disheartened by no discouragement, we may be sure that in due time our prayers will be answered, that "the Lord will send forth labourers into his vineyard."

38

WALTER LOWE CLAY, *THE PRISON CHAPLAIN: A MEMOIR OF THE REVEREND JOHN CLAY B.D. LATE CHAPLAIN OF THE PRESTON GAOL*

(Cambridge: Macmillan, 1861), pp. vi–viii, 351–352, 356–361, 364–366, 368–370

TO
M. D. HILL, ESQUIRE, Q.C.
RECORDER OF BIRMINGHAM,
ETC. ETC.

Dear Sir,
I dedicate this Book to you reverently, because you are a front-rank Soldier in that Holy War against Sin and Ignorance, in which my Father spent and lost his Life.

Your very faithful Servant,
W. L. CLAY.

Preface

The publication of this work is due to a combination of two reasons.

It was my father's intention, had he lived long enough, to compress his numerous pamphlets and reports, together with a great mass of fresh materials which he had collected, into a treatise ("to be made popular if possible") on the remedies for Crime. At his death, however, he had not even commenced the undertaking. He frequently asked me to carry out his design in case he failed to finish the task himself. In the present work I have attempted to discharge the duty laid upon me. I found that my father's MSS. were very fragmentary and imperfect; and, in consequence, I soon perceived that by merely editing his papers I should very inadequately fulfil his wishes. Eventually, I became convinced that an historical sketch of the Penal System of England would be at once a fitting monument to his memory, and, in some measure, an accomplishment of his scheme.

I had, however, another purpose to effect. Many of my father's friends urged me to write a memoir of his life. They wished to possess such a memoir for their own sakes, and they thought the life had been noble enough to deserve an effort to save his name, for a few years, from oblivion. It occurred to me that I might combine the gratification of this wish with my main intention; and I have, therefore, woven my father's biography into the history of the great cause for which he laboured. [...]

Chapter VI

The principles of criminal law, and the present penal system in England

[...] The phrase, "God's world," now so frequently in the mouths of the deepest thinkers of the day, (and of course echoed by crowds of half thinkers), is the expression of a great truth, which is already shining in noon-day glory on the minds of a few, and dawning on many more. We are, in fact, at last learning that God is the ruler of this world, as well as of the next; that His wish is to save mankind, not only from punishment hereafter, but from sin and darkness, and labyrinthine error here. We are at last beginning to believe that the Saviour came to save, not only men's souls, but literally, the world; to redeem, not only religion from all forms of idol-and devil-worship, but also science from intellectual arrogance, commerce from naked selfishness, politics from mundane craft, and law from unjust expediency.

When this truth is fully recognised, we shall at last perceive that all the problems, which mankind has to solve, resolve themselves into this,—first, to discover God's will, and then in all meekness to obey it. When we accept this as the real work given us to do, we shall try to make *our* laws the humble reverent copy of God's laws, *our* justice, as far as human infirmity permits, a facsimile of God's justice. [...]

[...] Now the theologians (and once more be it said, that legislators have but to apply the principles of true theology) have laid down four propositions with regard to God's law of punishment—three of which should form the basis of a nation's penal system. To cut up a great truth into propositions is always an unsatisfactory process; the logical anatomy seems to kill out the force and the life; besides, it is impossible to make the propositions exhaustive. But in this instance we must abide by the propositions in question, for the sake of clearness. The first of them is this;—that sin is often followed by penal suffering, in the natural order of cause and effect. The shattered nerves, the broken health and the early grave of a drunkard, for instance, form the *natural* punishment of his sin. In accordance with this we believe that heaven and hell, respectively, will be the natural results of righteous and sinful lives upon earth. But this great principle, of course, cannot be reproduced in human jurisprudence; the legislator has no concern with it. The eternal self-enforcing law, which developes sin into suffering, needs no help from a human administrator. Sometimes, unfortunately, when philanthropy sinks into sentimental folly, it ventures to meddle with the operation of this law, and to save the sinner from his appointed misery. Evil, however, in one shape or another is the sure result of such an interference. But besides this great fundamental principle, there are three others which the "higher power" among men, as the minister of God, is bound reverently to imitate. 1—In this present world, at any rate, besides the penal suffering which sin almost infallibly entails, we perceive what may be called a "supplementary justice" in God's dealings with men. Not only are sinful habits and sinful principles left to work out their own woe, but meet punishments are likewise arbitrarily assigned to sinful acts. Sometimes God Himself awards the penalty, as when He sends Elijah to pass sentence of death upon Ahab in the vineyard of Naboth; but in the ordinary course of His providence, He delegates the right of dealing out this supplementary justice to His human ministers; He appoints them His "revengers to execute wrath upon him that doeth evil." This then is the fundamental principle of human justice. Not for the protection of society, not for the "greatest happiness of the greatest number" (though ends like these will be surely accomplished), but in the name of God, the judge should sentence and the executioner strike.[1] Once establish this foundation-principle, and human justice will never run again, as it has run heretofore, into damnable injustice. This once acknowledged, we shall easily arrive at what ought to be the second and third principles in human justice—principles which, in all truth, are amply sufficient to regulate the entire administration of criminal law. 2—That the amount of guilt should be the measure of the punishment; this will save us from inflicting unjust cruelties in the unholy attempt to "deter by example." 3—That the object of punishment should be at once to expiate the guilt of the offence, and to lead the offender to repentance; this will save us, on the one hand, from maudlin benevolence, and on the other from the wickedness of so treating the criminal as to harden and degrade him.

These three principles form the true basis of criminal law. It is not intended here in any sense to prove their soundness, but taking that for granted, simply to offer a few suggestions on the method of application. [...]

[...] But to return to the three principles. To make them the frame-work of our criminal law, we must wholly repudiate Paleian and Benthamite theories. But the question now arises,—must we at once accept instead the doctrines of the modern philanthropic school? This editor, questioning with great diffidence the opinions of men whom he deeply reverences, is prepared to answer that we must not, without due qualification.

A thorough reaction against the un-Christian (or at any rate the non-Christian) treatment of criminals set in early in the present century, and has now almost reached its height. Men like John Clay, Alexander Maconochie, and Matthew Hill rebelled with their whole souls against the utter selfishness, folly, and injustice of the established principles and practice of English criminal law. They saw that the state herself, by her *vicious indifference* (which even law commissioners class as equally guilty with *direct criminal intention*) fostered crime. She protected drunkenness for the sake of revenue; she suffered pauper children to be bred up to delinquency in pernicious workhouses; she left the poor in heathen ignorance to battle with endless temptations; and, therefore, they questioned her right to punish crimes, in the guilt of which she shared herself. They saw that the upper classes— the society which demanded protection—in their shameful selfishness had done little to prevent the evils from which they suffered, and therefore they protested against their attempts to repress those evils by the single method of punishment. And besides all this they had learned by experience that, to deter by severity is, of all means, the most impotent for the prevention of crime.

Seeing, then, very clearly that punishment, as usually inflicted, was both unjust and ineffectual, many of the philanthropic school fell into the error of regarding it as a most objectionable instrument, which, though necessary sometimes, was always to be used as sparingly as possible. "The simple object of the state," they said, "is to prevent crime: the reformation of the criminal is the best means for the accomplishment of this object: in reformatory treatment, punishment must bear a part, but not one whit more should be applied than is absolutely necessary. A Christian, at any rate, whose highest aim is the salvation of souls, will not give his assent to any other view of the Criminal Question."

On very little examination this doctrine proves to be hyper-Christian. The salvation of souls is not the Christian's highest aim,—that itself is but the means to one still higher, the promotion of God's glory. To put all enemies under His feet, to bring every creature into subjection to His will and His law—this is the glory of God. We have no warrant for suspending a single Divine law, or for relaxing a single Divine penalty, even in the hope of saving a soul alive. And that man would be presumptuous indeed, who fancied that he could really further the eternal welfare of sinners by trying some plan at variance with the justice of God. When the Redeemer came to save men's souls, *He* did not repeal one jot or one tittle of the law. [...]

[...] From the hyper-Christian theory all notion of guilt, penalty, and expiation entirely disappears. "Pain," says one of the ablest exponents of that theory, "ought not to be inflicted in a vindictive spirit as retribution for the past, but administered strictly with the intention of producing the reformation of the offender." In accordance with this dogma the prison becomes a "moral hospital," where the criminal is treated with mental and spiritual surgery. He has no past crimes for which to atone; the moment he is reformed he may be dismissed as convalescent. In the actual state of English crime, the idea of a moral hospital is perfectly defensible; but viewed in the abstract, it is at variance with the whole tenor of Christianity. [...]

[...] When once punishment is meted out in due proportion, not to the legal character of the crime, but to the real culpability of the criminal, one of the chief difficulties of the hyper-Christians is cleared away. They say, and there is much truth in the assertion, that mere punishment hardens the culprit. To avoid this, they argue that we must make the punishment reformatory and not vindictive, and win the moral patient to feel that it is intended for his good and not for vengeance. Their end would be far better attained by making the punishment *just,* and leading the delinquent to acknowledge that it is so. Many philanthropists have suffered this word "vindictive" to mislead them. When punishment is inflicted to gratify anger, or revenge, it is "vindictive," but the word will bear no other meaning; and therefore to call the penalty inflicted by the state, "vindictive," is a mistake in terms. If the law has been used by revengeful witnesses or prosecutors, as the means for satisfying a private grudge, then the prisoner is truly the victim of vindictiveness, and his sufferings will almost inevitably produce a bad effect upon him. But though the state cannot be revengeful, she can be unjust. When to protect the selfish interests of society, or to deter by example, she inflicts a penalty out of all proportion to the offence, or when she rudely makes the crime and not the guilt the measure of her wrath, she acts with injustice; and it is under the endurance of injustice that the sufferer hardens his heart. But the retribution which is acknowledged to be righteous almost invariably softens. It is this which brings home to the sinner that awakening sense of guilt, which is the germ of repentance. If the philanthropists cast righteous retribution for the past out of their penal theories, they abandon one of the most powerful means which God has created for rousing that "Godly sorrow" which is the first beginning, and the only safe foundation for a genuine reformation of character. [...]

[...] It cannot be denied, in the first place, that it is justifiable, for the welfare of the community, to inflict sometimes a severer punishment on the delinquent than his guilt alone would warrant. But then, as was argued in the previous chapter, the offender, on whose liberties we are trespassing, has an absolute right to some compensation. To attempt, with all possible kindness, to turn the punishment into a blessing, to try to make it the means of winning him over to honesty and religion, is the best, perhaps the only feasible, compensation that we can offer. The evil that would otherwise arise from ultra-just punishment may thus be escaped. The attempt to reconcile a man to an over-measure of penalty, by the argument that society was a gainer by his suffering, would be labour in vain. But the prisoner's sense of wrong may be wholly dissipated, by convincing him, after an honest confession that he is hardly treated, that his own welfare, and not the selfish interests of the upper classes, is the main purpose of our unwilling severity. Many a time did Mr. Clay prove the efficacy of this argument in the cells of Preston Gaol. [...]

[...] It is easy to enunciate these truths, but to apply them would require knowledge far fuller and deeper than this editor possesses. In the following short sketch, therefore, of the present state of the Criminal Question in England, the attempt will not be made, except in some very slight and incidental fashion.

England has to deal with four wholly distinct classes of criminals: with men of good education; with children; with incidental offenders, who have stumbled into delinquency chiefly through their heathen ignorance; and lastly with habitual criminals. [...]

[...] The treatment of criminal children should be exactly the reverse of what is bestowed on gentlemen convicts. However heinous their crimes, or however depraved their natures, they have incurred so little guilt, that the state has no right to punish them severely. But in her own self-defence, and in mercy to them she is bound to provide education. Mr. Clay had been pleading for wiser and more Christian usage of criminal children, full thirty years before the legislature recognised their right to a better "house of discipline" than the common Gaol. In the medley of wickedness which filled the old Preston Bridewell, the certain ruin to which young delinquents were consigned by compulsory companionship with old gaol-birds was, in his eyes, the paramount evil. Year after year, by his reports and otherwise, he implored redress for this grievous wrong; and at last, when the separate system was introduced, to his infinite relief the justices decided that the first to be rescued from contamination, and placed in cells, should be the boys, whether tried or untried. The worst evil at length obviated, the question then arose whether cellular discipline was the kind of treatment best suited to children. Experience soon taught him the exact use to be made of such a prison as the Preston Gaol in the case of young criminals. Of late years, now that crime of all kinds, and juvenile crime in particular, has somewhat diminished, out of her annual crop of 70,000 offenders, England has about 6,000 children under the age of sixteen to provide for. For most of these, that is to say, for all who are not yet criminal by profession, nor possessed by that passion for thievery, so often seen even in the youngest children, Mr. Clay's version of the separate system would be, as a rule, thoroughly efficacious. He found that the great majority of such children, after the sharp lesson taught by a few months' isolation, might be returned to their friends so impressed and impressible, as almost to ensure their future good behaviour, unless grossly neglected. To avoid the danger of neglect, he would have made the parents responsible, under heavy penalties, for their subsequent honesty.

Note

1 The office of the executioner would never have sunk so low, if we had remembered that he is the minister, not of our ignoble selfi shness, but of Divine justice. The office involved no degradation in the old times, when "Samuel hewed Agag in pieces before the Lord in Gilgal." Truly, between Samuel in Gilgal and Calcraft in Horsemonger Lane, there is a wide gap; but not much wider than was the great gulf between the criminal law of God and the old criminal law of England. However, that gulf is narrower now.

39

[FRED W. ROBINSON],
FEMALE LIFE IN PRISON:
BY A PRISON MATRON

2 vols (London: Hurst and Blackett, 1862), vol. 1,
pp. 1–9, 44–50

Chapter I

Introductory

I wish it to be clearly understood that these are the honest reminiscences of one retired from Government service—that many years of prison experience enable me to offer my readers a fair statement of life and adventure at Brixton and Millbank prisons, and afford me the opportunity of attempting to convey some faint impression of the strange hearts that beat—perhaps break, a few of them—within the high walls between them and general society. I am anxious to set about this task earnestly, and in a good spirit—I will "nothing extenuate;" I have no reason to "set down aught in malice." I have the party-feelings of no clique to satisfy, no personal wrongs to seek to vindicate, and I am confident that the relation of these prison incidents can do no harm, and may, by God's help, effect some little good. For I am not alone in my conviction that these stories of erring and mistaken women—fallen sisters, but still sisters, whom we have no right to cast aside or shrink away from—do in many cases prove that there is no estate so low but that the elements of the better nature are existent, and still struggling for the light. [...]

[...] I believe I offer, for the first time, a true and impartial chronicle of female prison life; the mystery that has so long surrounded it, the official over-caution, there is no occasion for. The world is anxious to know, and has a right to know, the doings of its unfortunate and its misguided atoms;—shut from the society whose laws our prisoners have outraged, they are not shut out from public interest, or the prayers of honest men and women.

Whether I am fitted for the task, or have undertaken too much for my woman's strength—whether I have said too much, or too little—that world will fairly judge me in good time.

In those details of prison life which I am about to lay before the reader, I shall seldom keep to the anonymous. In those cases where the feelings of prisoners who

[FRED W. ROBINSON], *FEMALE LIFE IN PRISON*

have been discharged, and are, perhaps, attempting a new life, might be pained by the introduction of their names herein, I have, of course, forborne publicity, and contented myself with fictitious cognomens; but where the truth reflects credit on the woman whose name may at present be associated with all that is vile— or where the truth with respect to some dark natures has no power to harm— or where some characters well known to the public, through the medium of the newspapers, pass again across these troubled pages—I have not scrupled to give real names and dates. I shall be attaining my own ends, and offering a greater pledge of my validity, by such a course. Prisoners I would no more intentionally pain than prison-officers; but from a suspicion of mere book-making, I am anxious, even at so early a stage, to disabuse the public mind.

To avoid book-making, therefore, I shall pass very lightly over the ground trodden by former writers on this subject. [...]

[...] In conclusion, and as my chief reason for writing this work, let me state that it is the humble officers of our female convict prisons that have the greatest—nay, the only—opportunity of estimating the true characters of those whom they may have in charge. Directors may issue their annual reports, the governors of prisons may write their ponderous tomes upon the question, the chaplains may preach, and pray, and visit, but their opportunities of judging fairly and honestly are few and far between, and they are misled and deceived every week in the year. In men's prisons I believe it is the warder, and in female prisons I am convinced it is the matron, who alone has the power to offer a true picture of prison life. The matrons are in constant communion with the prisoners; seeing them not for a few minutes each in a daily or weekly inspection, but passing their lives in their midst; witnessing each minute some little slip of the mask which on visiting days the more cunning keep before their feelings; and often remarking some weakness, or passionate outburst, or wail over the past, or little trait of character that speaks of the old and better times, which it is not part of a matron's duty to report.

For a matron's duty is to report only offences against discipline; and even where the offence is trivial, much is looked over, and by some gentle-hearted prison authorities expected to be looked over, which even prison rules do not strictly countenance. And of that better side to prison character which a matron has the greatest chance of observing, of that evidence of affection for some kind officer who has screened offenders from a trivial punishment, or has listened to some little story in impulsive moments, about a mother, sister, brother, child, they loved once, the great report books utter not a word.

The report books are bristling with statistics, as the prison books are with sins of omission; Government can tell to a fraction the expenses of these large convict establishments—to a sailor's shirt or a door-mat the amount of work performed in six months—to a man or woman the number who attend chapel, or receive the sacrament, or are confirmed by my Lord Bishop—but of the life within the outward life that Blue Books speak of, and Parliament agitates concerning, there are no records kept.

With a hope of supplying that void in my own humble fashion, of adding my scraps of information, gathered by a little observation and no small experience, I have compiled this book. [...]

[...] It is a faint record of that inner life which I have recently alluded to. I have not attempted to probe too deeply into the strange workings of it, to see always sorrow and repentance therein, or to doubt in all cases the truth and honesty of those under lock and key. I have expressed my own convictions, often related my story and left the comments thereon to my reader—I am in many cases still perplexed as to the right motives and the true nature. There is but one Book that can fully reveal the awful mystery of such lives, that will one day tell the whole truth, and nothing but the truth!

Chapter V

Prisoners in general

I should be sorry to cast any undue romantic interest over the characters of female prisoners, although it will be presently my duty to direct a little attention to certain prisoners whose lives have had as much romance in them as most people's. And indeed that is not to be wondered at, when it is considered what a tempest-tossed life a woman's must generally have been, to have brought her to her dark estate.

But they are not all heroines, mourning over the error of their ways, and the faltering, downward steps that took them to an abyss of crime, and left them there—albeit they may be all women we can pity.

Charles Dickens, in one of his Christmas works, asserts eloquently that, however low they may have fallen, they grasp still in their hands some tufts and shreds of that unfenced precipice from which they fell from good, and that not to pity them is to do wrong to time and to eternity. And it is even possible—however deceptive outward appearances may be—that they all retain in their memory some fragmentary yearnings for the better past, the brighter days of their innocence and youth. But to see some of these women hour by hour, and listen to them in their mad defiance, rage and blasphemy, is almost to believe they are creatures of another mould and race, born with no idea of God's truth, and destined to die in their own benighted ignorance.

As a class, they are desperately wicked. As a class, deceitful, crafty, malicious, lewd, and void of common feeling. With their various temperaments there are various ways of humouring them into obedience, and here and there a chance of rousing some little instinct to act and think judiciously; but it can be readily imagined that there are all the vices under the sun exemplified in these hundreds of women, and but a sparse sprinkling of those virtues which should naturally adorn and dignify womanhood.

"For men at most differ as Heaven and earth,
But women, worst and best, as Heaven and hell,"

[FRED W. ROBINSON], FEMALE LIFE IN PRISON

asserts our greatest living poet; and no two lines, I fear, are more true to human nature.

In the penal classes of the male prisons there is not one man to match the worst inmates of our female prisons. There are some women so wholly and entirely bad, that chaplains give up in despair, and prison rules prove failures, and punishment has no effect, save to bring them to "death's door," on the threshold of which their guilty tongues still curse and revile, and one must let them have their way, or see them die. There are some women less easy to tame than the creatures of the jungle, and one is almost sceptical of believing that there was ever an innocent childhood or a better life belonging to them. And yet, strange as it may appear, these women are not always in for the worst crimes; there are few, if any, murderesses amongst them; they have been chiefly convicted of theft after theft, accompanied by violence, and they are satanically proud of the offences that have brought them within the jurisdiction of the law.

In the prison the teaching that should have begun with the women in their girlhood is commenced, and exercises in a few instances a salutary influence; but ignorance, deep, besotting ignorance, displays itself with almost every fresh woman on whom the key turns in her cell. It is the great reason for keeping our prisons full, our judges always busy; three-fourths of our prisoners before their conviction were unable to read a word, had no knowledge of a Bible or what was in it, had never heard of a Saviour, and only remembered God's name as always coupled with a curse. Some women have been trained up to be thieves, and worse than thieves, by their mothers—taking their lessons in crime with a regularity and a persistence that, turned to better things, would have made them loved and honoured all their lives. They have been taught all that was evil, and the evil tree has flourished and borne fruit; it is the hardest task to train so warped and distorted a creation to the right and fitting way. Praise be to those hard-working, unflinching prison chaplains who strive their utmost, and are not always unsuccessful; who have an open glorious repentance of one sinner to counterbalance the ninety and nine who scoff at all contrition, and do not, will not, understand, to use their own terms, "what the parson's driving at."

One of the most embarrassing positions for a well-educated prisoner—a lady-thief, or swindler—is to mix with these kinds of women. It is an additional torture to her punishment, for which she is wholly unprepared; they do not understand her or her ways; at Brixton Prison, where there is association, they will sometimes shun her. There are times even when, singularly enough, they taunt her with her education. "You was larnt better than us, and shouldn't ha' come here," I heard a woman say once. Cleaning their cells and scrubbing the stones appear the hardest trials. "Oh! dear," a lady prisoner said once over this kind of labour, "will this do, miss—or shall I try to scrub a little harder? I think I can!"

To hear some of the prisoners' excuses for their appearance in prison, is almost to believe in that disease of kleptomania which has been lately talked about—or in some familiar demon or tempter, as in the old books of James's time, constantly at these poor creatures' elbows, to suggest the profitable nature of sin, and the

SOCIAL AND POLITICAL REFORM

vanity of all that is upright and honourable. A returned woman—that is, a woman who has been let out on her ticket of leave, and has forfeited it by her misconduct, is arrested and sent back to Brixton Prison to work her time out—or who has been reconvicted, perhaps under a false name—always asserts that it wasn't to be avoided, *something* made her seek out the old pals, or steal her neighbour's goods again.

"I did try very hard, miss," she will sometimes say to the matron who may be interested in her; and if she believe in that interest the matron has more power over her and more influence with her than the chaplain; "I did try very hard, but it wasn't to be. I was obliged to steal, or to watch some one there was a chance of stealing from. I did try my best, but it couldn't be helped, and here I am. It wasn't my fault exactly, because I *did* try, you see, miss!"

There are other prisoners not so frank—and these prisoners form the majority—who stoutly maintain, to the last, their innocence of the crime for which they are incarcerated. However indisputable may have been the proofs alleged against them, they are always ill-used unfortunates, who have been made the victims of a foul conspiracy to place them there "in durance vile." They will assert these fabrications to chaplain, superintendent, matrons, and to each other, with a cool effrontery that no facts can diminish, and will quarrel upon the point amongst themselves occasionally. And though each is firm to her own story, she believes not a word of anybody else's—"That Ball—or that Matthews—was always such a liar!"

4.3

Philanthropic Organisations

4.3 Philanthropic Organisations

Philanthropic organisations mushroomed in the Victorian period. In addition to societies and institutions concerned with topics already covered in this section, such as the slave trade and prison reform, there were associations and organisations to deal with a whole range of social problems. Women played a great part in these organisations, as philanthropy was seen as a feminine virtue and an appropriate extension of their domestic mission. In London, in addition to supporting ragged schools, Sunday schools and other organisations for the young, women often visited slum neighbourhoods, providing charity along with advice on domestic arrangements and cleanliness. The Charity Organisation Society was the body that organised lady visitors for the slums. In addition to working on Charles Booth's survey, and living in the East End as part of this work, the Unitarian Clara Collet (1860–1948) worked with the Charity Organisation Society and wrote for its publication, the *Charity Organisation Review*. Meanwhile, Baroness Burdett Coutts (1814–1906) – an example of a High Church upper-class philanthropist – used the Coutts' fortune to build churches and model dwellings, fund ragged schools, and assist men, women and children to emigrate to the colonies.

In the article by Clara Collet reproduced here, she recommends George Gissing's London slum novels to those wanting to know more about the poor. Collet suggests that Gissing is engaged in remarkably similar work to that of the Charity Organisation Society, and counts him among her fellow (social) 'scientists'. Indeed, she argues that Gissing's plots are 'of little importance', compared with his depiction of individual members of the slum-dwelling class. Collet gives an insight into the COS's practices when she likens Gissing's novels to their case papers, arguing that both seek to read the characters of the poor and draw out lessons on ethical issues such as thrift. Rather than a problem of any one domain, the article shows how reading and writing the poor was a concern shared by social scientists, novelists and a philanthropic public.[1]

The short biography of Baroness Burdett Coutts was produced for the 1893 World's Fair exposition in Chicago (which had a section on 'women's philanthropy') and presented to the Board of its Lady Managers by Princess Mary, Duchess of Teck. It ensures that the Baroness's High Church credentials are front and centre by beginning with a record of the churches in England and the Bishoprics in the colonies that she endowed. The biography also details the training home for female ex-prisoners, Urania House, that Burdett Coutts established with the help of Charles Dickens – another novelist who wrote about the London poor. The biography quotes the letter that Dickens wrote to ex-convicts about the training home, in which Burdett Coutts appears as a Dickensian heroine, her heart bleeding for the women she sees outside her windows at night. Domesticity is believed to be the cure for these women, and at the home they are trained in household tasks. Ideal domestic conditions are also seen to be the cure for the slums in one of her other projects: in the model dwellings of Columbia Square in London, Burdett

Coutts' domestic, feminine charity is reported to have led to the disappearance of drunkenness as well as disease, and a revolution in cleanliness and tidiness.

Note

1 Ruth Livesey makes this argument in 'Reading for Character: Women Social Reformers and Narratives of the Urban Poor in Late Victorian and Edwardian London', *Journal of Victorian Culture* 9 (2004), pp. 43–67.

40

CLARA COLLET, 'GEORGE GISSING'S NOVELS'

Charity Organisation Review, May 1891,
pp. 375–380 [abridged]

Amongst optimistic philanthropists it is a common aspiration that the rich and the poor may learn to know each other better. With many this desire takes the form of a wish to be personally acquainted with the poor, to be brought into actual contact with them in such a way as to establish friendly relations with them. There is something a little pathetic or a little amusing, according to the frame of mind in which we may happen to be, in this supposition that we need only to be understood in order to be loved. Those of us who have come to the conclusion with regard to the majority of our own class that the less we have to do with each other the better friends we shall be find some difficulty in believing that frequent intercourse with persons with whom we have even less in common would be more fruitful in its results. Few people are unselfish enough or even intelligent and humane enough to be able to discern the real through the 'dust of the actual'; nor will all admit that the glimpses that can be obtained must necessarily be beautiful. Such doubters may find themselves more in touch with their fellow men through the medium of a great poet or a great novelist than by any intimate acquaintance with them.

They may be glad to understand everybody, but they do not want everybody to understand them. This section of the readers of the *Review* who wish to know about the working classes more particularly will find few better instructors than Mr. George Gissing.

Mr. Gissing is a realist. By this I do not mean that he is a lover of the unsavoury; he is nothing of the kind. Nor that he is a pessimist, although that he certainly is. Without pretending to understand what Aristotle meant by his definition of the soul, I quote it as conveying to modern readers the true meaning of 'realism.' 'It is, we have seen, a real substance which expresses an idea. Such a substance is the manifestation of the inner meaning of such and such a body…. The body is merely the material to which soul gives reality.' Only an idealist can describe the real; and it is the combination of idealism with the most accurate and deep knowledge of working class life that gives George Gissing's novel 'The Nether World' a place above all others in which the same task has been attempted.

289

The attitude which Mr. Gissing has successfully tried to adopt may be best expressed in the words of Harold Biffen in 'New Grub Street.' 'I want to take no side at all, simply to say, Look, this is the kind of thing that happens.' Of Richard Murtimer in 'Demos' the writer says with pity, 'and the chosen directors of his prejudice taught him to regard every fact, every discovery, as *for* or *against* something.' It is characteristic of Mr. Gissing that the moral indignation which pervades all his writings never moves him to curse individuals, classes, or society at large. 'Man is born unto trouble as the sparks fly upward,' fairly expresses Mr. Gissing's view of things; he does not even find fault with Providence, for so far as he knows there is no such thing, and he is far too logical an atheist to hate God.

Mr. Gissing's first novel, 'Workers in the Dawn,' although by no means worthless or unreadable, is not worth reading or discussing except in relation to his later works; and it is as a scientist, not as an artist, that he must be studied in these pages. Both in this first attempt and in his second novel published four years later, he handles a problem far beyond his powers and shows considerable power in doing so. That a writer with Mr. Gissing's determination to see things as they are and not as one would wish them to be should feel strongly attracted to the gloomy world of which the characters in 'The Unclassed' are inhabitants was inevitable. [...]

[...] Of the seven novels which have followed three only need be considered here—'Demos,' 'Thyrza,' and 'The Nether World.' Of the others, 'Isabel Clarendon,' 'A Life's Morning,' and 'The Emancipated,' are studies of character in the educated classes, while the title of 'New Grub Street' explains itself.

'Demos' is described as a story of English socialism. It is not, however, a socialistic story, and it differs from Mr. Gissing's other stories inasmuch as it definitely aims at showing the weakness of certain socialistic assumptions. Mr. Gissing hates politics and rarely argues, and his method of attack is one which makes defence singularly difficult. He merely points to human nature and relentlessly and yet sympathetically displays the defects and merits of the demos. Richard Murtimer, the socialistic agitator, becomes the owner of large estates and mining property, not in order to prove that the working classes are unable to bear sudden prosperity (the most zealous opponents of socialism have no fear of their being subjected to such an ordeal), but to throw into greater relief his selfishness and his want of moral perception. Most historians of Richard Murtimer's career would leave us with the impression that he was a contemptible ruffian. In some remarkable manner, Mr. Gissing conveys an impression of magnanimity in this socialistic leader whose actions and ideals were all ignoble.

Mr. Gissing never suggests remedies, and his plots are of little importance in a consideration of his novels. His intimate knowledge of the habits of life and thought of working people is all that I wish to dwell on here. To take the question of dress, it is surprising to find how much of character can be conveyed in a simple and detailed description of dress. What should we deduce from the following?

1   Her dress was very plain, and indicated poverty; she wore a long black jacket untrimmed, a boa of cheap fur, tied at the throat with black ribbon, a hat of grey felt, black cotton gloves.
2   She wore a dress of tartan, a very small hat trimmed also with tartan and with a red feather, a tippet of brown fur about her shoulders, and a muff of the same material on one of her hands.
3   She wore a plain, tight-fitting grey gown, a small straw hat of the brimless kind, and a white linen collar about her neck.
4   The boots upon her feet were sewn and patched into shapelessness; her limp straw hat had just received a new binding.
5   She wore a dark dress trimmed with velveteen, and a metal ornament of primitive taste gleamed amid her hair.

Totty Nancarrow's affection for pickles and jam is not peculiar to her, but the description of Clem Peckover's supper is a masterly character sketch.

'The sausages—five in number—she had emptied from the frying-pan directly on to her plate, and with them all the black rich juice that had exuded in the process of cooking—particularly rich, owing to its having several times caught fire and blazed triumphantly. On sitting down and squaring her comely frame to work, the first thing Clem did was to take a long draft out of the beer-jug; refreshed thus she poured the remaining liquor into a glass. Ready at hand was mustard made in a tea-cup; having taken a certain quantity of this condiment on to her knife, she proceeded to spread each sausage with it from end to end, patting them in a friendly way as she finished the operation. Next she sprinkled them with pepper, and after that she constructed a little pile of salt on the side of the plate, using her fingers to convey it from the saltcellar. It remained to cut a thick slice of bread— she held the loaf pressed to her bosom whilst doing this—and to crush it down well into the black grease beside the sausages; then Clem was ready to begin. For five minutes she fed heartily, showing really remarkable skill in conveying pieces of sausage to her mouth by means of her knife... She finished her beer in a long enjoyable pull. Her appetite was satisfied; the last trace of oleaginous matter had disappeared from her plate, and now she toyed with little pieces of bread lightly dipped into the mustard-pot. These *bonnes bouches* put her into excellent humour; presently she crossed her arms and leaned back.'

A district secretary of the C.O.S. said recently that Gissing's novels reminded him of the best specimens of case papers. None of those who have read 'The Nether World' will consider this a high compliment to anything but the case papers; but it is quite true that it would be possible to answer nearly every question in our case papers with regard to many of the characters in 'The Nether World' and 'Thyrza.' [...]

SOCIAL AND POLITICAL REFORM

[...] One more quotation may be given as a contribution to the ethics of thrift:

'We hadn't been married more than a month or two when I began to find fault with her, and from that day on she could never please me. I earned five-and-twenty shillings a week, and I'd made up my mind that we must save out of it. I wouldn't let *her* work; no, what *she* had to do was to keep the house on as little as possible, and always have everything clean and straight when I got back at night. But Jenny hadn't the same ideas about things as I had. She couldn't pinch and pare, and our plans of saving came to nothing. It grew worse as the children were born. The more need there was for carefulness, the more heedless Jenny seemed to get. And it was my fault, mine from beginning to end. Another man would have been gentle with her and showed her kindly when she was wrong, and have been thankful for the love she gave him, whatever her faults. That wasn't my way. I got angry and made her life a burden to her. I must have things done exactly as I wished; if not, there was no end to my fault-finding. And yet, if you'll believe it, I loved my wife as truly as man ever did. Jenny couldn't understand that—and how should she? At last she began to deceive me in all sorts of little things; she got into debt with shop-people, she showed me false accounts, she pawned things without my knowing. Last of all, she began to drink. Our fourth child was born just at that time; Jenny had a bad illness, and I believe it set her mind wrong. I lost all control of her, and she used to say if it wasn't for the children she'd go and leave me. One morning we quarrelled very badly, and I did as I threatened to—I walked about the streets all the night that followed, never coming home. I went to work next day, but at dinner-time I got frightened and ran home just to speak a word. Little Mike, the eldest, was playing on the stairs, and he said his mother was asleep. I went into the room, and saw Jenny lying on the bed dressed. There was something queer in the way her arms were stretched out. When I got near I saw she was dead. She'd taken poison.

'And it was I had killed her, just as much as if I'd put the poison to her lips. All because I thought myself such a wise fellow, because I had resolved to live more prudently than other men of my kind did. I wanted to save money for the future—out of five-and-twenty shillings a week. Many and many a day I starved myself to try and make up for expenses of the home. Sidney, you remember that man we once went to hear lecture, the man that talked of nothing but the thriftlessness of the poor and how it was their own fault they suffered? I was very near telling you my story when we came away that night. Why, look; I myself was just the kind of poor man that would have suited that lecturer. And what came of it? If I'd let my poor Jenny go her own way from the first, we should have had hard times now and then, but there'd have been our love to help us, and we should have been happy enough. They talk about thriftiness, and it just means that poor people are expected to practise a self-denial that the rich can't even imagine, much less carry out!'

Has Mr. Gissing any practical advice to give or any remedy to propose? Absolutely none. But it does not follow because he can offer no panacea for the woes of society at large that those who read him may not see their way more clearly to alleviate those of particular individuals.

41

BARONESS BURDETT COUTTS: A SKETCH OF HER PUBLIC LIFE AND WORK

(London: Unwin Bros, 1893), pp. 15–19, 21–23, 25–27, 105–110, 176–180

Introduction

[…] The Baroness is the youngest daughter of Sir Francis Burdett, Bart., one of the leading figures in the political history of the early part of the century, and long the champion of popular rights. She is the grand-daughter of the wealthy banker, Thomas Coutts, whose immense fortune—at that day perhaps unprecedented—was eventually bequeathed to her by his widow. This young English lady then found herself at the head of one of the great financial houses of the world, ranking in London next only to the Bank of England, while socially the unique character of her position conferred upon her informal privileges which almost constituted a prerogative. As one of many ambitions, the gratification of which thus lay within the grasp of the young heiress, a writer declared that, with her wealth, she might "purchase a principality."

But Miss Burdett-Coutts secured a nobler and wider rule. She enthroned herself in the hearts of the people and commanded the homage of those who represented all that was noblest and best in England. With a generous and ready sympathy she entered into the aspirations of the masses then struggling towards a better and happier life; while her character and position enabled her to direct aid and influence from many powerful sources into the same channel. None who fail to recognize this aspect of her life can in any way appreciate the Baroness' true position in the history of her time. She not only drew those around her into the circle of philanthropic work, but by means of an example, which women unknown to her in all parts of the world have recognized, she indirectly obtained vast and far reaching results in the cause to which her life has been devoted.

At her well known house in Stratton Street, London, she received sovereigns, princes, ambassadors, statesmen, and world-famed commanders. She was the friend of great scholars; and explorers, and missionaries came to her from the farthest ends of the earth. Young writers, actors and artists, their fame then first bursting upon the world, had already received from her the earliest and sweetest words of praise and encouragement. And yet amid a life of such high and absorbing interest her mind was ever silently working for the good of others, now on great schemes for the benefit of masses, now on some one of innumerable little projects for the benefit of individuals. It is with the first of these that this volume is specially concerned. Her vast work of private and individual charity is one of which no living hand can ever write the history, and she herself would probably be the first to desire that it should remain unwritten.

I
The Church of England

The earliest efforts of Miss Burdett-Coutts were devoted to the service of the Church of England, which it was her earnest wish to see firmly planted in the Colonies. In the year 1847, carrying this desire into effect, she endowed the Bishoprics of Capetown, South Africa, and of Adelaide, South Australia, both of them modeled exactly on the English system. About ten years later she founded the Bishopric of British Columbia; providing twenty-five thousand pounds for the Endowment of the Church; fifteen thousand pounds for the Bishopric; and ten thousand pounds towards the maintenance of the Clergy. In the interval she had been engaged at home in a munificent effort in the same cause.

In January 1846 a report was current that Miss Burdett-Coutts had signed a blank cheque, which she had handed to the Bishop of London with a request that he would fill it in for such a sum as might be required to build and endow "a handsome Church." It was also said that this cheque had been honored to the amount of thirty thousand pounds. The report was not exactly accurate; but as a matter of fact Miss Burdett-Coutts did build a Church, one of the most handsome erected in London in modern times. It was also true that a cheque for thirty thousand pounds proving altogether insufficient, a further sum of about sixty thousand pounds was provided to carry this magnificent work to completion. On the 20th of July, 1847, the first stone was laid of the Church of St. Stephen, Westminster—erected by Miss Burdett-Coutts to the memory of her father, Sir Francis Burdett, who for so many years had represented in Parliament the City of Westminster. The ceremony of consecration was performed on the 24th of June, 1850, the day being observed as a fête in Westminster, where some one thousand five hundred people, inhabitants, school children, and workmen, were publicly entertained. A few days afterwards a special visit was paid to the church and schools by the Prince Consort. [...]

[...] The building of the church involved provision for the purchase of a site, for the demolition of rows of poor houses and compensation to the tenants, and also for a permanent and liberal endowment fund. While St. Stephen's was in course of construction, Miss Burdett-Coutts provided a mission church and schools in which a congregation was first collected. From the date of the consecration, she has borne the cost of all repairs to the fabric, salaries of all officials, and all extraordinary expenditure for religious and educational purposes in connection with the church. But St. Stephen's is not, and obviously was never intended to be, only a church. Its Foundress conceived and carried out the idea of placing almost under the shadow of the great Abbey, but in the midst of a very poor district, a living example of all the work and influence, both spiritual and material, which can be included in a great parochial organization. This work has been gradually enlarged, and now includes Guilds for men, boys, and girls; Communicants' Guild for women: Missionary Lay-helpers; Working and Friendly Societies; Social and Benefit Clubs of various kinds; a Ringers' Guild; Temperance Societies; Bible Classes; an organization for District Visiting; and a Soup Kitchen, from which nearly seventy thousand dinners have been supplied to the poor within the last few years. The St. Stephen's Self Help Club, a most interesting experiment in co-operation, increased its operations from seven hundred pounds to two-thousand pounds a year within three years, and is still maintaining its extraordinary progress. In connection with the church were established the large and eminently successful St. Stephen's Schools, where fifteen thousand boys and girls have been educated. These Schools and a thriving Technical Institute which has grown out of them, are more fully referred to in the chapter which deals with the Baroness' work in aid of education.

VI
Columbia Square

THE gulf dividing the West from the East End of London, deep as it now is, was deeper twenty-five years ago. It was a subject on which Charles Dickens often dwelt. He speaks of the journey from the one district to the other as one of the most extraordinary transitions that could be experienced. In one of his articles he has written of the wealth and luxury, flowers and perfumes, the rich houses and luxurious equipages of the wealthy district, asking: "Are care, illness, sorrow, death, known in such a place? Who are all these people and how are all these palaces maintained, where do the inhabitants, where does the money come from?" Then he turned suddenly eastward to a locality where, in his own words, violence, cruelty, immodesty, and uncleanliness, were unmitigated and almost unconcealed. "Every thing is perverted. Childhood is old and careful. Infants, imitating the violence they have seen about them from their earliest recollection, are shrill and shrewish with the smaller infants placed under their care. The home is perverted from being a haven of rest, which the man longs to get to, and is become an earthly hell which he has cause to dread. The women are perverted to be unwomanly, and the men, for the most part, to be like the brute creation, with just enough humanity to make them more elaborate in brutishness. The air is perverted to carry from window to window the monstrous vapors encircled in a compound interest of corruption as it passes on. The sun's rays are perverted, and, instead of bringing wholesomeness and purity with them, draw up a new wealth of nastiness from every nook and corner, and, heating it to fever pitch, breed death far and near."

SOCIAL AND POLITICAL REFORM

In the center of this district, which Miss Burdett-Coutts visited with Dickens, was a spot known as Nova Scotia Gardens. There was a fine irony lurking in the poetic designation, for it was here that every evil of the neighborhood existed in an exaggerated form. There was a large piece of waste ground covered in places with foul, slimy looking pools, amid which crowds of half-naked, barefooted, ragged children chased one another. From the center rose a great black mound, formed of immense quantities of cinders, ashes, and animal and vegetable refuse, collected from the surrounding parishes. The stench continually issuing from the enormous mass of decaying matter was unendurable. Fever, and every other disease were never absent from the crime-stained locality, which was chiefly inhabited by starving weavers, thieves, courtesans, prize-fighters, and dog stealers.

It was characteristic of the Baroness that she should have picked out this Ultima Thule of poverty and degradation for the site of a new and noble enterprise, which, as in the case of so many other of her efforts, led directly to a far reaching and beneficent improvement in the condition of the poor of London. This spot was chosen for the erection of four blocks of model dwellings for the poor, the first buildings of the kind, and those upon which the Peabody buildings, and many other model lodging-houses, were afterward designed. The reeking mass of refuse was speedily removed, and by May, 1862, Columbia Square was in existence, affording accommodation for two hundred families, or about a thousand persons. Each house contains forty-five complete tenements, generally consisting of two, and sometimes of three rooms, one of which is provided with a good kitchen range. Remembering the habits of the class from which the tenants would be drawn, special attention was paid to secure abundant light and ventilation. Excellent drainage, lavatories, and baths, gave advantages to the inhabitants not at that time enjoyed by persons in much more favored circumstances, and at the top of each building was fitted an excellent laundry. A reading room and library of five hundred standard volumes were also provided.

It is rarely indeed that a pioneer effort anticipates to such a remarkable extent its own future development. These buildings, however, were so far in advance of the standard of that day that even now they are able to bear comparison with others recently erected, and designed to meet the requirements of the latest developments of sanitary science. They were immediately occupied, and have ever since been eagerly sought after; among the tenants, drunkenness and disease in great measure disappeared, and an almost Dutch-like cleanliness and tidiness are everywhere to be observed.

X
Stray Leaves

[...] One of her earliest efforts was the establishment of a home for women at Shepherd's Bush. In this, Charles Dickens spared neither time nor trouble. He superintended the purchase of land and buildings, the repairs and furnishing. He drew up rules, framed in a broad and truly charitable spirit, and with a view of making as easy as might be the new path which the inmates would strive to follow. He visited the prisons, and with the help of Governors and Magistrates selected the most hopeful cases. To these he sent an anonymous invitation to start a new life in a home where there would be no harsh or arbitrary rules, no distinctive dress, and no reference to the past. This invitation, which best explains the aim of the institution, is addressed "to a woman," to one who has lived miserably with no prospect before her but sorrow, nothing behind her but "a wasted youth;" and it continues:

"You are such a person, or this letter would not be put into your hands. If you have ever wished (I know you must have done so sometimes) for a chance of rising out of your sad life, and having friends, a quiet home, means of being useful to yourself and others, peace of mind, self respect, everything you have lost, pray read it attentively, and reflect upon it afterwards. I am going to offer you, not the chance but the certainty of all these blessings, if you will exert yourself to deserve them. And do not think that I write to you as if I felt myself very much above you, or wished to hurt your feelings by reminding you of the situation in which you are placed. God forbid! I mean nothing but kindness to you, and I write as if you were my sister. [...]

[...] There is a lady in this town who, from the windows of her house, has seen such as you going past at night, and has felt her heart bleed at the sight. She is what is called a great lady; but she has looked after you with compassion as being of her own sex and nature, and the thought of such fallen women has troubled her. She has resolved to open, at her own expense, a place of refuge very near London for a small number of women, who without such help are lost for ever, and to make it a *home* for them. In this Home they will be taught all household work that would be useful to them in a home of their own, and enable them to make it comfortable and happy. In this Home, which stands in a pleasant country lane, and where each may have her little flower garden, if she pleases, they will be treated with the greatest kindness; will lead an active, cheerful, healthy life; will learn many things it is good to know, and, being entirely removed from all who have any knowledge of their past career, will begin life afresh, and be able to win a good name and character. And because it is not the lady's wish that these young women should be shut out from the world after they have repented and have learned how to do their duty there, and because it *is* her wish and object that they may be restored to society, they will be supplied with every means, when some time shall have elapsed, and their conduct shall have fully proved their earnestness and reformation, to go abroad, where in a distant country, they may become the faithful wives of honest men, and live and die in peace."

This was the work at Urania College, Shepherd's Bush, and though it was afterwards found advisable to seek as inmates those who had taken only the first steps in vice, instead of those long numbered in the ranks of crime, yet the work had a great and a long success. By twos and threes, after probation, the girls were emigrated under careful supervision, and began the life which, in many cases, had been rendered impossible for them by the force of surrounding circumstances. For, says Dickens in one of his letters, "It is dreadful to think how some of these doomed women have no chance or choice. It is impossible to disguise from oneself the horrible truth that it would have been a social marvel and miracle if some of them had been anything else than what they are."

4.4

Social Purity

4.4 Social Purity

While philanthropists and city missionaries were often concerned with 'rescuing' prostitutes from the slums (for example, see this volume, The Salvation Army), the social purity movement challenged the sexual double standard it saw as responsible for prostitution itself. As well as campaigning for an improvement of morals among the people, social purity campaigners, such as Josephine Butler, opposed laws they believed enshrined the sexual double standard in law, such as the Contagious Diseases (CD) Acts. These Acts, introduced in the late 1860s, enforced a system of physical examination for women suspected of being prostitutes in garrison towns and ports throughout England. Campaigners, in line with their Christian beliefs, refused to countenance the theory that men were naturally promiscuous, and argued that the CD Acts had the effect of encouraging immorality – and in fact had not halted the spread of syphilis. In England the CD Acts were repealed in 1886, however, they remained in force in parts of the British Empire. The high-profile campaign against the CD Acts encouraged other social purity activism, including that of the White Cross Army (later the White Cross League), which was set up in 1883 by Ellice Hopkins (1836–1904) and supported by the Bishop of Durham as part of the High Church's increasing activism in response to social problems (see this volume, Christian Socialism). The Army used methods similar to those of the temperance movement to recruit working-class men to its cause and encourage them to lead more moral and sexually responsible lives (see this volume, Temperance). Other social purity societies used more repressive methods, for example, the National Vigilance Association used age of consent legislation to shut down brothels.

The Association for the Improvement of Public Morals worked for the establishment of Christian principles in society and used its journal, *The Sentinel*, to report on social purity campaigns. While the CD Act in Britain was repealed in 1886, and a resolution was passed in the House of Commons for the Act's repeal in India on 5 June 1888, many aspects of the Act remained in force in India for many more years, effectively licensing and encouraging prostitution in this part of the empire. The article from *The Sentinel* included here details campaigners' outrage at the official 'perfidy' of representatives of the Government of India in lying to the House of Commons about the repeal of the Act: they accuse officials of either intent to deceive or 'criminal ignorance'. As well as reporting on the activities of Parliament, the article also quotes the Indian press on this issue, which, in the quotation, addresses the British public as 'Christians and Patriots', mobilising Christian and national feeling against the authorities, in sympathy with the women of India. The article ends by suggesting that the situation has brought about a constitutional crisis, in which the people are come to 'doubt officials'. These officials are cast as the campaigners' enemies in a religious battle, in which 'The Lord will carry us through'.

Ellice Hopkins's White Cross Army recruited married and unmarried men and asked them to pledge to refrain from impure behaviour, such as bad language, excessive drinking, masturbation and sex outside marriage. The tract reproduced here is from the Army's 'White Cross Series', and featured the society's crest and motto 'Blessed are the pure in heart' on its front cover. As with tracts produced by other religious societies, the author is signalled only by a set of initials, in this case 'JEH', standing for Jane Ellice Hopkins. This concealment enables Hopkins to quote her own work, *Work Amongst Working Men*, and refer to herself as 'a well-known worker in the Cause of Purity'. In this tract she explicitly attempts to avoid the language of religion to counter men's explanation that their sins are caused by their 'Nature' (though this creeps back in towards the end, with references to death, destruction and hell). Instead, Hopkins uses comparison with animals and with her own definition of natural instincts in men to rhetorically assert the unnaturalness of impure behaviour. She is especially strong in her description of the perversion of women's 'natural' function by that great sin of cities, i.e. prostitution.

42

'ON THE REPEAL OF THE CD ACT IN INDIA'

The Sentinel, September 1888, pp. 109–110

Official perfidy

Professor Stuart, with a sturdy persistency for which we heartily thank him, endeavoured just before the House of Commons adjourned to extract from Sir John Gorst, who represents the Government of India in the House of Commons, some statement of what has been done in consequence of the passing of the resolution for Repeal in India. This is the sum of Gorst's replies as they were reported in *The Times* on August 3rd, 4th, and 10th. (1) Such directions have been given to the Government of India as will prevent the revival of the regimental system, which has already been wholly abolished. (2) The Cantonment regulations hitherto in force are to be so revised as to put a stop to the objectionable incidents in their administration. (3) The Bill of the Government of India dealing with the subject has not yet been received by the Secretary of State, and *he hoped that before the Bill arrived, the "Indian Budget" would have been discussed and the House would have adjourned.* (4) Till the Bill arrives he will make no further communication with the Government of India on the subject. (5) *Through an oversight* no steps had been taken to apprise the Government of India of the erroneous method in which Dr. Barclay and others had taken the averages in connection with the Lock Hospital reports.

We will not dwell on the impertinent sauciness of Gorst in openly declaring to Parliament his desire that the House of Commons would not be in session when the Bill arrives. There will be an Autumn Session. The Bill will be with us then, and our friends in Parliament will see to it that the Government shall carry out the spirit, as well as the letter of the resolution of June 5th. Nor do we stop to emphasise the singular "oversight" which Gorst had to confess. We only observe that these oversights are frequent, and only occur with respect to one class of communications. But Sir John says "the regimental system has already been wholly abolished," and when Mr. McLaren asked him if he could corroborate Lord Cross, the Secretary of State for India, who had said to a deputation, "that the whole of the regulations under the Cantonment Acts were *absolutely suspended and non-existent"* he replied "that if the Secretary of State has made such a statement, the Honourable Member ought to be satisfied with it, and should not require its corroboration." He left the House and the country to believe that the statement was true. If he knew it to be untrue it was his duty to correct the statement. Now the statement is absolutely false. Did Sir John Gorst know it to be false? If he did, then he shamefully suppressed the truth in order to mislead public opinion, and disgraced his commanding official position by giving continued vitality to a lie. If he did not know it was false, either he is a simpleton, the unenquiring tool of the India Office, or that Office is so grossly misconducted that it does not procure information of the highest importance which we possessed before Gorst was invited to confirm or deny the lie. From the most trustworthy source, we are assured that LICENSES TO SIN ARE STILL BEING ISSUED IN THE NAME OF THE GOVERNMENT OF INDIA TO WOMEN IN THE FOLLOWING PLACES AT LEAST, *namely,* LUCKNOW, SITAPUR, PESHAWUR, DEOLALI, MHOW, SECUNDERABAD, BELGAUM, BANGALORE. In how many other places the dreadful system is still maintained, notwithstanding the direct condemnation of it by the House of Commons, we are at present unable to say. We await further enquiries. We pledge ourselves to the accuracy of the statement that when the Secretary of State for India asserted "that the whole of the regulations under the Cantonment Acts were absolutely suspended and non-existent," and when the Under Secretary of State for India told Mr. McLaren he ought to be satisfied with that statement, and also told Professor Stuart that "the regimental system has already been wholly abolished," then and now, in eight important places, the Government of India was, and is, licensing women to sin as theretofore.

In addition to the private information to which we have referred, we have the testimony of the *Rast Goftar,* an Anglo-Gujarati weekly published in Bombay, which on June 10th said, speaking of the C. D. Act, "Its working has not been stopped in the Presidency towns as erroneously supposed. That the C. D. Act is still being vigorously worked in Bombay is a well-known fact requiring no proof whatever." Mr. W. J. Gladwin, of Bombay, in the course of a long and valuable letter addressed to the *Bombay Guardian,* says: "The public were told in May last by the highest official authority that the 'infamous Acts' were suspended in India. After that,—June 5th—the House of Commons unanimously voted for entire repeal. In the face of those facts read this later fact:—

"On the tenth day of July, 1888, the——Hospital at Belgaum, Bombay Presidency, was in full operation, with staff as follows:—

Surgeon	per month	Rs. 100
Hospital Assistant	"	" 25
Nurse	"	" 12
Female Detective	"	" 12

"Mark that last item, women of India and England! Think what it means, Christians and patriots! The British Government has female police in India! ...

'ON THE REPEAL OF THE CD ACT IN INDIA'

"I can speak out more plainly in papers directly devoted to this agitation. Here I can only say: (1) that Belgaum now has 150 female victims on the rolls of the Government of our Empress Victoria, (2) that compulsory registration, (3) compulsory weekly examination, (4) compulsory incarceration in a——Hospital,—are being enforced at the shake of the policeman's club.

"The Christian public of England and India may as well face the fact that the authorities in India do not intend to carry out the Repeal action of Parliament."

Yet the Chief Secretary says "the regulations under the Cantonment Acts" are "non-existent," and the Under Secretary says "the regimental system ... has already been wholly abolished." The statements are false. In the making of them there was either criminal ignorance, or the deliberate intention to deceive, which has succeeded. The country believes those statements. It is hard to convince the public mind that men of distinction, who occupy high offices of State, do make statements which are false in fact, and perchance false to their knowledge. Our enemies believe that if their statements are credited, public attention will turn to other subjects, well content to leave the women of India in fancied security. That is the end and aim of our defeated and desperate enemies, for then they will continue to set the will of Parliament and of the British nation at defiance, and will continue to maintain by stealth their wicked system of supporting vice. The palmy days of officialism are gone. The people have begun to doubt officials, and determine questions for themselves. The people have determined that Repeal shall be carried out in India. They will see it done, and when they find out that officials prevent them by falsehood and deceit, they will sweep away the officials, even Gorst, as well as the system. The people of England are ranged on the side of the women of India. God has marvellously aided those who have led the struggle on behalf of the afflicted outcasts of India. The Lord has taken out of their hands the cup of trembling, and has put it in the hands of them that afflicted them. The Lord will carry us through.

43

J. E. H. [ELLICE HOPKINS], *IS IT NATURAL?*

(London: Hatchards, [1885]), pp. 3–13 [abridged]

In a little book called *Work amongst Working Men*,[1] written by a well-known worker in the cause of Purity, the writer narrates:—

'I had been extremely annoyed at the bestial behaviour in the public-house of some of the drinking men who, I knew, were present; and having spoken with much warmth of my love for working men, and of all I had learnt from them, I couldn't help making an exception, and saying, that there was one place where I did not like working men at all, and that was in the public-house. "Out of a public-house a working man always knows how to behave to a lady; he would never think of demeaning himself by begging. I'd trust myself anywhere else to the care of working men. But in the public-house, if a lady ventures in and gives them a few papers, or asks them to meet her on a Sunday, what is the first thing they have to say to her? 'Gi'e us two-pence for a pot of beer.' 'Just like,' I added, with some asperity, 'a pig beginning to grunt for his wash the moment you approach his sty!' Up rose a hoary-headed doctor, and said, 'I think that's rather hard.' He paused. There was a suppressed stamping of feet and clapping of hands from the drinking-men,—then he went on in the same dry, quiet tone,—'hard, I mean, on the *pig*.' Sudden fall of countenance in the audience. 'Did you ever see a pig go into a gin-shop at all? and did you ever see a pig take a drop too much? and, above all, did you ever see a pig go home and knock about his sow?' This last question proved irresistible; a roar of laughter greeted it, the drinking-men felt they had got the worst of it, and nine of them joined the Temperance Club that night.'

Now there is a great deal of sense in the words of that good old doctor. I have often thought that we are very hard, not only on the pig, but on the whole animal creation in the way we have got into of speaking especially of the sins of the flesh as animal, brutal, bestial; and of using the common rough expression of the man who gets drunk or sins against his own manhood, that 'he makes a beast of himself.' Where can you find the animal that ever sins against its own nature, or that satisfies a want beyond the limit of the purpose for the attainment of which the want was implanted? Where will you find the animal that when it has satisfied its thirst persists in going on drinking till it has muddied its brain? Where will you find the animal that when it has satisfied its hunger goes on eating till it has overloaded its stomach and destroyed its digestion? Where will you find the animal that indulges in excesses that interfere with the propagation of its race and injure the health of its offspring? Where domestic animals have formed depraved habits, you will always find the origin of those habits not in the animal but in its master, man, the poor animal's evil 'divinity,' as Bacon calls him, who has occasionally shaped its ends to bad uses. [...]

[...] But if we find nothing like drunkenness in the animal world, still less do we find anything like those deeper evils which involve the suffering and the degradation of women, and which we so constantly speak and think of as the outcome of man's animal nature. But the Duke of Argyll points out, that in the whole of the animal creation man is the only animal that degrades and illtreats his female. 'There is nothing like it,' he remarks in his book on the Unity of Nature, 'among the beasts. With them the equality of the sexes, as regards all the enjoyments as well as the work of life, is the universal rule; and among those of them in which the social instincts have been especially implanted, and whose systems of polity are like the most civilised polities of men, the females of the race are treated with a strange mixture of love, loyalty, and devotion.' It is reserved for Man alone to illtreat and desert, and degrade and destroy, the being who is given to him to be the mother of his children and his devoted companion, and then to turn round and say that in so doing he has obeyed the dictates of Nature!

The dictates of Nature? When Nature, in noble scorn, points to her whole realm, and defies the man who thus belies her to find a single creature of her hand, however terrible or loathsome in aspect it may appear to us, that does not respect and cherish its female. She points to the little bird singing on his bough to his mate,—

'While bright eyes watch him from the nest,
A brooding wonder at her breast;'

or beating the air in joyous flight to find her food while she warms their young with her breast, or makes her tender wings a roof for them from the bird of prey or the storm. She points to the fierce hyena and the panther, that rend their fellows, but cherish and protect the creature with which they pair. [...]

[...] But, above all, let us clearly recognise that, of all unnatural things, the evil which is called 'the sin of great cities' is the most unnatural. Nothing is more painful in this painful question than the determined way in which men blink to themselves that a sin against Nature is inflicted on the woman, that all the divine functions of her womanhood are trampled out, and the very purpose for which she was made 'the mother of all living' defeated. And it is doubtless owing to the fact of its being thus an unnatural sin that it leads to such unnatural degradation. While mother-hood is still possible this unnatural degradation never takes place. Though in some of its aspects it may be still more awful that a man should be found to bring his child into the world through such a door of hell, the child to which he can perform no single duty of fatherhood, a child, in South's terrible words, 'not so much born as damned into the world' through the sins of its parents; still at least the infant hands bring to the unhappy mother the divine gift of tears, the divine possibilities of repentance; the feeble, outstretched infant arms, form the sacred sign of the cross athwart which the hosts of hell dare not cross the threshold to take possession of the mother's soul; at least, while she has her babe at her breast, the horrid laughter, sadder than the saddest wail, is stilled on her lip, the hard look in the eyes that seems to graze your inmost soul, is not seen, the mystery of degradation, which comes on one with a sort of crushing surprise, is not found. It is only after sin is finished and has brought forth death that these things are possible. Indeed, so grossly unnatural is the whole thing that a man well known in the literary world once told his intimate friend that on one occasion he got attached to an outcast girl, but the moment he entertained a touch of human feeling towards her he found it impossible to go on. There was only one thing possible to him then, not to degrade her, but at once to rescue her. What does this mean but that, in other words, the moment he had a touch of natural feeling the whole thing became impossible?

Nor is it less grossly unnatural on the side of the man. I earnestly contend, that men are by nature made just as modest and full of personal self-respect and delicacy as women; and had not all their natural and finer instincts been trodden down, not by the dictates of Nature, but by the dictates of the world and the low tone of social opinion, had not the very springs of their purity been fouled at their source by swines' hoofs, in the shape of coarse jocularity and unclean talk, it would be as repulsive to a man to give himself to a 'strange woman,' whom he neither knows nor cares for, as it would be to his sister, or to his wife and daughter, to act in the same way. And doubtless this sense of personal dignity, this natural self-respect, does keep many men from so debasing themselves. Their natural instincts are sufficiently strong and healthy to make them turn from it with loathing and disgust.

But even with forms of impurity that are less hideously unnatural than the trade of vice, and the existence of a pariah class of women, forms of impurity which are the outcome of strong, but ill-regulated, affection, before you can prove that, in yielding to them, you are yielding to the dictates of Nature, you have first to define *whose* nature. Do you mean the nature of an animal, or the nature of a man? For if you mean the nature of a man, you must take in all that belongs to that nature; not only his animal nature, but his conscience, reason, will, love. Is it according to the dictates of that nature to inflict a stigma on the very object of your love? Can a man show so much as a photograph of one he tenderly loves, and has perhaps lost, without instinctively passing his coat-sleeve over the glass, to wipe off the least speck of dust that may dim the sweet lips, or cloud the pure gaze? Is it natural to stain the very thing you most tenderly love, or to give the mother of your child a tarnished name for it to inherit? Is that tie a natural one, I ask, that makes it impossible for you to fulfil a single duty to the helpless child you have brought into the world, or to give it the daily guidance, the hourly wise watchfulness, the firm rule, which only your fatherhood can supply, and which makes the loss of a father such an irreparable one to a child, even when a stainless mother is still left? If you are capable of bringing into the world a being like yourself, with infinite possibilities of weal or woe, must it not, on the face of it, involve infinite responsibilities, the neglect of which forms the deepest violation of the dictates of your nature as a moral being? Is not marriage the only relation in which you can obey the real dictates of your nature, and secure the natural conditions involved in a human family?

As to those forms of impurity that partake more of the nature of suicide than of murder, the moral sense of mankind has branded them as in the highest degree unnatural, and too abhorrent to our nature even to speak about. 'When a man attempts to employ himself as a bare means to satisfy a brutal lust, he not only,' as the great philosopher Kant says, 'meanly abdicates his personality, and stands bereft of reverence of any kind,' but he abdicates his place in the kingdom of Nature as well as of God. Nothing in the least parallel to it can be found in the animal world.

Bear in mind that I am purposely keeping off all religious ground, and confining myself to the constantly reiterated assertion that Nature herself pleads a necessity for these sins. 'I speak unto wise men, judge ye what I say.' Is impurity natural? Does not the deep disorder of this part of our nature, the way it constantly defeats the purpose for which it was made, point to something that is unnatural, to man's rebellion against Nature, which makes him 'the Great Exception' to her universal harmony and order? [...]

[...] Impurity natural? The mountain peak from the heights of her unspotted snows saith: 'It is not with me.' The sea from the depth of her myriad crystal fountains saith: 'It is not in me.' Destruction and Death alone say, 'We have heard the fame thereof.' Hell alone from beneath is stirred at its coming, and proclaims, 'The worm is spread under thee and the worms shall cover thee.'

> 'Ah, wondrous blessèd world of ours!
> Ah, fountain opened evermore
> For all uncleanness! minister
> Of elemental love that everywhere
> About me flows and works in sea and shore,
> In fire and air, with love's absolving powers.
> O let thy gentleness make me great,
> That I may keep all day the simple state
> Of thy pure springs, thy blowing clover, skies
> Of morn and even, stars, and odorous sighs;
> Nor need again that voice from heaven:
> Go, sin no more;
> Thou art forgiven.'

Note

1 *Work amongst Working Men*. By Ellice Hopkins. Sixth Edition, Kegan Paul.

4.5

Christian Socialism

4.5 Christian Socialism

While socialism was often a secular movement, especially internationally, a number of British socialists were inspired by Christianity, and a number of members of the clergy saw socialism as a manifestation of the merciful spirit of Christ. Incarnation theology, such as that outlined by the Christian Socialist, F. D. Maurice, emphasised the humanity of Christ and prompted reformers to focus on improving social conditions in order to lessen sinners' physical, as well as spiritual, suffering. Millenarian beliefs also combined with the revolutionary atmosphere of the late nineteenth century to inspire Christian Socialists to prophesy the dissolution of society and the rise of alternative, utopian social formations (for more discussion, see Volume III, Mercy, and Volume IV, Owenism). While there was no single, coherent Christian Socialism, a unifying theme was the brotherhood of man, and the belief that the political economic system should reflect this. Similarly, Christian Socialists were united in their hatred of 'political economy'. Though Christian Socialists did not fully engage with economic socialism, they remained an important influence within the socialist movement.

Within the Church of England, the explicit socialist preaching of the Anglican minister, Stewart Headlam (1847–1924), caused considerable controversy and involved him in a number of disputes with the Bishop of London. Headlam was inspired by F. D. Maurice's Incarnationist faith in universal redemption, and his own love of the theatre, to work with actors and ballerinas. He defended this work in his sermons, such as those from 1881, reproduced here. His tone is often combative and colloquial as he instructs his congregation 'Don't think you can be religious by being more spiritual than He was'. He interprets the parables as calling on Christians to work on secular causes to improve society, and uses political terminology to comment on the disparity of the death rate between Belgravia and St Luke's and in calling for an 'organized society'. Finally, he goes so far as to explicitly claim Jesus as a 'Socialistic Carpenter' and calls for his congregation to be 'Christian communists'.

The Labour Church was founded by the Unitarian John Trevor (1855–1930) in Manchester in 1891. The *Labour Church Hymn Book* was collated by Trevor with his wife Eliza (d. 1894) and, as well as compiling hymns for the new Church, the edition extracted here set out the principles of the organisation. The first principle explicitly states that they saw the labour movement as religious, although the following principles make clear that this religion is anti-establishment and nonconformist. The Labour Church also describes the condition of labour in the country as a form of slavery, from which labourers can only escape through personal religious development. The preface admits that those who had abandoned traditional organised religion still felt a need for the familiar religious forms, such as hymns. In response to this need, the Labour Church therefore often adapted traditional religious songs; for example, in the hymn book extracted here, they provide a version of the National Anthem in which the working man, peasant and artisan are substituted for the Queen. At the same time, the collection brings together verses from the early nineteenth-century Chartist movement with new works by Edward Carpenter and E. Nesbit, and anonymous creations by labour organisations such as the unions, creating the impression of a movement with a strong history and wide membership. (For more discussion of the religion of the Chartist movement, see Volume I, Radical Christianity.)

Towards the end of the century, the Baptist minister John Clifford (1836–1923) contributed to the Fabian Society's collection of political tracts to discuss whether Socialism could be Christian and whether Christianity could be Socialist. Like Headlam, Clifford criticises Christians who believe that Churches should concern themselves with the higher, spiritual issues and not deal with the 'politico-economical conditions of the life of the people around them'. Clifford suggests that, by the time he was writing in the late 1890s, a large number of Christians had accepted the implications of Incarnation theology, and he paints a utopian picture of this 'regeneration of the social consciousness in the Churches of Christ'. Where he goes further than these Christians is in his commitment to changing the whole political-industrial system to one based on socialist collectivism, as a truer incarnation of Christ's teachings. He even approaches Marxism when he prescribes collectivism as the best economic base for a truly spiritual superstructure. In Clifford's tract there is an optimism based on modernity. He sees the possibility of collectivism in the developments in municipal infrastructure and services, and he uses the language of recent scientific discoveries to give his conclusion rhetorical force. Christ, he says, will transform the system, and usher in a utopia of socialist collectivism.

44

STEWART HEADLAM, 'THE SERVICE OF HUMANITY' AND 'THE STAGE'

In *The Service of Humanity and other Sermons* (London: J. Hodges, 1882), pp. 1, 3–7, 11, 13–18

The Service of Humanity

"If I wash thee not thou hast no part with me."—St. John xiii., 8.

Preached in Westminster Abbey on Maunday Thursday, 1881

It is the *grace* of our Lord Jesus Christ, the *beauty* of His life and character, which we want always to have with us. He is our Lord and Master, but He does not lord it over us: He does not frighten us by threats into obedience to Him, but He draws us to Himself with the cords of His perfect humanity, He binds us with the bands of His love. For us men and for our salvation He came *down from Heaven* and was *incarnate*. "His love" indeed "was of the valley:" it was *this* world which He felt demanded, and would in the end repay, His utmost care and attention. [...]

[...] The work of Jesus Christ and of His Church is then, in this Maunday Thursday event, as so often, shewn to be secular work: all work for Humanity, material as well as spiritual, is to-day revealed as being 'of Christ.'

Religious people, especially those who, owing to an evil environment or a fatal heredity, are not called to work for others in order to get their own daily bread; I say religious people, especially those of the leisure class, have a natural shrinking from this kind of thing: they prefer to think of Jesus Christ as the head of religious men, rather than as the head of every man, 'as the second Abraham rather than as the second Adam.' They shut their eyes to the secular side of Christ's work; to the Christian Communism of the Church of the Carpenter: they forget that we are a baptized brotherhood of equals; they think it more religious to have mystic sweet communion with those whose work is done, than to have real genuine fellowship though equally mystic and sweet with those whose work is going on; and so even St. Peter was shocked at our Lord's secular conduct, and when the Master came round to him with the bason and towel, like any common serving-man,

315

he said, "Lord, dost *thou* wash *my* feet? Thou who art the *Christ,* the Son of the living God: Thou who wilt restore again the kingdom to Israel, and introduce the true theology and re-establish the true religion; dost Thou degrade Thyself to the position of a mere serving man? and on *me* too! it is impossible." And then when Jesus had reminded him that the act was significant, and that the meaning of it would gradually dawn on him, he was still unconvinced and answered the more plainly "Thou shalt never wash my feet. Thou shalt establish a kingdom and teach a Theology, but never on my person degrade Thyself to secular service." He wanted in fact to be more religious than Jesus Christ was. There, my holy brethren, St. Peter spoke as religious men at all times have spoken: they have thought to do honour to Jesus by drawing clear lines between things secular and things religious; they have thought that the Church, the body of Christ, should confine herself to religious matters; that the material, political and social well-being of a parish, a nation, or of humanity, should be left to others, they have objected to the clergyman preaching politics, or the schoolmaster teaching the Bible, they have narrowed Church-work to mere clerical or semi-clerical work. [...]

[...] If therefore we members of Christ's Church are not doing secular work in the name of Christ, or if we fail to see Jesus at work side by side with everyone who is working for men, then no matter how religious we may be, Jesus says to each of us 'Thou hast no part with Me.' And on the other hand all who are ministering to the wants of humanity, no matter in how humble a fashion, all the proletariat as they call them, all the great working class, simply because they are the working class, all true artists, are so far following our dear Lord's Maunday Thursday mandate: it is for us to let them know that in as much as they have done secular work, as they have provided by their labour for food or clothes, or shelter, or artistic pleasure, or for any human need of one of the least of Christ's human family they have done it unto Him. [...]

[...] I say again don't think you can be religious by being more spiritual than He was. When He wanted to deliver people from the burden of their sin He did so; the poor paralyzed man, the impotent man at the pool of Bethesda, the woman whom the men with one law, a very free one, for themselves, and another, a very harsh one, for women, had condemned; these and many others Jesus absolved; He forgave them their sins and left to his Church the power and the duty to do the same; but when He cleansed the leper, when He healed the sick, when He washed the feet of His disciples, and left to us a mandate to do the works which He did, giving us an example, He meant us to do as He had done, and not to take the whole meaning out of the works by spiritualizing them; He meant us to work for health against disease, to fight against the evil circumstances which make the death rate of St. Luke's so much heavier than the death rate of Belgravia: He meant us to be an organized society, to work for the physical as well as for the moral and spiritual well being of the Humanity He lived and died to save. He meant us to do secular works in His name. [...]

[...] Again take those parables—those words of eternal life, of what do they tell? Of a life after death? Of a heaven beyond the grave? No! hardly a single word was uttered by Jesus about such a life or such a Heaven; they tell of a Kingdom of Heaven to be set up upon earth, of a righteous Communistic Society in which all were to be fed as surely as the birds, and clothed as beautifully as the lilies, of a real, genuine good news for the poor weary workers; the eternal life according to Jesus was to be enjoyed here and not merely hereafter, we are present inheritors and not only future heirs of the Kingdom of Heaven. [...]

[...] Holy Brethren, as you kneel to-morrow before the Crucified, remember that it is a Socialistic Carpenter whom you are worshipping, remember that He founded a Society in which equality and brotherhood were to be distinguishing features: think, therefore, how grievously you have failed since last Good Friday to do much to make that equality and brotherhood a reality: know that many of those infidels and heretics for whom you will pray are doing better secular work for humanity than you are; and that they *are* infidels and heretics because we have so grievously failed to let the true democratic light of the Church shine before men. And then on Easter morning when you make your great communion you will, as we obey the second Maunday Thursday mandate, get strengthened and refreshed by Jesus Christ Himself to live more really and practically the life of Christian communists. The body and blood of Christ sacrificed *for* you and received *by* you, will enable you boldly and cheerfully to do and to suffer far more than hitherto, in the fight to get the Kingdom of Heaven established upon earth.

The Stage

"Whatsoever ye do in word or deed do all in the name of the Lord Jesus."—Col. iii., 17.

Preached at St. Michael's, North Kensington, on August 7th, 1881

To-day you know is the festival of the Name of Jesus; and it is in His name that I wish to speak to you about the Church and the Stage: in His name whose grace or beauty we pray day by day may be with us: in His name who revealed God to be the Father, who wants His sons and daughters to be brave and happy.

And indeed in speaking to a Christian Congregation in vindication of the Stage, I am bound to take the very highest ground possible: and personally, if I may say so, I do so gladly; for my own enthusiasm for the stage is the result of strong religious conviction, and, unlike many of my clerical brethren, who left off going to the theatre when they were ordained, it is only during the nine years that I have been a priest that I have also been a regular and devoted theatre-goer.

The Athanasian Creed teaches us that the manhood has been taken into God; that it is necessary to everlasting salvation that we believe rightly the incarnation of our Lord Jesus Christ: that the Holy Spirit is incomprehensible, immense, boundless in His influence. These are the theological facts on which I base my vindication of the stage. Again, we of the latter part of the 19th century, influenced by the Oxford movement, have learned that the individual personal religion of the old Evangelical school is not enough, that the Church is a society into which we enter at our baptism: a society to carry on to the full, throughout the world, the work which Jesus Christ did in miniature in Palestine, and that every member of this society can in (and not in spite of) his vocation and ministry, truly and godly serve God. All work for humanity, however much the narrowly religious may sneer about it as secular, is claimed by us as church work: in endless guilds we are asserting and vindicating the rights and duties of the people in the Church. [...]

[...] Jesus Christ for us men and for our salvation came *down* from Heaven; He was made man: and has taken the *manhood*—the *whole* of human nature, and not merely our religious nature into God, and so we dare not say of any great sphere of human activity, of any persistent human qualities and faculties, that they are outside the range of God's spirit: and so the Church, the body of Christ and the temple of the Holy Ghost, cannot confine herself only to what we call religion, still less only to teaching men about a future life, but she is bound by loyalty to her Master and in virtue of her inspiration to take her part in all so-called secular matters: to encourage and support, and when necessary, to help to elevate and purify all who are in any way working for humanity. If, then, I can prove to you that theatrical art is calculated to do good work for humanity, then it becomes your duty as Churchmen to educate yourselves so as worthily to support that art, and to consider very seriously whether the policy of isolation which so many Churchmen, and especially Church officers, have pursued towards the Stage and its artists is not unchristian, and to be credited with most of the evil which has got associated with theatrical life.

45

ELIZA AND JOHN TREVOR, *THE LABOUR CHURCH HYMN BOOK*

(Manchester: Labour Church Institute, [1895]), pp. 1–7 [abridged]

The Labour Church

God is our King! Thy Kingdom Come on Earth. God and Liberty!

The Labour Church is Based Upon the Following Principles:—

1   That the Labour Movement is a Religious Movement.
2   That the Religion of the Labour Movement is not a Class Religion, but unites members of all classes in working for the Abolition of Commercial slavery.
3   That the Religion of the Labour Movement is not Sectarian or Dogmatic, but Free Religion, leaving each man free to develop his own relations with the Power that brought him into being.
4   That the Emancipation of Labour can only be realised so far as men learn both the Economic and Moral Laws of God, and heartily endeavour to obey them.
5   That the development of Personal Character and the improvement of Social Conditions are both essential to man's emancipation from moral and social bondage.

For further particulars, apply to the General Secretary, Labour Church Institute, Byrom Street, Manchester.

The nations that seemed dead have felt
His coming through them thrill:
Beneath His tread the mountains melt:
Our God is living still!

Gerald Massey

Preface

The compilation of this Hymn Book has been rendered necessary by the formation of Labour Churches in Manchester and other towns.

SOCIAL AND POLITICAL REFORM

The Labour Church is an organised effort to develop the religious life inherent in the Labour Movement, and to give to that Movement a higher Inspiration and a sturdier Independence in the great work of personal and social regeneration that lies before it. It appeals especially to those who have abandoned the Traditional Religion of the day without having found satisfaction in abandoning Religion altogether.

The Message of the Labour Church is that without obedience to God's Laws there can be no Liberty.

The Gospel of the Labour Church is that God is in the Labour Movement, working through it for the further emancipation of man from the tyranny, both of his own half-developed nature, and of those social conditions which are opposed to his higher development.

The Call of the Labour Church is to men everywhere to become "God's fellow-workers" in the Era of Reconstruction on which we have entered.

The first Labour Church Service was held in Manchester on the first Sunday in October, 1891. In reading, prayer, hymn, and song the traditional forms and phrases of religion have been discarded, and every effort has been made to emphasize the religion, not of creed or of history, but of actual everyday life, and especially of the great and growing Labour Movement. More recently Labour Churches have been formed in Bradford and other towns.

Grateful acknowledgment is made to the following authors and publishers, who have kindly granted permission to print the hymns appended to their names: Edward Carpenter (7), Messrs. J. Curwen & Sons (44, 58, and 67, from "General Gordon"), Havelock Ellis (15), George Gilbertson (16), Rev. J. Page-Hopps (51), William Isbister (75), Messrs. Macmillan & Co. (3), E. Nesbit (11), Messrs. J. Nisbet & Co. (59), Will Payne (31), H. S. Salt (10), Dr. Walter C. Smith (79), Miss Clara Thomson (42), Thias Walden (27 and 40), Joseph Whittaker (57).

Although this Hymn Book has been specially compiled for the use of Labour Churches, it is hoped that it may prove serviceable to the cause of Labour generally.

1

Union Hymn

Sung by 150,000 people at a Mass Meeting of Political Unions, at Birmingham, in connection with the agitation which preceded the passing of the First Reform Bill, 1832. See Miss Martineau's "History of the Peace."

Lo! here we answer! see, we come
    Quickly at Freedom's holy call.
We come! we come! we come! we come!
    To do the glorious work of all;
And hark! we raise from sea to sea }
The sacred watchword, Liberty!   } *Repeat*

E. & J. TREVOR, *LABOUR CHURCH HYMN BOOK*

God is our guide! from field, from wave,
  From plough, from anvil, and from loom
We come, our country's rights to save
  And speak a tyrant faction's doom.
And hark! we raise from sea to sea }
The sacred watchword, Liberty!   } *Repeat*

God is our guide! no swords we draw,
  We kindle not war's battle fires;
By union, justice, reason, law,
  We claim the birthright of our sires.
We raise the watchword, Liberty! }
We will, we will, we will be free! } *Repeat*

4

Truth is growing—hearts are glowing
  With the flame of Liberty:
Light is breaking—thrones are quaking—
  Hark!—the trumpet of the Free!
Long, in lowly whispers breathing,
  Freedom wandered drearily—
Still, in faith, her laurel wreathing
  For the day when there should be
  Freemen shouting—"Victory!"

Now, she seeketh him that speaketh
  Fearlessly of lawless might;
And she speedeth him that leadeth
  Brethren on to win the Right.
Soon the slave shall cease to sorrow,
  Cease to toil in agony;
Yea, the cry may swell to-morrow
  Over land and over sea—
  "Brethren, shout!—ye all are free!"

Freedom bringeth joy that singeth
  All day long and never tires:
No more sadness—all is gladness
  In the hearts that she inspires:
For she breathes a soft compassion
  Where the tyrant kindled rage;
And she saith to every nation—

"Brethren, cease wild war to wage!
Earth is your blest heritage."

From "Chartist Chaunt," by Thomas Cooper.

5

Now sound ye forth with trumpet tone,
    Let all the nations fear,
Speak to the world the thrilling words
    That tyrants quail to hear;
And write them bold on Freedom's flag,
    And wave it in the van—
They are the Fatherhood of God,
    The Brotherhood of Man.

Upon the sunny mountain brow,
    Among the busy throng,
Proclaim the day for which our hearts
    Have prayed and waited long;
The grandest words that men have heard
    Since ere the world began,
They are the Fatherhood of God,
    The Brotherhood of Man.

Too long the night of ignorance
    Has brooded o'er the mind;
Too long the love of wealth and power,
    And not the love of kind;
Now let the blessed truth be flashed
    To earth's remotest span,
Telling the Fatherhood of God,
    The Brotherhood of Man.

6

Men whose boast it is that ye
Come of fathers brave and free,
If there breathe on earth a slave—
Are ye truly free and brave?
If ye do not feel the chain
When it works a brother's pain,
Are ye not base slaves indeed—
Slaves unworthy to be freed?

E. & J. TREVOR, *LABOUR CHURCH HYMN BOOK*

Is true freedom but to break
Fetters for our own dear sake,
And with leathern hearts forget
That we owe mankind a debt?
No, true freedom is to share
All the chains our brothers wear,
And with heart and hand to be
Earnest to make others free.

They are slaves who fear to speak
For the fallen and the weak;
They are slaves who will not choose
Hatred, scoffing, and abuse
Rather than in silence shrink
From the truth they needs must think;
They are slaves who dare not be
In the right with two or three.

James Russell Lowell.

11

Come gather, O people, for soon is the hour
When princes must fall with their pomp and their power;
For the power of the future we know it shall be
A people united and sworn to be free.

Firm and fast we will stand,
Heart to heart, hand in hand,
In fair or foul weather,
Brothers together,
A people united and sworn to be free.

Come sharpen your wits, for our tongues are our swords,
To fight all our foes whether Commons or Lords;
Our tongues shall speak truly, whatever the cost,
And when clean are the weapons no fight can be lost.

Firm and fast, &c.

Our war cry is Freedom, and those who withstand
That cry have no place in our conquering band;
We strive for her sake from the cradle to grave,

SOCIAL AND POLITICAL REFORM

'Tis Freedom we fight for, and Freedom we'll have.

Firm and fast, &c.

E. Nesbit.

12

God save the working man,
    Peasant or Artisan,
    Where'er he be;
Let none his cause deride,
Be Thou, O God, his guide,
Make him his country's pride,
    Happy and free!

Let justice now arise
    To shame his enemies,
    And make pride fall;
Show them a nobler way,
Hasten the coming day,
On Thee our hopes we stay;
    God save us all!

Bless those in every land,
    Who work with head and hand,
    At duty's call.
They seek not vain applause,
But ask for righteous laws,
To guard the people's cause,
    God save them all!

46

JOHN CLIFFORD, *SOCIALISM AND THE TEACHING OF CHRIST*

Fabian Tract no. 78 (London: Fabian Society, 1897),
pp. 2–7, 10–11

An Address delivered by Dr. John Clifford *at the Annual Meeting of the Christian Socialist League, at Westbourne Park Chapel, February, 1895.*

One of the objections frequently brought against the application of the principles of Socialism to our industrial life is that such a process is opposed to the teaching and spirit of the Lord Jesus Christ.

Christianity, it is said, moves in a higher realm than that of humdrum toil, and operates for far higher purposes than those of settling the disputes of capital and labor, adjusting profit and loss, organizing production and distribution, fighting a dangerous plutocracy, and mediating peace between the masses of wage-earners and a narrowing number of wage-payers. It does not "preach a gospel of material blessedness." It ministers to a mind diseased by sin, banishes remorse, and prepares for death and eternity. It is not concerned with this fleeting life; so brief that "it is like a dewdrop on its perilous way from a tree's summit"; but with the infinite development of the human spirit through the eternity, and in the home, of God. In support of this eclipse of the life of the present by the stupendous and transcendent greatness of the life of the future revealed in Christianity, the saying of Jesus is quoted. "Work not for the meat that perisheth, but for the meat which abideth unto eternal life, which the Son of Man shall give unto you: for Him the Father, even God, hath sealed."

Hence, many Christians look with misgiving on Churches that venture to study the politico-economical conditions of the life of the people around them, touch with the tips of their fingers the problems for the abolition of poverty, and seek the up-lifting of the wage-earning classes by juster and healthier modes than those of spasmodic charity and unlimited soup. They denounce ministers who hold and teach that the laws of God run everywhere, even into wages and prices, into houses of toil and the sanitary conditions of factories and drapery establishments; and generally reason that the capacity of the mind for the hospitable entertainment of ideas is so sadly limited that no preacher can be faithful to Christ's message concerning sin and redemption, and at the same time agitate for a "fair living wage," or toil for the reorganization of the industrial life of the country on bases of justice and brotherhood. [...]

The Social Question

[...] Let me first of all fully recognize that these objecting Christians and Churches allow that the Christianity of Christ Jesus is not averse to the denunciation of the wrongs of modern society and the exposure of the miseries of our present condition. Indeed, it is eagerly maintained that Christ condemns every manifestation of *individual* selfishness, backs every earnest crusader against *personal* covetousness and greed, and justifies the strongest language we can use against the abuses of *individual* competition. All Christians agree in these outbursts of righteous indignation, and rather enjoy seeing the vials of oratorical wrath poured out on the heads of their neighbors; and some of them are beginning to think that after all the "accumulation of gold" is not the highest virtue, and that there is something wrong in that mediæval interpretation of the words of the Master, "The poor ye have with you always," which regards the continuance of poverty as a necessary condition to the exercise of the spasmodic charity of the rich. Many Christians, if not all, at last admit that there is a social question and that they must do something for it, if it is only to talk about it and to denounce somebody or something. They see the poor separated by a great social gulf from the rich, though geographically not far from one another. They lament overcrowding and ask what is the chance for chastity and health, for decency and comfort, to say nothing of happiness under such inhuman conditions. Here in West London—in *West* London—is a house of eight rooms and a small ante-room containing not less than forty-two persons; and it is a sample of the way in which we are violating God's idea of society, and destroying the very germ of social well-being in the extinction of the decencies and wholesomeness of the home.[1] The awful facts borne in upon us by the gathering masses of unskilled, decrepit, and hopeless laborers, the appalling armies of the unemployed, are forcing Christian men to think and to say "Something must be done." It is not wholly a question of "plenty of room at the top" for the men of tough fibre, clear brain and iron will; but of the "strong bearing the infirmities of the weak," and of brother caring for brother. The bitter separation of class from class, the tyranny of drink, the vice of gambling, the debasement and misery of early marriages, the degradation of women, "the huddling together of thousands of workers, the prey of the sweater"—all these increasing wrongs are, it is confessed, inextricably involved in our vast egoistic industrialism; men, women, and children are caught and crushed in the revolving wheels of this competitive machinery and then flung aside to perish in the workhouse, or to overweight the earlier efforts of their offspring. So that not a few observant souls are ready to accept the strong words of Ruskin and say, "to call the confused wreck of social order and life brought about by malicious collision and competition an arrangement of Providence, is quite one of the most insolent and wicked ways in which it is possible to take the name of God in vain."[2]

The Sense of Spiritual Brotherhood

[...] Some of the disciples of Christ will go further and give personal service. A real hearty, loving sympathy carries them to the homes of the poor and suffering, to feed patience, to brighten life, to uphold the afflicted, to sustain the workers in the fierce struggle with toil and want. They believe Christianity bids them preach justice, love, and brotherhood. They even plan for co-operative production. They inculcate stewardship and bid men remember that they have to give account of all they have and use to their Father in heaven. To them the social organism is a reality; and the spiritual brotherhood of men more than a phrase. They have seen God in Christ Jesus, and to them the Incarnation is the revelation of their obligations to their brother man, the widening of the definition of sin so as to include transgressions of the parish and city, of the nation and of humanity. No man lives to himself. Cain is anti-Christ. There is a solidarity of man. The kingdoms of this world are to become *the* kingdom of our God and of His Christ. Law and government are not beyond His policy; and even our industrial civilization may be shaped according to His will. It is a great change; and those who have experienced that regeneration of the social consciousness in the Churches of Christ are shaping the future of labor and of the life of the world.

Where Christians Part

[...] But it is when we come to a *social policy*, to a *method* or industrial re-arrangement, that the question arises whether we are moving along the lines of Christ's ideas, and are providing *the best industrial body for the incarnation* of *His spirit*. It is at this third stage we part. Christian men are agreeing more and more—(*a*) In their antagonism to individual greed and injustice; (*b*) in personal and sympathetic devotion to the welfare of the people; the parting of the ways is (*c*) as to the real basis on which modern industry shall organize itself. It is when scientific Socialism or Collectivism says—(*a*) Our industrial life should be based not on individual but on a collective ownership of the chief elements and material instruments of production, (*b*) that production should be managed not according to the will or caprice or might of private individuals, but collectively, and (*c*) that the results of toil should be distributed to all who have a share in the toil on the principles of absolute justice, *i.e.*, on the principles of equality in value;[3] it is then we are charged with opposing the teaching of the Master.

Now, let there be no mistake as to what this Collectivism is. It does not advocate the absorption of the individual by the State; or the suppression of the family; or the total extinction of private property; or the direction of literature, and art, and religion by the collective wisdom of the community; it does not involve the sudden overthrow of the machinery of industrial life; but in the light of the historical development of industry it seeks to accelerate the evolution of the industrial life,

SOCIAL AND POLITICAL REFORM

so that it shall free itself from the defects and evils that now belong to it, and shall fulfil its Divine mission in the enrichment of the whole life of mankind.[4] It seeks to build a far better body for the soul of Christ's teaching, and the spirit of His life and death, than this fiercely competitive system, through which He now struggles almost in vain to make His voice heard and His power felt.

The Possibility of Collectivism

[...] I may take it for granted that our present industrial *régime* is not final. Collectivism is at least *possible*. It is often forgotten that the present commercial system is not far advanced. It has scarcely travelled through its earlier and more crude years. There is no fixed necessity for regarding the present conditions of production and distribution of wealth as their final form. The era of Individualism, of syndicates and companies, of capitalists sitting round a green table and directing the movements of hundreds of laborers with no connection with each other except that created by what Carlyle calls the "cash-nexus," may give place to one in which State-industrialism, as seen in our police arrangements, post-office, the civic ownership and control of gas, water, electric lighting, and tramways, Government employment of labor in Woolwich and Portsmouth Dockyards and Enfield factories, enforcement of education, and the payment of teachers for the children of the nation, the provision by the rates of public baths, wash-houses, parks, gardens, art galleries, museums, hospitals, and asylums, will issue in a completely equipped co-operative commonwealth. All these may be. Human nature is confessedly very intractable; but British society may pass by certain stages from the limited Collectivism which now exists to one which covers the whole machinery of the lower part of life, and provides for that physical basis of human existence on which the spiritual structure is being slowly reared. [...]

What Collectivism Would Do

[...] Asserting, then, that there is nothing in Christianity against the change, and assuming that it is not impracticable, I now seek to prove that the Collectivist arrangement has at least four distinguishing merits, demonstrating its closer and stronger affinities with the teaching of Jesus Christ than the present method of administering the physical life of man—(1) It destroys the occasions of many of the evils of modern society; (2) it advances, elevates, and ennobles the struggle of life; (3) it offers a better environment for the development of Christ's teaching concerning wealth and brother-hood, and (4) fosters a higher ideal of human and social worth and well-being. I do not deny all ethical advantage to the individualistic system. I am aware it has developed that prodigious business capacity in a limited and distinguished few of our workers, which secured to Britain thirty years ago the commercial primacy of the globe. It has created the race of merchant princes, traders, paragons in developing and supplying new material wants.

JOHN CLIFFORD, *SOCIALISM AND CHRIST*

It has found the opportunity for builders of enormous industries in coal and iron, in the production of food and clothing, of machines and news, thereby bringing the produce of the world to our doors and the news of the world to our tables. It has fed legitimate ambitions and saved men from indolence, quickened the sense of responsibility, educated, drilled, and enriched inventive and business faculty.

Not for a moment would we forget these advantages; but we cannot blind ourselves to the fact that, as a system, it has not stirred the most unselfish desires nor fostered the most generous sympathies on any large scale. It has been egoistic, not altruistic. It is more in keeping with the gladiatorial than the Christian theory of existence. It provides for ruthless self-assertion rather than self-restraint. It does not inspire brotherly helpfulness, but the crushing of competitors and thrusting aside of rivals. Instead of co-operating in the struggle to save and enrich the lives of others, it tends to make its administrators forgetful of their claims, and renders it necessary to bring the power of legislation to the support of children in coal-mines and factories, to the protection and defence of weak women, to the limitation of hours of labor, and the imposition of sanitary conditions of toil. [...]

[...] On the other hand Collectivism, although it does not change human nature, yet it takes away *the occasion for many of the evils which now afflict society*. It reduces the temptations of life in number and in strength. It means work for every one and the elimination of the idle, and if the work should not be so exacting, responsible, and, therefore, not so educative for a few individuals, yet it will go far to answer Browning's prayer:

> O God, make no more giants,
> Elevate the race.

Hesiod teaches that "Work is the one road to excellence." "There is no shame in labor; idleness is shame." An effortless existence is intolerable, and leads to incalculable mischief. Individualism adds to the number of the indolent year by year; Collectivism sets everybody alike to his share of work, and gives to him his share of reward. [...]

[...] It is a new ideal of life and labor that is most urgently needed. England's present ideal is a creation of hard individualism; and therefore is partial, hollow, unreal and disastrous. But ideals are the main factors in the progress of the home, the parish, and the State. They are the forces that move individuals. Individualism fosters the caste feelings and the caste divisions of society, creates the serfdom of one class and the indolence of another; makes a large body of submissive, silent, unmanly slaves undergoing grinding toil and continuous anxiety, and a smaller company suffering from debasing indolence and continual weariness; begets hatred and ill-will on one hand, and scorn and contempt of man on the other. No! the ideal we need and must have is in the unity of English life, in the recognition that man is complete in the State, at once a member of society and of

SOCIAL AND POLITICAL REFORM

the Government—"a ruler and yet ruled"; an ideal that is the *soul* at once of Collectivism and of the revelation of the brotherhood of man in Jesus Christ our Lord, Son of God and Son of man.

Finally, I am sure that as we seek to build up our industries more and more on this basis we shall discover that we need a deep and wide-spread revival of the Spirit of Christ, a clearer insight into His ideas, so that we may suppress the passions that feed our individualistic system and sweep away the accumulated evils which have gathered round it, and at the same time to advance to perfection the Collectivist methods already operative in profit-sharing, in co-operative labor, and in Municipal and State industries. Collectivism will become an argument for a deepened spiritual life. Were we more Christian we should, as did the first Christians, seek with passionate ardor to incarnate a collective rather than an individualistic idea in society. Nothing more forcibly witnesses to the need of Christ than the failure of the Churches to cope with the evils of nineteenth-century life. It is Christ we need. Light both leads and kills. Science has just told us the swiftest and surest foe of the disease-spreading germs is the light. Christ is the light of the world. He shows us the way we should take; and He also will yet destroy the microbes of physical and moral pestilence and death in our modern industrial life, and render the animal the obedient servant instead of the tyrranical master of the human spirit.

Notes

1 *Time and Tide*. By John Ruskin; p. 9.
2 See Fabian Tract No. 5, *Facts for Socialists*; 1d.
3 *Socialism: its Nature, Strength and Weakness*. By Professor R. T. Ely; p. 9, *et seq.*
4 See Fabian Tract No. 51, *Socialism: True and False*; 1d.

4.6

Women's Suffrage

4.6 Women's Suffrage

Like socialism, women's suffrage is often treated as a secular movement, however, many women campaigning for the vote at the turn of the century were deeply religious, and were hungry for the civic responsibility enshrined in suffrage as well as its rights (for more discussion, see Volume I, Feminist religion). The Suffrage Movement had its roots in women's organisations of the 1850s that campaigned for women to have better educational and employment opportunities. Some of the women involved in these campaigns, such as the Unitarians Barbara Bodichon (1827–1891) and Bessie Rayner Parkes (who later converted to Roman Catholicism), formed the Langham Place Group, which presented the first petition to Parliament for the extension of the vote to women. They also produced the first feminist periodical, the *English Women's Journal*. The lack of parliamentary action on women's suffrage as the century wore on, despite the production of numerous petitions and pamphlets by women's organisations, increased feminists' feelings of outrage and, by the 1880s, the movement was organising large demonstrations across the country. By the twentieth century, parliamentary inaction led a breakaway group of suffragists, the Women's Social and Political Union, to promote militant action to pressure the government to heed their demands. The turn of the century also saw the formation of religious suffrage leagues, such as the Church League and the Quaker Friends' League, as some women argued that the answer to the Woman Question could be found in religion. While Jewish women took part in non-denominational feminist organisations, by 1912 women such as Gertrude Spielmann (1864–1949) decided that a Jewish suffrage league was necessary to take account of the particular context of Jewish society in Britain and the contribution Judaism could make to the cause.

Barbara Bodichon was a campaigner for women's suffrage in Britain, and a Unitarian. In the 1860s she formed one of the first suffrage committees, and supported Emily Davies to extend university education to women. Before this, in 1858 she was one of the women who set up the *English Women's Journal*, which was dedicated to discussing women's equality, especially their education and employment opportunities. In the article extracted here she expresses her 'faith' that British women have the natural ability to earn their own living and gain their independence, and argues that it is only the prejudices of society that currently render them unfit, by not preparing and educating them for such a career. Her argument is underpinned by a Christian fear of idleness, which she suggests is worse for women than the drudgery of manual labour. Interestingly, she does not argue that women's powers should be used in particular fields, such as social work, but only that women should be able to earn their own living – even in the field of business, which she portrays as perfectly noble and moral; the example she gives of a German female commercial traveller, was a missionary's widow. Ultimately Bodichon calls for women to sacrifice manners – those signs of femininity inculcated by society – in favour of the duty and virtue of independence.

Emily Wilding Davison (1872–1913) calls for a similar sacrifice of manners in her essay, 'The Price of Liberty'. A militant suffragette, famous for walking into the path of the King's horse at the Epsom Derby in 1913, her essay uses religious rhetoric to explain the motivations behind her actions. In a way that conflates civic and religious discourses, women's spiritual emancipation is interpreted as essential for human progress and God is translated into the 'Spirit of Liberty'. Like Bodichon, Davison argues that women should sacrifice social virtues like 'reputation' which, though they seem to an immoral society to be of highest importance, are not as valuable as a woman's soul. However, Davison's prose also expresses the suffering that women experience as they make sacrifices, ultimately evoking the Passion of the Christ, with militant suffragettes equated with the rejected Jesus (Anathema Maranatha), destined for martyrdom. Interestingly, Davison's personal Christianity also incorporates the Buddhist concept of nirvana (see Volume IV, Anagārika Dharmapāla and Modern Buddhism) – militant feminists are asked to sacrifice or transcend self entirely in self-immolation for the sake of future generations of women.

In contrast, the concept of self-sacrifice does not feature in Gertrude Spielmann's essay, 'Woman's Place in the Synagogue'. Instead, she calls for the Jewish community to raise the status in which women are held and to allow women to play a full role in Jewish social work and religious congregation. Following the example of Christian writers, who turned to Church history to justify women's role in religion (see this volume, Women and Authority in the Mission Field), Spielmann looks at the history of the treatment of women in Judaism. However, she disputes that religion in itself – Jewish or Christian – was the determining factor in the treatment of women, arguing instead that the culture in which the religion found itself was more significant. Spielmann does compare the Jewish culture unfavourably with the Christian culture of the early twentieth century, though, arguing that Jewish women wanting fulfilling employment in social work are often welcomed more by inter-faith organisations than those of the Jewish community. Although Spielmann argues for the equality of Jewish women, she does subscribe to a feminism of difference. Amongst the qualities of her 'strenuous' and well-educated women social workers, she singles out their 'tradition of disinterested service', and ultimately she writes that their 'sacred duty' is to cherish religion in the home, as wives and mothers.

47

[BARBARA BODICHON], 'HOW TO UTILIZE THE POWERS OF WOMEN'

English Women's Journal, vol. 3 (March 1859), pp. 34–35, 39–44, 46–47

ACCORDING to the last census of England, there were in this country three quarters of a million more women than men. This immense female multitude must consequently remain single all their lives, and in most instances provide for themselves. It is obviously very important, therefore, to multiply female employments, which in an old country, where every nook and cranny appears to be filled, is no easy matter. If we could prevail upon our rulers to superintend the exodus of the population to our outlying provinces, the inequality between the sexes here at home might be considerably diminished, because in more than one of our distant possessions there are five men to one woman.

But this is not the question at present before us. Taking the aggregate of surplus females to be what we have stated, the inquiry ought to be how we are to turn to the best account their powers of body and mind. We should be very sorry to propose that we should imitate any farther than we do at present the practices of the continent in rural districts, where women work in the field, until they become shrivelled and tanned like so many mummies, in the very flower of their age. In some respects, however, our continental neighbours act far more wisely than we do. Nearly all kinds of shops are given up to the management of women, whether it be that the young men are absorbed by the conscription, or that they take of themselves to more masculine callings. At any rate, the result is that thousands of women are able to earn their livelihood by means which here in England are entirely in the hands of men. In London alone there is a whole army of the stronger sex to be found behind counters, measuring out lace, longcloths, and ribbons, while the same number of young women, to whom these occupations are adapted by nature, are condemned to idleness with all the mischievous consequences of which it is almost necessarily the parent. Should society ever think of reforming itself, we trust that one of its first improvements will be to appropriate to the sexes the work for which each is best fitted. The army, the colonies, and many other fields lie open to the Lords of the Creation, while the Ladies of the

SOCIAL AND POLITICAL REFORM

Creation are much more restricted in their choice of crafts and mysteries by which to keep away the wolf from the door. [...]

[...] Our forefathers, a rough and ready people, gave women a much better chance than we do; and when in the ordinary paths of the world they found no room for them they draughted them off into a peculiar sort of factories where they earned their own bread, and by a wise contrivance rendered labor respectable. These factories were the convents in which women worked as girls do now in the cotton mills, though with much more moderation and in a different way. One of their occupations consisted in copying and illuminating manuscripts. [...]

But after all, society must to some extent be re-organised before women can be properly provided for, unless in these ancient hereditary drudgeries. In many parts of Europe they are the real hewers of wood and drawers of water to the community, and very good slaves they make too. Among mere savages the women do all the work, and are ill-used into the bargain; or if there be any department of labor, as hunting or fishing, which recommends itself by furnishing a little amusement, the men do that lest their women should become too sprightly. But even this state of things is perhaps better than what takes place in spurious and corrupt systems of civilization, where women are encouraged to be idle while young, that they may be more thoroughly despised afterwards. It would in our opinion be well if every woman, whether married or single, were able upon a pinch to earn her own living. The consciousness that she could, would give her a feeling of independence, a thing not to be despised in any walk of life. What is now called education, tends generally to make women good for nothing. Society abounds with coxcombs, who unquestionably think, if they are really able to think at all, that our sex are perfectly destitute of brains. If we do anything tolerably well, they tap us encouragingly on the shoulders, and exclaim, "Really, that is very wonderful!" They had evidently imagined previously that a woman and an owl were much the same thing. If we write, they criticise us with forbearance, obviously from the conviction that our productions will not bear the test applied to those of men. It is the same thing in all the other arts—our sculpture, our painting, our music, are very good considering! We are surprised that gentlemen of this class do not set up for prima donnas and dispute in matters of voice with the heroines of the opera. There, however, nature does actually seem to award superiority to women. No male singer has ever acquired the celebrity of Catalani, Pasta, Malibran, or Sontag. Among actresses too, the world has seen marvellous specimens of intelligence—intelligence equal to the comprehending of the greatest thoughts of Shakespeare.

If women can do this, we think it may be regarded as an indication that they are equal to the performance of many other things, demanding depth of thought, accuracy of judgment, and delicacy of taste. Apart from the production of ideas, a great actress is a great orator. If this be true, some of the greatest speakers of modern times have been women. What stands in the way of the development of female intelligence is the rooted prejudice of society, which prevents women during their early youth from entering upon studies calculated to give them genius, vigor, and originality. A thousand topics are proscribed to them which a man's mind may travel over at pleasure. An actress by her situation is necessarily emancipated from many of these intellectual drags, which we contend she may be, without at all impairing her character as a woman. Mrs. Siddons was probably as tender a mother and as good a wife as one English-woman out of ten thousand, and the same thing we believe may be said of Madame Pasta. We mention these two names because they belong to the history of Europe, but we might adduce many others from among those of the actresses of our own day.

One change in the social economy of England would naturally make room for many others. If several classes of shops in London were, for example, to come entirely, or almost entirely, under the direction of women, the next thing would be to have female commercial travellers, who, with regard to all articles of female dress or ornament, would be far better able to conduct throughout the country the business of the London house than any man whatsoever. Women, as it is, often travel alone; some for pleasure, others through the urgency of their affairs, and many from sheer restlessness, or an unquenchable desire for locomotion. These, when belonging to the proper classes, and duly instructed in the business to which they belong, would make excellent commercial travellers. We feel sure that very considerable departments of trade, if this view were taken of the matter, might fall into the hands of women, to the great advantage of employers and employed. Of course such a state of things would necessitate numerous changes in the system of female education, and instead of laboring to render girls timid, to strengthen their superstition and stimulate their nervous sensibility, mothers would endeavor to inculcate into their minds maxims of circumspection, self-dependence, and enterprise, with many other analogous qualities.

It is very probable, that to some extent this plan may have already been acted upon in England, it certainly has, in some few instances, on the Continent. We once remember in Tuscany to have met with an extremely pleasant and lady-like woman from some one of the smaller states of Germany, we forget which, who might have been called correctly enough a commercial traveller. The husband had been a missionary entrusted with the distribution of Bibles, but in what part of the world has escaped our memory. On his way out, however, he died at Rome, an event which his wife, who with her sister was on her way to join him, learned at Leghorn. Her funds were small, and, to render the matter still worse, her health also was very indifferent. When she wrote to her friends in Germany describing her circumstances, they, being probably themselves in business, hit upon the bright idea of commissioning her to go about for them, and conduct the affairs of their house in Italy. Her abilities were but ordinary, and so also were her personal attractions. She was honest, however, and diligent, and living on very little, both she and her sister soon contrived to surround themselves with all sorts of comforts. They went occasionally as far as Naples, and once I believe visited Palermo; but in general their operations were carried on in Northern Italy, where people are more addicted to business, and understand it better than in the South. As I felt an interest in their fate, I made many inquiries of them respecting their prospects, their mode of doing business, their profits, the character of those with whom they dealt, and many other points; and I found that they entertained a very favorable opinion of the Italians, who, according to them, were both pleasant and trustworthy. [...]

[...] These facts we have mentioned to show how much enterprise and courage women can sometimes display when inspired by no higher motive than the love of gain; but they would be able to do infinitely better if society were to reform its views respecting their claims and destinies. When the Nemesis of civilization blights their prospects, and blots out their names from the list of mistresses of families, they should be taught to regard themselves as of no sex, but simply as beings condemned to earn their own livelihood in the best way they can. If gifted with high self-respect, if their intelligence be well cultivated and directed betimes into the channels of business, there is no reason why they should not achieve independence, or even affluence, for themselves. It is impossible to map out the future, and therefore we cannot pretend to say what course the surplus female population of this country will hereafter be compelled by circumstances to take, but we are thoroughly persuaded that their situation will be much improved by learning to depend upon their own exertions. Even should they afterwards marry, they may be assured it will be no drawback either to their comfort or their happiness to be able to provide for themselves in case of emergency without the aid of any one. We know what class of persons God is said proverbially to help. Let women bear the wisdom of that old adage in mind, and study their own capabilities with reference to business. We need not be at all alarmed lest the progress of civilization should produce too many substitutes for human labor, and thus condemn a majority of Adam's children to eat the bread of idleness. All the operations of machinery need to be directed by intelligence, and have consequently a tendency to elevate those who overlook them in the mental scale. But there are innumerable processes which neither science nor invention, nor anything else, can take out of the hands of labor. These may be regarded as the perpetual inheritance of the children of toil, out of which bread springs up to them, like pleasant fruit on the way-side of life. We say pleasant fruit, because none but those who have tasted it can tell how sweet the earnings of labor are. Fortune, in her utmost munificence, can never bestow a delight equal to that which a man earns for himself when he eats what he has sown, and plucks from trees which he has himself planted.

It is one of the noblest characteristics of the present age that it is willing to recognise this truth. Still it is man chiefly that it contemplates. The surplus female population in the British islands have little or no care or attention bestowed on them. If they conduct themselves wisely and prosper it is admitted that they do well; but on the other hand no one is surprised or excited to very great commiseration if they are plunged over head and ears in ruin. Women, therefore, when they cultivate their understanding, and put forward their thoughts for the benefit of the public, should as far as possible direct their efforts to the improvement of their own sex. The loftiest minds among men have always been distinguished by unusual sympathy for the calamities and misfortunes of women, among which we must reckon the fact of being born in an old and over-peopled country. But men after all can rarely estimate at their full value the difficulties and obstacles with which women have to contend. When single and left to their own resources, two things are required of them almost wholly incompatible; first, in order to succeed they are expected to be bold and resolute; and second, it is demanded of them, to obtain the full approbation of men, that they shall never overstep the gentleness, reserve, refinement, and delicacy, for which in all ages and countries women have obtained credit. But she who has to fight the battle of life, without the least aid from any one, cannot practise much reserve. In the recesses of her own heart she may be delicate and refined enough, but her manners will inevitably contract from the circumstances of her position a certain masculine air not very reconcilable with that timidity which they are universally required to display.

To gain great things we must consent to sacrifice small ones. Manners are important enough considered by themselves, but sink into insignificance when thrown into the balance against duty and virtue. There are things which as human beings we must do, and great stress ought to be laid upon the way in which we do them, but obviously the main point consists, not in the mode, but in the fact.

These observations we make for the purpose of neutralising the objections which the world often makes to the bearing and demeanour of professional women. It is not with them, however, a question whether they shall be timid or intrepid. To keep their fortunes afloat they must bring into play all those faculties of the mind by which men are commonly differenced from women. It is the fault of society, not theirs, if fault there be. Wherever the civilization of a country provides homes for all the women of the nation, their manners are reserved, domestic, gentle. It is only when called upon to make their own way in life that they take to imitating men. Circumstances remove them from the fire-side, and place them out in the sunshine, dust, and bustle of the great arena of the world, and if they fail to advance by their own strength they are trodden down and lost. [...]

[...] What we have said may not be very encouraging to young ladies in search of a profession, but it is not our intention that it should have the contrary effect, we have an almost unlimited faith in courage. What people believe they can do, they either can or will soon be able to do. [...]

[...] Unless we totally misunderstand our countrywomen, they are quite as well fitted as any in the world—we mean by nature—to achieve independence for themselves, though in order to give them a fair chance, there must be an entire revolution in the theory and practice of education. Let women preserve the delicacy of their sex by all means, but while keeping this polar star in view, let them not be afraid to launch forth into the great ocean of knowledge, upon which, they may take our word for it, they will find themselves quite as able to float as men.

48

EMILY WILDING DAVISON, 'THE PRICE OF LIBERTY'

Suffragette, 5 June 1914, p. 129

The true suffragette is an epitome of the determination of women to possess their own souls. The words of the Master are eternally true:

> "What shall it profit a man if he gain the whole world and lose his own soul?"

And it is the realisation of this ideal that is moving the most advanced of the feminists to stand out at all costs to-day.

Men, as a sex, have not yet grasped the inevitability of the forging of this last link in the chain of human progress. Ever since history peeps out of the mists of time, the male of the race has made it his prerogative to give or deny the whole world to his partner, but has withheld from her that which is above all temporal things, namely, the possession of a soul, the manifestation of the Godhead within.

Forgetting the Mighty Spirit

They have beautified and decorated the shrine, but they have kept it empty of the divinity which gave a significance to the paraphernalia of the shrine.

Especially is this error noticeable and blameworthy in the latter days of the early Christian Church, when it was seriously discussed whether women even possessed souls, and sufficient doubt on the subject was raised to condemn the sex from that time onward to an inferior position in the community.

For centuries people have been groping after the dry bones of humanity, forgetting the mighty spirit which alone could make those dry bones live, till early last century the sons of men saw the need of the vivifying breath, and one man after another, one class after another, felt the quick, stirring process, and rose to the wonderous life of civic freedom.

Could the partners of men be untouched by this marvellous awakening? Could women any longer remain dry bones merely, or indeed even as a clod of earth in the valley? Could the newly-aroused and enlightened race owe its origin to an insensate and unintelligent creature?

The Parable of Militancy

The wonderful Renascence of Freedom has to extend its kindly influence to all! In the New Testament the Master reminded His followers that when the merchant had found the Pearl of Great Price, he sold all that he had in order to buy it. That is the parable of Militancy! It is that which the women warriors are doing to-day.

Some are truer warriors than others, but the perfect Amazon is she who will sacrifice all even unto this last, to win the Pearl of Freedom for her sex.

Some of the beauteous pearls that women sell to obtain this freedom which is so little appreciated by those who are born free are the pearls of Friendship, Good Report, Love, and even Life itself, each in itself a priceless boon.

Who will gainsay that Friendship is one of the priceless jewels of life? Did not the Elizabethan philosopher remind us that Friendship doubles our joys and halves our sorrows? Have not the poets sung the inestimable riches of Friendship?

Yet this pearl is sacrificed without a moment's hesitation by the true militant. And, indeed, the sacrifice is inevitable, even as the sun puts out the bright glow of the grate fire. Yet the Lares and Penates are valued gods, even if lesser lights, whilst on the sunniest day a bitter frost may necessitate the worship of the lesser but more comfortable flame.

Thus the sacrifice involves terrible suffering to the militant,—old friends, recently-made friends, they all go, one by one, into the limbo of the burning, fiery furnace—a grim holocaust to Liberty.

An even severer part of the price is the surrender of Good Report, one of the brightest and most precious of the gems in a woman's crown, as anyone can realise who knows how easily her fair fame is sullied.

Men have been able to go forward through good report and ill report, and so low has been the standard of morals for them that the breath of scandal but seemed to burnish more brightly their good qualities.

But owing to the same double standard the merest whisper of venomous tongues could damn a woman socially and politically, for to be safe she must be like Cæsar's wife.

Hence, to women, reputation is often as dear as life itself. Yet even this jewel has been sacrificed by the militant, for she has felt the truth of the Cavalier poet's song—

> "I could not love thee, dear, so much,
> Loved I not honour more."

And she has felt in her innermost soul that there was no chance of preserving any "honour" worth the name if she acquiesced in a state of society wherein women's souls and bodies were bought and sold.

"Ye cannot serve God and Mammon." What possibility for those who knew the existing evil to sit down and suffer it in comfort and peace? Better to be Anathema Maranatha for the sake of progress than to sit lapped in ignoble ease in the House of Good Fame! Better that all men should speak evil of her and revile her, fighting the eternal battle of glorious Liberty and Humanity!

But a more soul-rending sacrifice even than that of friendship and of good report is demanded of the Militant—that of the blood-tie. "She that loveth mother or father, sister or brother, husband or child, dearer than me cannot be my disciple," saith the terrible voice of Freedom, in accents that rend the very heart in twain.

"Even unto this price"

"Cannot this cup of anguish be spared me," cries the militant aloud in agony, yet immediately, as if in repentance for having so nearly lost the Priceless Pearl, in the words of all strivers after progress, she ejaculates: "Nevertheless I will pay, even unto this price," and in her writhing asks what further demand can be exacted from her.

The glorious and inscrutable Spirit of Liberty has but one further penalty within its power, the surrender of Life itself. It is the supreme consummation of sacrifice, than which none can be higher or greater.

To lay down life for friends, that is glorious, selfless, inspiring! But to re-enact the tragedy of Calvary for generations yet unborn, that is the last consummate sacrifice of the Militant!

> "Nor will she shrink from this Nirvana
> She will be faithful 'unto this last.'"

49

GERTRUDE SPIELMANN, 'WOMAN'S PLACE IN THE SYNAGOGUE'

Jewish Review, 4 (1813–1814), pp. 24–28, 31–34, 36

Woman's Place in the Synagogue[1]

[…] That the status of the Jewish woman, both in the religious and social life of the community, compares unfavourably with that of her Gentile sisters is hardly to be disputed. We have not only to consider her passive position in the synagogue, but also the very limited use made of her services on the Boards of our Communal Charities, to realise this fact. The peculiar gift of women in matters charitable and educational, is appreciated by the English as a nation. All over the country we find women serving on District and Urban Councils, and not only serving, but presiding over Boards of Guardians, C.O.S. Committees, School Committees, etc.; there is hardly a Royal Commission formed nowadays to inquire into matters affecting the interests of women and children but has a woman serving on it.

How does this compare with the position of women on the Boards of our various institutions? Do we welcome them? Do we encourage them to confront the many problems awaiting solution at the hands of our philanthropists and social reformers? It hardly looks like it, when we reflect that on all such bodies as admit women to serve on mixed committees, the number is severely restricted. Two or three women may be regarded as the maximum allowed to serve on any institution, though there is one institution which has ventured to enrol five women amongst its total of thirty-five members!

Men are elected on committees for a variety of reasons—not necessarily because they show capacity or evince any special interest in the subject; but where a woman is nominated, we may feel sure that her experience in some particular branch of the work is recognised. She is asked in the expectation that she will render steady and effective service, and it is not often that she disappoints; for deep in every true woman's heart is the overwhelming impulse to do what is in her power to relieve suffering, to help the helpless and to succour the distressed. Consequently we find many of the best workers of to-day preparing by systematic study and active training to enlarge the scope of their knowledge, the better to fit

SOCIAL AND POLITICAL REFORM

themselves for the work they have undertaken. The intelligent, strenuous girl of to-day, who prepares herself by studying sociology and kindred subjects, prior to training at a settlement or C.O.S. offices, is hardly likely to place her services at the disposal of our communal charities, under the conditions which prevail at present. She looks around and notes that with the exception of Care Committee work (which can scarcely be deemed communal work) there is practically no chance of her being admitted to active participation on any of our general charities for years. So what happens? She cannot afford to wait until one of the rare vacancies occurs, and so she turns away from the community, so sorely in need of trained and enthusiastic workers, and elects to serve where full scope for her powers will be accorded to her and where her efforts will be recognised and her standing on the committee advanced.

Of course, reference is now being made to the increasing number of women who show a strong bent towards public work and whose experience endows them with width of outlook and maturity of judgment. It is but a few years back since opinion has veered in favour of woman's entry into the public life of the community, limited though it still is; previously to that, custom and prejudice combined in attributing to her intrinsic inferiority. Nor could many men, in those days, appreciate the powerful and deep longing that women felt to raise the whole standard of their lives, to broaden their interests and to open their minds to nobler and higher matters than had occupied them thitherto.

On all sides we now note how these ideals have materialised. The feeling grows stronger and ever more insistent, that all what concerns the well-being of the community is the affair of woman as well as of man. The Union of Jewish Women is fully alive to the trend of events, and does all in its power to stem the drifting away from communal activities of its most promising women, by endeavouring to attract and secure them whilst young for work which will satisfy the demands of both brain and heart; but their further chance of usefulness to the community depends, to a large extent, upon the encouragement they will receive at its hands. With the education women are now receiving, and with their tradition of disinterested service, they should henceforth bring new and unexpected elements into public as well as into private life. And if this obtains in secular matter, how much more should it hold good in woman's connection with the House of Prayer. Is it not to the wives and mothers of Israel that we look to cherish the spark of religion in the home and to implant the love and knowledge of it in their children's breasts? And where do they hope to receive the knowledge and assistance for this sacred duty but from the synagogue? It is difficult to reconcile the conception of the Jewish woman as wife and mother, described in Jewish writings, with the actual position occupied by her in the synagogue of to-day.

To all intents and purposes woman has no place in the synagogue, whether as taking part in the service or in administering the affairs of the congregation; but the feeling is growing ever stronger, that the time has now come when Jewish women should strive to form a real and integral part of the congregation.

To thoroughly grasp the position and to appreciate the difficulties that confront us demands a study of past conditions. It would be well, therefore, to give a short survey of the position Jewish women held in Biblical times, subsequently showing how matters stood with them during the Middle Ages up to the present day, and finally indicating on what lines and in which direction reform seems desirable.

While sharing to some extent the universal Eastern conception of the inferiority of woman to man, the Judaism of Biblical times by no means sanctioned the total subjection of woman, subsequently authorised by Mohammedanism. It was only in accordance with contemporary Semitic custom in the countries surrounding Palestine, that women should take part in the religion of Israel, as we read that the Babylonian, Assyrian, and Phœnician religions allowed their women certain privileges in practising their religious cults.

The earliest allusion in the Bible to women's participation in public worship is that in Exodus xxxviii. 8, to the women who assembled to minister at the door of the "Tent of Meeting," of whose mirrors the lavers of brass were made; or one may perhaps consider it an act of public worship in Exodus xv. 20, when "Miriam the prophetess, the sister of Aaron, took a timbrel in her hand; and all the women went out after her with timbrels and dances." We have further examples in Hannah, and the wives and daughters of Elkanah, who attended the festival services at Shiloh; and again we read of the women who attended the sacrifices at David's feast on the recovery of the Ark.

Women were engaged in company with men in the Temple choir, as in Ezra ii. 64, 65, we read that "the whole congregation together was forty and two thousand three hundred and threescore, besides their menservants and their maidservants, of whom there were seven hundred thirty and six; and they had two hundred singing men and singing women."

Women appeared from time to time in the history of Israel as inspired prophetesses. Miriam is called a prophetess, so is Huldah, and Deborah appears both as prophetess and judge. [...]

[...] Now Christians generally maintain that the Church raised the position of women during the early centuries after the introduction of Christianity; and they attribute it to the following reasons:

1   Christianity taught the spiritual equality of both sexes.
2   Christianity maintained that marriage was a sacred and permanently binding contract.
3   Christianity made divorce difficult.
4   Christianity improved the legal status of woman and gave a new prominence and dignity to the female sex.

But it is difficult for us, as Jews, to subscribe to these views.

Christianity was not a great intellectual movement. It was the outpouring of a stream of religious emotion; but of the social problems of the time, it knew and cared little. Hence on secondary questions, like this of the treatment of women,

Christianity acquiesced in the feeling of its environment, and took its colour from the pagan countries around. [...]

[...] The Reform movement in the Christian Church affected the position of women but little until we reach the eighteenth and nineteenth centuries, when the formation of many dissenting and nonconformist bodies materially improved it. The Quakers, for instance, have always placed women upon a religious equality with men, and the Wesleyans, Congregationalists, Baptists, Presbyterians, and Unitarians followed suit. But amongst our people the religious emancipation of women is proceeding in extremely slow fashion, and the example set by the Reform Congregations of Germany, America, and here shows little chance, at present, of being followed by orthodox congregations. [...]

[...] In 1846 the Israelitish Council of Schwerin issued a mandate, which stated that women should be considered on an equal religious footing with man, their admission to confirmation being tantamount to the declaration of their religious majority; and in the same year Holdheim declared that woman was admissible to "Minyan." The Reform Congregation of Berlin, founded in 1845, was the pioneer one in the action taken in reference to the religious position of women; and in Dr. D. Philipson's words: "When the reform was introduced of seating men and women on the same floor of the House of Worship, the first step was taken towards the religious emancipation of women." In the Berlin Reform Congregation, therefore, they dispensed with the ladies' gallery, and the innovation has been followed by all the Reform and many of the Conservative Congregations in the United States.

I venture to think that in this respect reform has followed the right course, and one which, if followed, would solve many of the difficulties attendant upon the question of woman's place in the synagogue in England. Here, with the one exception of the Liberal Jewish synagogue, women take no part in the service, unless one includes the lady members of the choir, nor are they allowed any voice in the administration of the affairs of the synagogue, although a large proportion of the income of each congregation is provided by the lady seat-holders. It is true that amongst the Sephardim a woman is occasionally elected to serve as a "Yehida"; but, as far as I can ascertain, this is an honour more in name than in fact, as no "Yehida" can vote on the Board of Management of her synagogue, although her services may be requisitioned for a subcommittee. The West London Synagogue in Upper Berkeley Street is more democratic in its constitution, and allows ladies who hold seats in their own name, the right to vote at all meetings of seat-holders.

The Church of England is commencing to recognise the value of women having an equal voice with men in the management of Church matters; and there are several instances of women serving as churchwardens and sidesmen. It would, indeed, be a significant and happy augury if our Boards of Management viewed the question in the same light, and anticipated a demand which is bound to come in an age where the efforts of women of all ranks, of all professions and creeds, tend everywhere towards the recognition of women's services to the community. Whenever there is a general attempt on the part of women of any society to readjust their position in it, a close analysis will always show that the changed and changing conditions of that society have made woman's acquiescence in the *status quo* no longer desirable nor necessary. As Miss Pappenheim's article has shown, the feeling is strong, both here and abroad, that the time has now come when Jewish women should strive to form a real and integral part of the congregation. It may sound paradoxical; but in the opinion of many, the occupants of the ladies' gallery, being segregated and set apart altogether, cannot properly count as forming part of the congregation. No service would be held for them, unless a minimum number of ten men were present (ten male children of thirteen years of age would suffice), so how can they be regarded otherwise than as appendages of their husbands, fathers, or brothers? [...]

[...] It is earnestly to be hoped that the ardent spirit which moves the Jewess of to-day to take a more active part in the life of the congregation, will not be interpreted as a desire to break with the old things. No one recognises more than she does, how deeply the roots of our faith are embedded in the past; but at the same time, she cannot fail to see that the spirit now manifested among women is the spirit of an age which no longer allows them to be poor, inarticulate things—but human beings, with a voice, a will, a soul, an intellect urging them forward to a higher and fuller and nobler life.

Note

1 Abstract of two Papers read at meetings of the West End Jewish Literary Society in April and November, 1912.